Migration and Transformations

Regional Perspectives on New Guinea

Andrew J. Strathern and
Gabriele Stürzenhofecker,
Editors

UNIVERSITY OF PITTSBURGH PRESS
Pittsburgh and London

ASAO Monograph #15
Published by the University of Pittsburgh Press, Pittsburgh, Pa. 15260,
by arrangement with the Association for Social Anthropology in Oceania

Manufactured in the United States of America
Printed on acid-free paper

LIBRARY OF CONGRESS CATALOGING-IN-PUBLICATION DATA

Migration and transformations : regional perspectives on New Guinea / Andrew J. Strathern and Gabriele Stürzenhofecker, editors.
p. cm. — (ASAO monograph ; no. 15)
Papers presented over a three year period, beginning in 1988, at the annual meetings of the Association for Social Anthropology in Oceania.
Includes bibliographical references.
ISBN 0-8229-3782-4 (alk. paper). — ISBN 0-8229-5523-7 (pbk. : alk. paper)
1. Ethnology—New Guinea—Congresses. 2. New Guinea—Social life and customs—Congresses. 3. Culture diffusion—New Guinea—Congresses. I. Strathern, Andrew. II. Stürzenhofecker, G. (Gabriele) III. Association for Social Anthropology in Oceania. Meetings. IV. Series.
GN671.N5M63 1994
306′.0995—dc20 93-39287
CIP

A CIP catalogue record for this book is available from the British Library
Eurospan, London

Contents

Preface

The chapters of this volume have grown out of a three-year period of sessions at annual meetings of the Association for Social Anthropology in Oceania. They carry within them traces of the transformations that have occurred to our shared ideas along this migratory pathway. Initially, our intention in 1988 was to bring together scholars interested in working in Irian Jaya, the western half of the island of New Guinea, which had been effectively closed to anthropological research for several years. Our concern was twofold: to remind Pacific anthropologists of the continuing existence of Irian Jaya and its historical situation as a province of Indonesia, and to explore ways in which recent analytical approaches and theoretical themes in sociocultural anthropology could be applied to existing ethnographic materials on the province. Either way, we were concerned that Irian Jaya should not be forgotten. With this in mind, we constructed the next stage: to look for writers whose interests and topics could either span the artificial political divide between Irian Jaya and Papua New Guinea, or who could use theories and analyses based on the more recent and copious work done in Papua New Guinea to illuminate comparable data from Irian. At this early stage, we planned for a more balanced distribution of articles than is represented here; but along the way we have concentrated more on the establishment of linking themes and concepts, which do, in any case, overlap with a volume on Irian that has in the meantime appeared (Paul Haenen and Jan Pouwer, eds., *Peoples on the Move: Current Themes of Anthropological Research in New Guinea* [Nijmegen: Centre for Australian and Oceanic Studies, 1989]), and which depend on a broad transcription of what is meant by the term *migration,* opening up questions that are classic themes in culture history, such as the relationship between language and cultures, and the diffusion of cultural elements as against the physical movements of peoples. Consideration of these themes both takes us back to the work of theorists prior to the advent of the structural-functional emphasis within social anthropology and enables us to provide an alternative to the effects of the prolonged onslaught on supposedly orthodox ethnographic knowledge by post-modernist and deconstructionist writers. The positivist assumptions of the immediate postwar period have certainly been thoroughly picked apart, from a dozen different viewpoints. Who now believes in the pure stability and coherence of locally bounded sociocultural entities, even in New Guinea, that supposed haven of fragmentation and diversity? Recognition of the permeability of boundaries renders moot both classification and functionalist explanations. The answer, however, is not just to declare that the old ethnography is dead, but to use it in pursuit of a new understanding: the dynamics of cultural process over shorter or longer periods of time and encompassing varying scales of space. From this perspective, the focus is inevitably on process itself, on history and the possibility or otherwise of recovering it. Overall, the turn is therefore from deconstruction to reconstruction.

To complete the miniaccount of process here. In our second working session in 1989 we had two papers on Irian in addition to the one by Jelle Miedema that appears here: Gabriele Stürzenhofecker's reinterpretation of evidence regarding the spread of "Dani" forms of horticulture in and beyond the Baliem Valley, and Terence Hays's islandwide study of myths relating to perambulating penises and visiting husbands, a folkloric theme that itself appears to have migrated extensively and is certainly found on both sides of the border. Stürzenhofecker's paper is scheduled to appear elsewhere, and Hays's is still in progress, so they have been omitted here; but the papers that remain do form an adequate testimony to the range of exciting concerns we pursued in annual meeting places from Savannah to San Antonio and finally in 1990 to Hawaii, and the papers' aim is still to unite the two halves of the island intellectually, even though the island is politically divided.

Finally, we would like to record the benefit we derived from the participation in 1989 and 1990 of James B. Watson, who has for a long time advocated that Melanesianists take up the kinds of perspectives pursued in this volume. Watson's ideas—of organized flow, of the Ipomoean revolution, and most recently, in the paper draft he gave us in 1989, on international systems—have given extra impetus to our discussions and form a permanent part in the analytical framework of our study of the culture history in New Guinea.

In addition, we wish to thank others who kindly attended and contributed to our symposium discussions in 1990: Tim Bayliss-Smith, Aletta Biersack, Jan Godschalk, and Ed Langlas, to name some, and especially also Murray Chapman, who was pressed into service as our commentator and who described his task humorously as being similar to herding snakes of different sizes. He agreed to formalize his comments into a concluding chapter for this volume, but fieldwork and other commitments have prevented this, and we are extremely grateful to Tim Bayliss-Smith for stepping into the breach and providing an important set of comments seen from the perspective of human geography.

Acknowledgments

We wish to express here our grateful thanks to all the contributors who have waited so patiently for this volume to come into being; to the original participants in our ASAO sessions who helped to develop our discussions but whose work is not included, with special thanks to Terry Hays and James B. Watson for their stimulus and support; to the Office of the Dean, Faculty of Arts and Sciences, University of Pittsburgh, for institutional support; and to Patty Zogran for detailed work on manuscript preparation.

Migration

AND TRANSFORMATIONS

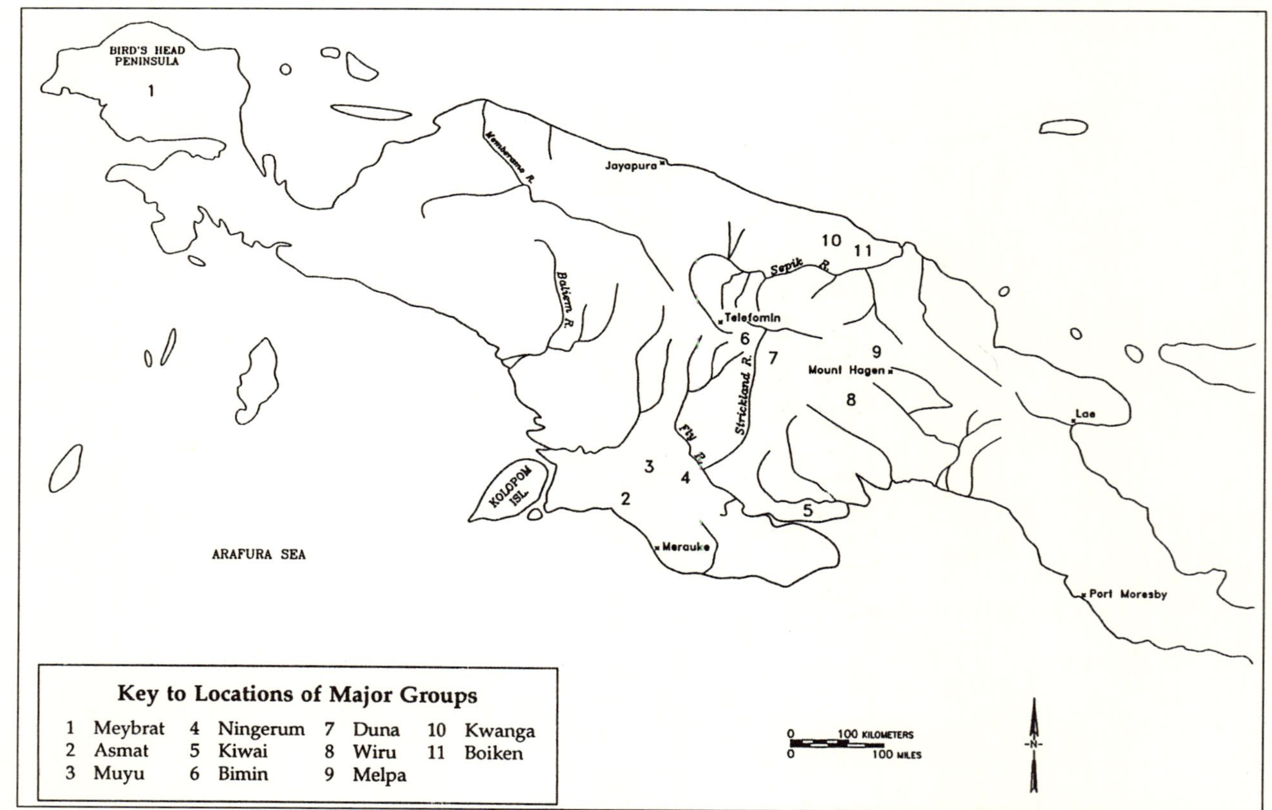

Map: Locations of major groups in Irian Jaya and Papua New Guinea discussed in the text.

INTRODUCTION

Andrew J. Strathern and Gabriele Stürzenhofecker

1

The two leading concepts that underpin this book are found together in its title. The term *migration* we use in an expanded sense that corresponds to the French concept of *circulation,*[1] referring to a total concept of movement of persons, practices, ideas, objects, cultigens, and so on, along tracks and pathways that can be at least partly delineated. We choose this term rather than *diffusion* because we do not wish to give too strong an impression of origin points and privileged cultural centers from which innovations spread to a periphery. Nevertheless, we are in a broad sense concerned with diffusion. In contradistinction to any simplistic notion of this process, however, we are interested both in the mechanisms by means of which the passage of persons and practices has taken place and also in the transformations of activity, identity, and meaning that occur along the way. The term *transformation* implies that changes are seen to take place from prototypical forms and these changes may also have a historical trajectory; but transformation does not imply all that would be signaled by the concept of evolution. It merely suggests that change is not random, that historical forces have shaped it, and that it may be possible to understand how contemporary populations exhibit features that can be related to their past. These two concepts, then—migration and transformation—replace in our usage the older concepts of diffusion and evolution, preserving a sense of the dialectics of change without committing us to any of the long-outmoded exclusivist positions that were at one time in the history of anthropology taken up under the banners of the two earlier terms.

Several confluences in the development of Melanesian and Pacific anthropology have led to the topic that we see here as formed by the intersection of migration and transformation. Most importantly, there is the realization that history is significant, followed quickly by the rider that the category of "history" is itself problematic: what kind of history are we appealing to? Is it history as another kind of nomothetic explanation of events, replacing in our pantheon the old god of social structure first enshrined by Alfred Reginald Radcliffe-Brown? Or is it history as the ideographic exposition of particularities, whether from the observer's or the people's own emic view? Postmodern influence is shown clearly in those studies that opt for the latter approach and implicitly or explicitly question whether there is such a thing as an objective account of events when these emerge, after all, from the subjective consciousness of people (Borofsky 1987; Biersack 1991; White 1991). Emic history, in this sense, also owes its impetus to the theme of the "invention of tradition" and to Marshall Sahlins's demonstration of misunderstood meanings in the interaction between Captain Cook and the Hawaiians (Hobsbawm and Ranger 1983; Sahlins 1981, 1985). Difficulties in the definition of tradition have also been pointed to by Pascal Boyer, who suggests that anthropologists need to develop a theory of tradition (Boyer 1989), and by Nicholas Thomas, who adds a critical discussion of how the observers' categories of Melanesia versus Polynesia, based on the concepts of chiefship and evolution, have emerged over time (Thomas 1989). Thomas himself cautiously embraces a version of regional-systems theory along with history as a way out of the impasse created by the uncritical use of evolutionary ideas (Thomas 1989:86–94; Thomas 1991). In more straightforward terms, a comparative and regional approach to cultural diversity, taking the physical environment into account, has long been practiced by geographers (see Brookfield with Hart 1971), and this approach easily accommodates further the consideration of data from geology, linguistics, and archaeology in the attempt to understand variation and change in the landscape of what Brookfield has called "old Melanesia." We follow this broad approach here, with the addition of some more specific concerns.

First, we are interested in the question of boundaries between social, linguistic, and ethnic groups, drawing the issue from Fredrik Barth's earlier work on ethnic groups and boundaries (Barth 1969). His classic exposition of this problem is found in his observation that boundaries persist despite constant traffic across them—an idea that gives us the key to at least part of the process whereby intercultural communication is achieved between differentiated units in New Guinea. The studies presented in this volume in some sense go one step further and question whether the concept of a boundary is at all applicable, when the traffic across the boundaries is great. At this point an emic turn is appropriate: we can look instead at the people's own concepts, and these certainly do include a sharp construction of differences as well as the appreciation of transactional flows between the differentiated categories. The chapters in this volume are concerned more with these transactional flows than with the boundaries they cross, but we have not succeeded in denying that boundaries exist, although we do stress their permeability.

Second, we have been concerned with questions of classification and reclassification, that result partly from Daryl Feil's recent synthetic theory of the evolution of societies in the Papua New Guinea highlands (Feil 1987) and partly from Maurice Godelier's exposition of the distinction between "great-men" and "big-men," which ranges these at least implicitly on an evolutionary continuum (Godelier 1982, 1986). Feil, like most theorists before him, grants considerable importance to the advent in central New Guinea of the sweet potato, a crop excellently adapted to the montane conditions found there and suitable for supporting large populations of both people and pigs. In this regard, the *moka* and *tee* exchange systems of the Melpa and Enga peoples come to stand at the highest point of the evolutionary continuum that Feil proposes, instantiating the ideal version of big-manship. Godelier starts from the same standpoint but is concerned more with the base of the supposed continuum—a base that he sees characterized by the great-man as leader, one who achieves his reputation as warrior or religious expert, and not by any special relationship to labor, resources, or exchange networks. This emphasis on expertise in war or religion, he suggests, is the prototypical form of leadership and should be used as our basic representational icon of the leader rather than the big-man. Problems arise with these two approaches, because empirical realities do not fit neatly into the categories invented. In principle this does not matter if the categories are presented as models; but, although the big-man concept can be fairly clearly defined, the great-man in fact embodies a heterogeneous diversity that is difficult to subsume under a single label other than by appealing to the absence of characteristics found in the big-man case (see also Godelier and Strathern 1991).

In this volume, Bruce Knauft's study shows that regional areas we have looked upon as lacking big-manship in fact display many characteristics of this type. Jelle Miedema's study of trade, migration, and exchange in the Bird's Head of Irian Jaya further shows that warfare and exchange went hand in hand there, rather than exchange replacing warfare as in Feil's Papua New Guinea–derived model. In general, we can recognize elements of big-manship emerging also in those areas confidently assigned to the great-man type, the Ok region, for example (and I return to this point below). What is remarkable is that complexes of practices—including those of leadership—appear to have been exported from group to group, along with cult practices such as the Female Spirit complex described earlier for the Mount Hagen area (Strathern 1970, 1979), elements of which can now be traced over a much wider geographical scale, as the papers here by Gabriele Stürzenhofecker, Fitz John Porter Poole, and Andrew Strathern indicate. A crucial link between "the highlands" and "Ok" is provided by the Duna people, and Stürzenhofecker in her chapter first establishes, by the use of attribute clusters, how the category "Duna" stands (with respect to known significant variables) in relationship to other cultural entities around it. She then proceeds to exemplify the interstitial status of the Duna area with regard to its cultural connections with Ok. (Subsequent fieldwork during 1991 in a part of the Duna area that borders on Ok has amply and directly confirmed the indications obtained from this prefieldwork study.)

A specific concern that is shown in at least two chapters of this volume is a concern that also resonates with Feil's discussions of the Papua New Guinea highlands societies. Miedema's discussion of the Bird's Head area and Robert L. Welsch's discussion of the Upper Fly-Digul area, which belongs both to Irian and to Papua New Guinea, both recount the expansion of regional systems of exchange. These systems can obviously become the bearers of cultural traits and practices also, as Paul B. Roscoe has shown for the long-yam complex in the Sepik (Roscoe 1989). Their character is often intrusive, instigating patterns of regional integration among diverse ethnic groups along pathways of exchange that can carry with them other functions such as trade, as we have long known for the Massim *kula* system and the Melpa *moka*. Both studies presented here show us new facets of this phenomenon, which stand again in useful contrast to Feil's model. Miedema shows for the Bird's Head that the expansion of exchange can take place on a basis other than that of intensified agricultural production (as in Feil's model), that is, the intensification of the slave-cloth trade nexus at the intersection between the hierarchical political systems of Indonesia and the relatively egalitarian ones of New Guinea. An obvious historical difference here is that in Miedema's case study, the process is driven by exterior forces; whereas in Feil's purview, only endogenous forces are primarily at work. This historical difference in itself, however, indicates to us the difference that geographical scale can make to analysis. If Miedema had confined himself to the local level of the Meybrat, he could not have reached a proper explanation for the phenomenon he is examining; and even for the Papua New Guinea highlands, it is probably important to include the ways long-distance trade in shells and plumes affects intensifying local agricultural production, its effects acting as relevant factors in the efflorescence of exchange. Welsch's study, however, shows us that a regional network can emerge even without intensified production or external influence, merely by the extension of credit relations as the basis for fiduciary social relationships in general. Such arrangements are inherently expansive and potentially inflationary (see Strathern 1969).

The overall topic for the chapters of this volume is the flow of communication between social groups, and the concomitant patterns of regional variation that result from this flow. It is not necessary for this purpose to make a rigid definition or demarcation of what "a region" is in general or of what any given region is in particular. Our concept is one of translocal processes and the classifications that emerge from these, and our viewpoint is therefore elastic and relational rather than fixed and typological. However, it is possible—as Stürzenhofecker's and Knauft's chapters, utilizing quite different methods, show—to uncover new configurations or to test old ones by means of this approach. Roscoe also, by a rigorous juxtaposition of ethnohistorical, biological, and linguistic data, substantially redraws the prehistoric map of the Sepik region and generates suggestions about process that are highly germane to our overall topic. Because our interest is not primarily in establishing new regions but more in discussing connections between areas, however, it is not necessary for us to adopt any overall mapping methodology. Regions can be seen as emergent entities, deriving both from our own interests as writers as well as historically from the development of a people's own consciousness. Often, we are working with fragmentary data that can be manipulated or interpreted with insight, but that do not provide us as yet with a firm basis for generalizations. These chapters, therefore, are an exploration, revealing important perspectives at all levels, from the local group described by Karen Brison in the first chapter to the islandwide survey of terms for sweet potato by Richard Scaglion and Kimberly A. Soto in the last case study.

In the rest of this introduction, we pass now to a more detailed outline of the chapters, considered in sets, which can act as a guide or a signpost to the reader, pointing out how the studies relate to each other and the main thrust of each individual discussion.

2

The first two chapters are on the Sepik: Karen Brison's study of migration into and out of Kwanga local groups and Paul Roscoe's exposition of migrations and interactions between ethnic and linguistic groups throughout the Sepik. These two studies correspond to the more strict definition of the term *migration* (as employed by geographers), as well as to traditionally established methods of analysis in social and cultural anthropology. Brison draws a good deal of her inspiration from James Watson's seminal concept of organized flow, but she is equally concerned with the transformation that emerges from the absorption of individual migrants into the local group, or the conversion of flux into stability. The Kwanga, like other peoples in New Guinea, appear to outside observers to have set themselves a structural problem by proclaiming their groups as patrilineal and combining this with rules of exchange partnerships that require a minimal slotting into each family of persons of the correct sex and age. They have solved their own problem neatly by regularly adopting others into these slots; and these in turn are permitted to retain their historical ties with the areas from which they came. Each local group, then, has a patrilineal exoskeleton, but its actual personnel form a "mosaic"—to borrow Poole's elegant term—of other local groups, and these ties are used for alliances and for refuge in case of conflict. Many studies of local groups in the highlands—beginning with the work of Watson himself (Watson 1970)—have depicted similar processes, albeit with special permutations. Indeed, the highlands first became famous anthropologically on the basis of this problem of "nonagnates" in the local group. In the present context, Brison's study is significant not only in showing that the same problem has to be tackled when analyzing different Sepik groups, but more so in revealing the very specific microlevel mechanisms that are needed to allow cross-local migration to occur at all in situations where local groups are already established in an area. There are both push factors (sickness, conflicts, subsistence needs) and pull factors that act in correlation (the slots that must be filled in social groups). Together, these push and pull factors enable continuous movements of people to take place. Brison also observes that immigrants often bring new ideas and practices with them, and this presumably is a factor that makes them valuable to their hosts as well as a source of cultural change. This insight could then be applied back to all the highlands cases that have not been considered from that perspective before.

At first sight Paul Roscoe's chapter is on such a different scale from Brison's chapter that it is hard to discern where they intersect. At the broadest level, Roscoe is concerned with the prehistoric interactions of the anciently established Torricelli speakers and the later immigrant populations of Ndu speakers in the context of long-term ecological changes, especially the retreat of the Sepik inland sea from about 6000 B.P. until it reached the present configuration about A.D. 1000. Roscoe uses ethnohistorical materials to suggest the main pathways of migration of peoples over this time span and then turns to consider that ancestors of the Abelam and Boiken peoples "almost certainly moved through an already resident, probably Arapesh-related, Torricelli population." From genetic evidence, it can be deduced that the Boiken intermarried more with the earlier residents than did the Abelam. Correspondingly, the Boiken language shows more Torricelli linguistic influence than does Abelam. It seems the Abelam were more inclined to violence—killing settlers and thus maintaining both linguistic, genetic, and, we should add, cultural separateness. Roscoe argues that the "Abelam" model has hitherto been taken as general (it corresponds also to old European models of Indo-European prehistory); and he offers the "Boiken" model as a contrast.

It is here that Brison's study comes into play, since she has shown one way that assimilation—with recognition of diversity—can work in a contemporary context. By extension, this could also provide a model for prehistoric processes (a point that Roscoe himself recognizes), and Roscoe suggests contemporary field sites where further fine-grained studies could be carried out. At the end of the chapter, he raises another point that could lead to important comparative applications. Regardless of broader overall movements of peoples, over time there are asymmetrical flows between groups of women in marriage, and Roscoe suggests that these could result in acculturative features of women's culture being transmitted to their children (an idea that conveys to us also that it would be important to pay attention to the roles of women among the Kwanga, for example). These network processes would cause a certain diffusion of female-related cultural elements separately from the transactionally engineered transmission of male elements connected with cult complexes. In other words, cultural changes have to be seen separately for the two genders, and our concentration on the transmission of cults and rituals might obscure these more everyday processes that nevertheless are cumulatively important.

It remains true, however, that major institutions, whether male dominated or not, can carry with them "packages" of cultural elements that are spread as a secondary or concomitant effect of the spread of the institutions themselves. It is therefore important to understand how such major institutions themselves expand over time in patterns of areal integration such as have been examined for the north coast of New Guinea by Theodore Schwartz (1963) and Thomas Harding (1967); for the Massim by numerous writers (for example, Leach and Leach 1982); for the Sepik by Deborah Gewertz (1983); and for the highlands by Andrew J. Strathern (1971), M. Meggitt (1974), and Daryl Feil (1984, 1987).

Robert Welsch's study here differs markedly from these earlier works, since he is dealing with an area lacking high population density, prominent big-men, intensified production, and hierarchical chiefship. In a sense he offers us a "pure" demonstration of the unintended effects of the extension of lines of credit, in a system without high production of the basic exchange item, which is pork. "A little pork goes a long way" seems to be the conclusion. But because pork does not keep well, it is necessary for all the networks of recipients to converge on the feasting site, and this therefore brings together, if briefly, persons of diverse ethnic and linguistic backgrounds. The intersection of this system with the Muyu people's overriding interest in cowries as currency provides the driving force for expansion, since cowries were obtained by pork transactions at feasts. The demand for cowries therefore fueled also the pig festivals and expanded the networks of people interested in them, and this pressure was maintained because the number of cowries in circulation was much less than the numbers owed in transactions between partners. To the motto regarding pork we can therefore add the motto "a few cowries make the world go round." We also see the influence of the Muyu culture on its neighbors, pig festivals being one of the prime mechanisms whereby that expanding influence was exercised in the Upper Fly-Digul area.

Jelle Miedema's study illustrates the results of the articulation of two forms of exchange: coercive slave trading, generated from Indonesia, and an exchange of cloths for marital rights in the interior societies of the Bird's Head. The predatory character of the external trading complex replicated itself historically within the Irianese populations because these became themselves involved in it as traders and since slave traders, having acquired cloths, moved inward from the coast to displace established leaders and to transform further the local social systems. Here, then, we definitely find "big-men" of an exploitative kind, but they are also involved in warfare as a business directed toward the taking of slaves, a process that has also been important in transforming local social structures elsewhere, notably in West Africa (Wolf 1982:195–231). Miedema suggests that they were also therefore in a sense "great-men." This cannot be in the sense proposed for that term by Godelier, since Godelier links the category to a kind of social system in which the principle of the equivalence of wealth and human life has not (yet) developed, whereas the entrepreneurial "new big-men" in the Bird's Head were involved in the construction of a brideprice system out of a former system of restricted exchange characterized as "sister exchange." The exact terms of Godelier's model are therefore not involved here.[2] Instead, it is the historical specificity of the account that is striking. The new big-men gained their power partly by bringing with them imported cloths that formerly had been excluded from trade and were regarded as *kain pusaka* 'sacred heirlooms' as opposed to *kain jalan* 'cloths for exchange'. They then, in entrepreneurial manner, converted these to exchange items and used them to organize marital networks, thus buttressing their own power and incidentally ensuring an enhanced control over women's marriage choices.[3] The development of the new big-man system thus arguably worsened rather than improved the situation of women in the society (another finding that runs counter to Feil's conclusions regarding the Papua New Guinea highlands). The finding does not invalidate Feil's work; it rather shows us that the transformational tendencies of social systems may lead in several directions. Miedema's chapter also shows that a predatory influence at a point of power may cause large-scale population movements, as peoples who are less powerful migrate away from the source of power rather than toward it.

Bruce Knauft's chapter, distilled from a monograph-length manuscript (Knauft 1993), continues this theme of the examination of exchange systems in regional perspective, in this case for a range of societies on the south coast of Papua New Guinea and Irian Jaya. Knauft's task is complicated because he is largely dependent on archival and published data that were produced at a time when anthropological interests were cast more in the mold of Sir James Frazer and hence paid close attention to mythology but less attention to social organization. Knauft aims to remove the label of "homosexual societies" from this region. First, it is questionable whether one should take such a label as a metonym for the whole society even where ritualized homosexuality is found; and second, not all of these societies did in fact practice homosexuality. He suggests instead that a focus on their handling of sexuality as a whole—in which there certainly was an enhanced or heightened interest—would provide a more balanced perspective. Having cleared the ground, so to speak, he is able to look again for linking features in other domains of social life. Here he finds a surprising number of elements that we usually associate with the big-man model. The effect of his careful inquiry is thus to overturn an earlier set of ethnographic classifications and to reveal, beneath these, features that enable us to discuss these societies in comparison either with each other or with societies from all across New Guinea. As do Welsch and Miedema, he finds features that are different from those of the Papua New Guinea highlands (as identified by Feil): politico-economic intensification in this part of New Guinea "does not depend on high population density or a high degree of subsistence localization. It is rather based on extensive subsistence exploitation and a high degree of geographical mobility both in amassing foodstuffs and aggregating population in pulsating movements." What Knauft depicts here is in fact an intensified form of the movements Welsch found in pig festivals in his case study. In particular, the mechanism of "pulsating movement" is a powerful one within the social dynamics of this area.

From these three studies by Welsch, Miedema, and Knauft, which deal with regions of New Guinea that either have not been considered comparatively or have been presented as polar opposites of the highlands Papua New Guinea case, it becomes possible for us to make classifications that are on a broader scale and to pinpoint different bases from which politico-economic development can take place. These regions thus become more "like" the highlands of Papua New Guinea, while also exhibiting distinct features of their own. A "highlands model" is useful as a tool for examining these cases, but only up to a point, and the most crucial factors for comparison are those that differentiate the systems from one another. "Migration" as such is less important as a factor here than the transformational capacities of the systems in question.

The last four chapters in the volume are closely related and show in tandem the linked themes of migration and transformation. Richard Scaglion and Kimberly Soto's chapter on linguistic evidence of the diffusion of the cultivar sweet potato throughout New Guinea sets the scene for the more locally detailed chapters by Fitz Poole, Gabriele Stürzenhofecker, and Andrew Strathern. It is here also that the spirit of James Watson most clearly imbues the text, for it was Watson who first argued for the significance of the sweet potato in the historical transformation of societies in interior montane New Guinea.

The chapter by Richard Scaglion and Kimberly A. Soto has two, in principle separate, aims. The first is to review the evidence regarding the time depth of the sweet potato in New Guinea. From its presence, potential or documented, in archaeological and other records on Polynesia and eastern Melanesia, they argue that this time depth may be as great as a thousand years rather than as short as the three hundred years that have been more often hypothesized. Their second aim is to show from linguistic evidence that the terms for the sweet potato fall into a limited number of linguistic sets, and they argue that the geographical distribution of terms may give us clues to the possible pathways by which the sweet potato moved into the interior of the country. Detailed refinements of their results will be forthcoming; here we can suggest that there is a carryover from Indonesian terms since the Indonesian *ubi* is clearly related, for example, to the Dani *mbi,* and the term *siabulu* is found not only in the Papuan Plateau area but also in a Dani-related area at Angguruk, where it appears as *suburu* (V. Heeschen pers. comm.). There is also the possibility that the term applied to taro or yam in one area may be related to the term nowadays used for sweet potato in another area. Or there may be more than one term, as in Pangia within the Southern Highlands Province of Papua New Guinea, for example, where the lexeme *mondo* relates to sweet potato as it is grown in mounded garden beds, a practice that has diffused southward from Ialibu (ex–Mount Hagen) into the Wiru-speaking area of Pangia (and is also found much more widely distributed, for example, as far west as the Duna); while the term *tia,* possibly in use before the term *mondo,* seems to be cognate with the *siabulu* set.

These complications aside, the overall evidence of diverse sets of terms—clustered at least in part geographically—supports the contention that the sweet potato entered New Guinea by more than one route. Such a hypothesis would help us explain the singularity of the Ok region, right at the hub of montane New Guinea, where most cultural emphasis is placed on taro rather than on sweet potato, whereas to both the west and the east the major populations are dependent on the sweet potato (Mek, Dani, and Ekagi peoples in Irian, and Central Highlands groups from the Duna eastward in Papua New Guinea). In this scenario, the sweet potato could have entered eastern New Guinea and proceeded slowly into the interior and thence westward, facilitating expansions and migrations of populations and ending at the watershed of the Strickland Gorge with the Duna people; while from the west it entered Irian from Indonesia and proceeded east, terminating with the Mek peoples, and thus leaving only Ok as the prehistoric bastion of taro-growing. From this perspective, further interesting questions arise. First, if the sweet potato traveled westward in Papua New Guinea, then the traces of its passage should show most clearly in those areas far to the west, near Ok. Second, if the sweet potato helped to engender social changes, then these may be reflected in stories of ritual forms that began in core areas and passed in a chainlike manner from place to place.

Andrew Strathern's chapter takes up this theme, relating it to the Female Spirit cult and its diffusion from the apparent ritual center of Tambul in the Western Highlands Province, with traces also in the Southern Highlands as one passes from Mendi to Nipa, and thence to Tari and finally Lake Kopiago. It is here that the two chapters by Stürzenhofecker and Poole come into play, operating at different scales and in different modalities of regional scope.

Gabriele Stürzenhofecker's chapter is designed, first, to set the Duna people into relief within the general regions to which they, in overlapping fashion, seem to belong. We have long been used to intuitive assessments of cultural or structural similarity between highlands groups, usually based on dendrograms of linguistic interrelations. More systematic comparison demands that one codes complex variables in a standardized manner, thus losing in subtlety but gaining in cross-cultural "reach." Stürzenhofecker's paper does this by selecting a set of variables that are likely on ethnographic grounds to be useful in making such cross-cultural comparisons and coding these for a range of peoples east, west, and south of the Duna. The overall results clearly indicate the significance of certain variables in distinguishing peoples and suggest that the "big-man complex" of wealth-based competitive leadership is among the most important of these attributes. More specifically for the Duna, the clusters established show the Duna to have close links not just with the Huli to their south, but also with the Paiela to the east and the Bimin (with whom Poole worked) to their west. Rather than being just a "fringe highlands" people, then, they are better seen as an "in-between" group, showing facets that belong now to Ok, now to the Papuan Plateau, and now to the Central Highlands societies. This classificatory exercise helps to contextualize specific overlaps at the ritual level between the Duna and their western Ok neighbors, including the Bimin themselves, a part of whose origin story links them to their eastern neighbors.

Fitz Poole's paper locks in with this point, showing in considerable and even poignant detail the Bimin-Kuskusmin people's own ethnohistorical awareness of their ties both with other Ok populations and with the highlanders across the Strickland Gorge, that is, the Duna and the related Bogaia and Agala. These people are aware of themselves as an ethnic agglomeration, resulting from diverse streams of migration that are recorded in remarkable detail. Poole's account gives us a high degree of insight and indicates the riches that can sometimes be tapped by ethnohistorical methods of study. The Bimin-Kuskusmin are an amalgam, expressed by a moiety division, in that the "Bimin" regard themselves as originally influenced more by ancestors from the east, and the "Kuskusmin" regard themselves as influenced by ancestors from the northwest (that is, Ok). The original migrating ancestors from the east are described as having cultural practices very like those of Central Highlanders today, centering on the sweet potato and pig herding.

Most remarkable of all, these traditions regarding the sweet potato are also represented in mythology as having been brought into the area by the powerful culture heroine Afek, who originally came from the east and taught people about the sweet potato. She then passed to the west and on her return displaced the sweet potato with taro and its associated cult practices based on the central cult house in Telefomin. The Bimin-Kuskusmin, in their historical and ecological niche, thus inverted the order of prehistory elsewhere in the highlands, where taro is usually represented by the people as having been cultivated long before the sweet potato. Such a permutation could simply be because of their geographical position at the intersection between Ok and the Central Highlands of Papua New Guinea. It shows in any case that there are traditions of both novel cults and novel crops, and that Afek as she came from the east is depicted as bringing with her the sweet potato. Poole's finding raises the whole issue of what the Afek stories in the Ok region are about. We have been accustomed to hive them off as something sui generis. Undoubtedly myth can accrete much into itself, but it is still possible to suggest that we gain a glimpse here into the kernel of history across regions, catching sight of peoples migrating, crop changes, and ritual innovations, all in a single package.

Linguistic evidence again may support this view, since the term *kamok*—used for a leader in exchanges—is found in Bimin and among the Nalumin (Atbalmin) as well as among the Mianmin further to the west, and it is cognate with terms having the same referent in all of the Enga-related languages to the east (*kamongk* in central Enga and *kamanggo* in Wiru, for example). The occurrence of this term, out of its linguistic context as it were, may represent a trace of the processes of change that accompanied the passage of the sweet potato crop through the New Guinea landscape. The term *mondo,* among the Duna, for mounded (that is, intensive) sweet potato gardens largely tended by women may be another trace, or mark, of the same cultural history. Another set of marks may be the stories of a culture heroine who is variously associated with pigs, sweet potatoes, or cult stones, and the tracks of this theme are explored consecutively by Strathern and Stürzenhofecker, ending on the eastern banks of the Strickland then taken up again by the Bimin to the west in the transformed shape of the androgynous Afek.

Many more questions are raised than can be answered by the discovery of these "tracks" of passage in prehistory, which cross over the boundaries of language and culture that we have tended to conceptualize in our analyses and which indicate, rather, the ways groups are permeable to flows of new communication, in ways that can also be deduced, in different modes, from Fredrik Barth's discussions of the communicability of symbols in various Ok cultures (Barth 1987) and Ron Brunton's exposition of volatility in Melanesian cultures at large (Brunton 1989). Overall, however, we can argue that ritual forms may in prehistoric times have been the vehicle by which other innovations could persuasively or legitimately be exported from one area to another, in a way analogous to the manner in which ceremonial exchanges were the vehicle of—and in time replaced—trading relations between diverse groups (the examples of the *kula* and the *moka/tee* nexus again may be cited here). Ritual switch points (as Strathern calls them)—such as can be located in Tambul for the Female Spirit cult—may then prove to have been very important generally for determining the frontiers and directions of cultural innovations.

The arguments presented in each of these chapters, then, highlight the permeability, passage, and creative permutations of culture in New Guinea through time and space. Both peoples and cultural practices appear to have moved across the landscape, in concert or separately, causing that particular blend of heterogeneity with the continuity of themes that characterizes the intercultural picture of the island as a whole. An excellent term for this aspect of the human condition has appeared recently in the work of Appadurai, who coined the term *ethnoscape* to refer to postcolonial circumstances. In fact it is equally applicable to precolonial history as discussed in this volume (Appadurai 1991).[4] We are well aware that these chapters touch only on certain aspects and on certain themes of the overall situation, and that we cannot at this stage draw from them a set of general propositions. Such a set would have to take into account at least two further general matters—warfare and trade—that have not formed the main focus of the investigations reported here (but see Wiessner and Tumu n.d.). Obviously warfare created frontiers and boundaries, while trade—like ceremonial exchange, marriage, and the diffusion of ritual—caused a reticulated network of communicative ties across such "gaps." General studies of warfare and trade (such as those by Knauft [1990] and Hughes [1977], for example) could be used as a basis for this further stage of reintegrating and reconceptualizing regional contexts of life in the recent prehistory of New Guinea. Here we have been content with a number of more modest aims, in line with the intentions of our sessions at the ASAO: to knit together Irian Jaya and Papua New Guinea by studies that show their cultural interconnections; and to break down, also, the picture of cultural boundaries into one of historical change and movement, forming what James Watson called New Guinea's indigenous "international systems."

Since these aims were formulated and our introduction first completed in 1990, a number of studies have appeared that move in the same directions as we propose here. We mention two. Terence Hays has taken up the question of whether the term *New Guinea Highlands* is to be seen as referring to a region, a culture area, or a fuzzy set. He concludes that essentialist definitions are not the best way to grasp our subject matter and that an alternative program is to study the ramifying networks of interconnections between peoples that cross-cut formal linguistic or other boundaries. In other words, he proposes a shift of emphasis from morphology to process (Hays 1993:141–164 with comments). Second, Simon Harrison has described the process of interchange between peoples as "the commerce of culture in Melanesia," stressing the fact that cultural practices pass from place to place via transaction, subject to reworking and reinterpretation along the way (Harrison 1993). Harrison cites both the Duna Kiria Pulu and the Melpa Female Spirit cults in this context. Relying on Modjeska (1977, 1991) Harrison suggests for the Kiria Pulu that it represents a ritual forerunner among the Duna of the secular *moka* exchanges in the Mount Hagen area. It is not necessary to accept this particular evolutionary argument (see Strathern n.d.), but Harrison's overall argument regarding the circulation of prestige-bearing knowledge and/or valuables fits neatly with our own emphasis on cross-boundary flows and interstitial configurations.

REFERENCES

Appadurai, Arjun
1991 Global Ethnoscapes: Notes and Queries for a Transnational Anthropology. *In* Recapturing Anthropology. R. Fox, ed. Santa Fe: School of American Research Press.

Barth, Fredrik
1987 Cosmologies in the Making: A Generative Approach to Cultural Variation in Inner New Guinea. Cambridge: Cambridge University Press.

Barth, Fredrik, ed.
1969 Ethnic Groups and Boundaries. Oslo: Universitetsforlaget.

Biersack, Aletta, ed.
1991 Clio in Oceania. Washington: Smithsonian Institution Press.

Borofsky, Robert
1987 Making History: Pukapukan and Anthropological Constructions of Knowledge. Cambridge: Cambridge University Press.

Boyer, Pascal
1989 Tradition as Truth and Communication: A Cognitive Description of Traditional Discourse. Cambridge: Cambridge University Press.

Brookfield, Harold, with Doreen Hart
1971 Melanesia. London: Methuen.

Brunton, Ron
1989 The Abandoned Narcotic: Kava and Cultural Instability in Melanesia. Cambridge: Cambridge University Press.

Feil, Daryl K.
1984 Ways of Exchange. St. Lucia: University of Queensland Press.
1987 The Evolution of Highland Papua New Guinea Societies. Cambridge: Cambridge University Press.

Gewertz, Deborah
1983 Sepik River Societies. New Haven: Yale University Press.

Godelier, Maurice
1982 Social Hierarchies Among the Baruya of New Guinea. *In* Inequality in New Guinea Highlands Societies. A. J. Strathern, ed., pp. 3–34. Cambridge: Cambridge University Press.
1986 The Making of Great Men. Cambridge University Press.

Godelier, Maurice, and M. Strathern, eds.
1991 Big-Men and Great-Men. Cambridge: Cambridge University Press.

Haenen, Paul, and Jan Pouwer, eds.
1989 Peoples on the Move: Current Themes of Anthropological Research in New Guinea. Nijmegen: Centre for Australian and Oceanic Studies.

Harding, Thomas G.
1967 Voyagers of the Vitiaz Straits. Seattle: University of Washington Press.

Hays, Terence
1993 The New Guinea Highlands: Region, Culture Area, or Fuzzy Set? Current Anthropology 34 (2):112–141 (with comments).

Hobsbawm, Eric, and Terence Ranger, eds.
1983 The Invention of Tradition. Cambridge: Cambridge University Press.

Hughes, I. M.
1977 New Guinea Stone Age Trade. Research School of Pacific Studies, Department of Prehistory, Australian National University. Terra Australis 3.

Knauft, B.
1990 Melanesian Warfare: A Theoretical History. Oceania 60: 250–311.
1993 South Coast New Guinea Cultures, History, Comparison, Dialectic. Cambridge: Cambridge University Press.

Leach, Edmund R., and Jerry W. Leach, eds.
1982 The Kula: New Perspectives on Massim Exchange. Cambridge: Cambridge University Press.

Meggitt, M.
1974 Pigs Are Our Hearts! Oceania 44:165–203.

Ohnuki-Tierney, Emiko, ed.
1990 Culture Through Time: Anthropological Approaches. Stanford, Calif.: Stanford University Press.

Roscoe, Paul B.
1989 The Pig and the Long Yam: The Expansion of a Sepik Cultural Complex. Ethnology 28(3):219–233.

Sahlins, Marshall
1981 Historical Metaphors and Mythical Realities: Structure in the Early History of the Sandwich Island Kingdom. Ann Arbor: University of Michigan Press.
1985 Islands of History. Chicago: University of Chicago Press.

Schwartz, Theodore
1963 Systems of Areal Integration: Some Considerations Based on the Admirality Islands of Northern Melanesia. Anthropological Forum 1:56–98.

Strathern, A. J.
1969 Finance and Production: Two Strategies in New Guinea Highland Exchange Systems. Oceania 40(1):42–67.
1970 The Female and Male Spirit Cults in Mount Hagen. Man n.s. 5:571–585.
1971 The Rope of Moka: Big-Men and Ceremonial Exchange in Mount Hagen. Cambridge: Cambridge University Press.
1979 Men's House, Women's House: The Efficacy of Opposition, Reversal, and Pairing in the Melpa *Amb Kor* Cult. Journal of the Polynesian Society 88:37–54.
n.d. Ritual Movements Reconsidered. *In* Papuan Borderlands: Huli, Duna, and Ipili Perspectives on the New Guinea Highlands. A. Biersack, ed. University of Michigan Press, in press.

Thomas, Nicholas
1989 Out of Time: History and Evolution in Anthropological Discourse. Cambridge: Cambridge University Press.
1991 Entangled Objects: Exchange, Material Culture and Colonialism in the Pacific. Cambridge, Mass.: Harvard University Press.

Watson, J. B.
1970 Society as Organized Flow: The Tairora Case. Southwestern Journal of Anthropology 26:107–124.

White, Geoffrey
1991 Identity Through History: Living Stories in a Solomon Islands Society. Cambridge: Cambridge University Press.

Wiessner, Polly, and Akii Tumu
n.d. The Oral History of Trade and Ceremonial Exchange in Enga. Paper presented to the conference The Mek and Their Neighbours, in Seewiesen, October 17–22, 1990, sponsored by the Forschungsstelle für Humanethologie in der Max-Planck-Gesellschaft.

Wolf, Eric
1982 Europe and the People Without History. Berkeley: University of California Press.

NOTES

1. We are grateful to Murray Chapman for pointing this out in his comments at the 1990 symposium session in Kauai, Hawaii.

2. In a comment on this proposition Miedema further wrote: "Probably I should have made more clear that the big-men/great-men combination is valid for the whole interior of the Bird's Head but only with respect to warfare; whereas it is more or less valid for the *eastern* Bird's Head from both

the 'warfare' and the 'sister-exchange' point of view. During the process, in that the restricted exchange of women was gradually replaced by the brideprice system . . . in the eastern Bird's Head, both 'sister exchange' and the brideprice system have seemingly existed side by side. (Initially Kebar women were married off to the southern Meax in order to acquire the imported *kain timur* cloths, whilst the restricted exchange of women among the Akari has only relatively recently been abandoned." Miedema adds that the possibility of labeling systems by means of the big-men/great-men stereotypes is easier now than before since "it seems that Godelier's 1991 big-men/great-men model is more flexible—and more realistic—than his 1986 model" (Miedema pers. comm. 1992, edited).

3. In a further comment on this part of the text, Miedema noted that the new big-men gained access to the heirloom cloths by manipulating exchanges with the indigenous big-men/great-men and thus broke their monopolistic control over communications, for example their monopoly of contact with the ancestors. In the past, cloths for exchange, at least in the western Bird's Head, were sometimes converted into heirlooms after they had circulated for a long time, but this had always been a one-way process, for, once defined as sacred, they could not be converted back into cloths for exchange. Yet this is precisely what the new big-men did. Miedema noted also that these new big-men gained control over others through cloth exchanges, by their accusations of witchcraft against women, or by their cultivation of a reputation for sorcery (Miedema pers. comm. 1992).

4. Strathern thanks Maria Lepowsky for introducing him to this term of Appadurai's at a working session on regional histories during the 1992 ASAO meetings in New Orleans.

ORGANIZING THE SOCIAL FLOW IN AN EAST SEPIK VILLAGE

Karen Brison

THE CONTRIBUTORS TO this volume have shifted the focus of analysis from the local group, which was the conventional unit of anthropological research, to regional systems instead, because in many areas of precontact Melanesia people, artifacts, customs, ritual complexes, myths, and magic often moved between local groups. Considering each local group in isolation would, therefore, give a distorted or at best incomplete view of social structure, culture, and the processes of change. In the following pages, I will examine the migration of people between local communities, particularly among the Kwanga of the East Sepik Province of Papua New Guinea, and will analyze the implications that the frequency of this migration has for our understanding of local group organization.[1]

Researchers have suggested that there was a great deal of migration in precontact Melanesia (Chapman and Prothero 1985; Hamnett 1985; Waiko 1985; Watson 1970, 1983, 1985): whole villages often relocated because of enemy attacks, natural disasters, or fears of sorcery (Chapman and Prothero 1985:8); individuals, groups of several families, or even whole lineages frequently left one community and either formed new communities or affiliated themselves with existing local groups. In fact, James Watson (1983:222) argues that the migration of people between local groups was the norm among the northern Tairora of the Eastern Highlands of Papua New Guinea, and possibly also in other areas of Melanesia, because local communities had "centripetal" and "centrifugal" tendencies, which ensured a steady circulation of people into, and out of, them. Warfare, which produced refugees and also created the need to recruit people to maintain large communities for purposes of defense, was one source of such tendencies (Watson 1983:230–231, 1985:35). But characteristics of social and political relations also ensured that insiders would leave the local groups and be replaced by recruits from other communities (Watson 1983:219, 232–235). Edward LiPuma (1988) similarly suggests that Maring clans actually encouraged some of their members to migrate, at least temporarily, and to take up residence with other clans in order to gain access to those groups' resources and also to build up and cement alliances. In short, migration between local groups was both frequent and may even have been thought desirable in many areas of precontact Melanesia.

The high rates of migration and the ease with which outsiders were integrated into local groups have led many scholars to suggest that ethnographers may have initially misinterpreted the principles of local group formation and organization, particularly in the Papua New Guinea Highlands. John Barnes (1962) started a lively debate when he suggested that, since Highlands groups contained a high proportion of nonagnates, ethnographers had been mistaken in calling these communities localized descent groups. He argued that anthropologists had imported models of local group organization based on unilineal descent from Africa; New Guinea Highlanders themselves did not think in terms of descent from common ancestors but, instead, felt only that it was best for sons to follow their fathers—although men could also select their residence group by other principles. In the New Guinea Highlands, then, local groups comprised a high proportion of agnates, but in fact, these groups were not constituted by principles of patrilineal descent. Andrew Strathern (1969, 1972) and Marie de Lepervanche (1968), among others, responded that patrilineal descent models were not just imposed on Highlands societies by anthropologists: Highlanders often spoke of local groups as patrilineal descent groups even if many group members were, in fact, nonagnates. But H. W. Scheffler (1985:12–13) has recently argued that even this limited claim about the salience of patrilineal descent principles to Highlanders was untenable; there is little evidence that Highland groups even represent themselves as descent groups. Scheffler suggests that male members of groups speak of themselves as "brothers" or "sons of one father" (even if some group members are in fact nonagnates) but that such talk does not indicate they think of local groups as ideally being agnatic descent groups. Rhetorics of brotherhood simply indicate that people think that patrifiliation is a sufficient (though not necessary) condition for group membership and that they think of local group members as being like brothers to each other; talk of brotherhood does not indicate that Highlanders think of group members as patrilineal descendants of a common ancestor, as would be the case in a patrilineal descent group.

More recently, several scholars have also argued that anthropologists have unwittingly imported assumptions to their analysis of Pacific local groups and so have fundamentally misunderstood them. Specifically Jocelyn Linnekin and Lyn Poyer (1990), Watson (1983), and LiPuma (1988) all argue that Western notions of kin and group identity may not be shared by Pacific peoples: both Western scholars and people in many areas of the Pacific speak of the bonds that unite members of kin groups as being based on shared 'substances' (such as blood and semen). But, while Westerners tend to view such 'substance' as something that can only be inherited, many Pacific people believe that the 'substance' which unites group members can also be acquired (and passed on to one's children) through such activities as eating food grown on a group's land (LiPuma 1988:6–7 [and particularly ch. 3]; Strathern 1973; Watson 1983:10). Thus, Pacific peoples may not see descent from a common ancestor as necessary for the sharing of common 'substance' and, consequently, they may view immigrants and their children, who have participated in group activities and shared in group food, as "brothers" and "sisters" indistinguishable from those who claim membership in the group through unilineal descent. In short, according to this view, it is Western scholars—not the local people—who think that local group members should be recruited through unilineal descent and who are bothered by the fact that many local group members are not, in fact, descendants of clan ancestors.

In this chapter, I will examine local group organization in an area of the East Sepik Province where, as in the Highlands, localized corporate groups contain a high proportion of nonagnates.[2] I lived and worked in two villages of the Kwanga language group, Inakor and Asanakor, located in the Dreikikir district. I will argue that while Kwanga villagers clearly did not regard patrilineal descent as the sole, or even the primary, principle by which new members should be recruited to local groups, they did, nevertheless, make a distinction between people who were patrilineal descendants of lineage ancestors and those who had been recruited to the group according to other principles. This was even true of descendants of people who had been recruited to a local group from outside the core patrilineage several generations in the past. Villagers, for instance, said that the grandchildren and great-grandchildren of immigrants were not "true" members of their current groups, but were only "filling holes" or "taking places" in these groups. In tracing lines of descent over several generations in this fashion, Kwanga villagers showed that they were not—as Barnes (1962) and Scheffler (1985) suggested is the case among Highlanders—thinking in terms of patrifiliation, in other words, merely thinking that sons should follow their fathers, without being concerned with unilineal descent from a common ancestor. If villagers were thinking solely in terms of patrifiliation, they would not distinguish men who took their group membership from a father who had been adopted into a group from others, since sons of adopted lineage members become members of their father's group through a rule of patrifiliation. Instead, when Kwanga villagers say that the children and grandchildren of immigrants are not "true" members of their current groups, the villagers show that they are concerned with what Scheffler, quoting Fortes (1959:207), terms patrilineal descent, that is, "a generalized connection recognized between a person and one of his ancestors" (Scheffler 1985:2). Thus, I will suggest that, at least in some areas of Melanesia, ethnographers have found "descent models" not because they have imported inappropriate assumptions to their analyses but because Melanesians speak in these terms. In making this argument, I will reaffirm the position of those like A. Strathern (1968, 1972) who argue that at least some Papua New Guineans use rhetorics of unilineal descent that have sociological significance even if they are not followed strictly as principles of recruitment to local groups.

Specifically, I will argue that among the Kwanga and perhaps also in other regions of Melanesia, dogmas of unilineal descent are an important part of a regional level of social organization. Patrilineal ideology is used to create a "structure" of relationships between fellow villagers; but the various "slots" in this structure can be filled according to a number of principles of recruitment. This system helps to integrate immigrants into villages. Patrilineal principles also help to maintain regional networks that are important to individual survival. People go to some lengths to remember their patrilineal ancestry and to stress that they are only "taking a place" in an adopted group because this allows them both to participate as full members of their adopted community and to maintain ties with (and access to the resources of) their ancestral group. Thus, the Kwanga go out of their way to promote the idea that descent groups exist both in order to integrate the local community in face of frequent migration between villages and to maintain a system of regional alliances.

MIGRATION AMONG THE KWANGA

Kwanga villagers think that the men and women of today are descendants of a number of ancestors who emerged from various water holes. Villagers say that ideally land should be occupied by the patrilineal descendants of the first person to have arisen from it. But villagers also recognize that, in fact, there was a great deal of migration traditionally and that most of the residents in any area are the descendants of people who are known to have migrated to Inakor and Asanakor quite recently.

Traditionally there was a great deal of migration among the Kwanga. Donald Tuzin (1976)—following D. Laycock (1965) who bases his conclusions on linguistic evidence—hypothesizes that the Kwanga were originally a Sepik River group who pushed north when overcultivation destroyed their own land. There was also a great deal of migration related to warfare. Inakor and Asanakor residents told stories of several villages that were forced to relocate by enemy attack. Several Kwanga villages in what is now a large stretch of unoccupied bush to the west of Inakor and Asanakor were driven out by Wasera-Abelam speakers from the village of Nungwaiya to the south in the late 1920s or early 1930s (Forge 1966:24), and the refugees from the captured villages went to Inakor, Asanakor, and Apangai, an eastern Kwanga village to the south. All of these immigrants are now dead, but their children and grandchildren still speak of their immigrant heritage and, in the past twenty years or so, have started to use some land to the west of Inakor, which they usually speak of as their native ground. My informants also said that two of the other eastern Kwanga villages had originally been located somewhere to the west of Inakor and Asanakor and had been forced to move several times because of enemy attack.

Inakor and Asanakor had, themselves, suffered several attacks. Each village, for instance, claimed to have at one time burned down the other, forcing the residents to take refuge for a few years with nearby villages before returning to their original location. The village residents now speak of their temporary hosts as their "mothers" and say that strong alliances were forged between themselves and their "mothers" during this period. Inakorians and Asanakorians also said that their fathers and grandfathers had taken part in raids on other villages and they could point to certain blocks of land they said had been won in warfare.

There was also evidence of migration that was not related to warfare. Watson (1970, 1983) says that much Tairora migration is caused by the pressures of living in close proximity with kin for long periods of time. He suggests that:

> In many cases grievances fester and accumulate for long periods of time with no real resolutions. A relatively small complaint or a minor disagreement concerning only two individuals can break the fragile

> truce within the group, releasing stored resentments that quickly escalate both the size of the contending parties and the gravity of their dispute. Physical violence is possible. Houses may sometimes be burnt, people beaten or shot. Deaths now and then occur. It is perhaps not too much to speak of a cumulative contamination of co-residence. The potential for fission among co-residents, I therefore suggest, builds perennially and cannot be postponed forever. (Watson 1970:121)

There was evidence of similar tendencies in Kwanga villages. The Inakor lineage of Bwandanger, for instance, was believed to have immigrated to the village from the north. According to legend, the original Bwandanger village broke up when a woman deliberately put some pig feces at her husband's brother's door. The victim was so offended by this gesture that he went to his sister's husband in Inakor and asked him to organize a group to attack and destroy the Bwandanger village. According to legend, the traitor and his family were the only survivors of the resulting raid. This legend indicates that there was considerable suppressed aggression between co-residents, which could cause village fission. Ethnohistories in many areas of the country trace the fission of local groups to similar trivial grievances.

My Inakor and Asanakor informants also claimed that their two villages had once been one, located on the present site of Inakor. Several lineages in the two villages claimed to have once been part of the same corporate group. According to local legend, just before it divided the original village was very crowded, and this led to frequent fights over "land, pigs, and women," and also to several deaths through sorcery. Consequently, several lineages divided and the new groups founded the village of Asanakor (primarily on land that had been captured in warfare).

Tensions within villages also caused individuals to emigrate, sometimes for short periods of time and sometimes permanently. One of the most prominent families in Inakor, for instance, claims to be the descendants of one man (the grandfather of the present senior generation of this group), who took refuge in Inakor and was adopted by a lineage headman who had no male heirs. More recently, this man's grandson Hapandi, an Inakor sorcerer, took refuge in his grandfather's home community for several years after he was accused of ensorcelling several people and was run out of Inakor.

Pressures associated with a relatively egalitarian political system in which every ambitious man wanted to be leader of his own group also created centripetal tendencies. Watson says that among the Tairora there was relatively little ascribed hierarchy. Ambitious individuals rose to power by building a faction, and they sometimes preferred to recruit people from outside the local group (perhaps refugees of war) since immigrants were dependent on their sponsor for protection and for access to resources and were, therefore, more likely to be loyal than local followers. But the growth of one strong man's faction almost inevitably threatened other ambitious men and their followers, who would sometimes try to escape domination by forming an independent village or by joining with another community in the region. Thus, the Tairora political system ensured a steady turnover of local group personnel (Watson 1985:35–36).

The Kwanga political system may also have been a source of centripetal tendencies in villages, though in a somewhat different way. Kwanga communities comprise a number of lineages. There are nineteen lineages in Inakor each with between one and twelve adult male members (with an average of three). The genealogically senior male of each lineage is the headman and controls the group's hunting and gardening magic and secret origin myth. He also allocates land and other resources.

Lineages tend to fission at the point where genealogical links between members are forgotten (usually people remember little more than two or three generations back in time), and ambitious junior brothers want to become headmen of their own groups. In the C case, for instance (see figure 1), the genealogical relationship between Mike and the rest of the group has been forgotten. He and Anakwa (whose genealogical connection with the rest of the group is remembered but distant) retain C as their totem but have separate resources and exchange obligations from the rest of the group.[3] Hikuto, the most junior of the four "grandfathers," was clearly an ambitious and successful man. He had three wives, which is almost always a sign of success, and numerous offspring. His desire to increase his own power and that of his direct descendants apparently contributed to the division of C into separate branches. This was evident in the fact that Hikuto's son Henry, the genealogically senior male, had the group's myth. Henry told me that he would pass on his knowledge, not to Mike, the senior member of the next generation, but to his brother's son, Walafuku, the senior man of the next generation in Henry's own line, thus furthering the structural separation of the branches of C.[4] Thus, as among the Tairora, a relatively egalitarian political system—in which many men strive to become leaders and few are content to remain subordinate to their elder brothers—produces a tendency for local groups to split and perhaps also to replace the community members who have left with outsiders.

When lineages fission, the two new groups usually divide the

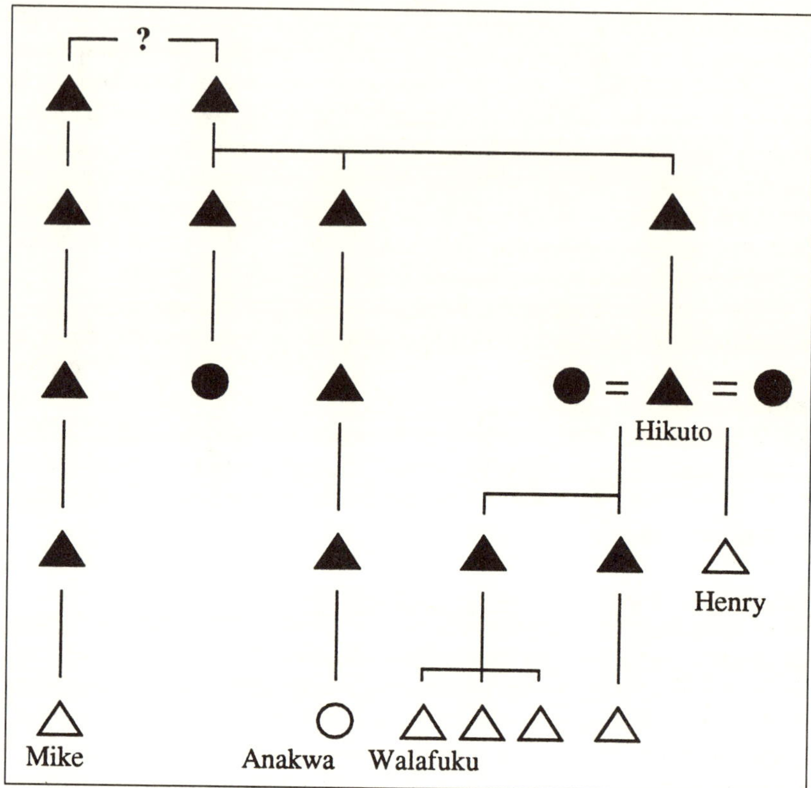

Fig. 1. Lineage C: ? = classificatory siblingship, relationship unknown.

original estate between them and remain within the same village. But in some cases one branch of the lineage moves to new land. In the case of the Inakor and Asanakor split, for instance, several lineages divided and one of the halves remained in Inakor while the other moved to the new site of Asanakor, which was vacant land that had been captured in warfare.

The circulation of people through the region was paralleled by a great deal of trade: in ritual complexes, magic, myths, and to a lesser extent, material artifacts. In fact, immigrants usually brought ritual and magical knowledge to their host villages. Kwanga men were (until 1978) initiated into six grades of a male initiation cult. My informants claimed that only one of the initiation grades (the penultimate) was really "their own," and told me myths about how they had adopted various of the other grades from neighboring language groups.[5] One of my informants said that, according to legend, one male cult festival had been brought to Inakor by his ancestress who had left her natal village and sought refuge in Inakor after having a violent fight with her co-wife.

People also said that much of their magic had been imported from other groups. People told me, for instance, that their own fathers had learned the magic necessary to grow the long yams that are a central part of the ritual complex of the neighboring Bumbita, Ilahita Arapesh, and Abelam, from the Bumbita Arapesh to the north. Before that time, my informants said, the Kwanga had grown only short yams. People also said that the most powerful war and rain magic had come to Inakor with a refugee from a village to the southwest of Inakor. Descendants of this refugee still, in fact, retained ties with their ancestral community and frequently visited there to purchase love and card-playing magic.

In short, traditionally and to a lesser extent in modern times, there was a great deal of migration among the Kwanga related to warfare and to conflicts within villages. The movement of people was paralleled by a movement of ritual and magical complexes. Furthermore, the apparent triviality of many of the reasons why people migrated to other groups suggests that there was no strong normative pressure against such behavior and that it may (as LiPuma suggests) even have been encouraged in some cases. Thus, migration of people between local groups was not an exception to a general rule of stable residence; instead, it seems to have been an accepted fact of life before pacification.

PATRILINEAL DESCENT: IDEOLOGY AND REALITY

My Kwanga informants often seemed to me to hold two contradictory models of their own society simultaneously. On one hand, they said that society should be organized by principles of patrilineal descent. Villages should comprise a number of lineages, whose first ancestors had emerged from the ground on the land now used by each group. Men should inherit lineage membership, rights to land and other resources, and exchange partnerships from their father. Within the lineage, the genealogically senior male should control the hunting and gardening magic necessary for group prosperity and make the decisions about resource allocation and ceremonial exchange obligations. People admitted that lineages sometimes adopted sisters' sons and immigrants from other villages but said that these people should always remain subordinate to the "true" members of the group.

On the other hand, my informants were not at all reluctant to admit that their community did not conform very well to the rigid patrilineal model. Many people said that their "ignorant" ancestors lived "wrong." By this they meant that there was a great deal more flexibility in determining actual group membership, leadership, and resource allocation than the more rigid patrilineal model suggests. Lineages traded blocks of land with each other, so the land now owned by any lineage had little relation to where their first ancestor emerged. Furthermore, due to liberal adoption practices many members of lineages were not patrilineal descendants. Even lineage headmen were as often as not nonagnates. Individuals also freely admitted that most villagers were the descendants of immigrants. People from other villages slyly hinted that Inakor and Asanakor had come to occupy their present sites only recently and that the ancestors of all present residents emerged from the ground at a place well to the west. Many of my Inakor and Asanakor informants said that this legend was true.

I will argue that the Kwanga retain these two, apparently contradictory, views of their own society because, together, they form a system that helps create a stable, orderly community in face of a great deal of migration into and out of the group; at the same time, the two models of local social organization help to maintain a system of regional alliances.

Andrew Strathern (1968:38)—following Scheffler (1964, 1965, 1966) and de Lepervanche (1967–1968)—argues that unilineal-descent constructs can serve a number of purposes. They can serve as a principle of recruitment. But they can also foster unity within groups by creating kinlike relations. Thus unilineal-descent models may be a significant component of social organization even if they do not determine the way people are recruited to groups. There is some evidence among the Kwanga to suggest that, although people do not necessarily recruit group members according to patrilineal principles, these principles are still sociologically significant.

Patrilineal descent is only one of several principles through which members are recruited to lineages. In fact, one young informant told me the rule was that the first son was a member of his father's group and all the younger sons were distributed to take places in other groups. Another man said, "In the past we lived wrong. We were always giving our children away to other groups. But then the white men came and taught us that children should always follow their fathers," also indicating that, as a principle of recruitment, patrilineality was never very strong even as an ideal. A census of Inakor, in fact, revealed that only 67 percent of adult married men are, in fact, in the lineage of their father (10 percent are in the group of their father's brother; 7 percent are in their mother's brother's or father's mother's brother's lineage; 3 percent are in the group of their mother's second husband, and 11 percent are in an unrelated lineage.) Many men have taken places, or as the local people say, they are "filling holes" (*wa rairo* 'went down in a hole') in other lineages (see Brison [1992] for an extended description of adoption among the Kwanga).[6]

The transfer of a man to another group has varying implications. The move is arranged by the father of the man and a senior member of the adopting group. Though the agreement is often made when a boy is still a child, the actual transfer will not occur until he is married and ready to take his place in the exchange system. When asked to name their lineage affiliation, men will almost always give their natal rather than adopted group, and people often say that they use resources from both their natal and their adopted groups. Residence is usually with the adopted group but sometimes with the natal group. The offspring of an adopted man will often join his adopted group (and in this case they are less likely to use the resources of their father's patrilineage). In some cases, however, a shortage of men in their father's patrilineage will lead to one or all of his sons being sent back to that lineage. What the shifting of a man to another lineage invariably implies is that he will take up the exchange and initiation obligations of the adopted group. Most often he will relinquish the obligations associated with his patrilineal totem, but in a few cases, particularly those of ambitious and promising individuals, exchange and initiation obligations associated with both the natal and adopted groups are held simultaneously.

There are many reasons why men are traded between lineages. One common reason for transferring sons to other lineages has to do with the demands of the exchange and initiation system. Each man has an exchange and initiation partner. These two partners initiate each other's sons into the male cult and engage in a series of associated food exchanges and their sons, in turn, become exchange partners to each other. People either adopt sons or allow some of their sons to be adopted to make sure that exchange partners have an equal number of sons to pair off as exchange partners in the next generation.[7]

The flexible system of recruitment to lineages also allows for the correction of demographic imbalances in the local group created by migration or by deaths and births. For instance, since lineages are quite small, flukes of reproduction will leave some groups without male heirs. This will leave "holes," which can only be filled by recruitment from other groups. The alternative, allowing the group's population to disappear, could easily lead to conflict over ownership of the group's resources.

Adoption also facilitates the integration of immigrants into the village. For example, one refugee was taken in by a man from the group F which had no sons. He gave one of his daughters to the immigrant to marry and made him his heir. The couple had numerous descendants who now occupy one branch of F and have also filled places in many other lineages that have died out. In another case, when a group of immigrants came from the west, there were too many of them to be adopted into existing lineages. Many of the immigrants took on the exchange and initiation obligations of one branch of Inakor lineage F, which had no male heirs. But others of the immigrants retained their original lineage totem and were given land by one of Inakor's existing lineages (see also Tuzin 1976). New exchange partnerships were created with the other lineages of Inakor. As well, new exchange partnerships were created within the group of immigrants, and a few people were dispersed to fill places in other lineages that were short of men. Similarly when group H came in mythical times from the Bumbita Arapesh area to the north, they were given a block of land in Inakor and also took on the totem I. No one was able to say whether the totem I was a new totem created for this group or whether it had belonged to a group that had died out. I-H members were also dispersed to fill places in groups that lacked heirs.

When immigrants were given places in a preexisting social structure, they became an integral part of the community with ties binding them to other village members. This bound the village together, something which was clearly desirable in a situation of endemic warfare where a larger population was advantageous for defense (see Tuzin 1976 on the integration of immigrant groups into Ilahita). This was, for obvious reasons, useful for the immigrant and was also advantageous to the host village whose fighting strength was enhanced. There was no shortage of resources, so there was little cost to this system.

Moreover, despite the ideology that gave primacy to "true natives," the flexible system allowed immigrants to become full members and even leaders of the villages into which they were adopted.

The case of I-H will illustrate this point. The I-H case (see figure 2) chiefly concerns one man, Hambamjeri (now dead), and his sons (now men in their sixties). Hambamjeri was by birth a member of I-H. Because of their immigrant history, this group had less land than most of the other Inakor lineages. Hambamjeri married and had a son who took a place in I. Later, Kebu—a man of another Inakor totem, G—died leaving a widow, Naromwa. As G was short of men, they invited Hambamjeri to marry Naromwa and take the place of Kebu in G. Naromwa bore two sons by Hambamjeri. Her father asked that one of these sons be given to his totem, C, since this group was short of men. Accordingly the elder son took his father's place in G and the younger son took a place in C. When the older son died, the younger son, Hilanda, took both his own place in C and his older brother's place in G. Hilanda himself had several wives and passed on his C place to the son of his first wife and the G place to the sons of his second wife. Hambamjeri acquired a third wife by stealing a young woman who had come to marry another man, Nakumini, of another branch of the G totem. In compensation for the loss of the girl, Nakumini requested that one of her sons become his heir in G. Accordingly, Hambamjeri gave him his youngest son by this woman. Hambamjeri's older two sons by his third wife were also given to other lineages. The eldest, Narombor, was given to Hambamjeri's brother who was, himself, filling a place in lineage J, which had died out. The second son, Saimbor, was given a place in lineage K, which was also without true heirs. Thus the five sons of Hambamjeri all became senior men of different lineages. Two of them were ritual artists; two had hunting magic.

This case is extreme but not unique in kind. The four surviving sons of Hupakumba, another prominent big man of Hambamjeri's time, also are each senior men of different lineages. Thus immigrants and other nonagnates can become lineage headmen.[8] This flexibility is advantageous in a situation where intervillage migration is common. The immigrant need not face the prospect of life as a second-class citizen. Members of a host village realize that they themselves might easily be forced by warfare to take refuge in another village and can expect to be full citizens of their new village.

This system fosters village solidarity in a number of ways. First, villages are also divided into cross-cutting initiation classes and moieties, which are involved in a variety of exchanges of food, valuables, magic, and labor associated with the male-initiation cults and also with deaths of group members. Each married man has two exchange partners, one in the same initiation class and the other moiety, and

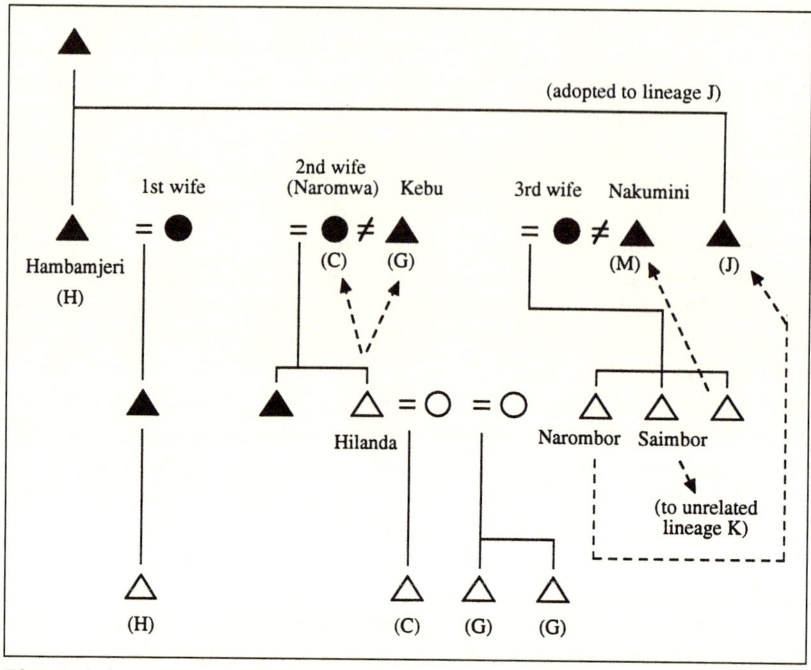

Fig. 2. Adoptions of Hambamjeri's sons: ≠ = marriage ended by death or divorce; ↗ = adoption.

the second in the same moiety but the other initiation class. Individual exchange partners often compete with each other in the context of larger exchanges and festivals between moieties or between initiation classes. Thus, when someone "goes into a hole" in a particular lineage, he also becomes a member of a moiety and an initiation class and takes on a series of obligations and relationships associated with that role. He engages in a number of common activities with these groups and shares common interests. An initiation class, for instance, will initiate the other class's sons into the male cult and will also present that class with pigs, yams, and shell valuables. All members of the initiation class have a common interest in ensuring that the initiation and exchanges go well since this reflects on each person's reputation. Relationships between moieties are similar. Joint activity and common interests foster a sense of group solidarity.

Second, adoption prevents, at least in some cases, the rivalry between brothers (Tuzin 1976) that can lead to lineage fission. Men like Hambamjeri with several sons arrange for the younger sons to "fill holes" in other lineages, and they may become headmen of these lineages. Perhaps this is one reason why eastern Kwanga villages tend to be somewhat larger (between 300 and 500 people) than those of the northern Tairora (under 200 people). Political tensions inherent in a relatively egalitarian system in which every ambitious man wants to be leader of his own group are alleviated by an adoption system that allows ambitious younger brothers to escape the domination of their elders.

While patrilineal principles do not determine lineage membership, such principles are important in Kwanga social organization. People make a clear distinction between those who are "true" members of a lineage and those who are just "filling holes," even if the man "filling a hole" has inherited the position from his father and grandfather. While informants (some of whom I quoted above) sometimes said they had learned patrilineal principles from the Australian colonial administration, there were indications that the emphasis on patrilineal principles is not solely a result of local people internalizing Western models of local organization. People tend to conceive of the relationships within lineages in a patrilineal idiom (even if some current lineage members are nonagnates). People also can trace patrilineal descent several generations back in time, to before the Australian administration was an active presence in the region. People distinguish their de facto lineage membership from their "true" affiliation through patrilineal descent and even reactivate ties with members of "true" patrilineages that their families have not been active members of for several generations. This all indicates that there is an indigenous emphasis on patrilineal ties.

While Kwanga villagers know that many lineage members are not agnates, they do conceive of the relationship between group members in terms of patrilineal principles. These are used, in combination with exchange partnerships associated with the male-initiation cult, to create a "structure," and then whoever happens to be available is recruited to fill each slot.[9] The case of lineage N (see figure 3) illustrates this process. Relationships within the original N patrilineage are used to structure relationships between the current members of N, several of whom have been recruited from outside the patrilineage. Originally N comprised two classificatory brothers. When the elder brother had no sons, a man was recruited from lineage M to take his place. The M man had two sons, creating two new structural slots. The elder son has been succeeded by his son Takuto who, having no sons, has recruited his mother's brother's son's son to take his place. Takuto's father's brother had no heirs, and so Gara, a

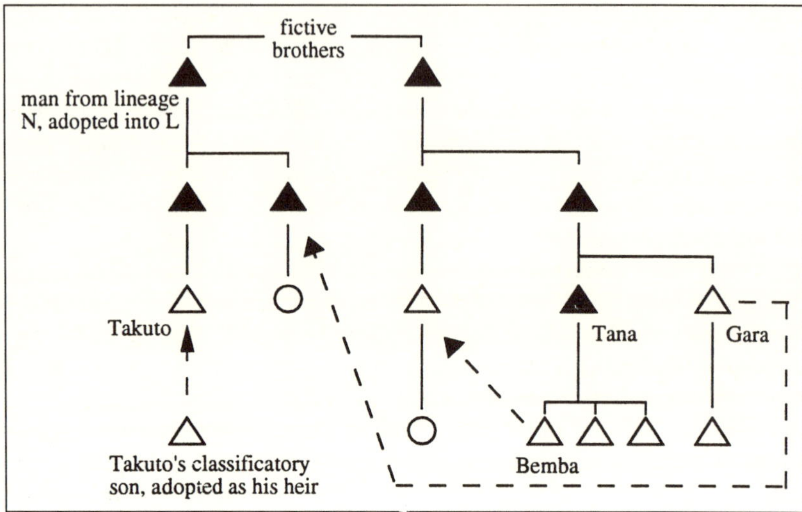

Fig. 3. Adoptions in Lineage N: ↗ = adoption.

member of the junior branch of N, has taken this place. The junior N grandfather also had two sons. The eldest son's son had no male descendants, so Bemba, a descendent of the younger grandfather, has taken his place. The younger son had two sons, Tana and Gara, and so the extra son, Gara, was given to the senior line of N. In short, each father must be replaced with a son, so those without male children must recruit heirs from other sources and those with more than one son often allow the younger sons to be adopted into other groups.

The patrilineal ideology is evident in the way people conceive of relationships within N. Each man occupies a "hole" in an imaginary genealogy of N that would have been actualized if each of the "true" members of N had had one or two sons. Patrilineal principles are important to people: they say that current members of lineage N are entitled to use N land because they occupy "holes" created by an imaginary line of descent from the first person to have emerged on N land. Similar thinking was apparent in other cases where all the "true" members of certain lineages had died out years before and their places had been taken by immigrants from other villages. Villagers still spoke of the estates of these lineages as being held in trust for the patrilineal descendants of the first ancestors. Current lineage members based their claims to the lineage's resources only from the fact that they were "filling holes" left by the original lineage members.

The importance of patrilineal descent to the Kwanga is also evident in the fact that people who have been "filling holes" in other lineages make some effort to keep track of their patrilineage. Far from forgetting about their immigrant pasts, many Kwanga villagers make some effort to remember histories of adoption and migration. Many people proudly told me that they were just "filling holes" in Inakor lineages and really came from another area. There is evidence that this is true in other areas of the country as well, where, for instance, migration patterns are preserved in myths. Similarly, when people are adopted into other lineages within the same village, they retain a strong sense of identification with their natal lineage and descendants will retain this.

There are several reasons why people distinguish between true and adopted lineage members. First, there is no particular reason to disguise adoption. In the local view, belief in common unilineal descent is not necessary to foster group solidarity. Fellow lineage, moiety, and initiation-class members do not always trace feelings of solidarity to ties of 'substance' and, when they do, they are just as likely to trace these ties through female links, since many lineages have adopted matrilateral kin (see also Wagner 1967). Kwanga kinship terminology makes little distinction between matrilateral and patrilateral kin, and people seem to remember relationships through women as much as they do those through men. (In fact, one informant told me that traditionally the Kwanga believed an infant was formed of blood drawn from both mother and father, but that they had learned from the Australians these ideas were wrong—the infant was formed only from his father's semen and the mother was just an "empty netbag" in which the fetus grew.)

Patrilineal-descent idioms serve, instead, to create a structure that locates the individual in the rest of community (through exchange partnerships, and through moiety and initiation-class membership) and allocates him resources. It is not necessary that people believe they share common blood, only that each knows his place in the system.

Second, it can be advantageous to remember ties to other groups. As in many areas of Papua New Guinea, Kwanga oral histories are shaped by social and political conditions: people remember things they think might be useful to them and forget things that are potentially detrimental to their welfare (Lacey 1981; Watson 1983:138). Among the Kwanga, there seems to have been little cost in being an immigrant, as Hambamjeri's case indicates, and there were many potential benefits to remembering an immigrant past. Some people even went out of their way to retain ties with ancestral villages. One of my neighbors, for instance, had sent one of his several sons to live with a relative in his ancestral village (village of his father's father) in order to retain ties with his distant kinsmen there. Such ties can have a number of purposes. First, people can take refuge in their ancestral village, at least temporarily (and perhaps permanently), if they run into trouble in their current residence. After the Inakor sorcerer Hapandi, for instance, was accused of killing several people in Inakor, he went and lived for several years in his father's father's natal village until feelings cooled in Inakor. On another occasion, Hapandi also joined several other individuals from surrounding villages in trying to reclaim a section of unoccupied bush where they believed their ancestors had lived, probably just before the Wasera-Abelam invasion of the 1920s. Another Inakor man also moved to (and stayed in) the same community after being accused of ensorcelling one of his Inakor neighbors.

As these examples indicate, people do not usually leave their adopted village unless their situation there is dire. In fact, the only two cases I recorded involved people who had been accused of practicing sorcery. The "ancestral" communities they returned to were ones that kinsmen had occupied no more than two or three generations before.

There are several other reasons people made an effort to remember ties to other villages and lineages. For one thing, allies and relatives in other villages are useful sources of valuables, carvings, and pigs during male-cult initiations. Men accumulate prestige by soliciting such gifts and loans from friends and relatives in other villages to present to their exchange partners in the course of an initiation. Second, people learn and purchase new magic and rituals from relatives in other villages, and this is another source of prestige and power. Third, many Inakor and Asanakor groups now use land they claim as their ancestral estate. This can also be a source of prestige and influence within the village since several of the descendants of immigrants have loaned plots of their ancestral estates to their current neighbors and friends.

The pragmatic nature of Kwanga ethnohistories is well illustrated by the case of the lineage Tumbutakwile. This lineage immigrated to Inakor in the 1920s. Men from this group told me that they had reclaimed their ancestral land, which was an easy walk to the west from Inakor, and were using this land for coffee and yam gardens. However, closer investigation (and conversations with members of other lineages whose ethnohistories were shaped by different agendas) revealed that most people agreed Tumbutakwile's "real" ancestral land was much farther to the southwest of Inakor (too far, in fact, to be used by anyone living in Inakor) and that the land reclaimed by the Tumbutakwile group in Inakor had been won in warfare from another group. Tumbutakwile had lived there for a short time before taking refuge in Inakor. In this case, descendants of immigrants in Inakor remembered just enough of their history to lay claim to some land they could conveniently use, and they "forgot" the more distant past, which suggested that the only land they had rights to was much too far away to be of any use to them.

In short, memories of past migrations form the basis of a current system of alliances between villages and between lineages within a village. People remember enough of their history of migration to be of use to them in particular situations and do their best to forget, or at least temporarily conceal, the rest.

PACIFICATION, CASH CROPPING, AND CHANGE

The usefulness of keeping track of patrilineal descent is also shown by recent changes. Several factors have led people to reevaluate the importance of patrilineal ties. First, the area was pacified soon after World War II. Cessation of warfare greatly decreased the need for migration. Second, local entrepreneurs began to actively encourage cash cropping soon after World War II, and now most villagers have coffee gardens from which they reap an average annual income of 150 kina per family. Coffee gardens are most often planted on prime land close to the village. This creates a shortage in land close to the village, which is also the most coveted garden land. That situation has led to land disputes. Third, improvement in medical facilities has brought about a decrease in the infant mortality rate. More children survive and, consequently, there are fewer empty "slots" to be filled by recruitment outside the patrilineage. Fourth, the land allocation policies of the national government have been a source of concern to villagers. The Kwanga say that the new land courts recognize only patrilineal rights to land and believe that the national government is in the process of returning all land to its rightful owners, that is, to the descendants of those who emerged from that ground. Thus they worry that land captured in warfare several generations ago will be taken away and that everyone will have to return to their "true" ground.

All of these changes increase the costs of flexible principles of recruitment, decrease the benefits they provide, and thus have led to a shift toward more rigid patrilineal principles. The increased pressure on resources created by cash cropping and the decreased infant mortality rate means that there are greater costs to adopting new members to groups. Perhaps for the first time, there are shortages in valued resources. Also, pacification has decreased the benefits of a flexible system. People no longer fear they will be forced to seek refuge in other villages and so no longer value the flexible principles that facilitated this. A large village is no longer necessary for defense, either, so additional population is not beneficial. In short, changes in migration patterns have led to changes in emphasis in the ideas of social organization.

There are indications that patrilineality as a principle of recruitment is becoming stronger. People express reluctance to give their sons to other lineages, saying that these sons will have inferior rights as adopted members. There are also cases now of "true" (that is, patrilineal) members of lineages attempting to evict adopted members. In the case of the lineage L (see figure 4), for instance, Tomba the "true" member of the group had lived and worked for years in

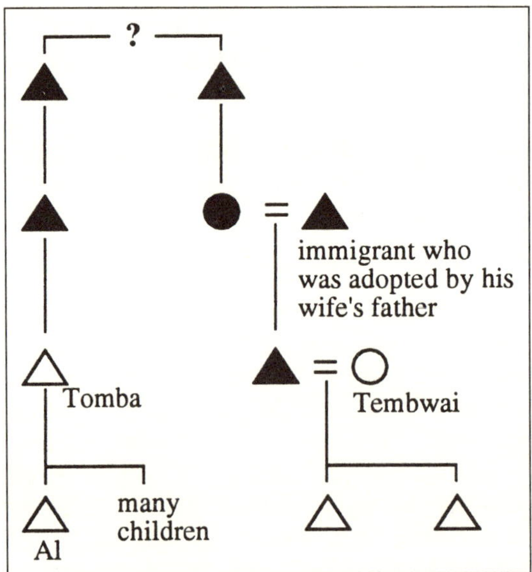

Fig. 4. Lineage L: ? = classificatory siblingship, relationship unknown.

Maprik, a local town. There he had three wives and numerous children. In 1986 he returned briefly to Inakor bringing with him one of his sons, Al, whom he left in the village. Before returning to Maprik, Tomba went to the village Councillor asking that the widow Tembwai and her two adult sons be ejected from L. He said that they had no right to use L's resources because they were not "true" members of the group and, in fact, Tembwai's husband's father had been adopted into L, when he came as an immigrant to the village and married the daughter of a man without male heirs. (This attempt to evict Tembwai and her offspring had met with little success at the time I left the village.)

CONCLUSIONS

In conclusion, while Kwanga local groups contain a high proportion of immigrants and their descendants, villagers promote an ideology of patrilineal descent by distinguishing "true" group members from people who are "just taking places" and by going to some length to remember their histories and to maintain ties with their ancestral communities. Although ideas of patrilineal descent do not determine group membership, they are an important part of a regional system of social organization in which people are assigned "slots" in a structure of relationships that is at least partly created through patrilineal principles and in which memories of "true" ancestry create a regional system of alliances.

I have also commented more generally on the role of local ideologies about social structure. Statements about group composition and history—among the Kwanga and probably also elsewhere—represent attempts to impose structure on a complex social field in order to achieve particular purposes. When people say they are living on the same land from which their first ancestors emerged, they are not necessarily describing what they believe to be the history of the situation; instead, they are asserting that they have a right to the land. When people say they are not "true" members of a community but are only "filling holes," they are likely thinking of the benefits associated with retaining ties with their ancestral communities. When situations decrease the benefits associated with asserting certain versions of social structure and history and increase the costs, then we would expect peoples' stories about their communities and their histories to change accordingly.

I have examined the flow of people into and out of a single village and have suggested that a patrilineal ideology is not a fiction created by anthropologists but is one of the principles of social organization that facilitates this flow of people. Although my analysis has focused in some detail on a single case, I suggest that the processes operating in this case are typical of other areas as well and that, therefore, an understanding of these mechanisms is important to the study of larger, regional, migrations of people over longer periods of time than I have dealt with in the Kwanga case.

REFERENCES

Allen, Bryant
1976 Information Flow and Innovation Diffusion in the East Sepik District, Papua New Guinea. Ph.D. dissertation. Department of Geography, Australian National University.

Barnes, John
1962 African Models in the New Guinea Highlands. Man 62: 5–9.

Brison, Karen J.
1992 Just Talk: Gossip, Meetings, and Power in a Papua New Guinea Village. Berkeley: University of California Press.

Chapman, Murray, and R. M. Prothero
1985 Circulation Between "Home" and Other Places: Some Propositions. *In* Circulation in Population Movements: Substance and Concepts From the Melanesian Case. Murray Chapman and R. M. Prothero, eds., pp. 1–12. London: Routledge and Kegan Paul.

Eyre, Stephen L.
1992 Alliance Through the Circulation of Men: A System of Name-Assigned Residence. Ethnology 3:277–290.

Forge, Anthony
1966 Art and Environment in the Sepik. Proceedings of the Royal Anthropological Institute for 1965, pp. 23–31.

Fortes, Meyer
1959 Descent, Filiation, and Affinity: A Rejoinder to Dr. Leech. Part 2. Man 59:206–212.

Hamnett, Michael
1985 Precontact Movement Among the Eivo and Simiku Speakers in Central Bougainville. *In* Circulation in Population Movements: Substance and Concepts From the Melanesian Case. Murray Chapman and R. M. Prothero, eds., pp. 39–56. London: Routledge and Kegan Paul.

Kaberry, Phyllis

1941 The Abelam Tribe, Sepik District, New Guinea: A Preliminary Report. Oceania 11:233–258, 345–367.

1967 The Plasticity of New Guinea Kinship. *In* Social Organization: Essays Presented to Raymond Firth. M. Freedman, ed. London: Frank Cass.

1971 Political Organization Among the Northern Abelam. *In* Politics in New Guinea. Ronald M. Berndt and Peter Lawrence, eds., pp. 35–73. Seattle: University of Washington Press.

Lacey, Roderic

1981 Traditions of Origin and Migration: Some Enga Evidence. *In* Oral Traditions in Melanesia. Donald Denoon and Roderic Lacey, eds., pp. 45–56. Port Moresby: University of Papua New Guinea and the Institute for Papua New Guinea Studies.

Laycock, D.

1965 The Ndu Language Family (Sepik District, New Guinea). Pacific Linguistics, series C, no. 1. Canberra: Australian National University.

Lepervanche, Marie de

1967–68 Descent, Residence and Leadership in the New Guinea Highlands. Oceania 38:134–158, 159–189.

Linnekin, Jocelyn, and Lyn Poyer

1990 Introduction. *In* Cultural Identity and Ethnicity in the Pacific. Jocelyn Linnekin and Lyn Poyer, eds. Honolulu: University of Hawaii.

LiPuma, Edward

1988 The Gift of Kinship: Structure and Practice in Maring Social Organization. Cambridge: Cambridge University Press.

Losche, Diane

1978 The Exchange of Men: The Abelam Balancing Act. Paper delivered at American Anthropological Association Meetings in Los Angeles.

Mead, Margaret

1938 The Mountain Arapesh. Vol. 1, An Importing Culture. Anthropological Papers of the American Museum of Natural History 36(3).

Sahlins, Marshall

1965 On the Ideology and Composition of Descent Groups. Man 65:104–107.

Scaglion, Richard

1976 Seasonal Patterns in Western Abelam Conflict Management Practices: The Ethnography of Law in the Maprik

Sub-Province, East Sepik Province, Papua New Guinea. Ph.D. dissertation. University of Pittsburgh.

Scheffler, H. W.
1964 Descent Concepts and Descent Groups: The Maori Case. Journal of the Polynesian Society 73:126–133.
1965 Choiseul Island Social Structure. Berkeley and Los Angeles: University of California Press.
1966 Ancestor Worship in Anthropology: Or, Observations on Descent and Descent Groups. Current Anthropology 7:541–548.
1985 Filiation and Affiliation. Man 20:1–22.

Strathern, Andrew
1968 Descent and Alliance in the New Guinea Highlands: Some Problems of Comparison. Proceedings of the Royal Anthropological Institute of Great Britain and Ireland, pp. 37–52.
1972 One Father, One Blood. London: Tavistock.
1973 Kinship, Descent and Locality: Some New Guinea Examples. *In* The Character of Kinship. J. R. Goody, ed., pp. 21–34. Cambridge: Cambridge University Press.

Tuzin, Donald F.
1976 The Ilahita Arapesh: Dimensions of Unity. Berkeley and Los Angeles: University of California Press.
1980 The Voice of the Tambaran: Truth and Illusion in Ilahita Arapesh Religion. Berkeley, London, and New York: University of California Press.

Wagner, Roy
1967 The Curse of Souw: Principles of Daribi Clan Definition and Alliance. Chicago: University of Chicago Press.

Waiko, John
1985 Na Binandere, Imo Aueri? We are Binandere, Who Are You? *In* Mobility and Identity in the Island Pacific. Murray Chapman and Philip Morrison, eds., pp. 9–29. Pacific Viewpoint 26, special issue.

Watson, James
1970 Society as Organized Flow: The Tairora Case. Southwestern Journal of Anthropology 26:107–124.
1983 Tairora Culture: Contingency and Pragmatism. Seattle and London: University of Washington Press.
1985 The Precontact Northern Tairora: High Mobility in a Crowded Field. *In* Circulation in Population Movements: Substance and Concepts From the Melanesian Case. Murray Chapman and R. M. Prothero, eds., pp. 15–38. London: Routledge and Kegan Paul.

NOTES

Some of the figures and extracts in this chapter were previously published in Karen J. Brison, *Just Talk: Gossip, Meetings, and Power in a Papua New Guinea Village* (Berkeley: University of California Press, 1992), copyright The Regents of the University of California, and are reprinted here with the kind permission of the publisher.

1. I conducted research in the East Sepik Province from August 1984 to October 1986. Funding for research among the Kwanga was provided by Donald Tuzin with a National Science Foundation grant. I will refer to "the Kwanga" for convenience, but the statements in the chapter apply to eastern Kwanga villages (speakers of the Kwanga Two dialect) and not to the western, Kwanga One, villages. Most of the information for this chapter was collected in the two eastern Kwanga villages Inakor and Asanakor.

2. Phyllis Kaberry (1967), Richard Scaglion (1976), and Donald Tuzin (1976) all note that patrilineages among the Kwanga's neighbors the Abelam and the Ilahita Arapesh contain a high proportion of nonagnates.

3. Anakwa remains a member of C, even though she is female, because she has no brothers. She married an immigrant from another village and together they succeeded her father in C. This is a common practice.

4. Tuzin (1980:201–202) describes similar processes within the Ilahita subclan where junior branches attempt to assert their autonomy by introducing a new spirit statue into the tambaran house. Scaglion, working among the Western Abelam, also notes that the basic corporate unit of Abelam society—the lineage—is prone to fission: "After a time, the eldest brother's authority is challenged by a younger brother as the lineage becomes too large and unwieldy to administer" (1976:65, 66). Kaberry, too, mentions the tendency of Abelam corporate groups to fission when they "become too large" (1941:254).

5. Tuzin (1976) similarly argues that the neighboring Ilahita Arapesh adopted their largely similar male-initiation cult from the Abelam language group to the east.

6. Tuzin (1976:236) says that 35 percent of Ilahita men are not in the same ritual unit as their true brothers, and Kaberry (1971:58) says that in the Abelam village of Kalabu, only 71.2 percent of adult men gave the name of their natal clan when asked for their clan membership. These figures both indicate that shifting of personnel among patrilineal descent groups is common in the region.

7. Tuzin (1976) says that the principle is that each man should have an heir.

8. Tuzin (1976:237–240) also presents a case of a promising younger brother being shifted to a new lineage group.

9. Eyre (1992) describes a somewhat similar system among the neighboring Urat language group. The Urat remember patrilineal ties, but individuals are frequently affiliated with (that is, use resources of and take on exchange obligations of) groups other than their own patrilineage.

WHO ARE THE NDU?

ECOLOGY, MIGRATION, AND LINGUISTIC AND CULTURAL CHANGE IN THE SEPIK BASIN

Paul B. Roscoe

INTRODUCTION

A combination of developments in recent cultural anthropology has conspired to divert the field increasingly from questions that once were considered quite basic. The generative processes behind regional cultural permutation are a case in point. Where once culture-area dynamics were a consuming interest in American cultural anthopolgy, the narrow ethnographic foci of modern analyses and a rising preoccupation with ethnographic construction and representational rhetoric have rendered questions about the larger cultural matrix within which a field site is located almost quaintly anachronistic. To the extent the larger matrix is examined, the questions posed tend to focus more on the How than on the Why: the regional distributions of symbolic systems associated with marriage, personhood, or whatever, may be described in exquisite semantic detail, but issues connected to why they take this distributional form are ignored. The implications of historical process—at least over the *longue durée*—nowadays excite little analytical interest.

In light of the extreme difficulties of reconstructing all but the colonial and postcolonial history of most societies, such omissions would be more justifiable were it not that the methodological problems have been allowed to dictate theory. Where a detailed historical record is available, history often features heavily in the analysis; where it is absent, culture tends to be analyzed as though it were without history. In the case of Melanesia, the latter contingency reigns, and history has tended to drop out of the analysis of Melanesian culture. And yet, of course, Melanesia had a prehistory, and were we acquainted with it, very likely our analyses would take very different tacks than they do now.

In this chapter, I attempt to inject a little prehistory into our understandings of language and culture in the Sepik basin of Papua New Guinea, a particularly apt stage for such an analytical expansion given its extraordinary linguistic and cultural heterogeneity. I begin with an outline of current hypotheses concerning Sepik prehistory, and then attempt a reinterpretation in the light of legendary, genetic, and dermatoglyphic (that is, fingerprint) data—evidence that hitherto largely has been neglected but that cast doubt on many details of the established picture of the Sepik's past. Because of the limited scope of these data, the examination necessarily is restricted to the people of the Middle and Northern Sepik, in particular those who speak the Ndu language of the Middle Sepik Stock, Sepik Sub-Phylum of the Sepik-Ramu Phylum (see map 1). In representative terms, though, this is less limiting than it seems: Ndu speakers comprise some 47 percent of all Sepik-Ramu Phylum speakers and around 32 percent of Sepik basin dwellers as a whole.

Because the ethnographic breadth of the exercise and the complexity of the data necessarily render much of the analysis rather complex, I draw its main results together in some detail in the concluding section. Readers unenchanted by technicalities, therefore, may care to go directly there from the end of the following section. There, too, they will find the contention that Sepik ethnographers have incorporated overly simplistic historical processes into the explanation of local cultural permutations. The more detailed processes revealed by this present study open up new avenues for understanding linguistic and cultural process in the Sepik (and, by extension, Melanesia) and suggest potentially fertile new foci for ethnographic fieldwork and analysis.

PREVIOUS VIEWS OF SEPIK AND NDU PREHISTORY

The Sepik basin of New Guinea lies like a great, flat-bottomed trough scooped out of the top of the island from the mouth of the Sepik River in the east to the Border Mountains between Irian Jaya and Papua New Guinea in the west (see map 1). The ridges turned along the rims of this sprawling trench make up the Bewani, Torricelli, and Prince Alexander mountains in the north, and the Central and Schrader ranges of the central New Guinea cordillera in the south. Between these two chains, the Sepik River tumbles to the floor

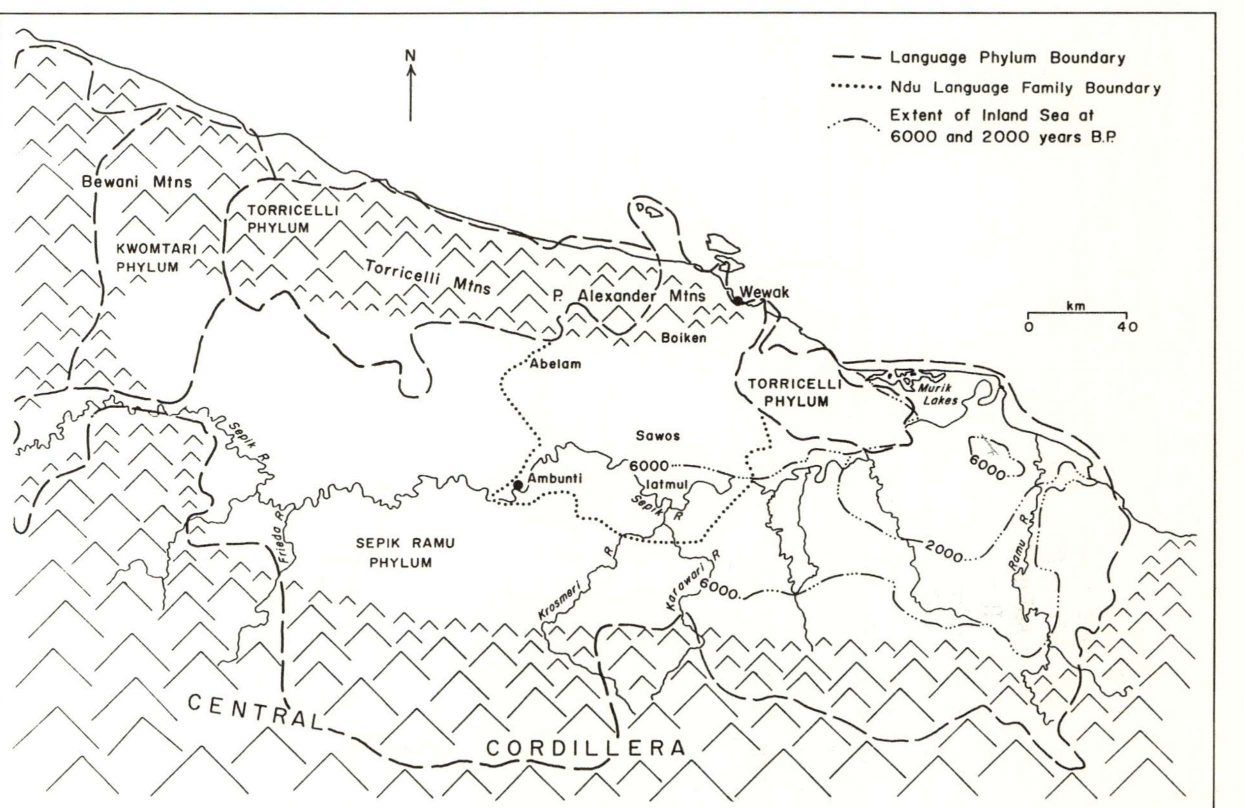

Map 1. The Sepik Basin of Papua New Guinea.

of the trough from its headwaters in the Thurnwald Range, thence following a serpentine path to the Bismarck Sea.

In truth, the Sepik Basin was not formed by any primordial excavation. Instead, it is part of the Intermontane Trough, a major geostructural feature that extends through the entire island from Geelvink Bay in Irian Jaya to the Huon Gulf in Papua New Guinea, continuing as a submarine depression into the New Britain Trench (Löffler 1977:12). It was formed by a complex geological history of sedimentation, uplift, flooding, and erosion that began between fifteen and twenty million years ago, when sediments from the already emergent central New Guinea cordillera started to accumulate on the floor of the unbroken ocean to the north. A few million years ago, following marine regression and offshore thrusting and uplift, these marine deposits broke the ocean surface as the ancestral forms of the coastal and Border ranges; block-faulting and erosion then began sculpting them toward their modern relief.

Until a million years ago, the great elongated crescent this newly emergent relief formed with the central cordillera enclosed a vast inland sea. Subsequently, as sediments from the surrounding mountain arc accumulated on the floor of the embayment and as ocean levels rose and fell with the advance and retreat of the Pleistocene ice ages, the coastline of the bay lapped back and forth several times along the east-west axis of the Sepik Basin. Around 17,000 years ago, as glacial snow and ice from the last ice age began to melt, sea levels started their most recent rise, and around 6,000 years ago, the ocean finally stabilized at its modern level. At this point, the Sepik-Ramu Basin was a huge, probably mangrove-fringed inlet stretching as far west perhaps as Ambunti and with a large island, now the Bosman Plateau, at its entrance (see map 1). Over the next few thousand years, the shoreline of this embayment began a final retreat eastward, infilled by elongating bird's-foot deltas associated with the Sepik and Ramu river systems. Behind the advancing shoreline, the change from marine to freshwater conditions was rapid, and in its later stages, the inland sea may have become a vast and shallow freshwater lake. Finally, around A.D. 1000, the coastline reached its present extent, leaving the Sepik much as we know it today (Haantjens et al. 1972:37–41; Reiner and Mabbutt 1968:65–67; Swadling 1990; Swadling et al. 1988:14–15; Swadling et al. 1989).

The Sepik region has been inhabited for at least 14,000 years (Swadling et al. 1988:18) and very probably for much longer. Consequently, it seems probable that the ecological transformations wrought by these movements of the Sepik sea to and fro precipitated a multitude of migrations among prehistoric Sepik peoples. Coupled with the region's ecological heterogeneity, these movements produced a cultural diversity that is perhaps without parallel in world history. At contact, the region was home to an extraordinary diversity of economic, political, ritual, and artistic forms, reflected in an equally heterogeneous linguistic scene (Lutkehaus and Roscoe 1987): crammed into an area only 270 by 400 kilometers, a population of no more than about 400,000 people still speak over 170 languages, a diversity made the more incredible by a profusion of dialects (Laycock 1973:54).

Sepik prehistory is evidently fundamental to a comprehensive explanation of this linguistic and cultural variation but, unfortunately, our data on Sepik prehistory are poor and—in the absence of extensive and sustained archaeological research—will remain so for the foreseeable future. Nonetheless, three sources have attempted a sketch of the region's past.

From an analysis of trade relations, art styles, and environment, Frank Tiesler (1976) has argued for four major Sepik settlement phases. In the first, the Sepik's earliest immigrants moved down the Sepik coast from Irian Jaya, some spreading inland over the Prince Alexander, Torricelli, and Bewani mountains into their southern foothills, others being channeled inland east of the Sepik delta along the northern fall of the central cordillera (see map 1). During this first settlement phase the Sepik floodplain was uninhabited, but it began to fill, in the second phase, as migrants filtered further south from the coastal chains and others moved north from the foothills of the central mountains. At the same time, centers of "consolidation" formed in what is now Northern Abelam, Iatmul, and Kwomtari territories and in the Frieda River area. The third settlement phase saw further immigration to Iatmul territory and outmigrations east and west along the Sepik River. From the Middle Sepik, migrations also occurred downriver to the Murik Lakes; and upstream migrations occurred along the Upper Sepik. Finally, during the fourth settlement phase, the Murik Lakes area received Austronesian-speaking immigrants from overseas and, together with the Iatmul, underwent "cultural radiations" ("kulturelle Ausstrahlungen").

Tiesler's Sepik prehistory bears only passing resemblances to the second (and most influential) sketch of Sepik prehistory, which derives primarily from linguistic data supplemented by findings from archaeology and physical anthropology (Laycock 1965, 1973; Wurm et al. 1975; Wurm 1982:261–275; Wurm 1983). This outline deals with the migrations of languages rather than people, although its authors frequently equate the two. The first language migration was borne by

Australoids spreading from Southeast Asia, between about 40,000 to 10,000 years ago, through what was then a single New Guinea–Australian continent. The second and third language migrations were Papuan and passed through the Sepik from the northwest to the southeast around 15,000 and 10,000 years ago, respectively. The second of these migrations is important as the probable parent of the Torricelli Phylum languages, which today are spoken by some 27 percent of Sepik people.

Several further language migrations then occurred between about 5,500 to 4,000 years ago. Along the coast, Austronesian speakers spread to several islands and took up residence in a chain of pockets on the mainland. A little later, offshoots of a third and main Papuan language migration entered the Sepik-Ramu Basin from a dispersal point somewhere around the southern half of the modern PNG–Irian Jaya border. Another language migration moved from Vogelkopf along the northern coastal areas into and through the Sepik coastal mountains, possibly causing a southward movement of Torricelli Phylum languages. And still in this time frame, yet another movement—carrying ancestral forms of the Sepik-Ramu Phylum languages—sprang from the present-day northern Irian Jaya–PNG border area. One offshoot spread along the coastal region into the Sepik-Ramu Basin; the other—bearing ancestral forms of modern Ndu and related languages—apparently advanced south into the highlands, then north into the Middle Sepik area, and on toward the north coast.

It is on the migrations of the Ndu-speaking people (the Abelam, Boiken, Iatmul, Manambu, Ngala, and Sawos) that Donald Laycock (1965, 1973) focused most of his attention. In his earlier work (and it is unclear whether he retained the view), he speculated that the ancestors of the Iatmul—and probably also of the Abelam, Boiken, and Sawos—migrated into the Middle Sepik from the foothills at the head of the Karawari and Krosmeri rivers (see map 1):

> the Karawari River (including the Krosmeri system) . . . joins the Sepik exactly in the middle of the Iatmul-speaking area, and almost due south of the whole bulk of Ndu-family population. Iatmul villages exist on the banks of the Karawari and Krosmeri, and the names of villages further upstream show similarities to those of Ndu-family villages. (Laycock 1965:195–196)

Encountering the Sepik River, the ancestors of the Iatmul, Manambu, and Ngala then spread east and west along the river itself. The ancestors of the Abelam, Boiken, and Sawos—migrating through the middle Sepik region before, contemporaneously with, or after these arrivals—pushed further north into the Sepik plains and southern foothills of the coastal mountains, with the Boiken penetrating the peak land to populate a section of the coast and several offshore islands.

Subsequently, Laycock's scenario of middle Sepik prehistory became concretized in the literature as a migration of rather imperial Ndu speakers, fighting their way toward the coast, exterminating or ejecting whichever luckless Torricelli speakers got in their way. Thus, Forge viewed the Abelam as:

> moving gradually north from the river, consuming the original vegetation on the plains and displacing the previous inhabitants . . . the result of the jostling together of large, fairly densely packed Abelam villages, fighting each other and gradually moving as a whole in a northerly and later westerly direction. (Forge 1966:24–25; see also Tuzin 1976)

The third and most recent attempt to reconstruct Sepik prehistory is the most sophisticated. Drawing on linguistic, archaeological, and ecological data supplemented with settlement histories, Pamela Swadling (1984) begins a "speculative reconstruction" of Sepik cultural history with the ancestors of the Torricelli speakers who, she suggests, probably have been in the Sepik since Pleistocene times, possibly occupying—albeit sparsely—the plains, hills, and coast. Subsequently, Torricelli speakers east of the Sepik River were separated from those to the west by the last movement inland of the Sepik coastline. At some point, possibly over 5,000 or 6,000 years ago, ancestral forms of the Sepik and Ramu Sub-Phylum languages emerged, the former containing the rudiments of Ndu languages and spoken by founding settlers probably living on alluvial plains along the southeastern shores of the flooded basin. With the retreat of the Sepik sea, drainage conditions in this region may have deteriorated and back swamps begun to form, encouraging migration westward to the Sepik Hills, the plains and hills of the Upper Sepik, the levees of the Sepik meander floodplain, and the Middle Sepik plains. Migrants to the Middle Sepik region, the early Ndu speakers, would have competed with already resident ancestral Torricelli populations, who eventually were encouraged to move to their present foothill, mountain, and coastal locations.

Painstaking as these reconstructions are, they do not exhaust the data available on Sepik prehistory. In particular, they draw sparingly or not at all from a plethora of indigenous settlement histories and from several studies of blood grouping and dermatoglyphics among Ndu and neighboring Torricelli populations. To remedy this situation, therefore, I first present a review of available Sepik settlement-history data, and then a summary of the blood and fingerprint evidence. Next, I discuss the implications of these data for Sepik prehistory. Finally, I speculate on how some of the more puzzling aspects of my conclusions might be further explained.

SEPIK MIGRATIONS: THE SETTLEMENT-HISTORY DATA

Among many Sepik peoples, kin groups recount narratives that include information on the provenance and subsequent migrations of their apical ancestors. As part of the grand corpus of Melanesian oral tradition, these settlement histories have resided in something of an anthropological limbo with regard to their status as history, as accounts having some validity in depicting the particulars of what happened when. It is not uncommon, for example, to find them implicitly afforded historical validity and used to flesh out ethnographic accounts or to advance analytical theses; or to the contrary, to find them denied this authenticity on the implicit assumption that, as "myths and legends," they are purely cultural constructions. Elsewhere (Roscoe 1989), I have closely analyzed this question for 371 legends dealing with the prehistoric migrations of the Boiken. The internal coherence of this corpus and its concordance with linguistic, genetic, and ecological data strongly suggest that the geographical dimensions of these traditions have some foundation in prehistoric occurrences. In other words, when a settlement history states that the founding ancestor(s) of kin segment X migrated to village Y from place Z, these claims appear in general to reflect historical reality.

Notwithstanding their geographical validity, however, Sepik settlement traditions contain several serious flaws that limit their usefulness in establishing Sepik prehistory. To begin with, they are much better represented in the oral histories of some groups than in others. The traditions of the seminomadic Sanio-Hiowe of the Sepik Hills, for example, link clan totems to places currently inhabited but make no mention of ancestral migrations (Townsend pers. comm.). By contrast, almost every clan and quite a few subclans among sedentary coastal foothill dwellers such as the Abelam and Boiken have detailed legends of their ancestors' wanderings. Second, it is probable that the more recent the migration, the more likely it will be remembered and represented in the oral corpus. As we shall see, for example, Iatmul settlement histories exhibit a high degree of coherence and clarity, but this corpus may represent only a relatively recent migrational movement. There may well have been earlier migrations, since lost from the oral record.

Finally, the diachronic validity of Sepik settlement histories is suspect. Although origin stories frequently mention the time of an ancestor's arrival relative to other early immigrants, this ordering often conflicts with other narratives in a village. My own research in the Yangoru Boiken village of Sima indicates that a detailed knowledge of a village's settlement patterns, social structure, and environment can establish a village's approximate settlement diachrony, but such an analysis demands many months of fine-grained data gathering.

Nevertheless, settlement data constitute a seriously neglected source of information on Sepik prehistory, and to my knowledge this is the first attempt to collate broad-scale information from published and unpublished Sepik migration legends (see maps 2 and 3).[1] Since the general tendencies are easy to lose in the detail of map 2, map 3 is an attempt to summarize overall patterns. However, I should emphasize that, since sample densities on map 1 are insufficient for the use of more objective methods such as cluster analysis (see Roscoe 1989), this summary is only subjective.

The settlement-history data support Laycock's linguistic-based proposition that the Iatmul spread east and west along the Sepik River, and the data also suggest that the Nor-speaking Murik Lake dwellers had similar origins (see map 3). The evidence also unequivocally supports Laycock's further contention that the Abelam and Boiken moved north from the river toward the coast. The data provide no support at all, however, for his hypothesis that Ndu speakers migrated down the Korosameri and Karawari river systems—or any other southern Sepik tributary for that matter. In the whole collection of Ndu legends, including those of the Iatmul, there is not a single reference to a migration from south of the Sepik River into present-day Ndu territory; if anything, the picture is reversed, with Iatmul settlement histories indicating a migration south from the Gaikarobi area and thence east and west along the river.

The data are in accord, however, with the recent suggestion by Swadling et al. (1988) that the Ndu migrations were linked to the disappearance of the Sepik's inland sea:

> There is little doubt that major cultural traditions such as the Iatmul splitting from the Sawos [i.e., the people around Gaikarobi] to occupy

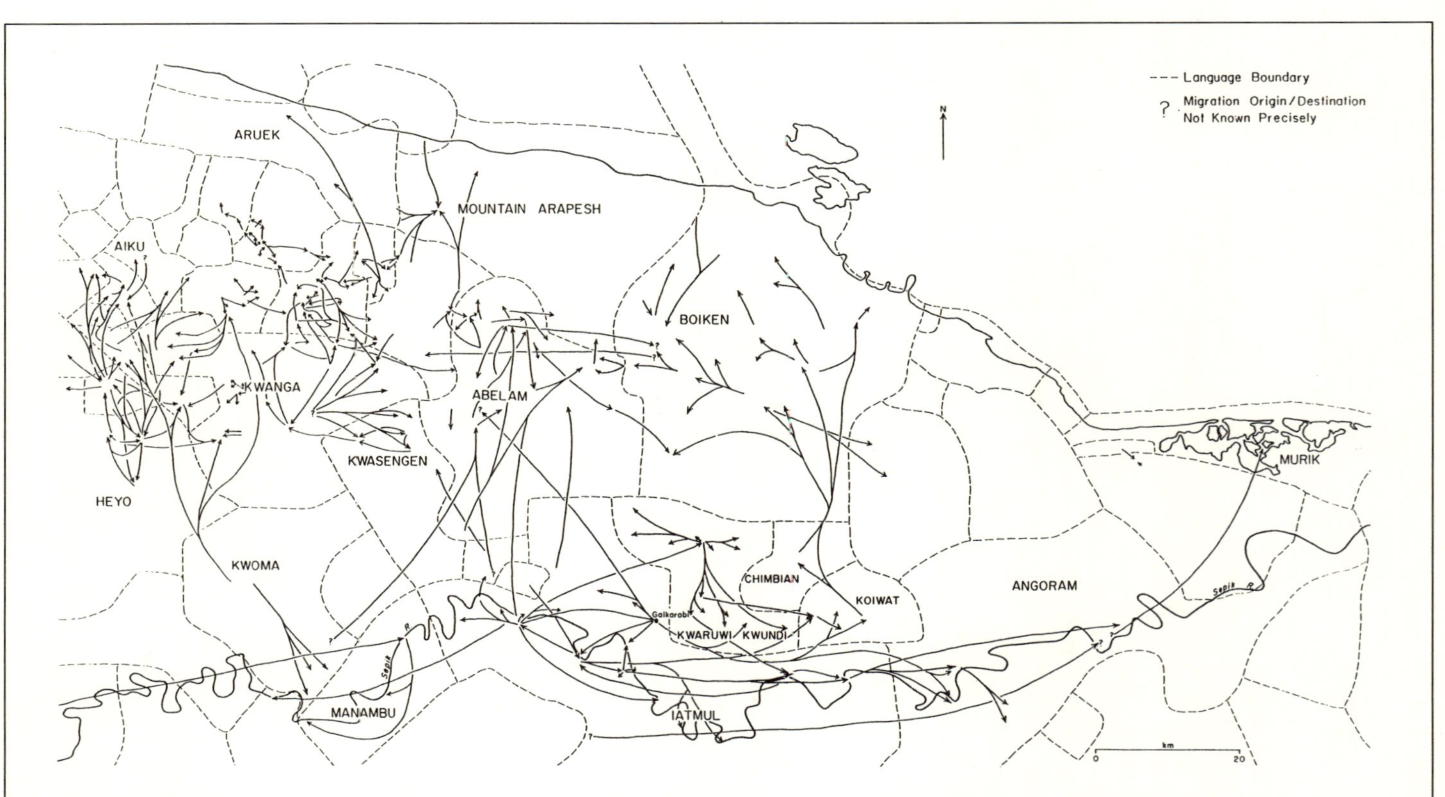

Map 2. The prehistoric migrations of the Ndu and their neighbors (raw data).

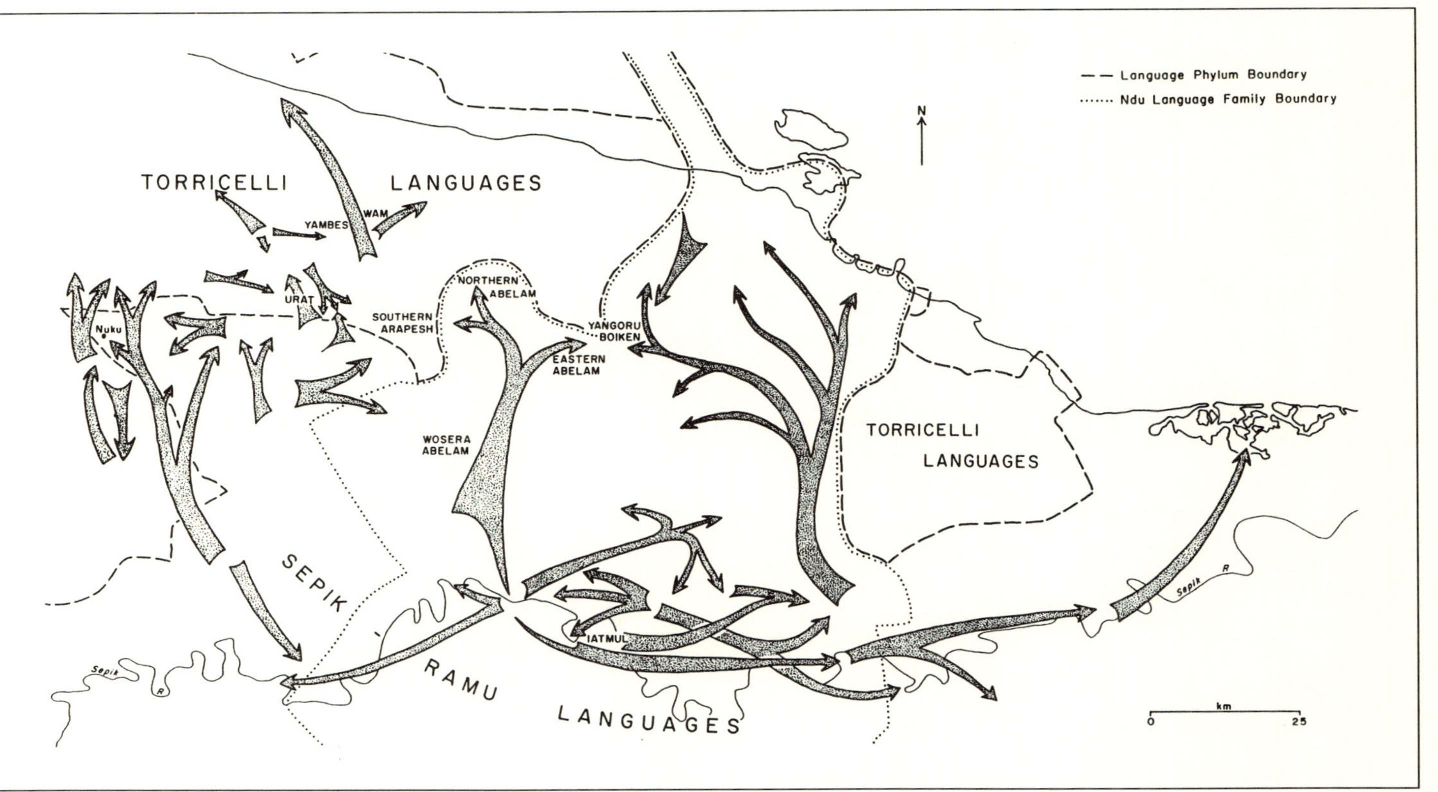

Map 3. The prehistoric migrations of the Ndu and their neighbors (smoothed data).

> the river banks of the Sepik and the departure of the Muriks from Moim Lakes and their settlement some time later at the Murik Lakes actually coincide with significant natural events. (Swadling et al. 1988: 14–15)

If the inland sea still existed during the Ndu migrations, then it should not surprise us to find no evidence of their migration down the Korosameri and Karawari river systems: until 2,500 or 3,000 years ago these locations were still underwater, and for an undetermined time afterward they remained waterlogged swamp and lagoon.

This does not mean, however, that Laycock was wrong to contend, on the basis of several Trans New Guinea Phylum affiliations in the Ndu languages, that the Ndu came from the southern foothills of the central cordillera. These foothills would have formed the southern shores of the Sepik's inland sea, and it is possible that early Ndu people migrated across the water in canoes to the northern shores. In other words, although the Iatmul may not have migrated down the Korosameri and Karawari rivers, they still may have come from the foothills in which these rivers now rise. Other, non-Ndu traditions of movements onto what was once the seabed—such as those of the Karawari people who claim to have migrated from the foothills at Samariap (Newton 1967:206)—presumably refer to migrants who followed the Ndu after the waters' retreat.

Another possibility is that the ancestors of the Sepik-Ramu speakers simply migrated east, following the recession of the Sepik embayment and shedding offshoots north and south, which included the Ndu among the later ones: assuming these early people were marine adapted, they would be inclined to follow their retreating livelihood in preference to finding a new one. Such a scenario is not too different from Wurm and Laycock's suggestions that the Sepik-Ramu Phylum languages appeared in the extreme west of the Sepik Basin some 5,000 years ago, subsequently swinging south and then east and northeast as far as the country between the lower Sepik and Ramu rivers (see, for example, Laycock 1973:55; Wurm 1982:271). Certainly, this picture would tie together the final retreat of the Sepik shoreline some 5,000 or 6,000 years ago and the spread of the Sepik-Ramu languages from around the same time; and it would account for the distribution of this phylum across the region once covered by the inland sea (see map 1).

In light of the common suggestion that the northward-expanding Ndu pushed previously resident groups before them, it is worth noting that several non-Ndu speakers—including especially the

Tama-speaking groups around Nuku and the Torricelli Aiku, Kayik, Lou, and Aruek—do exhibit such a northward-migratory trend. On the other hand, the remove of some of these groups from Ndu territory raises questions about whether Ndu movements could have been solely responsible. Perhaps, instead, these movements were prompted by the northward movements of more westerly Sepik-Ramu speakers. Surprisingly, the Kwanga—a group linguistically related to the Ndu and subject more directly to Ndu expansion—display less of a northward movement and more of a centrifugal tendency eastward, westward, and northward from the now-uninhabited heart of their territory. According to oral testimony, the reason was serious warfare (Allen pers. comm.). Finally, some Kwoma people seem to have migrated counter to any northward trend, and Ross Bowden (1983:4) speculates that originally they may have come from the foothills of the Torricelli range.

Although Sepik settlement histories seem to furnish important clues to the region's prehistory, there also is an aspect in which they are very misleading. First, they are overwhelmingly male-centered narratives: with few exceptions, they describe the migration of male ancestors or small kin groups led by males. In this largely virilocal land, however, it probably has been the women rather than the men who have done most of the migrating from one village to another. Second, clan traditions frequently ignore numerous subsequent immigrations by men who, for military or demographic reasons, settled with an established clan and took up its resources, thereby becoming members. Indeed, in the Yangoru Boiken village of Sima, the members of most clans are descendants not of the founding ancestors referred to in clan traditions but of subsequent immigrants from adjacent settlements, who shifted because of conflict or shortages of resources in their natal homes. Much the same, it seems, is true of the Abelam (see, for example, Gorlin 1973:45; Lea 1965:196) and the Kwanga (Brison, this volume). The point is that usually only the founding ancestral migration (and not these subsequent immigrations) is mentioned to the casual inquirer after village traditions, and in all probability, memories of quite a few other such movements have been lost entirely. The net result is that the settlement histories analyzed above probably are skewed toward early, longer-distance migrations at the expense of later, more localized migrations. This is analytically advantageous to the extent that localized "noise" in the migrational record is filtered out, revealing the earlier, more salient movements. Nonetheless, these localized migrations are important when we come to interpret Sepik prehistory from the genetic evidence.

SEPIK MIGRATIONS: THE BLOOD AND DERMATOGLYPHIC EVIDENCE

Blood grouping (Schanfield 1977; Simmons et al. 1965; Steinberg et al. 1972) and dermatoglyphic data (Plato and MacLennan 1975) from the Sepik Basin constitute two further, largely unexploited sources of data that bear on the region's prehistory. Unfortunately, only one of these sources provides any straightforward concordance with the conclusions of the linguistic and legendary evidence: Kevin Kelly (1990:201) suggests that the exceptionally high frequencies of certain Gm polymorphisms among the Abelam, Iatmul, and Yambes are due to the migratory origins of these people in the main area of the Sepik River, where prehistorically, he claims, malaria was absent (Kelly, citing van Dijk and Parkinson 1974). The remaining data are more difficult to interpret but nonetheless suggest some intriguing conclusions about Ndu prehistory.

The main sources of genetic data are several studies of ABO, MNS, and Rh blood groups for the Torricelli-speaking villages of Wahlen (Yambes language); Arisili, Bana, Luwaite, and Warengene (Wam language); Musimbelim and Daihonge (Urat language); and Ilahita (Southern Arapesh language); and for the Ndu-speaking villages of Stapigum and Jama (Wosera dialect of Abelam); Suanumbo (Eastern dialect of Abelam); Maprik (northern dialect of Abelam); Suapmeri and Kanganum (Iatmul language); and Boim and Kwolyik (Yangoru dialect of Boiken) (see summary in Simmons et al. 1965).

We can probe these data by applying a method devised by Henry Harpending and Trefor Jenkins (1973, 1974) that transforms gene frequencies into a matrix of coefficients of kinship (or relationship) among the groups in question using the equation

$$r_{ij} = \frac{(P_i - \overline{P})\,(P_j - \overline{P})}{\overline{P}\,(1 - \overline{P})}$$

for any allele. Here, P_i and P_j are the gene frequencies of the allele in question in populations i and j respectively, and P is the weighted mean gene frequency of the allele in the study array. The matrix of sample coefficients is calculated for each allele, and these matrices then are averaged to yield one overall matrix of sample coefficients.

Table 1 displays the resulting matrix for the Sepik data.[2] The table shows, for example, that the coefficient of relationship between the two Torricelli groups Wam and Southern Arapesh is quite high (0.008), as we might expect; whereas the coefficient between Southern Arapesh and Urat, also Torricelli, is rather low (−0.009), which we

Table 1
Coefficients of Genetic Relatedness of Selected Sepik Groups

	Urat	Yambes	Wam	S. Arapesh	N. Abelam	E. Abelam	W. Abelam	Y. Boiken	Iatmul
TORRICELLI									
Urat	.0059								
Yambes	.0079	.0545							
Wam	−.0050	−.0202	.0141						
S. Arapesh	−.0092	−.0111	.0082	.0220					
NDU									
Abelam									
Northern	.0069	.0094	−.0031	−.0078	.0110				
Eastern	.0023	.0029	−.0107	−.0049	−.0036	.0272			
Wosera	.0072	−.0026	.0016	−.0081	.0129	−.0058	.0218		
Y. Boiken	−.0054	−.0140	.0056	.0082	−.0094	.0026	−.0139	.0250	
Iatmul	−.0107	−.0269	.0095	.0026	−.0163	−.0101	−.0132	.0011	.0639

might not expect. To facilitate further interpretation, this matrix was analyzed into its principal components (Wilkinson 1988) to produce a genetic map. Attention was restricted to the first three eigenvectors, which accounted for 81 percent of the total variance (see table 2); inspection of the next two vectors indicated no serious vitiation of the conclusions drawn below. The resulting plots of the component loadings (that is, the eigenvectors multiplied by the square root of the corresponding eigenvalues—to avoid spherical distortion) are combined into a single, three-dimensional plot in figure 1.

In some respects, figure 1 holds no surprises. The Northern and Wosera Abelam and the Wam and Southern Arapesh pairs are each relatively undifferentiated, as might be expected given their supposedly common ancestral origins and speech patterns. Given the common presumption that modern Ndu and Torricelli speakers represent different stocks, however, it is surprising to find that on no component axis is there any clear differentiation of Ndu speakers as a whole from Torricelli speakers. Applying simple Chi-square tests to the

Table 2
Component Loadings of the Kinship Matrix

Population	*Component Loadings (eigenvector × square root of corresponding eigenvalue)* 1	2	3
TORRICELLI			
Urat	0.060	0.028	0.001
Yambes	0.188	−0.038	−0.111
Wam	−0.081	0.033	−0.060
Southern Arapesh	−0.066	−0.053	0.053
NDU			
Northern Abelam	0.078	0.062	0.025
Eastern Abelam	0.039	−0.094	−0.008
Wosera Abelam	0.056	0.119	0.059
Yangoru Boiken	−0.067	−0.106	0.056
Iatmul	−0.207	0.050	−0.135
Eigenvalue	0.108	0.047	0.044
Cumulative Percentage of Total Variance Explained	44	63	81

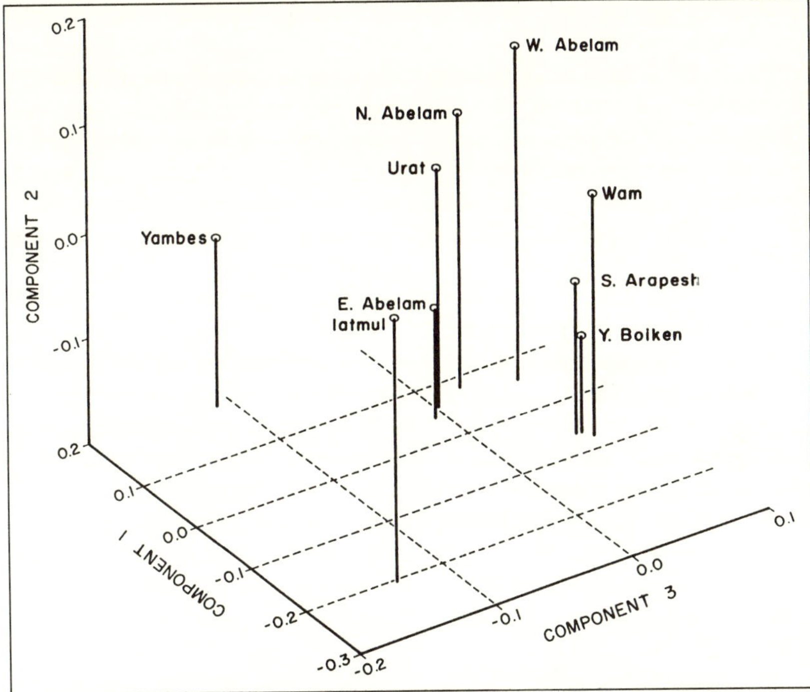

Fig. 1. Populations plotted on first three component loadings.

same data, Simmons et al. (1965:229, 231) reached a similar conclusion, suggesting that "in spite of cultural, linguistic and language family groups," the results "could probably be accounted for by the origin of these people from a common stock."

Subsequently, this startling conclusion was echoed in Chris Plato and Robert MacLennan's (1975) analysis of fingerprint data from villages throughout the Torricelli-speaking Wam; from the Ndu-speaking Eastern Abelam villages of Bugitu, Suanumbo, and Walangai; and the Ndu-speaking Wosera Abelam villages of Isogum, Gulakim, Saragum, and Stapigum. The authors found a greater similarity exhibited between the Wosera and Eastern Abelam in their dermatoglyphic frequencies than either of these exhibited with the Wam, as might be expected from their linguistic affinities. But they found, nonetheless, that Wosera Abelam and Wam frequencies were very similar and suggested that the Wam and Wosera Abelam "originated from the same stock despite their evident linguistic and cultural differences" (Plato and MacLennan 1975:213). Applying Harpending and Jenkins's method to Plato and MacLennan's data, Paul Lin et al. (1983) later calculated a principal components-type eigenstructure to reveal that the Wam and Wosera Abelam groups consistently were less differentiated from one another than from the Eastern Abelam populations. In other words, the fingerprints of the Ndu-speaking Wosera Abelam were more like those of the Torricelli-speaking Wam than those of their supposed Ndu congeners, the Eastern Abelam.[3] The blood-group data show that the Eastern Abelam are at least as differentiated from the Wam and Wosera Abelam as the Wam and Wosera Abelam are from each other (see figure 1).

Origin in a common stock may be one explanation for the absence of a clear differentiation between Ndu and Torricelli speakers in these data, but it is not the only one. We know that numerous localized migrations probably followed the Sepik's major migratory intrusions, and the resulting genetic drift could explain a significant amount of the Ndu-Torricelli genetic homogeneity. Certainly, as S. W. Serjeantson et al. (1983) suggest for populations elsewhere in northern Papua New Guinea, localized genetic drift partly could account for a tendency to homogeneity between the Eastern Abelam and Yangoru Boiken (see figure 1).

But geographical propinquity and localized genetic drift hardly explain the lack of differentiation between the Urat and the Northern and Wosera Abelam on the one hand and the Southern Arapesh and the Yangoru Boiken on the other (see figure 1). The Torricelli-speaking Urat are some 32 kilometers from the Ndu-speaking Northern Abelam; the Torricelli-speaking Southern Arapesh some 40 kilometers from the Ndu-speaking Yangoru Boiken (see map 3). Neither the linguistic nor the legendary data shed much light on the Urat-Abelam similarities. There is no ethnohistorical evidence of Abelam migrations into Urat territory or vice versa (see map 2). And although southeastern Urat villages appear to have absorbed a large number of refugees from the Kwanga (a group that like the Abelam speak a Sepik-Ramu, though not an Ndu, language), this seems insufficient to explain such a close affinity between the two groups (Allen pers. comm.; see map 2).

By contrast, as I have argued elsewhere (Roscoe 1989), linguistic and ethnohistorical evidence offers a very plausible explanation for the surprising finding that the Yangoru Boiken have greater genetic similarities to the Southern Arapesh than to their Ndu-speaking cousins the Abelam and Iatmul. Boiken territory, it appears, once was populated by Torricelli speakers of ancestral Arapesh. At some later time, Ndu-speaking immigrants began to move north from the Koiwat fenlands on the northern banks of the Sepik River into what is now Boiken territory (see map 3). Reaching the Prince Alexander Range, they then spread along the southern and eastern falls of the mountains, finally penetrating to the coast and offshore islands. In the course of this migration, they appear to have settled and intermarried with the resident Torricelli population, in the process imperially assimilating the language of their hosts to their own. The reason for the lack of genetic differentiation between the Southern Arapesh and Yangoru Boiken, therefore, is simply that the Ndu-speaking Boiken are to a considerable degree biologically Arapesh.

It would be surprising if this process were not repeated elsewhere in the Sepik; indeed, the fact that the Eastern Abelam are no more genetically differentiated from the Southern Arapesh than from the Northern and Wosera Abelam (see figure 1) may reflect another instance. In sum, given extensive migrational intermixing and more localized genetic drift due to intermarriage and movements among adjacent villages, there may be no need for the suggestion—the counterintuitive suggestion, given the linguistic and cultural patterns—that the Ndu and Torricelli speakers originated from a common stock.

What this does not explain, however, is why the Ndu-speaking Northern and Wosera Abelam are differentiated so much more from the Southern Arapesh than are the Yangoru Boiken, especially given their physical proximity to the Southern Arapesh in modern times (see figure 1 and map 3). If the Yangoru Boiken exhibit marked Arapesh affinities, why do not these two Abelam groups? One possibility is that every Ndu group advanced as much or more by mating as by might, but that there were far more Ndu intruders into the Northern Abelam areas than into other regions, genetically swamping the resident Torricelli speakers. In support of this scenario, Abelam population densities have throughout recorded history been significantly higher than those of the Boiken. Moreover, some Northern Abelam villages—such as Kalabu (Kaberry 1971:47–48)—contain clans of Arapesh origin, and there are mixed Abelam-Arapesh settlements along the Northern Abelam border (see Scaglion n.d.:3, for example), which suggests immigration and intermarriage in both cases.

Finally, this scenario would fit the eastward retreat of the Sepik sea, which passed due south of the Northern and Wosera Abelam some 5,000 years ago but passed Koiwat, the Boiken homeland, only about 2,500 years ago. Thus, if the ecological transformations set off by this marine retreat had stimulated Ndu speakers to move north, they would have been migrating into the Northern Abelam region for very much longer (and hence in greater numbers) than into Boiken territory. The problem with this scenario is that, if Ndu intruders into Abelam territory came in greater numbers over a longer period of time, it is difficult to explain why the Abelam language, unlike that of the Boiken, failed to reach the coast.

A second possibility is that, to a greater degree than the Boiken, the Northern and Wosera Abelam moved northward by force, displacing or exterminating the Torricelli speakers in their path. By this measure, they would have preserved their genetic distance from the Arapesh. And the scenario would explain why the Abelam, in contrast to the Boiken, never penetrated to the coast: their military onslaught eventually created an equal and opposite Arapesh reaction, much as Tuzin (1976, 1988) has theorized, explaining also their greater population density.

This argument finds other support in the lower frequency of autochthonous origins in Abelam settlement traditions. Throughout the Sepik, one encounters a subset of traditions in which founding ancestors are depicted not as immigrants but as émigrés from nearby holes in the ground, trees, stones, water holes, and so on. I have argued elsewhere (Roscoe 1989) that these clans appear to be of greater antiquity than those of migratory origin and, in the case of the Prince Alexander–Torricelli foothills, may represent clans of Arapesh ancestry. Among Boiken groups closest to Arapesh territory, these autochthonous tales represent between 24 and 31 percent of all settlement traditions (ibid.:146); among the Abelam, however, they are much rarer (Hauser-Schäublin pers. comm.)—as one might expect if the Abelam advance relied more on extermination or displacement of Arapesh residents. Unfortunately, this scenario of a more warlike Abelam advance raises the question of why some Ndu groups might advance more through military might while others advanced more through marital delight (an issue to which I shall return).

Whatever scenario we construct, however, the blood and dermatoglyphic data suggest that Sepik languages and genes have not migrated in lockstep. Although this is trivially obvious in localized intermarriage across linguistic boundaries, the data suggest a much more profound differentiation. In some areas, notably the modern territory of the Boiken, language seems to have flowed much more freely relative to genes than in areas such as modern Northern Abelam territory. The corollary of this point is that, contrary to prevailing anthropological opinion, the current cultural and linguistic configuration of the Sepik is not a simple product of groups speaking one language jostling aside groups speaking another, displacing or exterminating them by armed might. In some areas at least, "intrusions" may have involved no use of arms and may have been preceded or followed by mating and marriage. Nor should this surprise us. Although there are instances in oral history of whole villages being appropriated through extermination or displacement en masse (Hokmori 1977; Kaberry 1971:43; Roscoe 1989:148), more common by far are tales of migrations by refugee individuals or small kin groups, units that were far too small by themselves to exterminate or displace the settlements they encountered. Instead, the newcomers made peace, settled, and intermarried with their new hosts.

SEPIK MIGRATIONS: THE DIACHRONIC PERSPECTIVE

So, although genetic, dermatoglyphic, and settlement data suggest certain conclusions about the whence and whither of the Sepik's prehistoric migrations, they largely fail to illuminate the chronology of these migrations. But a few points can be made nonetheless.

Several authorities have suggested that the migrations of some Ndu people are relatively recent. From an analysis of Sepik River genealogies, Newton (1967:204) estimated that the Iatmul populated the river from the inland Sawos village of Nggaigorupi (Gaikarobi) beginning around 1775. Markus Schindlbeck (1980:548) argues, also from genealogical data, that Gaikarobi was founded from a nearby village, Ngetupma, around 1810. Similar claims have been made of other, non-Ndu groups. The Nukuma-speaking Kwoma, who belong to the same language stock as the Ndu, claim to have migrated to their present location about six or seven generations ago, that is, about 150 years ago (Bowden 1983:4). And, although he is skeptical of his evidence, David Lipset (1985:73) calculates that genealogical data put the beginnings of the ancestral migrations of the Nor-speaking Murik at about 200 or 250 years ago, which one might expect if they were displaced by an Iatmul expansion around this time. In support of this "short chronology" as I shall call it, we may note the coherence and comprehensiveness of the Iatmul settlement-tradition corpus: there is very little of the "noise" that characterizes the Abelam and Boiken corpora and presumably reflects the accumulation of small-scale, back-and-forth migrations over a long period of time (see map 2).

William Foley (1986a:23) suggests that given the central location of the Sawos languages among the Ndu family, and "with the usual comparative linguists' assumption that areas of oldest occupation exhibit the highest linguistic diversity,'' the Sawos were the ancestors not only of the Iatmul, but also of the Abelam and Boiken. If Douglas Newton and Markus Schindlbeck are correct, therefore, this might indicate that the migrations of the Abelam and Boiken peoples also occurred within the last few centuries. Donald Tuzin, reconstructing the history of the Southern Arapesh village of Ilahita, suggests precisely this for the northward thrust of the Abelam:

> Ilahita's complex social organization was intelligible as a systemic response to a dramatic increase in local population *beginning in the middle to late 19th century. . . .* According to my reconstruction, this increase was due mainly to the influx of refugees retreating before the Abelam as they migrated northward from the area of the Sepik River. (Tuzin 1988:84, emphasis added; see also Tuzin 1976:44, 53)

If these arguments are correct they refute the linkage suggested earlier between the retreat of the Sepik's inland sea and the migrations of the Ndu people, since the former occurred several thousand, not several hundred, years ago.

There are grounds for questioning a ''short chronology'' of Ndu migrations, however, especially where the Abelam and Boiken are concerned. To begin with, the basis for some of these short-chronology estimates is questionable. Newton, Schindlbeck, and Lipset all calculate their chronologies from genealogical histories. But, as Lipset points out, genealogies are subject to telescoping, and this phenomenon seems particularly probable given the characteristic shallowness of New Guinea genealogies. Among the Yangoru Boiken, for example, a legend associated with modern millenarianism traces the origins of the black and white races to events that took place on the slopes of Mount Hurun six generations before the current middle-aged population (in other words about 150 years ago), which is patently an absurd conclusion. In Yangoru, in fact, it was very common to find significant past events attributed to the *woranga* generation (that is, the great grandparental generation of perhaps 125 years ago), even though, on other evidence, they could not possibly have occurred then.[4] The *woranga* generation, however, was just beyond the living memory of Yangoru people, and it appeared to act as a sort of cultural receptacle for events assigned to the time after the events of creation but prior to living memory. Significantly, perhaps, the Iatmul also have this ''warangka'' generation (Bateson 1958:312). In the absence of independent corroborating evidence, therefore, we might accept that the Iatmul migrations occurred at least between 180 and 225 years ago, but we should be cautious about accepting that they occurred at this time. Regarding Ilahita's apparently recent origins, Tuzin's sources are unclear, but they may be genealogical (see, for example, Tuzin 1976: 62–67). If so, then the same cautions must apply.[5]

There are several grounds, in fact, for suggesting that the migrations of the Abelam and Boiken at least are of considerably greater antiquity than Tuzin's "short chronology" implies. In arguing that by the middle or late 19th century the Abelam had thrust close enough to Ilahita to start a rapid increase in the region's population density, Tuzin implies that the northernmost Abelam villages of today probably did not reach their present positions until a century or so ago, if not half a century later, when warfare—the means of Abelam expansion, according to Tuzin—was quenched by the Pax Australiana. If so, then the Northern Abelam village of Kalabu would have been created—or, at the very least, would have undergone a dramatic increase in size—within the lifetime of older people living in the village in 1939; and Arapesh villages to the north and west would have undergone significant structural transformations within the lifetimes of these same elders. Yet Phyllis Kaberry, who arrived in Kalabu in that year to conduct fieldwork, makes no mention of either occurrence (immediate and remarkable though they surely would have been in local minds had they occurred).

In fact, Kaberry's (1971:47–48) comments suggest that the majority of Kalabu's hamlets had been in existence for several generations at least; and Brigitta Hauser-Schäublin (1989:20), who worked in Kalabu in the late 1970s and early 1980s, comments that the Abelam advance north had ended at least a hundred years before. My own detailed historical and ethnohistorical analysis among the Yangoru Boiken similarly indicates that most clans had been in place for at least 100 to 150 years, and probably much longer. Furthermore, since the ethnohistorical evidence indicates that the ancestors of the Northern Abelam came from the vicinity of the Sepik River about 45 kilometers to the south, while those of the Yangoru Boiken originated about 75 kilometers away in the Koiwat fenlands on the northern shores of the Sepik (see map 2), then for these two groups to be in place at least a century ago, the migrations of their ancestors must have begun considerably earlier.[6]

A second difficulty with a "short chronology" of Abelam and Boiken prehistory is the glottochronological evidence. According to Laycock's (1965:181) figures, the Ndu family of languages split up over a period roughly from 3,000 to 1,000 years ago, with the Iatmul, Abelam, and Boiken separating over a period roughly from 2,000 to

1,300 years ago.[7] These dates are temptingly close to the environmental transformations precipitated by the retreat of the Sepik Sea, but Laycock raises several concerns about their interpretation, and today only those virginally innocent in linguistic theory would accept glottochronological dating at face value. First, there is no evidence for a uniform vocabulary retention rate for New Guinea languages. Second, assuming a uniform retention rate, the rate constant for New Guinea languages is still unknown and is probably rather higher than that used in Laycock's glottochronological calculations. If so, then his calculated splitting dates would be rather earlier than the actual dates. Third, the method assumes no contact between the languages concerned subsequent to their separation. If such contact did occur, then calculated splitting dates would be rather later than the actual dates. And fourth, the evolution of linguistic diversity is not necessarily the product of intrinsic linguistic mutation alone, as glottochronology assumes, but can also come about when two or more linguistically distinct populations intermix, one assimilating but being changed by the other or others. If such mixing does occur, then calculated splitting dates will be rather earlier than actual splitting dates. This point is important in light of my foregoing suggestions that, in migrating to their current locations, the Ndu speakers probably intermixed in some degree with already resident Torricelli-speaking populations.[8]

The direction of the likely errors introduced into the calculations suggest that the actual splitting dates of the Abelam, Boiken, and Iatmul were probably rather later than Laycock's figures. Quite how much later is difficult to say, but I find it hard to believe that the errors could account for a difference of from 1,000 to 2,000 years (that is, an error of from 400 to 800 percent) as a "short chronology" would imply. To approach the matter from another direction, the "short chronology" suggests that the marked linguistic differences among the Abelam, Boiken, and Iatmul arose within the space of a couple of centuries. Since early historical and ethnographic records indicate no more than minor linguistic changes within these groups over the last 50 or 70 years, this proposition is difficult to accept.

Finally, there is the blood group evidence. Figure 1 reveals that, on all but component 3, the Iatmul are more differentiated from the Northern and Wosera Abelam and the Yangoru Boiken than they are from the Torricelli groups. It is difficult to imagine how this could have come about if the Abelam and Boiken had split from the Iatmul just a couple of hundred years ago.

The weight of evidence, I suggest, indicates that the Abelam and

Boiken started their migrations from the Sepik River rather more than a couple of centuries or so ago. And it does not contradict the possibility that these migrations are sufficiently ancient to have been prompted by the ecological transformations wrought by the last recession of the Sepik Sea.

This does not mean, however, that the Iatmul migrations are necessarily of similar antiquity. The difficulty here is that Laycock failed to include the Sawos languages in his glottochronological analysis of the Ndu languages. Thus, it is entirely possible, given the evidence, that the Abelam and Boiken split from early Sawos/Iatmul languages many centuries ago but that the Iatmul did not move from the Sawos area until much more recently, as Newton and Schindlbeck suggest. In fact, Philip Staalsen's subsequent glottochronological studies of the Sawos and Iatmul languages strongly support a recent split. Three Sawos "languages" (including the Gaikarobi "language") turn out to have cognacies with Iatmul of 97 percent or higher, which leads Staalsen to list them as dialects of Iatmul (Staalsen 1969:11). And the Iatmul villages themselves have a cognacy rate in the vicinity of 99 percent (Staalsen 1969:70), far greater than that found among the Abelam and Boiken (Wilson 1976:59–61; Freudenburg 1976).

CONCLUSION

Given the intricacy of much of the foregoing analysis (unfortunately required by the complexity and breadth of the data), it is worth concluding with a summary of what now can be said of Sepik prehistory. These findings conveniently divide into conclusions about scenarios and process.

With regard to scenarios, it seems safe to say that modern Torricelli languages are descended from those spoken by an early population that immigrated to the Sepik some time ahead of a second immigrant population speaking ancestral forms of Sepik-Ramu languages. The limitations of the data render any conclusions concerning these Sepik-Ramu languages highly speculative, but it is possible they were spoken by an immigrant population that moved from the west some 5,000 or 6,000 years ago, initially migrating through the central cordillera, or through the intermontane trough farther north, possibly as a marine-adapted population following the retreat of the Sepik sea.

Nor can we be dogmatic about subsequent events. Settlement traditions indicate that the ancestors of western Sepik-Ramu speakers such as the Kwanga and Tama moved south, away from what is now the Sepik River, as did the ancestors of their Torricelli-speaking neighbors immediately to the west. But it is presently impossible to say whether these migrants reached their present positions from the central cordillera across the inland sea, following its retreat over its drying bed, or simply from its northern shores.

It does seem probable that the early Sepik-Ramu population spawned the ancestors of the Ndu-speaking groups now spread across the lands from the Middle Sepik to the northern mountains and that these proto-Ndu arrived first in the Middle Sepik region, quite possibly in what is now Sawos territory. However, it is impossible to say whether they immigrated from what are now the headwaters of the Karawari and Krosmeri rivers (as Laycock suggests), or from the alluvial plains in the southeast (as Swadling prefers). If they did come from either of these places, however, then the settlement traditions suggest an arrival over water before the recession of the inland sea rather than by foot across its infilling bed. Alternatively, if ancestral Sepik-Ramu speakers followed the sea's retreat east, then the Ndu speakers probably would have reached the Middle Sepik from farther up the Sepik River.

Subsequent history becomes a little clearer. The balance of evidence suggests that the Ndu presence in the Middle Sepik is ancient rather than recent and that the ancestors of the Abelam and Boiken began moving north many hundreds of years ago. In so doing, both populations almost certainly moved through an already resident, probably Arapesh-related, Torricelli population. Their interactions with these residents may have been very different: where the Boiken commonly seem to have married, settled with, and linguistically assimilated their Torricelli hosts, the Abelam may have been more inclined to violence. Finally, within the last few hundred years, the Iatmul seem to have split from western Sawos speakers and moved south to their present location on the banks of the Sepik River.

To those readers who are not Sepik specialists, perhaps the point of greater interest in all this is what it implies about process, about the influence of migration on the generation of and regional permutation of linguistic and cultural forms. To date, Sepik anthropology has largely reflected the general anthropological literature on migration (Adams et al. 1978) in focusing overwhelmingly on society-level migrations, the movement of whole peoples from one place to another en masse. As a result, regional linguistic and cultural permutations in the contact era are usually explained as the historical products of peoples who, bearing distinctive languages and cultures, were migrating and exterminating or thrusting other peoples aside.[9] In this view, biological, linguistic, and symbolic features to some extent may permeate from one people to another, but by and large the genes, language, and culture of any particular people today represent the direct evolutionary descendants of their ancestors—as though these physical and symbolic features all migrate together in hermetically sealed quanta.

As William Adams et al. (1978) note, however, movements of whole peoples have occurred much less frequently in the course of recorded human history than migrations of isolated individuals or families. Concomitantly, the idea of Sepik migration as society-wide movement recently has fallen into question (see Allen 1986; Filer 1984; Foley 1986b, for example), and the data presented in this chapter strongly suggest a more complex picture. Major population movements do appear to characterize Sepik prehistory, but the fine detail of the ethnohistorical evidence, the difficulties in clearly differentiating Ndu and Torricelli populations by blood type and dermatoglyphics, the pronounced affinities between the Torricelli-speaking Southern Arapesh and the Ndu-speaking Yangoru Boiken, and similar affinities between the Torricelli Urat and Ndu Abelam indicate that, in many places, the contact-era cultural and linguistic scene was as much the product of individuals or kin fragments settling with, marrying, and sometimes assimilating ethnically different neighbors.[10]

These revisions in the established picture of Sepik prehistory invite us to rethink how migratory movements contribute to regional linguistic and cultural permutation. Here, I should like to consider two questions: Why should some peoples resort more to armed might in their advance, when others rely more on marriage? and How can language and culture advance to some extent independently of genes? The Abelam and Boiken are particularly appropriate cases for considering these issues. On the one hand, despite their common ancestry, the northward-advancing Ndu component of the Abelam seems to have used armed force more readily than that of the Boiken. On the other hand, in the Boiken as opposed to the Abelam case, Ndu speech patterns seem to have advanced much more rapidly north than Ndu genetic flow, penetrating in fact to the coast.

An answer to the first question that might find favor with Abelam ethnographers (such as Forge [1990], for example) is that the Abelam's Ndu ancestors had a particularly aggressive ethos. Disposed more to advance through extermination or displacement of the resident Arapesh, they would preserve the integrity of their genes, language, and culture, at the same time creating an Arapesh resistance that would impede the movement of these features north. As simple as this explanation seems, however, it resolves one question by begging another: Why are the Abelam more aggressive? And it sheds no light on the mechanisms by which the Ndu patterns in Boiken speech advanced ahead of Ndu genes—as opposed, say, to Arapesh linguistic patterns maintaining their hegemony, as one might expect if the Ndu intruders were mainly individuals or small kin groups.

What might resolve the puzzle, I suggest, are the marital strategies employed by the Ndu components in the Boiken and Abelam populations. Commenting on the linguistic influence of the Alamblak on the Yimas, south of the Iatmul, Foley (1986b:25) has pointed out that in small virilocal communities exogamous marriage can be an important instrument of language change. Through most of their childhood, children of both sexes often spend most of their time with their mothers and relatively little with their fathers, and so they are more influenced by their mother in the acquisition of their native language. In consequence, the more the women of one population marry and move into another, and the more asymmetric this flow is, the more predatory may be the propagation of the inmarrying women's language.

Although we lack any substantial data on prehistoric marriage patterns, evidence from recorded history indicates that the Boiken may have inclined much more than the Abelam not only toward the outmarriage of women but also toward accepting some asymmetries in the direction of this flow. To judge by Diane Brady Losche's (1982: 89–93) remarks, for example, the Abelam place a much greater emphasis than the Yangoru Boiken on marrying close to home, and this is reflected in village endogamy rates (table 3). Over about the last century, between 45 and 60 percent of women in the northern Yangoru Boiken village of Sima have married out of the village, compared with between 15 and 35 percent among the Northern and Wosera Abelam. If these differences prevailed in the past, then (all other things being equal) the Boiken's Ndu-speaking female ancestors routinely may have moved into Arapesh-speaking territory, propagating their speech patterns, with significantly greater frequency than the Abelam's Ndu-speaking women.

Were Arapesh women returning in equal numbers, then the Boiken linguistic advantage would be significantly attenuated. With Torricelli and Ndu linguistic features flowing each way at similar rates, the result would be a symmetric linguistic miscegenation, not the triumph of Ndu over Torricelli patterns. If present practice is our witness, however, the Boiken contrast to both the Abelam and

Table 3
Village Endogamy Rates Among the Abelam and Yangoru Boiken

Village	*Period*	*Population*	*Rate (%)*	*Source*
NORTHERN ABELAM				
Apangai 1 & 2	mid–1970s	552	83.3	Losche 1982:402
Kalabu	1939	489	73.4	Kaberry 1971:43
Yenigo	1962	234	65.2	Lea 1964:57
WOSERA ABELAM				
Nungwaigo 1	1969	265	82.5	Gorlin 1973:45
Pukago 1	1969	360	84.6	Gorlin 1973:45
Stapikum	1962	152	62.9	Lea 1964:57
YANGORU BOIKEN				
Sima	1880–1980	150?–350	37.5–55.5	Roscoe, field notes
Sima	1971–1980	350	49.0	Roscoe, field notes

Arapesh in preferring an asymmetric marriage pattern. Where the Abelam and Arapesh prefer a direct or delayed exchange of women between kin groups, the Boiken prefer the asymmetric "iai" marriage of the Iatmul, in which a man marries his FMBSD.[11] Thus, the Ndu ancestors of the Boiken may have been more disposed than the Abelam to have women move into Arapesh territory, rewarded not by a return in kind but by the eventual triumph of their language over that of their in-laws.

Although this hypothesis is little more than conjectural history, it need not remain so. If these processes were at the heart of the differential spread of Ndu speech patterns in the coastal mountains, then there is every reason to suppose that they continue today and that fine-grained ethnohistorical, linguistic, genetic, and cultural analyses will reveal them. An ideal field site for such research would be the area north of Warrabung, where Eastern Abelam, Kaboibus-Arapesh, and Yangoru-Boiken borders converge, permitting the simultaneous investigation of Abelam-Arapesh, Boiken-Arapesh, and Abelam-Boiken interactions.

Nor need such a project be limited to the transmission of language. If women flowing asymmetrically into alien communities transmit features of their natal language to their young, there is no reason why analogously they might not transmit features of their natal culture. The interesting feature of such a process would be the resulting gender-based cultural division. Women marrying asymmetrically into alien communities could transmit to their children only those features of their natal culture to which they had access. Thus, we might expect them to inject into their husbands' cultures aspects of their natal female culture such as child care, food cultivation and gathering, beliefs about female physiology, contraception, and so on with relative ease. With similar ease, we might expect them to propagate public aspects of their natal symbolic culture—for example, sorcery beliefs, songs, and children's stories. But we would hardly expect them to spread secret male culture, such as Tambaran cults or long-yam-growing ritual. Viewed across a region, in sum, we might expect that a process of cultural transmission through the asymmetric flow of women from one community to another would result in cultural aspects of the donor community being differentially spread into the receiver community, with traits accessible to females reaching further than those accessible only to males.

REFERENCES

Adams, William Y., Dennis P. Van Gerven, and Richard S. Levy
1978 The Retreat From Migrationism. Annual Reviews in Anthropology 7:483–532.

Allen, Bryant
1986 Some Environmental Considerations in Sepik Culture History. Paper presented at the Wenner-Gren symposium Sepik Culture History: Variation and Synthesis. Mijas, Spain.

Aufenanger, H.
n.d.a The Passing Scene in North-East New-Guinea. Collectanea Instituti Anthropos 2. St Augustin: Anthropos Institute.
n.d.b The Great Inheritance in Northeast New Guinea: A Collection of Anthropological Data. Collectanea Instituti Anthropos 9. St Augustin: Anthropos Institute.

Bateson, Gregory
1958 Naven. Stanford: Stanford University Press.

Bowden, Ross
1983 Yena: Art and Ceremony in a Sepik Society. Oxford: Pitt Rivers Museum.

Bragge, Lawrence W.
1984 The Japandai Migrations. Paper presented at the Wenner-Gren symposium Sepik Research Today. Basel, Switzerland.

Brison, Karen J.
1988 Gossip, Innuendo, and Sorcery: Village Politics Among the Kwanga, East Sepik Province, Papua New Guinea. Ph.D. dissertation. University of California, San Diego.

Filer, Colin
1984 The Cultural Configuration of Nuku District. Paper presented at the Wenner-Gren symposium Sepik Research Today. Basel, Switzerland.

Foley, William A.
1986a Language Change and Language Allegiance in the Sepik. Paper presented at the Wenner-Gren symposium Sepik Culture History: Variation and Synthesis. Mijas, Spain.
1986b The Papuan Languages of New Guinea. Cambridge: Cambridge University Press.

Forge, Anthony
1966 Art and Environment in the Sepik. Proceedings of the Royal Anthropological Institute for 1965, pp. 23–31.
1971 Marriage and Exchange in the Sepik: Comments on Francis Korn's Analysis of Iatmul Society. *In* Rethinking Kinship and Marriage. Rodney Needham, ed., pp. 133–144. London: Tavistock.
1990 The Power of Culture and the Culture of Power. *In* Sepik Heritage: Tradition and Change in Papua New Guinea. Nancy Lutkehaus, Christian Kaufmann, William E. Mitchell, Douglas Newton, Lita Osmundsen, and Meinhard Schuster, eds., pp. 160–170. Durham, N.C.: Carolina Academic Press.

Freudenburg, Allen
1976 The Dialects of Boiken. Working papers in Papua New Guinea Languages 16:81–90.

Froelich, J. W., and E. Giles
1981 A Multivariate Approach to Fingerprint Variation in Papua New Guinea: Implications for Prehistory. American Journal of Physical Anthropology 54:73–92.

Gorlin, Peter
1973 Health, Wealth, and Agnation Among the Abelam: The Beginnings of Social Stratification in New Guinea. Ph.D. dissertation. Columbia University.

Haantjens, H. A.
1965 Morphology and Origin of Patterned Ground in a Humid Tropical Lowland Area, New Guinea. Australian Journal of Soil Research 3:111–129.

Haantjens, H. A., P. C. Heyligers, J. C. Saunders, J. R. McAlpine, and R. H. Fagan
1972 Land Systems of the Aitape-Ambunti Area. *In* Lands of the Aitape-Ambunti Area, Papua New Guinea. H. A. Haantjens, comp., pp. 36–59. Canberra: Commonwealth Scientific and Industrial Research Organisation.

Harpending, Henry, and Trefor Jenkins
1973 Genetic Distance Among Southern African Populations. *In* Methods and Theories of Anthropological Genetics. M. H.

Crawford and P. L. Workman, eds., pp. 177–199. Albuquerque: University of New Mexico Press.

1974 !Kung Population Structure. *In* Genetic Distance, James F. Crow and Carter Denniston, eds., pp. 137–165. New York and London: Plenum Press.

Hauser-Schäublin, Brigitta

1989 Kulthäuser in Nordneuguinea. Berlin: Akademie-Verlag.

Hokmori, Patrick

1977 Tuonumbo Village in the East Sepik Province. Oral History 5(4):69–74.

Kaberry, Phyllis M.

1971 Political Organization Among the Northern Abelam. *In* Politics in New Guinea: Traditional and in the Context of Change. Ronald M. Berndt and Peter Lawrence, eds., pp. 35–73. Seattle: University of Washington Press.

Kelly, Kevin M.

1990 Gm Polymorphisms, Linguistic Affinities, and Natural Selection in Melanesia. Current Anthropology 31:201–219.

Laycock, Donald C.

1965 The Ndu Language Family (Sepik District, New Guinea). Pacific Linguistics, series C, no. 1. Canberra: Australian National University.

1973 Sepik Languages—Checklist and Preliminary Classification. Pacific Linguistics, series B, no. 25. Canberra: Australian National University.

Lea, D. A. M.

1964 Abelam Land and Sustenance. Ph.D. dissertation. Australian National University.

1965 The Abelam: A Study in Local Differentiation. Pacific Viewpoint 6:191–214.

Lin, Paul M., V. Bach Enciso, and M. H. Crawford

1983 Dermatoglyphic Inter- and Intrapopulation Variation Among Indigenous New Guinea Groups. Journal of Human Evolution 12:103–123.

Lipset, David M.

1985 Seafaring Sepiks: Ecology, Warfare, and Prestige in Murik Trade. Research in Economic Anthropology 7:67–94.

Löffler, Ernst

1977 Geomorphology of Papua New Guinea. Canberra: Commonwealth Scientific and Industrial Research Organisation and Australian National University.

Losche, Diane Brady

1982 Male and Female in Abelam Society: Opposition and Complementarity. Ph.D. dissertation. Columbia University.

Lutkehaus, Nancy C., and Paul B. Roscoe
1987 Sepik Culture History: Variation, Innovation, and Synthesis. Current Anthropology 28:577–581.

Mead, Margaret
1947 The Mountain Arapesh. Vol. 3. Socio-Economic Life. Anthropological Papers of the American Museum of Natural History 40:159–232.

Nekitel, Otto
1975 The History of Womsis. Oral History 3(3):2–32.

Newton, Douglas
1967 Oral Tradition and Art History in the Sepik District, New Guinea. *In* Essays on the Verbal and Visual Arts. June Helm, ed., pp. 200–215. Seattle: American Ethnological Society.

Plato, Chris C., and Robert MacLennan
1975 The Dermatoglyphics of the Maprik Sub-District of the Sepic District of New Guinea. Zeitschrift für Morphologie und Anthropologie 66:208–216.

Reiner, E., and J. A. Mabbutt
1968 Geomorphology of the Wewak-Lower Sepik Area. *In* Lands of the Wewak-Lower Sepik Area, Papua New Guinea. H. A. Haantjens, comp., pp. 61–71. Melbourne: Commonwealth Scientific and Industrial Research Organisation.

Roscoe, Paul B.
1989 The Flight From the Fen: The Prehistoric Migrations of the Boiken of the East Sepik Province, Papua New Guinea. Oceania 60(2):139–154.

Scaglion, Richard
1976 Seasonal Patterns in Western Abelam Conflict Management Practices: The Ethnography of Law in the Maprik Sub-Province, Papua New Guinea. Ph.D. dissertation. University of Pittsburgh.
n.d. Pacification and the Reorganization of Abelam Settlement Patterns. Unpublished manuscript.

Schanfield, M. S.
1977 Population Affinities of the Australian Aborigines as Reflected by the Genetic Markers of Immunoglobulins. Journal of Human Evolution 6:341–352.

Schindlbeck, Markus
1980 Sago bei den Sawos. Basel: Ethnologisches Seminar der Universität und Museum für Volkerkunde.

Serjeantson, S. W., R. L. Kirk, and P. B. Booth
1983 Linguistic and Genetic Differentiation in New Guinea. Journal of Human Evolution 12:77–92.

Simmons, R. T., J. J. Graydon, D. C. Gadjusek, F. D. Scholfield, and A. D. Parkinson

1965 Blood Group Genetic Data from the Maprik Area of the Sepik District, New Guinea. Oceania 35(3):218–232.

Staalsen, Philip

1965 Brugnowi Origins: The Founding of a Village. Man 65:184–188.

1969 The Dialects of Iatmul. Pacific Linguistics, series A. Occasional paper. Canberra: Australian National University.

1975 The Languages of the Sawos Region (New Guinea). Anthropos 70:6–16.

Steinberg, A. G., D. C. Gadjusek, and M. Alpers

1972 Genetic Studies in Relation to Kuru, No. 5. Distribution of Human Gamma Globulin Allotypes in New Guinea Populations. American Journal of Human Genetics 24 (supplement):95–110.

Swadling, Pamela

1984 Sepik Prehistory. *In* Sepik Heritage: Tradition and Change in Papua New Guinea. Nancy Lutkehaus, Christian Kaufmann, William E. Mitchell, Douglas Newton, Lita Osmundsen, and Meinhard Schuster, eds., pp. 71–86. Durham, N.C.: Carolina Academic Press.

Swadling, Pamela, John Chappell, Geoff Francis, Nick Araho, and Baivu, Ivuyo

1989 A Late Quaternary Inland Sea and Early Pottery in Papua New Guinea. Archaeology in Oceania 24:106–109.

Swadling, Pamela, B. Hauser-Schäublin, P. Gorecki, and F. Tiesler

1988 The Sepik-Ramu: An Introduction. Boroko, Papua New Guinea: Papua New Guinea National Museum.

Swadling, Pamela, Claudia Hyles, and Simon Lohia, eds.

1980 Traditional Settlement Histories and Legends From the Sepik and Madang Provinces. Oral History 8(9).

Tiesler, Frank

1976 Besiedlungsgeschichte und Stilprovinzen in Nord-Neuguinea. Ethnographische Archäologie Zeitung 17:479–489.

Tuzin, Donald F.

1976 The Ilahita Arapesh: Dimensions of Unity. Berkeley and Los Angeles: University of California Press.

1988 Prospects of Village Death in Ilahita. Oceania 59(2):81–104.

van Dijk, Wjom, and A. D. Parkinson

1974 Epidemiology of Malaria in New Guinea. Papua New Guinea Medical Journal 17:17–21.

Wassmann, Jürg

1990 The Nyaura Concepts of Space and Time. *In* Sepik Heritage: Tradition and Change in Papua New Guinea. Nancy

Lutkehaus, Christian Kaufmann, William E. Mitchell, Douglas Newton, Lita Osmundsen, and Meinhard Schuster, eds., pp. 21–35. Durham, N.C.: Carolina Academic Press.

Wilkinson, Leland
1988 SYSTAT: The System for Statistics. Evanston, Ill.: SYSTAT.

Wilson, P.
1976 Abulas Dialect Survey. Working papers in Papua New Guinea Languages 16:51–79.

Wurm, Stephen A.
1982 Papuan Languages of Oceania. Tübingen: Gunter Narr Verlag.
1983 Linguistic Prehistory in the New Guinea Area. Journal of Human Evolution 12:25–35.

Wurm, Stephen A., D. C. Laycock, C. L. Voorhoeve, and T. E. Dutton
1975 Papuan Linguistic Prehistory and Past Language Migrations in the New Guinea Area. *In* Papuan Languages and the New Guinea Linguistic Scene. S. A. Wurm, ed., pp. 935–960. Pacific Linguistics, series C, no. 38. Canberra: Australian National University.

NOTES

Some of the data on which this paper is based were gathered during 1979–1981 and 1987 in field trips sponsored by the Department of Community Medicine at the University of Papua New Guinea and funded by the Emslie Horniman Scholarship Fund, the Ford Foundation, the University of Rochester, and the Faculty Research Committee of the University of Maine. Other data were most generously provided by Bryant Allen, Patrick Gesch, Colin Filer, Brigitta Hauser-Schäublin, and Patricia Townsend. Steve Bicknell executed the artwork. The assistance of these persons and institutions is very gratefully acknowledged. I should also like to thank Pamela Swadling for drawing my attention to the importance of the Sepik Sea in the region's prehistory and Henry Harpending for advice on transforming blood-group data into indices of genetic relatedness. None of these individuals is in any way responsible for the errors I probably have made.

1. On map 2, the migrations of the Boiken people are schematized from the nearly 300 migrations marked on Roscoe (1989) map 2. Sources for this map include Allen pers. comm.; Aufenanger n.d.a:73–75, 102, 278, 299; Aufenanger n.d.b:318; Bowden 1983:3–4; Bragge 1984:appendix C; Filer 1984: 31; Gorlin 1973:37–40; Kaberry 1971:47–48; Lea 1964:48; Lipset 1985:72–73, and pers. comm.; Losche 1982:29; Nekitel 1975; Newton 1967:203–206; Roscoe 1989, and field notes; Scaglion 1976:49; Staalsen 1965:184, 1969:70, 1975:9–10; Swadling et al. 1980; Wassmann 1990:26–28.

2. The Wosera-Abelam figures were calculated as a weighted mean of the Jama and Stapigum data.

3. Citing studies by J. W. Froelich and E. Giles (1981), the authors suggest an explanation of gene flow into East Abelam from the "Kanaken, a Melanesian-speaking coastal population" (Lin et al. 1983:118).

4. For example, when directly queried, some Sima informants were of the opinion that the two principal pig-exchange ceremonies began in the *woranga* generation. But the structure of the moiety, submoiety, and sub-submoiety systems—coupled with the ethnohistories of several individual pig-exchange submoieties—indicate a much earlier origin.

5. I should emphasize that even were Tuzin's "short chronology" in error, it would not invalidate the rest of his argument about the growth and evolution of the Ilahita polity. The evolutionary process he describes could as well have taken place several centuries ago, or over a period of several centuries.

6. It is commonly presumed that the Sepik grasslands are the deforested results of the Abelam and Boiken northward advance, and certain of their microgeomorphological features attributable to the activities of large earthworms and slope wash suggest that they—and by implication the Abelam and Boiken northward advance—have some antiquity (Haantjens 1965; Swadling 1984:21). Unfortunately, the dating of these features comes from Laycock's glottochronology and hence cannot serve as an independent dating of Ndu migrations. In any case, we cannot be sure that it was the Ndu and not some earlier Torricelli population that created the grasslands.

7. Laycock was unable to obtain data for the Sawos groups, but he hypothesizes a split around 1,800 or 1,900 years ago (1965:187, 181).

8. Loath as I am to take on linguists on their home ground, this factor also leads me to question Foley's suggestion that the degree of linguistic differentiation in the Sawos region indicates it was the Ndu homeland. This may have been so, but linguistic differentiation seems, in this case, hazardous ground on which to base the case.

9. For the Sepik, for example, see Forge 1966; Laycock 1965; Lea 1965:205; Swadling 1990:81–84; and Tuzin 1976, 1988.

10. The unfortunate methodological consequence of this point is that, since small-scale movements leave few distinctive archaeological traces, it is doubtful that Sepik archaeology will provide many rapid advances in our understanding of the Sepik's migrational prehistory or of its implications for Sepik cultural permutations and distributions.

11. For the Abelam, see Forge (1971:137), Kaberry (1971:50), Lea (1964:57), and Losche 1982:96. For the Arapesh, see Mead (1947:182–183) and Tuzin (1976:100–104).

PIG FEASTS AND EXPANDING NETWORKS OF CULTURAL INFLUENCE IN THE UPPER FLY-DIGUL PLAIN

Robert L. Welsch

South of New Guinea's central cordillera lies a vast but thinly populated plain, blanketed by a dense rainforest and extending across an area as large as Papua New Guinea's central highlands. This plain straddles the border between Indonesia and Papua New Guinea, from the great Digul River system of Irian Jaya in the west to Papua New Guinea's mighty Fly River in the east. The upper portion of the plain consists of low-lying hills and ridges drained by the many tributaries of these two major rivers. To the south the Upper Fly-Digul plain becomes less hilly, eventually opening out onto the savannahs and swamps of the South Coastal Plain (map 1).

One of the most striking features of the Muyu, Mandobo, Yonggom, Ningerum, and other societies that occupy the Upper Fly-Digul Plain is an elaborate pig-feast cycle that is a frequent social event during the dry season (roughly from November to April). Large pig feasts attended by hundreds of guests are not uncommon in New Guinea, particularly in the highlands where populations are both large and dense. What is so unusual about pig feasts in the Upper Fly-Digul area is that, despite the region's low population density and small autonomous settlements, feasts are routinely attended by several hundreds and sometimes by two or three thousand guests.

I would like to examine how these feasts—together with the patterns of credit, debt, and social obligations that accompany them—integrate these small dispersed communities. In particular, I consider how individual social and economic ties are linked through feast activities to create socioeconomic networks that stretch far across the plain. Often, the social networks invoked during a feast include in-

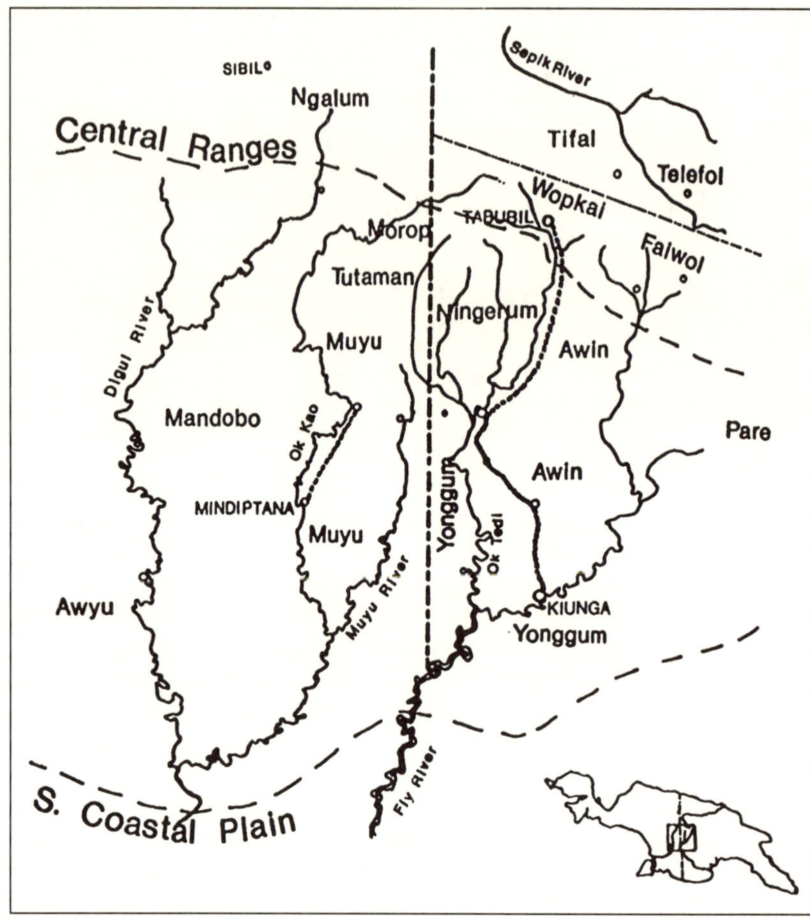

Map 1. The Fly and Digul river systems: – – – = international border.

dividuals and families from several different ethnolinguistic groups. In this sense, feasting is a regional phenomenon in the Upper Fly-Digul area, even though each ethnic group has its own local conventions about how feasts should be organized and conducted.

My purpose here is to suggest that the socioeconomic ties invoked in staging a feast on the Upper Fly-Digul Plain are inherently expansionist. Once invoked, they tend to incorporate an expanding number of individuals and settlements into a loosely integrated economic structure that stretches across most of the Upper Fly-Digul. It is doubtful that any participants are aware of how far these economic networks extend across the plain, nor do individuals directly perceive the expansionist—and in some respects inflationary—character of the system. Nevertheless, the economic relations that are most pronounced among the Muyu at the center of the plain appear to have expanded to the east and west into the Mandobo, Ningerum, and Yonggom areas, in a process I refer to as the economic Muyu-ization of non-Muyu (Welsch in press).

Economic expansion of the Muyu has not led to larger social groups or more encompassing political alliances. Wider and more active networks do not seem to have created big-men or given leaders greater authority—as they may have done among the Melpa and the Enga (see Strathern 1971; Feil 1984). Nor has economic Muyu-ization meant political or even economic hegemony of Muyu people over non-Muyu.

The expansion of Muyu-style feasting into non-Muyu areas has undoubtedly facilitated the spread of certain customs, practices, and goods across the plain, most notably into the Mandobo area (see Boelaars 1970:17). But my concern here is less about the diffusion of particular customs or practices than about the socioeconomic mechanisms that led individuals and communities on the Muyu frontier to be drawn increasingly to participate in Muyu-style pig feasts and to share the Muyu people's preoccupation with cowrie-shell money and other shell valuables.

The pig feast is not the only institution involved in creating and maintaining social and economic linkages between communities in the Upper Fly-Digul area. But feasts build on and invoke these other socioeconomic and political institutions, particularly marriage and affinal relations, social payments, and (formerly) alliances for defense and raiding. By bringing together individuals from widely scattered communities, feasts offer concrete evidence of how relations between individuals in autonomous local groups are integrated into socioeconomic networks that extend far and wide across the region.

Several times each year, feasts brought together large numbers of individuals from a wide area, often involving communities whose local customs and languages differed. Feasts are unmistakably the most important and exciting social events on the Upper Fly-Digul Plain. Moreover, the organization of feasts has a dynamic quality that encourages expansion along preexisting networks to incorporate larger numbers of people.

In local neighborhoods, feasts were instrumental in reaffirming affinal and kin relations, in managing social payments (such as brideprice, childprice, death payments, and other debts), and in promoting trade. For individuals living 50 kilometers or more from one another, pig feasts provided a forum that facilitated establishing and renewing social relations between unrelated or distantly related individuals.

J. W. Schoorl (1957) noted that social relations in this region focused on ties between individuals rather than on ties between groups. Even when social groups formed for some purpose, the persistent social units involved rarely consisted of more than a small extended family or lineage. Larger social groupings periodically coalesced around preexisting relationships between individuals in different families; but such groupings rarely comprised the same set of personnel. Pig feasts exhibit the most visible example of how large but temporary social groupings form around individual relationships—usually building on relationships between people living in nearby homesteads or hamlets. These ephemeral social groupings are tangible evidence of the extensive social networks that crisscrossed the rainforest and linked households from one end of the Upper Fly-Digul Plain to the other.

COMMUNITY ORGANIZATION IN THE UPPER FLY-DIGUL REGION

Scattered over some 35,000 square kilometers of rainforest are many small settlements inhabited by perhaps as many as 40,000 people speaking at least a dozen different languages in the Awyu-Dumut, Ok, and Awin-Pa families.[1] Despite important linguistic differences the Upper Fly-Digul peoples share a number of common cultural patterns that differ markedly from neighboring peoples in the mountains to the north and from the peoples inhabiting the coastal plain to the south (Welsch in press; Barth 1971; Busse 1987).

Beginning in the 1950s, the government and missions encouraged people in the Upper Fly-Digul to form central villages, but previously they had no villages as such; their settlements characteristically consisted of tiny hamlets made up of one or two houses built high up in trees.[2] These tree and pole houses were built on patriclan territories near sago swamps and were usually surrounded by extensive banana gardens.

The inhabitants of each hamlet were linked through ties of kinship and marriage to the residents of most neighboring hamlets. With these kinsmen neighbors they routinely cooperated in a variety of joint activities, but the largest enduring corporate group was the small co-resident group that occupied a single tree house or small hamlet. Only rarely do co-resident groups appear to have numbered more than 20 or 30 individuals (see Schoorl 1957:19–20).

Local groups in the Upper Fly-Digul typically formed around a set of closely related agnates, ideally a set of brothers and their families. These men are members of a named patrilineal clan. As a co-resident group, these agnates—together with their wives and children, and often a handful of sundry other relatives from moribund clans—comprise a local clan segment. Members of local clan segments often see themselves as related to other local clan segments with whom they putatively share descent from a common ancestor or ancestral clan in the distant mythological past.[3] But such affiliations have no significance in reckoning rights over land and natural resources, which are held by individuals on behalf of their families and local groups.

High mortality rates had a powerful impact on local groups and local group memberships. The deaths of middle-aged parents, for example, frequently left children and young adults as orphans, to be adopted or taken in as foster children by relatives in other clans (Welsch 1982). Small group size and high mortality also appear to have brought the demise of many smaller patriclans (Schoorl 1957). Conversely, as local group size increased, more successful local groups tended to fragment, usually as a result of suspicion of sorcery and mistrust following the death of a prominent adult (Schoorl 1957; Welsch 1982). Frequent suspicions of sorcery and a tendency to suspect agnates of foul play made larger corporate groups unstable and susceptible to fragmentation along lineage lines. This pattern of fragmentation corresponds to the large number of clans bearing the same or related clan names found in many parts of the region.

Modern ethnic affiliations—such as Muyu, Mandobo, Ningerum, Yonggom, and Awin—formerly played no role in structuring local communities or their group activities. Each local patriclan segment controlled its own lands, held its own secret men's cult rituals at its own sacred sites, arranged its own marriages with surrounding homesteads, and managed political relations through its own kinship and affinal ties with neighboring clan segments. Insofar as ethnolinguistic identities existed before contact, they were primarily labels applied to peoples who spoke different languages or practiced different customs. Such designations were generally names for others and were rarely used to indicate one's own linguistic or cultural associations, for which a clan name had much more salience and specificity.

Ethnolinguistic labels do not seem to have discouraged interaction between ethnic groups, nor do they appear to have been been especially important in encouraging interaction among peoples speaking the same language. Marriages were commonly arranged with all of a clan segment's neighbors, with little regard for the language they spoke. In addition to local kin ties with neighboring hamlets, each local patriclan segment had its own friends or trade partners living as far as a hundred kilometers away with whom they periodically visited and traded for exotic goods. Such partners were typically members of other ethnic groups.

In short, the societies of the Upper Fly-Digul were highly fragmented into small, autonomous, land-owning groups. They had no central villages or religious institutions that united their communities into large congregations or political associations, such as occurred in the head-hunting societies on the south coastal plain or around the centralized men's cults found in the Mountain Ok societies. At the time of contact, Upper Fly-Digul communities were small dispersed hamlets that pursued their own local interests.

CULTURAL CONTINUITIES ON THE UPPER FLY-DIGUL PLAIN

From the beginning of European contact in the first decades of this century, observers have repeatedly noted a number of striking cultural features that distinguished the Upper Fly-Digul area from the coastal peoples and their neighbors along the middle Fly and Digul. The earliest accounts emphasized the essential homogeneity of peoples living upstream from the head-hunting communities of the lower and middle reaches of these river systems.

In the late 1920s, for example, H. Geurtjens (n.d.:75–81) noted marked differences between the Digul people (his name for the Upper Digul groups) and the coastal Marind with whom he had had many years' experience. These differences were recognized around the Dutch concentration camp at Tanah Merah by L. J. A. Schoonheyt (1936) who perceived the various Upper Digul groups as generally similar to one another but strikingly different from the fierce Mappi and Djair groups to the south. Schoonheyt recognized three Upper Digul groups—the Kaoh, the Moejoe (Muyu), and the Mandobo Papuans—each named for the major river around which they lived.[4] But while each of these three areas exhibited linguistic and cultural differences, what Schoonheyt found most striking were their obvious commonalities.

As government officers and missionaries learned more about the

Upper Digul peoples, they increasingly acknowledged many subtle differences in local languages, customs, and practices. But observers generally considered these differences to be insignificant when compared with what they saw as obvious similarities. For example, although R. den Haan (1955) noted the different terms and languages used in the Kaoh, Muyu, and Mandobo areas, he nevertheless wrote about their pig feasts as the same phenomenon. Similarly, when writing the first detailed ethnographic account from the region, Schoorl (1957) felt comfortable treating the Muyu as an ethnographic unit, although he recognized that the Muyu spoke a number of different dialects or languages.[5]

Leo Austen's (1923a, 1923b) reports from his Northwest Patrols provided the first ethnographic notes on the Papua New Guinea side of the border.[6] He noted that different languages were spoken on the east (Awin) and west (Yonggom) sides of the Ok Tedi but found the cultures of these two groups so similar that he described them together (Austen 1923a:134; 1923b:340). Such similarities gradually tapered off north of the Birim River but disappeared only when he reached the upper foothills of the Star Mountains.

The Upper Fly and Digul River peoples looked and dressed very much the same: instead of the large shell phallocrypt commonly worn in the south, men wore round or flat nuts ("tree seeds"), occasionally penis gourds further to the north; women wore two-piece skirts made from a kind of bulrush. The characteristic house style was a tall tree or pole house, often built sixty feet above the ground, though somewhat lower in the northern areas on the plain. This house form was quite distinctive, differing both from the kinds of houses seen near the coast and from those found in the mountains to the north.

Throughout the region, sago and bananas were the staple foods, supplemented by tubers, greens, and fruits from small mixed gardens as well as pork, fish, and wild game. While mixed gardens show considerable variation across the plain, in some areas being carefully fenced and in others hardly maintained, extensive unfenced banana gardens are characteristic of the area as a whole. Only in the extreme north near the mountains has the monocropping of taro been reported, usually replacing sago as the major staple, a pattern common in the mountains.

Perhaps more important than any of these characteristics was the observation that virtually the whole of the Upper Fly-Digul Plain participated in an elaborate pig-feast cycle quite unlike the feasts in the surrounding areas. There were numerous minor variations in how these feasts were arranged, staged, and hosted. Between some communities there were also differences in the relationship between public pig feasts on the one hand and secret men's cult feasts on the other. In some places, for example, men's cult activities were held in the bush away from the gaze of women and children; in others a temporary cult house was erected in the public feast compound. The mythological charters that explain these feasts vary also, identifying culture heroes with different names, slightly different stories about how feasts came to be, and so on. But on the whole, the feast cycle is surprisingly similar from the Digul to the Fly, having few parallels with feasting outside the region.

Early observers also recognized the importance of pig feasts throughout the plain (Muller 1931, 1955; Beharell 1938) and the large numbers of people who attended them (Schoonheyt 1936:238–242; Hosking 1954; den Haan 1955).[7] By the 1950s, the general commonality of Upper Fly-Digul feasts was generally recognized by observers (Nieland 1953, 1955; den Haan 1955; Schoorl 1957) as were the fundamental differences between feasts held in the Upper Fly-Digul and those among the Djair or Mappi. Dutch observers were especially cognizant of the important role that shell money played in feasts and social relations generally in the Upper Digul and the rather minor importance of shell money in the south (Adatrechtbundels 1955; Nieland 1953).

To outsiders, the Upper Fly-Digul Plain presented sharp contrasts with the coastal and riverine communities. The small scattered peoples in the interior were not headhunters and were generally felt to be less warlike. Their most elaborate and important ceremonial occasions were pig feasts rather than celebrations surrounding the taking of heads, and while the coastal groups seemed preoccupied with heads, the Upper Fly-Digul peoples seemed preoccupied with shell money.

LINGUISTIC DISCONTINUITIES ON THE UPPER FLY-DIGUL PLAIN

In spite of cultural similarities, the inhabitants of the Upper Fly-Digul region speak a number of mutually unintelligible languages in three main language families: the Awyu-Dumut, the Ok, and the Awin-Pa families. Although these families have been identified as members of the Trans–New Guinea Phylum, they are in fact quite different from one another (see Voorhoeve 1975b). These language families share few cognates, have quite different pronoun systems, and exhibit many other grammatical differences, all of which suggest a common linguistic origin no more recent than 3,000 years ago (Healey 1970). Indeed, while their attenuated linguistic relationships may reflect a common origin in the very distant past, such linguistic similarities as do exist would not lead us to expect common cultural characteristics of great importance at the time of European contact in the early 20th century.

In adjacent language families to the south, which are no more different from these three families (and equally members of the Trans–New Guinea Phylum), almost none of the distinctive Upper Fly-Digul characteristics have been observed (see Busse 1987; Welsch in press). The widely separated Upper Fly-Digul communities exhibit a variety of cultural continuities that are difficult to explain on the basis of linguistic relationships, even if linguistic groupings suggest a common (but very ancient) origin.

The strongest argument against a common origin hypothesis to account for observed similarities across the Upper Fly-Digul is the fact that each of the three families present on the plain has close relatives outside it. In each instance the cultural similarities within the plain are far stronger than those within any of the language families.

The lowland Ok Ningerum and Muyu, for example, have obvious linguistic affinities with their mountain Ok neighbors—such as the Faiwol, Telefol, and Ngalum (Ok Sibil). Yet the subsistence economy, community structure, feast practices, and men's cult organization found in the mountain and lowland Ok areas have very little in common (see Barth 1971; Reynders 1962; Schoorl 1956; Welsch in press). Similarly, the Mandobo and Wambon peoples in the Dumut subfamily share very little with their Awyu subfamily neighbors to the south aside from an obvious linguistic relationship. It is precisely because such linguistic relationships exist in the absence of obvious cultural similarities that we are inclined to ask what mechanisms could account for the observed homogeneity within the Upper Fly-Digul at all.

If the Upper Fly-Digul region forms a kind of culture area, it is not because these peoples shared a common origin in the distant past; rather it is the result of factors internal to the region that appear to have generated these broad commonalities.

Two factors seem both important and relevant to understanding the mechanisms responsible for the observed cultural continuities that stretch over this wide area: (a) common adaptations to a common environment; and (b) participation in a regional network of socioeconomic relations.

Ecologically, despite some variation in altitude and rainfall, the Upper Fly-Digul region is remarkably uniform and clearly different from the adjacent regions in the mountains or on the coast. This ecological uniformity may have encouraged similar kinds of settlement patterns, land-tenure systems, subsistence strategies, and horticultural practices. The high rainfall and poor soils found in the region require long fallow periods and encouraged nonintensive shifting cultivation (see Reynders 1962). Thus, dispersed settlements rather than large central villages appear to be an adaptive and efficient response to such poor environmental conditions. Where large villages have formed since the 1950s—as a result of government pressure or as a way of being near modern facilities—local people now report a significant reduction in the productivity of garden lands, sago swamps, and streams, all of which is attributable to the increased demands large settlements have placed on the environment (see Welsch 1979; Kirsch 1989).

Such common ecological factors may have promoted reliance on sago and bananas throughout the region. Small settlement size may have encouraged house types built high up in trees as a defensive measure where larger settlements were not adaptive. The pattern of small dispersed settlements undoubtedly required each hamlet to form social and political relations with neighboring hamlets for common defense and marriage. But within these ecological constraints, many different kinds of social organization or patterns of socioeconomic relationships seem possible besides those actually found in the region.

To phrase this somewhat differently, the ecological constraints that may have encouraged or supported major cultural differences between the Upper Fly-Digul and the south coastal peoples are insufficient as an explanation for the pronounced cultural continuities observed across the Upper Fly-Digul Plain. For this, we must consider how socioeconomic networks operated in the region, in particular, how shell money, social relations, and pig feasts were (and continue to be) linked to one another.

THE SOCIOECONOMICS OF SHELL MONEY

Schoorl (1957, 1976) was the first anthropologist to study any of the Upper Fly-Digul peoples in any depth. He was first drawn to the region while in the Dutch colonial service, when he was assigned to investigate the Muyu people's preoccupation with cowrie-shell money. Both the mission and the government believed the use of shell money was obstructing Muyu social and economic development. Missionaries were most concerned about the cowrie shell's association with sorcery. For them, Muyu desire for shell money stemmed from its role as the local medium of exchange used for all debts; most worrisome was the cowrie's use in murders for hire and in sorcery. The Dutch government disliked the cowrie shell for some of the same reasons, but the main concern was that Muyu people's preoccupation with shell money prevented the rapid introduction of guilders as a currency; the Muyu devoted too much energy to obtaining shells and, thus, had little desire to participate in the cash economy, especially contract labor.

After several months of field research on the shell-money problem, Schoorl (1954, 1976:36–47) determined that the assumptions held by the mission and government were fundamentally incorrect. Sorcery might result from nonpayment of debts or other social obligations but had little to do with the particular medium of exchange in circulation. Moreover, cowrie shells were not a barrier to the use of guilders; rather, it was the scarcity of guilders in circulation and the virtual absence of stores with imported goods to sell that had prevented Muyu from accepting foreign money as a general medium of exchange in the local economy.

But Schoorl's analysis went much further, asserting that shell money was a true money and that virtually every aspect of Muyu life was monetized and regulated by the exchange of shell valuables. Both Schoorl (1976) and den Haan (1955) published price lists for a wide range of domestic and imported goods in the 1950s, in which each item's value was computed as a set number of cowries, to demonstrate the cowrie's important role in ordinary economic transactions. And not unexpectedly, brideprice payments included a large number of money cowries and other shell valuables.

But local trade and brideprice payments were only the most obvious arenas in which shells circulated as a local currency. Shell money was also used for a wide variety of minor compensations and indemnities for transgressions. Shells were even used in real estate transactions: buying and selling land, sago palms, and fruit trees.

Pig breeding was the primary way for Muyu to obtain money cowries (den Haan 1955; Schoorl 1957, 1976). A piglet purchased for one or two cowries might bring as many as thirty as a mature hog. But while a few pigs were sold to consumers as an ordinary commodity, the vast majority of adult pigs were sold at pig feasts. In the 1950s, Schoorl's informants claimed that their main reason for holding feasts was to obtain shell money from selling their pork. Even the secret men's cult feasts were held primarily to obtain money from the sale of pork to their guests.

Money cowries were not the only kind of shell money in general use among the Muyu, though they were the standard unit against which other valuables were pegged. Nassa shells sewn into headbands, small baler shells used as ornaments, and dog's teeth sewn onto belts also circulated as money in the local economy. All of these valuables were required, together with a substantial number of cowrie shells, for brideprice payments. In addition, nassa shells and dog's teeth were important as smaller units of value, or small change, used for buying goods of less value than a single cowrie. Convertibility of one kind of shell valuable for another supported the far-reaching monetization of the social economy. Convertibility also allowed Western currencies to enter the economy, at first as a less important valuable but then becoming the primary unit of value in the 1960s.

The Muyu were not the only Upper Fly-Digul people whose lives were profoundly influenced by the circulation of money cowries. The Yonggom, the Mandobo, the Ningerum, the Morop, and other groups living in the foothills to the north shared the Muyu's keen interest in obtaining shells. The Ningerum to the east and the Mandobo to the west appear to have been somewhat less preoccupied with shells than were the Muyu (Welsch in press; Boelaars 1970). Only among the Awin and their eastern neighbors did cowries play a rather minor role in the local economy, although at least some Awin groups used cowries in trading with their Yonggom neighbors.[8]

The demand for money cowries as a local currency declined very rapidly in the Ningerum area between 1962 and 1964 when they were virtually replaced by Australian pounds as the local medium of exchange. Data from other parts of the region are limited, but I suspect that the general pattern was quite similar in Yonggom and Muyu. Within a matter of months, cowries, baler shells, dog's teeth, and the smaller sizes of nassa shell lost their value. Only large nassa shells remained in circulation alongside modern currency. Although this devaluation of the local currency happened more than a decade before my research in Ningerum, even as late as 1990, nassa shell headbands are still an essential part in many brideprice payments. The largest part of brideprice payments consists of PNG kina, just as it formerly was made up of cowries. The Ningerum extended their term for money cowries, *kiwo,* to refer to all forms of modern currency, whether Australian pounds or dollars, PNG kina, Dutch guilders, or Indonesian rupiah. Modern currency is understood as a replacement for the old money cowries; kina notes now appear to play precisely the same role in social and economic transactions as cowries formerly did.

One might be tempted to believe that Schoorl exaggerated the significance of cowries in Muyu and the comprehensiveness of the cowrie shell's penetration into so many aspects of social and economic life. But my own impressions, drawn primarily from research among the eastern groups, is that he is fundamentally correct. Discussions and disputes about money and shells for brideprice, child-price, and other social payments were such frequent topics of conversation in Ningerum and many surrounding communities in the late 1970s that it is difficult to imagine that shell money was any less important in the past over a large part of the Fly-Digul area.

If Schoorl's analysis errs, it is in understating the importance of credit in the economy, particularly long-term debt. The wide use of credit for simple economic transactions as well as social payments like brideprice was only partly a consequence of the relatively small numbers of cowries and other shells in circulation in the past and the short supply of modern currency today. Having a number of creditors and a number of debtors was essential for maintaining relations with individuals in other corporate groups. The truly wealthy or influential man was not the one with the most shells or cash in hand, but the man who could obtain credit beyond his productive means whenever he needed it.

To understand how the local economic system operated, it must be remembered that while shells were formerly used for virtually every kind of economic activity (purchases of local goods such as string bags, skirts, tobacco, and so on, payments for pork, and in all social payments), relatively few shells actually changed hands at any one time. The number of shells levied as prices in these transactions were markers of value, irrespective of how much of the price was paid at the time the transaction was made. The use of credit in virtually every segment of the social economy thus allowed the total value of transactions to exceed many times over the actual number of shells in circulation.[9]

Central to the economy were the long-term debts created to mark and cement social relationships between individuals. Lacking any form of sister exchange, most social relations were inherently asymmetric: a man was obligated to his wife's father and brothers, nephews were obligated to their mother's brothers, matrilateral cross-cousins (classed as uncles) had rights over their patrilateral cross-cousins (classed as nephews), and even the relationship between brothers was asymmetric granting an older brother authority over a younger brother. The rights and obligations that surrounded these diverse social relationships were expressed in economic obligations.

Every individual in these societies is beset by numerous economic obligations from which it is impossible to be free. There is never enough specie in circulation to cover all these obligations, so goods are sold on credit or partial credit, brideprice is partly paid and the balance reckoned as an unpaid debt, and so forth. The most important aspect is that the local economy is structured to prevent anyone from extricating themselves from an onerous set of outstanding debts, most of which are unpaid social payments.

At birth, children are indebted to their mother's brothers for a matrilateral payment to protect them from sickness. At marriage, a man incurs additional obligations, first a smaller payment at engagement to mark his bride (one of the few payments that are usually paid in full) and then a much larger brideprice. With the birth of each child, the father owes a childprice payment to his affines entitling the children to remain members of his household. This payment parallels the child's own matrilateral payment and is sometimes confused with it, but in most cases it seemed only part of a son's childprice was actually paid during the father's lifetime. And foster parents invariably claim rights to their foster children in compensation for the hard work and food they have invested in the child.

When a father dies, his sons inherit all his outstanding debts and obligations in the same way they inherit his lands. When a man's wife dies, he must pay a death payment to her kin. In return, he receives a burial price from her agnates for the "hard work" of handling the body, although he must pay a burial price to his brother-in-law when his own sister dies. Any number of relatives in other clan segments may demand a payment to compensate them for their grief whenever any of a man's co-resident agnates die. In sum, economic obligations defining social relationships accumulate, quite literally, from birth to grave, and even at death they are passed on to a man's heirs.

Such economic obligations comprise an onerous kind of "social mortgage," from which no Muyu or Ningerum or Mandobo or Yonggom man is ever free. The value of these social payments is set unilaterally by the senior party in the relationship, such as a father-in-law, an uncle, or a foster father, usually after a certain amount of negotiation. But the prices charged are usually high enough that no one ever expects them to be paid in full. The costs of childprice, brideprice, and death duties are set according to a fluctuating scale that charge rich men more than poor men. At least since the introduction of wage labor, which allowed some men to increase their wealth unpredictably, these social obligations can be reassessed to a much higher rate should anyone experience windfall profits.

While every person has a number of creditors who demand payments at more or less regular intervals, each individual also has a number of debtors from whom he can demand payments. But demands for repayment or even partial repayment of debts sets off a "chain reaction" of demands that spreads from one local group to another (Schoorl 1976:22). Politically autonomous clan segments thus become linked into wide-ranging economic networks by transfers of shells or money as well as by the creation of debts.

The key to the Muyu and Ningerum world of finance was to put enough pressure on one's debtors so they would pay something when money was needed, while simultaneously trying to avoid making so many demands that debtors become angry and refuse to pay anything at all. Angry debtors were especially dangerous because they might elect to end the relationship permanently by hiring someone to murder an unreasonable creditor (see Schoorl 1957; Welsch 1982). But by the same token, creditors who are angry over nonpayment of debts are also a force to be reckoned with, since they too may want to terminate the relationship through violence, sorcery, or murder by hire. The threat of violence, but especially sorcery, is a powerful force that motivates the circulation of valuables and gives men reputed to be sorcerers considerable leverage in obtaining new credit. If successful in avoiding this Scylla and Charybdis, a man can obtain enough money from his debtors to satisfy his creditors, proving himself too good an investment for anyone to consider having him killed as a recalcitrant deadbeat or as an unreasonable creditor.

A social mortgage is a kind of insurance policy that protects people from sorcery and murder, but only so long as payments and goodwill gestures continue to be made from time to time. One opportunity for making payments, of course, is at pig feasts. And it is at pig feasts that individuals can at the very least offer token gifts to maintain goodwill with both their debtors and their creditors.

It should perhaps be noted here that in most communities on the Upper Fly-Digul Plain individuals developed a network of relationships of various kinds with all their neighboring settlements. As a result of marriages strategically placed over the past two generations, most households had at least one persisting social obligation (or social credit) with every other household or hamlet within their neighborhood. Given the dispersed settlement pattern that existed at contact, such social ties with neighboring households provided an extremely safe defensive arrangement. If all of one's neighbors were kinsmen with ongoing socioeconomic ties, one could count on them for protection against a dawn raid. At the very least, one would not have to fear that neighbors would launch a raid themselves. But on the other hand, this arrangement also meant that nearly all of one's neighbors had to be placated periodically with gifts of pork or payments of shells to guarantee their amiability and continuing goodwill. Pig feasts and the secret men's cult feasts offered the most public forum for expressing these positive social connections.

THE ORGANIZATION OF PIG FEASTS

Pig feasts are the height of the social calendar throughout the Upper Fly-Digul area.[10] They vary in size from small family affairs where one or two pigs are butchered to major social events with upward of thirty pigs and many hundreds of guests. Den Haan (1955) observed one Muyu feast attended by an estimated 3,000 people at which only 15 animals were killed. In 1979 I attended a Ningerum feast with 32 animals and about 700 guests. In the mid 1980s even larger feasts were still being held in the southern Yonggom (Kirsch pers. comm.).

Preparations for a large feast are arduous, and often the bulk of the work falls on the co-hosts and a small number of their closest kin. It can take six months to process enough sago and even longer to build the feast compound and round up all the pigs to be killed. I attended one feast at Kungim in the northern Yonggom where the construction of the large feast house and sleeping quarters for the guests took nearly eighteen months to complete. In this case, construction took so long that the women had to replace about half the sago after it had spoiled.

But although for the co-hosts feasts take months to prepare, for the guests they last only a single night; but it is an intense, activity-filled 24 hours. Most guests set off for a feast in the morning, going first to the next hamlet or village to meet other guests. Here they eat some sago, gossip, and smoke for about an hour or so. Joined by friends from this hamlet who will also attend the feast, they set off together for the next settlement on the way, where they eat and talk once more. Stopping two or three times more they are joined by a growing number of guests. Finally, late in the afternoon they arrive at a small clearing in the bush, set off a few hundred meters from the feast compound.

At this clearing they will be joined by other groups of guests, each of which has also made their way to the clearing by stages throughout the day. Each group began at the most distant settlement along a particular track in the bush as a group numbering only ten or twelve men, women, and children; when they arrive at the clearing each group consists of from 50 to 150 guests. The majority of guests live only a few hours' walk from the feast, but at all but the smallest feasts there will be some guests from hamlets two or three days' journey away. At large feasts there may be three or four separate clearings for guests arriving from different directions.

At the clearing in the bush, the guests stop once more to decorate themselves for a dramatic, warlike entry into the feast compound. Here they wait until the hosts tell them all is ready. Then the men dance into the feast compound in single file, each brandishing bow and arrows, a club, or a stick, and singing a war chant.

The feast compound consists of a large, square feast house situated at the end of a long narrow plaza. Here the hosts and their families have slept for the past week or two as they completed all the preparations. On either side of the plaza is a long row of sleeping quarters for the guests. At the head of the plaza near the feast house is a row of wooden cages where the pigs are kept until the morning of the feast when at dawn they are shot with arrows through the slats in the cages. While the guests are making their way to the feast, the hosts are busy butchering the pigs, performing various rituals, and finishing up last-minute details. When everything is ready, the hosts send word to the guests, and five or six men from the host group climb onto the roof of the feast house to greet their guests as they make their war dance into the compound.

The guests arrive in the order prescribed by their hosts. Each line of warriors dances with their weapons into the long narrow compound, while the women and children straggle in behind them carrying bamboos of water and whatever possessions each family brought with them. With war chants and great excitement the warriors assemble at the head of the compound, forming a large cluster in front of their waiting hosts, who sit or stand with stern countenance and drawn bows on the roof of the feast house. It is an exciting but tense moment as each band of armed guests enters the compound. Should violence erupt between guests and hosts over some unresolved conflict, it will happen as the guests arrive with their bows drawn. Although such overt hostilities are unusual today, in the past, feasts occasionally turned into armed raids.

After the guests from each clearing have arrived, the hosts or owners of the feast welcome their assembled guests. They give several speeches, cryptically explaining the reasons for holding the feast and exhorting all to tie up their bows and arrows and to refrain from hostility. The guests retire to the long row of sleeping quarters to await the distribution of uncooked pork, while the hosts climb down from the roof and return to the feast house where the butchered pork is ready for distribution.

The host group performs several minor rituals and soon emerges from the feast house in single file carrying large portions of butchered pork. Although there are usually some pieces still available for sale, most of the meat is already promised to particular individuals. Finally, the owners of the feast begin distributing the fresh pork by holding up a leg or a back, and with a few whoops begin calling out the names of the recipients. Those presenting the pork jump up and down shouting as they wait for their guests to come and fetch the meat as they are called. The recipients come running with similar shouts and take the meat from their hosts. Each of the hosts then takes another piece of meat and calls out to another guest. Within a few moments all of the hosts are shouting out names, jumping and whooping as before, until the entire compound is filled with a torrent of shouting and motion.

Occasionally a portion of meat will be kept by the guest to whom it was given. But more typically the meat has already been promised to someone else. In such cases, those who have received pork become the givers, and they immediately call out for the next recipient to come get his pork with the same whooping and jumping as before. And if this person has promised it to someone else, he takes the meat and immediately calls out the name of the next recipient, and so on, until each piece of pork has been formally given to its ultimate recipient.

At most of the feasts I attended, the meat usually passed through three or four sets of hands before being set aside in the sleeping quarters. Occasionally, however, a single piece of pork was passed on to seven or eight different people. Women as well as men can both give and receive pork, but it is nearly always a man who calls out the recipient's name and receives the meat on behalf of a kinswoman.

After ten or fifteen minutes of intense activity, all the meat has been given out, and quiet and calm returns. The hosts retire to the feast house once more, shortly to return bearing other foodstuffs, particularly sago, bananas, and tubers. All of these foods are for cooking with the pork or to be eaten during the nightlong vigil as the meat cooks.

Many feasts are accompanied by a men's cult feast. Among the lower Ningerum, these are held in the bush some distance away from the main feast compound at one of the host clan's sacred sites. In the upper Ningerum, the hosts build a temporary cult house adjacent to or as part of the feast compound. In either case, after the distribution of pork at the main feast, the men turn their attention to the distribution of sacred men's cult pork among initiated men. Distribution of sacred pork follows the same pattern as at the public feasts. If the men's cult feast is held in the bush, initiated men adjourn to the bush compound. After this distribution, most of the men return to the main feast to ready their feast pork for cooking, while the recipients of men's cult pork remain in the cult area to cook their pork there.

At large feasts one or more dances are performed during the night to entertain the hosts and guests alike. Anyone who wishes may participate in the dancing or sit around as spectators. At these dances or just milling about the compound, young people find an opportunity to meet eligible members of the opposite sex from communities they may rarely visit. Hosts discourage sexual liaisons at their feasts because illicit relations, if discovered, often lead to conflicts. Nevertheless, young men like to perform in front of the girls they are attracted to, and both sexes find opportunities to catch the averted glances of potential spouses. Older people also enjoy dancing as well as the chance to see friends and relatives living in distant settlements.

During the night, everyone catches up on gossip while the pork slowly cooks. Some people take short catnaps; others use the time to sell the wares they have brought with them. Women roast tubers or bananas for their families and friends, and there is always plenty of talk, food, and satisfying fellowship with friends and family in the orange and yellow glow of cooking fires scattered around the compound.

By about 9 A.M. the meat has finished cooking, and at the signal from the hosts the men gather together with their own group to open and cut up their pork and sago. After eating some of the meat and after the women have received their share, the men prepare small pieces of meat and sago for a generalized exchange of cooked pork. Soon the cacophony increases, as guests call out the names of individuals to come get pieces of cooked pork and sago. These small prestations of cooked pork are reciprocated shortly thereafter and serve to mark in a public way that a positive relationship exists between the pairs of individuals involved.[11]

Everyone continues eating and exchanging cooked pork for as much as an hour, by which time the guests have begun to leave for home. Packing up what few belongings were brought with them as well as the remaining food to be taken back to the relatives at home, the guests depart without ado. Heading home without stopping at the hamlets where they had rested and waited the day before, the return journey takes a fraction of the time the outbound trip took. And once home, they share their pork once more with those not able to attend.

THE SOCIOECONOMICS OF PIG FEASTS

Distributions of pork at a feast take on several different meanings depending on whether the pork is cooked or uncooked, whether it is given as a whole pig or as single portion, or whether the transaction is arranged as a gift or a purchase. Among the Muyu, relatively little of the pork is given outright as gifts; most is formally sold to recipients at prearranged prices. This same pattern holds true for distributions of Ningerum men's cult pork, although at public feasts in Ningerum most distributions are arranged as outright gifts between affines, kinsmen, or friends. Whether formally arranged as a gift or as a purchase, such transactions usually require some future return gift or purchase that follows a pattern of delayed reciprocity over a number of years.

Feasts are typically co-hosted by two men from different clan segments or from different lineages within a clan segment. Each host has as many as three or four of their own mature pigs for the feast, while other pigs are contributed by agnates in each clan segment and sometimes by kinsmen in allied clans. The owner of each pig retains the right to give it away or sell it to whomever he wishes. Each owner is responsible for prearranging the distribution of his pork and for preparing sleeping quarters for his guests. Each co-host takes half of the feast house for the use of his own family and the individuals he invites to contribute pigs. Despite such allocations of space and responsibilities, the entire set of contributors should act cooperatively, serving jointly as hosts of the affair.

At most feasts, the two co-hosts reciprocally exchange at least one pig. This balanced exchange typically provides the pork eaten by their respective families during the feast itself.[12] Such reciprocal exchanges symbolize the harmony and cooperation that should exist between co-hosts.

All of the other pigs are given out or sold to individuals with whom the co-hosts have some social tie. Hosts may use a pig to pay part of their brideprice, childprice, matrilateral payment, death payments, and the like. These gifts never satisfy such social debts in full and rarely are feasts the venue for making a major prestation toward any of these payments. Nevertheless, these gifts will be reckoned along with other payments as part of a brideprice, childprice, or other obligation. Hosts use the rest of their pork to recognize other social relationships or repay other obligations.

Gifts of uncooked pork always mark some social relation and frequently an ongoing obligation. Often, the recipient is a long-term creditor to the pork giver—such as a wife's brother or an uncle. But the roles may be reversed, so that the creditor makes prestations to an individual he intends to demand shells or money from. The giver may repay a gift of pork he received some time before, or if the piece of pork is being sold, the sale may be an effort to recover shells or money he paid for pork he was obliged to buy in the past. Or the prestation may be used to create a new relationship or to stimulate one that has become strained by excessive demands or inadequate attention. When guests pass on a portion of uncooked pork they have received, it rarely contributes directly to paying off outstanding social mortgage debts. Nevertheless, such prestations often draw upon these kinds of relationships and are part of each individual's attempts to manage personal social networks.

Whatever the precise character of the prestations, they mark in a tangible and public way that a positive, mutually supportive relationship exists between the two parties. Despite the complex and sometimes Byzantine implications of these transactions, feasts offer an opportunity as well as an obligation to establish or reestablish cooperative ties between any two parties and their immediate kin groups.

Cooked pork at a feast plays a rather different role from uncooked pork. It defines two kinds of social relationships depending upon whether it is being shared or exchanged.

Sharing occurs within each group of guests that arrive together. When the bundles of cooked pork and sago are opened, they are opened cooperatively by the same men who came to the feast as a group. Such groups include men from the same local clan segment, but they also include men in many other clans. Together they squat around the bundle of food, cutting the meat and sago into portions and eating together. Their womenfolk sit together in the sleeping quarters nearby, and they too share the fruits of the nightlong vigil.

Hosts and guests do not as a rule share their cooked pork. Once one of the guests receives his portion of fresh pork, it leaves the active sharing network of its original owner. But sharing occurs among families of the hosts, who in preparing the meat for cooking act as cooperatively as any group of guests.

Where exchanges of cooked pork occur, as they do in Ningerum, the typical pattern is one of direct and immediate balanced reciprocity. Individual men from each group sharing pork make gifts to men in other groups. Minutes later these recipients make return gifts of comparable size. Unlike gifts of fresh meat, cooked pork creates no lasting obligations. These prestations merely symbolize the network of solid supportive relations that each man possesses. And it often happens that men who share pork at one feast may exchange it at another.

One striking feature of feasts in Muyu, Yonggom, and Ningerum is that the act of cooking the pork confuses the distinction between pork-givers and pork-recipients, which is so publicly marked in the formal distribution after the guests arrive. While uncooked pork physically changes hands passing from one guest to another at the initial distribution of meat, both parties will in fact share the meat once it is cooked. In addition, of course, they will share it with all the women, children, and other relatives who accompany them to the feast. This is, perhaps, one of the few times that someone can both give away their pork and eat it too. Uncooked pork is available for the social purpose of becoming a gift, but after having been given, it is eaten together by both the giver and the recipient.

During the many transactions involving a particular piece of pork at any feast, a variety of different social relations are marked and publicly expressed for individual participants. At another feast these relations may be marked differently, corresponding to the particular personnel who attend. Thus, for a brief time each feast configures individual social ties into broad and more encompassing networks.

Irrespective of the specific relations expressed through pork, each relationship emanates from the peculiar social networks of particular individuals. Each individual relationship is marked as being cooperative and mutually supportive. But in the aggregate, what emerges at a feast (unless it is spoiled by violence) is large groups of individuals temporarily linked together into enormous social networks that stretch out across the rainforest in every direction.

MAPPING SOCIOECONOMIC NETWORKS

Feasting in the Upper Fly-Digul region requires considerable coordination among individuals scattered over a wide area. Organizing the activities of so many people in such a way that they all arrive on the proper day and time is a remarkable feat in and of itself. In the past this task was made more difficult by the absence of a formal calendar and by the tendency for feast preparations to take longer than most hosts anticipate.

Like most other activities in the region, however, coordination among these dispersed kin groups is arranged through the individual social ties that link them. The process of organizing a feast begins when co-hosts determine how many pigs will be available for distribution and who will receive which portions of these pigs. Each pig owner then begins sending out invitations to his guests, usually many months before the event takes place.

Each pig-owner host invites his guests in person, visiting each in turn and promising each a specified part of a particular pig. The host and guest discuss the social and economic arrangements involved in the transaction. This includes whether the pork will serve as part of a major social payment (such as a brideprice payment), whether it is given in repayment of some particular debt, or whether the pork is being sold to the guest. Once a promise of pork is accepted by a kinsman, he is then free to pass it on to another kinsman that he wants to invite to the feast. He then visits his own prospective guest, arranging for this kinsman to accompany him to the feast and accept his pork. This guest may pass it on to someone in his social network, and so on.

Invitations are the first phase in displaying the social relationships that will be fostered and managed at a feast. The details seem to vary a bit from place to place, but the pattern I observed among the Ningerum illustrates how they generally operate.

Butchered pigs are always divided up into seven portions: head, back, belly, two hands, and two legs. These are standard measures or units of meat whose only variation comes from the size and quality of the animal. In making a promise of a future prestation of a pig, the host gives his would-be guest a leaf containing seven small leaflets, each leaflet representing a specific portion of the pig.

While whole pigs are given when important social relations are to be acknowledged, less important ties may be expressed with half a pig—the head, hands, and belly, or the back and two legs. These may be further subdivided into individual portions, and I have even seen back portions split into two small pieces. If half the pig will be given to a guest, he receives the prerequisite three or four leaflets representing the hind end or the front end respectively. If only one leg is to be given, the guest receives one leaflet with the understanding that it represents a particular leg, and so on.

To promise a portion of meat, the host visits the prospective guest bringing the appropriate leaflets with him. After receiving one or more leaflets the guest now has possession of a sort of future contract on the meat. It is up to him to pass it on to one of his creditors or kinsmen as he sees fit. If he wants to send it on, he walks to the prospective recipient's house and gives him the leaflet. Then this man (or woman) may take it on to one of his creditors and so on.

Thus, when a piece of pork is promised to a guest, a leaflet begins its long journey from bush house to bush house, always following links in the individual social networks that emanate from one set of hands in each house. One must bear in mind that formerly extended families lived in scattered tree houses or hamlets. Even today people usually maintain a bush house in addition to a house in their village. As leaflets are sent out in all directions from the host's hamlet, they slowly work their way from house to house along the walking tracks or across the ridges until they reach their final destinations.

With each prestation of a leaflet comes an implicit invitation for the family of the recipient to attend the feast. And this invitation is extended to the close kin of each recipient as the leaflets make their way along their tracks. With each transfer of leaflets from house to house through the rainforest, more and more guests are invited to the feast. Most of the leaflets will stay within a single day's journey of the feast compound, but for larger feasts, some leaflets will end up two or three days' walk away. It is only because these markers can travel a great distance through many hands, adding five or ten guests at each set of hands, that large feasts with thousands of guests are possible.

Co-hosts, who usually contribute the largest number of pigs, have more guests to invite than anyone else. But even with three or four pigs, a host's distributions rarely extend to more than a dozen guests. One pig is exchanged within the feast house, one or two others may be given as half a pig, and another may be given as individual portions. Moreover, because the host is primarily concerned with managing his most vital social ties, nearly all of his distribution will go to individuals in neighboring hamlets. While his leaflets may travel two or three days' journey, his own responsibilities rarely extend beyond a few hours' walk.

During the long months of preparations, hosts make periodic visits to their invitees to apprise them of their progress and finally to announce the day scheduled for the feast to begin. This news spreads out across the countryside following the same paths as the leaflets. As the feast day approaches, each invitee makes arrangements with his guests as to when and where they will meet. People at each stop on the way to the feast prepare sago and bananas for the guests who will assemble on their way. None of these preparations are as arduous as the preparations of the hosts, but families nearer the feast compound must entertain much larger numbers of people than those further away. Such arrangements require a considerable amount of information to move back and forth along the tracks well in advance of the feast.

Each leaflet follows the same path that the guests will themselves take on their journey to the feast—though, of course, the leaflet goes in the opposite direction. For every feast these leaflets etch out across the countryside a composite mapping of all the individual social networks that will be invoked at the actual feast. But while the path each leaflet follows represents no single individual's social network, on the feast day it defines a new composite social grouping: people who will sit together to share the meat. If the leaflet's path is short, most of the people involved will inevitably be kinsmen and old acquaintances. But when the path is long, it may bring together many individuals from distant places, many of whom are strangers or who barely know one another.

In establishing new social bonds between individuals, even if these ties are only temporary and expressed as a relationship between social equals, feasting opens new channels for a variety of possible social relations. Feasts may set the stage for future marriages; they may open up new avenues for obtaining credit; and frequently feasts create new trading partners in distant places. Before pacification, the social bonds initiated at feasts also offered prospects for creating new political alliances by establishing ties between local groups that already had relationships with the same intermediary hamlet.

The new social relations fostered at feasts are temporary and may never develop into more enduring ties. But at the very least, they establish options that may not have existed before. Subsequently on long trading expeditions or at other feasts, individuals always have a few friends and acquaintances they can visit and stay with when they are far from home. But like every other aspect of finance and feasting, once invoked, such relationships must be reciprocated and carefully managed. Not to do so could be hazardous because unreciprocated relations always raise the threat of sorcery or other hostilities. On the other hand, relations between individuals in distant settlements are generally immune to the intense social demands that regularly exist between neighbors.

Each feast builds a network of individuals that begins at a different place and spreads out along different sets of relations. No two feasts are ever attended by precisely the same people, and yet one may always expect to see a certain number of the same people at any two feasts. During the course of a single season most people will attend five or six feasts, which offer an opportunity to reciprocate past invitations and strengthen ties that extend out in many different directions. And in each case, relations that are sealed through the distribution and sharing of pork today must be reciprocated by one of the parties in the future.

CONCLUSION

In the course of describing pig feasts and the socioeconomic obligations that accompany them, I have outlined a number of key features of the Muyu, Yonggom, Ningerum, Mandobo, and other societies that inhabit the Upper Fly-Digul Plain. Perhaps the most important feature of social relations in these societies, much as it is in most New Guinea societies, is the principle of reciprocity—the imperative to repay social and economic obligations.

In the Upper Fly-Digul region this imperative to reciprocate was and continues to be enforced by the constant threat of sorcery or other personal violence. If the fear of sorcery were not as pervasive in these societies as it seems to be (see Boelaars 1970; Schoorl 1957; Welsch 1982), social networks might take rather different forms from those historically observed. But with sorcery a constant threat, even today, the peoples of the Upper Fly-Digul region remain attentive to managing the demands of their personal social networks. Reciprocity and the pervasive fear of sorcery provide at least one aspect of the economic system's internal dynamic.

While socioeconomic relations are negotiated and played out around virtually every aspect of daily life, nowhere are the extensive social networks they create so visible as at pig feasts. My first objective has been to demonstrate how pig feasts in the Upper Fly-Digul area economically integrate most of the nearly 40,000 people who inhabit the region. Large feasts develop exclusively around relationships between individuals, primarily relationships between individuals in neighboring hamlets or local clan segments. But through the imperative to reciprocate past invitations and to manage long-term social obligations, each participant tends to add his own social linkages to those of others, building larger and larger networks that stretch far across the rainforest-covered plain. Despite many local variations in the way feasts are staged and organized, pig feasts are a regional phenomenon that integrates communities speaking a number of different languages and dialects.

One of the paradoxes of social life across the Upper Fly-Digul Plain is that while the vast majority of marriages take place within a few kilometers of home, they create extensive social networks that integrate large numbers of people as far as 100 kilometers away. (A few marriages are arranged with men from distant groups living several days' walk away, but these cases are quite unusual.) But despite this pattern of concentrated social ties within small local neighborhoods, most men have personal social networks that extend a great distance, sometimes across two or three different languages. It is the dense, overlapping social networks with nearby households that generate a much less dense but still wide-ranging set of social relations that stretch out across the rainforest. These social networks are a direct consequence of the kind of pig feast found in the region, because feasts provide the context and opportunity for small personal networks to develop into much larger and longer networks.

Historical and prehistoric data about the development of pig feasts in the Upper Fly-Digul area are extremely limited. All we know is that the feast cycle I have just described was well established among the Muyu, Yonggom, Ningerum, and Mandobo by the time outsiders first encountered these peoples. Without archaeological data it is unclear how long the Muyu or any other Fly-Digul society has practiced pig feasts with the enthusiasm they do. Nor is it possible to know how long these groups have been so preoccupied with the acquisition of shells and other valuables. What is unmistakable, however, is that the self-perpetuating cycle of social obligations observed in the region has considerable potential for intensifying the desire (and social needs) for shell money. For the Muyu, this desire for shells translated into an intensification of pig feasts, which they hosted principally as a way of obtaining cowrie shells.

The Muyu at the center of the Upper Fly-Digul Plain appear to have had the greatest population pressure, reaching as high as 17 people per square kilometer in one small area (Schoorl 1957:12). While this density is low in comparison with many other parts of New Guinea, it is high for the local communities concerned here. Such a density would have put strains on the local social economy, even if it did not overtax the local environment.

Whether as a result of population pressure or as a consequence of the ordinary workings of their economy, the Muyu economy appears to have expanded across much of the plain.[13] Muyu intermarried heavily with Mandobo groups on their western frontier. Through these marriage ties (and the brideprice obligations that accompanied them) Muyu-style feasts appear to have spread westward across

Mandobo country (see Boelaars 1970). To the east, Muyu-style feasts were found throughout the Ningerum and Yonggom areas, and Muyu were intermarried with these groups along their eastern frontier. Muyu-style feasts may also have expanded across these eastern groups, although it is more difficult to demonstrate such an expansion into these areas, since both groups are linguistically very closely related to Muyu. In the 1970s, there was some evidence that unrelated Awin (Aekyom) groups further to the east were gradually becoming tied into Ningerum and Yonggom trade, affinal, and feast relations. The Awin economy was not yet Muyu-ized or Ningerum-ized to any great extent, certainly not to the extent that the Mandobo economy was. Whatever economic expansion may have been occurring prior to pacification has now largely ceased, with the various new economic options that have now appeared with the Ok Tedi mine.

Muyu intermarriage with groups that did not already participate in feasts (and with the cowrie shell economy more generally) probably offered various economic advantages that marriages with other Muyu did not. It is clear, for example, from early Muyu responses to the introduction of Western goods that Muyu were ready to take economic advantage of their more remotely situated brethren by charging higher prices for imported goods than they could obtain closer to home (Schoorl 1976). In the same way, marriages with local groups on their frontiers might have offered lower brideprices and opportunities to acquire shells with less effort.

Muyu-ization of non-Muyu economies might begin with intermarriage, but I suggest that expansion occurs as a socioeconomic process ultimately linked to brideprice payments, not because intermarriage leads to some diffuse blending of cultures. In short, economic penetration of the Muyu economy might begin with marriage, credit, or participation at feasts. But once new players become linked to individuals who had a vested interest in the system, those new players became increasingly obliged to reciprocate and participate more intensively. Feasts not only offered opportunities for expansion, but the organization of feasting encouraged its expansion.

The wide regional integration that accompanied Muyu-style feasts did not require local corporate groups to yield any of their local autonomy. Feasting built on and invoked local social relations and the broad networks that emerged at a feast could expand cumulatively like the tiles in a game of dominoes. Each link in the chain of relations was formally independent of all others, yet over time these relations become interconnected as the cumulative result of participation at many feasts. In this way, extremely local events—such as one man's demanding a payment of shells from another—could set off a chain reaction that might be felt throughout most of the region. It is in these terms that we can understand the large size of many feasts and the economic integration of the Upper Fly-Digul region, despite the autonomy and small size of its constituent local groups.

REFERENCES

Adatrechtbundels

1955 Huwelijk en echtscheiding bij de bevolking der Onderafdeling Boven-Digoel (1930–1953–1954). Sections: (a) Ontleend aan het dagboek van assistent-resident R. H. Muller van Tanah Merah, Zuid-Nieuw-Guinea, Dec. 1930, Jan., Maart, en April 1931, betreffende de Moejoe- en Kaubevolking; (b) Ontleend aan het tournee-verslag van de onderafdelingschef van Boven-Digoel van 30 Oct.–4 Nov. 1953, c. Uit het tournee-verslag van bestuursassistent B. Frank van 18 Febr.–6 Maart 1954. 's-Gravenhage: Martinus Nijhoff, 1910–1955. Adatrechtbundel 45, no. 92, pp. 529–531.

Austen, Leo

1923a Report of a Patrol of the Tedi (Alice) River and the Star Mountains W.D. Papua Annual Report for 1920–21, pp. 122–134.

1923b The Tedi River District of Papua. Geographical Journal 62: 335–349.

Barth, Fredrik

1971 Tribes and Intertribal Relations in the Fly Headwaters. Oceania 41:171–191.

Beharell, J.

1938 Patrol Report, Daru no. 3 of 38/39.

Berghuys, F. H.

1937 Varkensfeest te Kawolinggam. Koloniaal Tijdschrift 26: 190–205.

Boelaars, Jan

1950 The Linguistic Position of South-Western New Guinea. Leiden: Brill.

1970 Mandobo's tussen de Digoel en de Kao: Bijdragen tot een Etnografie. Assen: Van Gorcum.

Busse, Mark

1987 Sister Exchange Among the Wamek of the Middle Fly. Ph.D. dissertation. San Diego: University of California.

Drabbe, P.

1954 Talen en dialecten van Zuid-West Nieuw-Guinea. Micro-Bibliotheca Anthropos 11. Freiburg: Anthropos Institute.

Feil, D. K.
1984 Ways of Exchange: The Enga Tee of Papua New Guinea. St. Lucia: University of Queensland Press.

Frank, B.
1954 *See* Adatrechtbundels

Geurtjens, H.
n.d. Op Zoek naar Oermenschen. Roermond—Maaseik: J. J. Romen and Zonen.

Haan, R. den
1955 Het Varkensfeest zoals het plaatsvindt in het gebied van de rivieren Kao, Muju en Mandobo (Ned. Nieuw Guinea). Bijdragen tot de Taal-, Land- en Volkenkunde 111:92–106, 162–190.

Healey, Alan
1964 The Ok Language Family of New Guinea. Ph.D. dissertation. Australian National University.
1970 Proto-Awyu-Dumut Phonology. *In* Pacific Linguistic Studies in Honour of Arthur Capell. S. A. Wurm and D. C. Laycock, eds., pp. 997–1063. Pacific Linguistics, series C, no. 13. Canberra: Australian National University.

Hosking, D. R.
1954 Patrol Report, Kiunga no. 2 of 53/54.

Jones, Barbara Ann
1980 Consuming Society: Food and Illness Among the Faiwol. Ph.D. dissertation. University of Virginia.

Kirsch, Stuart A.
1989 The Yonggom, the Refugee Camps Along the Border and the Impact of the Ok Tedi Mine. Research in Melanesia 13:20–30.

Muller, R. H.
1930 *See* Adatrechtbundels

Muller, W. J.
1931 Eenige mededeelingen omtrent de bevolking aan de Moejoe en Kaurivier. Memories van Overgave, microfiche no. 775.
1955 Volksordening bij de Moejoe-, Mandobo- en Djair-bevolking der onderafdeling Boven-Digoel (1930–1953). Reports by R. H. Muller, N. A. Nieland, and B. Frank. Adatrechtbundels 45, no. 56, pp. 317–321.

Nieland, N. A.
1953 Memorie van overgave der onderafdeling Boven-Digoel; 23–2-'51 t/m 5–2-'53. Memories van Overgave, microfiche nos. 766–767.
1955 Goede en Kwade Zijden van Feesten. Adatrechtbundels 45, no. 22, pp. 31–32.

Reynders, J. J.
1962 Shifting Cultivation in the Star Mountains Area. Nova Guinea, Anthropology 3:45–73.

Salim, I. F. M. Chalid
1973 Vijftien jaar Boven-Digoel: Concentratiekamp in Nieuw-Guinea, Bakermat van de Indonesische onafhankelijkheid. Amsterdam: Contact.
1977 Limabelas Tahun Digul: Kamp konsentrasi di Nieuw Guinea tempat persemaian kemerdekaan Indonesia. Transl. Hasil Tanzil and J. Taufik Salim. Jakarta: Bulan Bintang.

Schoonheyt, L. J. A.
1936 Boven-Digoel. Batavia: N. V. Koninklijke Drukkerij de Unie.

Schoorl, J. W.
1954 Rapport van het bevolkingsonderzoek in het Moejoe-gebied. Memories van Overgave, microfiche nos. 776–778.
1956 Tournee-verslag over de tournee naar de Sibil-vallei van 14 november tot 19 december 1955. Memories van Overgave, microfiche nos. 683–684.
1957 Kultuur en kultuurveranderingen in het Moejoe-Gebied. Leiden: Proefschrift from Rijks Universiteit.
1976 Shell Capitalism Among the Muyu People. Irian: Bulletin of Irian Jaya Development 5(3):3–78.

Strathern, Andrew
1971 The Rope of Moka: Big-Men and Ceremonial Exchange in Mount Hagen, New Guinea. Cambridge Studies in Social Anthropology 4. Cambridge: Cambridge University Press.

Voorhoeve, Clemens L.
1975a Central and Western Trans-New Guinea Phylum Languages. *In* Papuan Languages and the New Guinea Linguistic Scene. S. A. Wurm, ed., pp. 345–459. New Guinea Area Languages and Language Study, vol. 1. Pacific Linguistics, series C, no. 38. Canberra: Australian National University.
1975 Languages of Irian Jaya: Checklist and Preliminary Classification, Language Maps, Word Lists. Pacific Linguistics, series B, no. 31. Canberra: Australian National University.

Welsch, Robert L.
1979 Resources, Land Tenure and Ownership in the Ok Tedi Mine Area. Report prepared for the PNG Department of Minerals and Energy.
1982 Experience of Illness Among the Ningerum of Papua New Guinea. Ph.D. dissertation. University of Washington.
in press Cultural Continuities Between the Upper Fly and Digul Rivers: What Evidence for a Fly-Sepik Corridor? (to appear in Oceania).

NOTES

The research upon which this paper is based was largely conducted between 1977 and 1980 and was supported in part by a Fulbright-Hays Dissertation Fellowship (1977–78) and by a National Science Foundation Dissertation Improvement Grant (1977–79). Additional observations and insights about Kiunga District were facilitated by the PNG Department of Minerals and Energy, for whom I was a consultant (1978–79 and 1980). More recently I had an opportunity to visit Kiunga and Ningerum in 1990 while I was pursuing other research in Papua New Guinea that was supported by the National Science Foundation, Walgreen Company, and Field Museum of Natural History. I gratefully acknowledge the financial support of all these institutions. In addition I would like to thank the following institutions in Papua New Guinea who so generously offered logistical support and encouragement: The University of Papua New Guinea, the PNG Department of Minerals and Energy, the Department of the Western Province, the PNG Institute of Medical Research, the Institute of Papua New Guinea Studies, the Institute of Applied Social and Economic Research, the National Research Institute, the Ok Tedi Development Company, and the Montfort Catholic Mission. I would like to thank Terence Hays, Stuart Kirsch, Andrew Strathern, Gabriele Stürzenhofecker, John Terrell, and Sarah L. Welsch, all of whom made many useful comments on earlier drafts of the paper and helped improve its tone and argument considerably. Any errors, of course, are my own. Most important, I would like to thank the people of Kiunga District whose constant friendship and hospitality so generously offered made this paper possible.

1. The major languages spoken by peoples inhabiting the Upper Fly-Digul Plain are set out below. Estimated numbers of speakers are derived from Voorhoeve (1975a; 1975b), except for Ningerum and Morop, which are estimated by the author. For the most part these estimates are derived from population estimates made in the 1950s and are assumed to be very rough. Relationships between many of these languages are poorly understood, and several languages within the Awyu-Dumut and Ok families may constitute dialect chains rather than distinct languages. In the late 1970s, I recorded a

Awyu-Dumut Family		*Ok Family*		*Awin-Pa Family*	
Wamggom	1,000	N. Kati (Muyu)	8,000	Aekyom (Awin)	6,000
Wambon	1,000	S. Kati (Muyu)	4,000	Pa (Pare)	1,500
Kaeti (Mandobo)	4,000	Yonggom	2,000		
Kotogut	1,000	Ningerum	4,500		
Aghu (Djair)	3,000	Iwur	1,000		
		Morop	500		
	10,000		19,500		7,500

variety of names for different languages along the Ningerum-Muyu frontier such as Vengwap, Okbari, and Tutaman. These seem to denote dialect differences between clusters of local clan segments rather than mutually unintelligible languages. Of the ethnolinguistic groups listed above, the Awin and Pa in the east and the Aghu (or Djair) in the southwest appear to be the least integrated with other communities in the Upper Fly-Digul area (see Welsch in press). My discussion here primarily concerns socioeconomic integration among the Mandobo, Muyu, Yonggom, and Ningerum.

2. In the southern part of the plain, where the people were often the target of head-hunting raids from the south, settlements were somewhat larger and consisted of up to six or seven houses (see Austen 1923a). According to Schoorl (1957:17), settlements of one, two, or three tree houses were much more characteristic.

3. In Ningerum, for example, one finds Daupka clan segments in the north as well as the south, but these local groups are completely autonomous. In the southern or lower Ningerum there are some Mwitka clan segments that occupy neighboring territories. These clan segments are distinguished as Mwitka Avya, Mwitka Op, Mwitka Kim, and so on. Each is autonomous and has a separate territory, but if asked to explain how they can all be Mwitka, people say they are descended from a common founding ancestor. Marriage is frequent between these different Mwitka groups, but quite uncommon within a local clan segment. Schoorl (1957:19–20) observed a similar pattern in both Kawangtet and Yibi.

4. This usage appears to have been customary in government reports into the late 1950s (see Muller 1931, 1955; Nieland 1953, 1955; den Haan 1955) and probably dates to Muller's period and the early years of the internment camp at Tanah Merah.

5. P. Drabbe (1954) distinguished two dialects of Kati (his term for the people since identified as Muyu): the Ninati dialect in the north and the Metomka dialect in the south. Both Jan Boelaars (1950:77) and J. W. Schoorl (1957:12–13) accepted Drabbe's linguistic analysis that these were dialects rather than different languages. Schoorl, however, suggests that there are other dialects in the Muyu area, particularly in the north near Tumutu. Schoorl also noted a number of cultural differences that corresponded to the differences in language identified by Drabbe, and his text is filled with qualifications as to whether the discussion refers only to the northern or southern communities or to both. More recently, Alan Healey (1964) and Clemens L. Voorhoeve (1975a, 1975b) have distinguished these two dialects as different languages, which are now called Northern and Southern Kati, respectively.

Although linguists have repeatedly distinguished Yonggom from both these languages (Healey 1964; Voorhoeve 1975a, 1975b), Yonggom's position as a distinct language remains problematic (see Kirsch 1989). Kirsch (pers. comm. 1990) sees Yonggom as mutually intelligible with the language spoken in both the northern and southern Muyu.

6. In later reports, Austen distinguished the different groups he met as

Ionggom, Awin, Worom, and so on. But in his first reports from these patrols, he referred to the various groups according to the rivers that passed through their territories: the Tedi natives, and so on.

7. Perhaps the first published description of a feast is that by F. H. Berghuys (1937), whose description of a feast witnessed in 1936 is excerpted in I. F. M. Chalid Salim's account of his internment at Boven Digoel (Salim 1973:329–331; 1977:419–421). Salim's awareness of the importance of feasts suggests how obvious the importance of local feasts must have been to residents from outside the Upper Fly-Digul area.

8. Austen (1923a) reported trade between Awin and Yonggom, and I heard some reports of such trade south of Ningerum station. At Matkomnai I also heard cowrie shells referred to as "Yonggom" money.

9. The use of credit had an inflationary aspect as well, just as it does in Western economies. In the 1950s, for example, after the Dutch government had removed a substantial number of cowries from circulation in Muyu by levying fines for misdemeanors in terms of set numbers of cowries, Schoorl (1976:62) conservatively estimated that there were about 31,595 actual shells in circulation. This amounts to five cowries per person.

10. This description of the staging and organization of pig feasts draws primarily upon my observations of more than a dozen feasts held in and around the Ningerum area between 1977 and 1979. Most of these feasts were held in the lower Ningerum (Alisi Ningerum) area where I was living around Hukim, Yongtau, Minipon, Tengkim, Bankim, and Wambom villages. Besides these feasts, I also attended one feast at Kolebon on the eastern ridge, two near Bankim No. 2 village along the border, several in the upper Ningerum (Kasuwa) area around Ambare and Kwikim, one along the border in the upper Ningerum area north of old Irimkwi (which was heavily attended by people from Irian Jaya), and one large Yonggom feast at Kungim (attended by a large Muyu group from across the border and many Ningerum guests whom I accompanied). Although I observed some differences among these feasts, their general organization was quite similar.

11. Stuart Kirsch (pers. comm.) reports that these minor exchanges are absent in the southern Yonggom, and I am not certain how widespread this practice is beyond Ningerum and a few nearby villages.

12. In Ningerum there is no strict taboo on eating one's own pigs (see Jones 1980), but it is not desirable. Each host avoids eating his own pig by exchanging a pig with his co-host. Following this exchange, when the time comes to share cooked pork, each co-host may share the other's pork since it no longer belongs to the original owner.

13. The principal mechanism of economic Muyu-ization was marriage, with its obligations for brideprice, childprice, and other related payments. Once a man from a hamlet that was as yet un-Muyu-ized married a woman from a Muyu (or Muyu-ized) community, he and his descendants were almost inevitably incorporated into lifelong economic obligations with their

Muyu-ized kin and affines. In effect, they were obliged to participate in an economic system if they wanted to maintain contact with the bride's kin. In the modern period, a few Ningerum broke such ties by moving away from the region, but for most people the social costs of losing touch with one's relatives were too great to contemplate.

TRADE, MIGRATION, AND EXCHANGE

THE BIRD'S HEAD PENINSULA OF IRIAN JAYA IN A COMPARATIVE PERSPECTIVE

Jelle Miedema

1. INTRODUCTION

In this paper, through a description and analysis of the interrelations of slave trade, migrations, the prevailing exchange complex, and correlated phenomena, I hope to provide a developmental perspective by means of which the comparative study of the Bird's Head cultures can be carried out more systematically. As this matter has previously been dealt with only in a preliminary way (Miedema 1988), this study can be considered a further elaboration of the theme. This is an urgent matter: as more ethnographic data about the Bird's Head region and other regions of Irian Jaya become available (BKI 1988), the volume of interregional and indeed trans–New Guinea comparative studies will certainly increase, but studies of this kind cannot be carried out successfully without an adequate framework.

As far as the Bird's Head is concerned, the ethnographic picture is still very incomplete. Regarding the thirty or so ethnolinguistic groups of the Bird's Head peninsula, only four ethnographies have been published—on the Meybrat (Elmberg 1968), the West Ayfat (Schoorl 1979), the Kebar (Miedema 1984), and the Moi (Haenen 1991). Additional ethnographic data about other tribal groups are scarce and fragmentary, and in particular the southern part of the Bird's Head is still practically unknown from an anthropological point of view.

Yet despite this limitation, it can also be stated that the developmental perspective I am concerned with is not merely dependent on what is known about the Bird's Head. This area can also be regarded as part of a wider field of study. Investigations carried out in other areas can help to provide more insight into the ethnographic past and present of the Bird's Head cultures. We are dealing here with a special area, for the Bird's Head peninsula can be considered a transitional region between Asia and Oceania. Whereas from an overall cultural point of view the peninsula must be classified under Oceania, it is historically and politically situated in the periphery of Asia. This is reflected in the best-known cultural phenomenon of the Bird's Head, the so-called *kain timur* exchange system.[1] On the one hand, this system cannot be fully understood without insight into the former trade relations between the Moluccas and the west coast of Irian Jaya—particularly the northern shore of the MacCluer Gulf. On the other hand, neither can it be understood without insight into similar exchange systems, both in other parts of Irian Jaya and in Papua New Guinea.

The *kain timur* complex is significant for this study because it is one of the most important phenomena of the Bird's Head cultures. Various anthropological studies have provided evidence that the *kain timur* exchange system plays a dominant role in almost all spheres of life among most of the ethnolinguistic groups of the Bird's Head.[2] In a process of mutual adaptation, myths, social structures, and cultural codes have been modified since the arrival of the *kain timur*, imported cloths that for hundreds of years have gradually been distributed across the Bird's Head through trade and ceremonial exchange on occasions of marriage, birth, sickness, and death. Up to now, however, the impact of the *kain timur* has predominantly been dealt with in a limited context and with regard to particular groups. The development of the *kain timur* system in its entirety has hardly been studied, at least not systematically. Therefore, in the following sections, I will first present a description and analysis of the conditions under which the *kain timur* system emerged, the directions in which it expanded, and the extent to which it was accepted in particular cultural settings. This approach is the most promising starting point for a comparative study of developments in both the Bird's Head and other areas of New Guinea.

It will be evident that this research strategy is not new. An important contribution to the systematic analysis of the emergence, distribution, and variety of adaptation of exchange systems has recently been made by Daryl Feil with regard to the *tee* and *moka* exchange systems in the highlands of Papua New Guinea (Feil 1987). Referring to that study, I have previously indicated that it makes quite a difference whether an exchange system arises through (surplus) production in the agricultural sphere or through trade (Miedema 1988: 505).

I will further elaborate the importance of a comparison between the rise and expansion of the *kain timur* system on the one hand and the *tee* and *moka* systems on the other hand in the final section (section 5) of this study. In the following sections, I will first focus attention on the emergence (section 2) and expansion (section 3) of the *kain timur* system. As these aspects have also been dealt with in previous studies (mainly published in Dutch), in section 2, I will mainly confine myself to a short recapitulation of the results of the investigations involved. In section 3, the scope of analysis will be broadened by elaborating on the interrelations of slave trading, migration, and exchange. Next, in section 4, I will discuss the impact of the expansion of the *kain timur* exchange relationships on the cultural settings into which the system expanded, and vice versa. Among other topics, section 4 contains a correction concerning the west-east axis that has thus far often implicitly been used in studies dealing with the cultural heterogeneity of the Bird's Head. Finally, in section 5, I will reconsider the theoretical significance of the Bird's Head data with regard to the development of exchange systems as such.

2. THE SLAVE TRADE AND *KAIN TIMUR*: CENTER AND PERIPHERY

Various anthropological studies have shown that the center of the *kain timur* complex is situated in the Ayamaru area in the interior of the western Bird's Head. The evidence at issue concerns the following facts: (a) compared to other Bird's Head ethnolinguistic groups, the Ayamaru people (the Meybrat and Meysawiet) have the most elaborate classification of cloths; (b) in the Ayamaru region, we are confronted with surplus-manipulating big-men, whose role is less pronounced in other areas; (c) the *kain timur* reached the Bird's Head exclusively by way of the south coast, from where they were gradually traded and exchanged to the hinterland—mainly via the Ayamaru area (see Elmberg 1968; Miedema 1984, 1986).[3]

To start with the route along which the *kain timur* reached the Bird's Head, for hundreds of years slaves and birds of paradise were exchanged, particularly for *kain timur*, and these cloths were bartered only along the south coast of the Bird's Head. Slave trading was also carried out along the north coast of the Bird's Head (Miedema 1984), but here slaves as well as tobacco, rice, and birds of paradise were exchanged for common cotton fabrics or other trade goods. Slave trading was practiced along the south coast on a much bigger scale than along the north coast. Unlike the north coast, the south coast was permanently inhabited by trade agents who operated as middlemen between the war leaders in the interior and the well-known great slave traders of West Irian, the *raja-raja* (*raja* means 'king') of Rumbati, Patipi, Kokas, and Arguni (see also Pouwer 1955; van Lochem 1963).[4] Through *sosolot* trade relationships (Müller 1857:101; Miedema 1984:73), each of these *raja-raja* had his particular sphere of influence. The export of slaves lasted until the end of the last century, whereas in the interior of the Bird's Head, slave trading still occurred up to one generation ago (Barnett 1959; Miedema 1984, 1988, 1989). Centers of slave export were found along the lower reaches of the Kais, Kamundan/Ayfat, Wiriagar/Aimau, and Sebjar rivers (see map 1). From there, the trade agents went upstream to trade and raid in the hinterland, particularly the upper Inanwatan or Aytinyo area (the southern Ayamaru area). It is important to note that slaves were not simply exported. In the interior of the Bird's Head they were also much sought after as reserve capital and cheap labor (Barnett 1959: 1015), or as cheap marriage partners and as a means to enlarge a small kinship group (Miedema 1984). However, the exportation of slaves can in general be regarded as a mechanism resulting in the importation of *kain timur*.

The importance of these *kain timur* is that they were regarded as having not only a practical value but also a prestige value, and that the prestige value is directly linked to the emergence of brideprice payments and an elaborate ceremonial exchange system (Elmberg 1968, Schoorl 1979).[5] Whereas initially a woman could be exchanged only with another woman, gradually (as the quantities of *kain timur* increased) cloths became the new medium in the exchange of women between kinship groups, an exchange that until then had been characterized by forms of an elementary exchange (direct sister exchange, or indirect exchange postponed to a following generation; see section 4). What is more, whereas *kain timur* were initially used to obtain a wife, later, women were subsequently used (through forced marriages to outsiders) to acquire *kain timur* (Miedema 1980, 1984).

Unfortunately it is difficult to be more specific about the temporal sequence of events. As far as the south coast is concerned, the only thing known is that written sources that mention barter of *kain timur* for slaves date from at least the last decades of the 16th century (Boxer and Manguin 1979). This implies that in the direct hinterland of the south coast, the Ayamaru area, the *kain timur* system emerged in a rudimentary form at least as early as four hundred years ago. Nor is it possible to be more specific concerning the present-day periphery of the *kain timur* complex. With regard to the northeastern

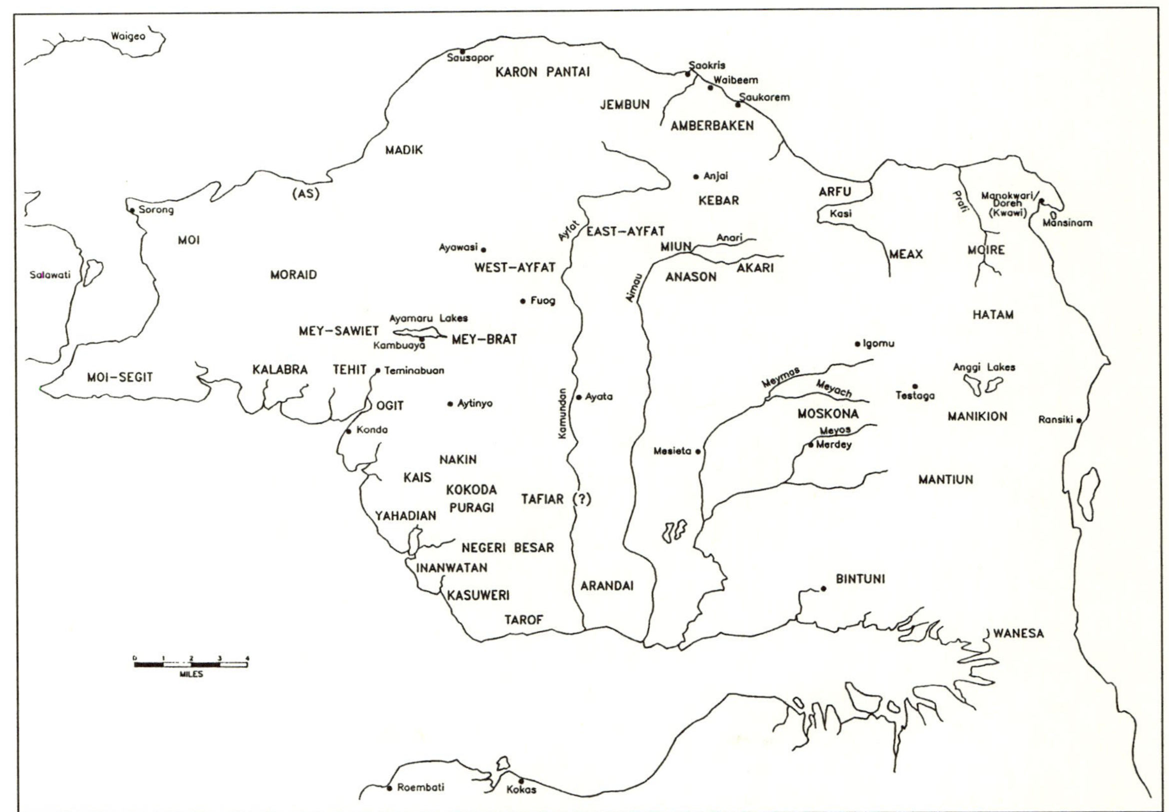

Map 1. Tribal groups (in capital letters) in the Bird's Head.

Kebar area, it is known only that the *kain timur* reached the Kebar mainly (but not exclusively) by way of the southern Meax (see section 3), and mainly through marriage relations. This is known because unbalanced marriage relations between the Kebar and the Meax (in favor of the latter—Kebar women were purposefully married off to acquire *kain timur*) are reflected not only in their present-day (1979–80) marriage relations but also in former marriage relations as revealed in the relevant genealogies (Miedema 1984). It is further known that the first Meax people migrated to the north coast (again see section 3) by way of the eastern Kebar area as early as 1777–1817 (Miedema 1984:80). It is therefore likely that *kain timur* contacts were established in the northeastern periphery of the *kain timur* complex at least as early as two hundred years ago.

Regarding the emergence and expansion of the *kain timur* system, reference has thus far been made to the center and just one peripheral area: the Ayamaru area, and the Kebar plains area including its immediate surroundings. However, the periphery of the *kain timur* complex has to be further specified. As this subject will also be dealt with in the following sections, it suffices here to note that, like the Kebar, the Ayfat and Moi peoples (in the northern interior and the northwestern coastal area) also have a less elaborate classification of cloths than that current among the Ayamaru people (Kamma 1961:212; Schoorl 1979:167; Miedema 1984:82). However, a difference is that, like the Ayamaru people, the Ayfat and Moi peoples distinguish different categories of cloths: *kain jalan* 'wandering cloths' or cloths for exchange, versus *kain pusaka* 'hereditary cloths' and male versus female cloths.[6] But the elaboration of these specific categories is less specific among the Ayfat and Moi than among the Ayamaru people.

In the foregoing, I have confined myself to some general notes with regard to the conditions under which the *kain timur* system emerged, and the directions in which this system expanded. Both aspects have to be further specified, but this is only possible by dealing first with another phenomenon that is highly intermeshed both with slave trading and with the development and expansion of the *kain timur* system: migration.

3. TRADE AND MIGRATION

In 1960, Pans gave a detailed reconstruction of the migration routes of almost all the ethnolinguistic groups in the eastern Bird's Head region. He saw that, in the course of many generations, several migration waves occurred from the south in a northeastern and

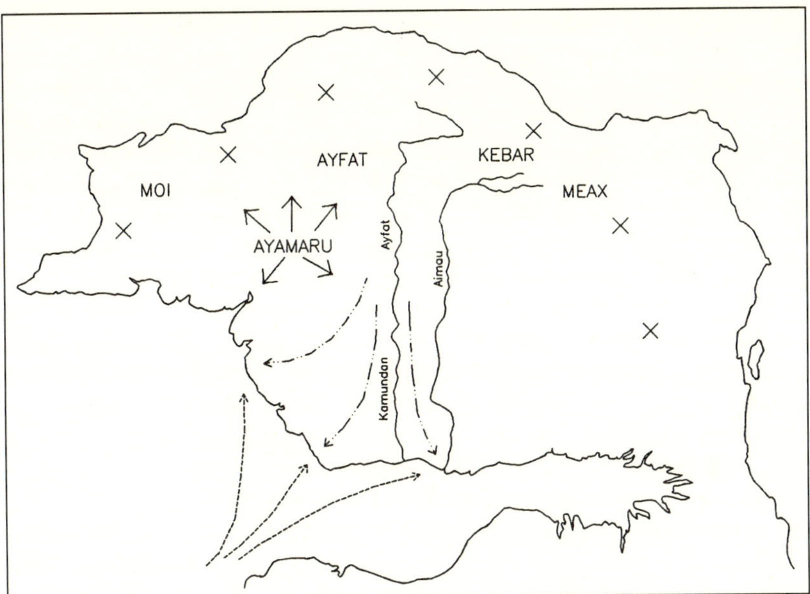

Map 2. Center and periphery of the Bird's Head *kain timur* complex: ↖↑↗ = center; × = periphery; – ·· – = export of slaves; - - - - = import of *kain timur*.

northern direction. And although Pans mentioned, as important contributing factors, population growth, soil exhaustion in the southern regions, and exchange trade along the northern and eastern coast of the Bird's Head, he regarded raids and slave-trading activities along the south coast as "perhaps the *most important* cause" of the migration waves (Pans 1960:46, 47, 54, 60, my italics).

Because of the existence of the slave-trading centers along the south coast, and because the Kamundan/Ayfat and Wiriagar/Aimau river systems and the adjacent steep mountain ranges—which run from north to south in the center of the Bird's Head region (see map 1)—form a natural barrier between the eastern regions and the western regions of the Bird's Head, predatory activities in the hinterland of the south coast resulted in divergent migration routes of the peoples affected. Whereas population groups in the eastern Bird's Head migrated mainly in a northeastern direction, groups in the western Bird's Head migrated mainly in a northwestern direction. Examples are respectively the Meax, Hatam, and Moire peoples (Pans 1960), and the Anason, Anari, and Miun peoples (Miedema 1984) in the eastern Bird's Head; and the Ogit (Van Rhijn 1956:2), the Ayfat (Schoorl 1979:141–142), and probably also the Meybrat in the western Bird's Head.

Migrations are important for obtaining insight into the routes along which peoples, objects, and ideas moved across an area. However, these routes are not usually found along straight axes between the center and periphery of the objects and ideas concerned. Both spatial and temporal perspectives must be taken into account, and this is especially true for the comparative study of the Bird's Head cultures—whose peoples have been characterized as "peoples on the move" (Pans 1960). Although it seems that the natural barriers and divergent migration waves I have noted imply a split between the western regions and the eastern regions of the Bird's Head, there is important evidence that this split is rather artificial, at least from a temporal point of view. My argument is that, given the ecological conditions in the central Bird's Head, the predatory activities along the south coast and in its adjacent hinterland have driven a wedge northward between the former inhabitants of the hinterland. This implies that there were formerly closer contacts between the peoples in the area concerned (that is, the peoples east and west of the Kamundan/Ayfat and Wiriagar/Aimai rivers), and this can be attested by tracing cultural as well as linguistic similarities between the groups east and west of these rivers.

A first similarity between the groups concerned is the occurrence of trickster stories, or rather, striking similarities with regard to parts and sequences of events mentioned in these stories (Miedema 1986: 37), the so-called *siwa* and *mafif* stories of the Ayamaru people in the western Bird's Head, and the *jubewi* and *junon* stories of the Kebar people in the northeastern Bird's Head. The latter stories are found only among the South Kebar Anari people, who trace their provenance from southern areas (Miedema 1984:124). (The importance of this detail will be dealt with later.)

A second link between the cultural areas east and west of the Kamundan and Aimau rivers are the so-called *rumah adat* or *adat* houses (*adat* means traditional values, rules, and customs), used for initiation practices (Elmberg 1968; Schoorl 1979). As far as the eastern Bird's Head is concerned: in 1979, I happened to obtain some information about these (secret) houses during an expedition to the then unknown Akari people (see map 1). Only a small amount of information could be obtained from South Kebar Anari men, who were directly related to Akari men who, in turn, had been initiated in the *adat* houses of the southern Anason (Miedema 1984). Just two characteristics of these *adat* houses were mentioned. First, they had something to do with Bauk (a well-known mythological figure from the western Bird's Head), and second, initiates were not allowed to eat parts of food touched by others and offered to the initiates by the cult leaders (which is an aspect also of former initiation cults in the western Bird's Head; see van Rhijn 1960:24–32).

A third connection between groups east and west of the Ayfat and Aimau rivers is found in the field of language. In a recent article, Voorhoeve noted that the Brat language (*Brat* means 'Meybrat/East Ayamaru') "is spoken in five major dialects, Ayamaru, Marei, Karon Dori, West Ayfat and *East Ayfat*" (Voorhoeve 1987:5, my italics). In the same study he wrote,

> The postulated presence of Brat in the eastern Bird's Head, and the migration towards the centre which must have followed may perhaps provide the answer to a number of cognates with *Meax* for instance, or the *sharp break* between it [Brat] and its present neighbours to the west and north, and the absence of any close relatives. (Voorhoeve 1987:9, my italics)

Evidently Voorhoeve's findings support the idea of the central Bird's Head cultural area's being divided by a wedge. Whereas, long ago (with a time perspective of thousands of years), a Brat language group moved from west to east, later (time perspective hundreds of years), this Brat group split up into the Meybrat and the East Ayfat and became divided from their then eastern neighbors, the Meax. The Meax dispersed in a northeastern direction, while evidently the Brat moved in a northwestern direction (the Meybrat having no close relatives to the west and north; see also Schoorl 1979:140–142). After moving northward, representatives of both language groups moved to the center again. This concerns the Karon Dori and the Miun (Meon) at the western and eastern upper reaches of the Ayfat and Aimau rivers respectively (Miedema and Welling 1985).

The data concerned show not only that the Bird's Head cannot just be split up into an eastern part and a western part, but also that migrations—triggered off by raids and slave trading along the south coast—resulted in a decrease of intertribal contacts along an west-east axis, and at the same time in an increase of contacts along (semicircular) south-north axes in the eastern part as well as the most western part of the Bird's Head (see map 3).

This reconstruction of particular migration routes, which is valid mainly for the prepacification period, supports the view (based on additional ethnographic data) that the northeastern Kebar obtained

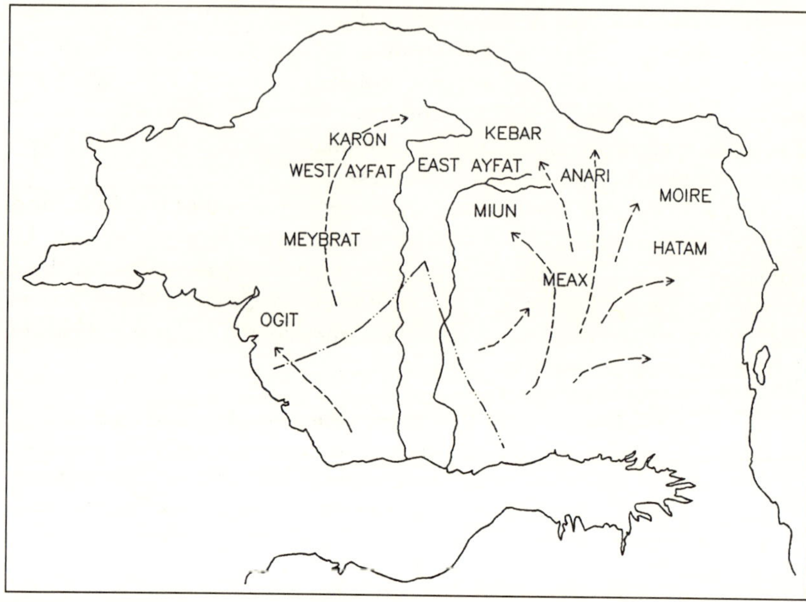

Map 3. Divergent and semicircular migration waves in the Bird's Head peninsula: – ·· – = wedge; - - - - = migration routes.

their *kain timur* mainly by way of the then southeastern Meax (and not by way of the western Karon or the southwestern Ayfat), whereas it also explains why the Ogit along the southwest coast of the Bird's Head have only recently become involved in the *kain timur* complex (as the Ogit originate from the Inanwatan area, where the *kain timur* are unknown).[7]

After having explored the effects of slave trading on migrations, I will focus attention on the effects of the abolition of slave trading. In that context, I shall not be concerned with the recent tribal moves triggered off by the process of village building, but more particularly with the move of the coastal trade agents (see section 2) into the interior of the western Bird's Head. The immigration of this category of men is very important, as these men and their descendants became highly involved in the *kain timur* exchange complex.

When slave trading gradually decreased and was formally abolished also in the Sultanate of Tidore and adjacent areas, including Dutch New Guinea (see Miedema 1984), the trade agents along the southwest coast of the Bird's Head had to look for a new focus of exchange to consolidate positions of power and prestige. Obviously relying on the long-standing network of trade relationships with war leaders or big-men (see section 5) in the interior, these trade agents started to move inland.[8] Here they married women in exchange for many cloths, axes, or even *kain pusaka* 'sacred, inherited cloths' thus obtaining the right to settle locally (Miedema 1986).[9] However, once settled inland, these "immigrant-*bobot*" (Elmberg 1968) started to compete with the local *bobot-telaga* (*bobot* means 'big-man' and *telaga* means 'lake', referring to the lakes in the Ayamaru area [see Elmberg 1968]) on the local *kain timur* market. Here the immigrants from the south coast managed to achieve a new position of power through the introduction of new initiation cults. These cults were practiced in "non-traditional initiation societies, called UON and TOCH'MI, both of which maintained a connection with medicine-men and axe-men of coastal villages" (Elmberg 1968:204; Miedema 1986). The importance of this detail is that the connections referred to were only with the south coast and with the west.[10] Other connections with the west, or Salawati, are mentioned in the myths of origin of Ayamaru big-men: whereas six of the seven big-men in the village of Ayamaru (former Mefkotiam) claimed to be descendants of immigrants from the south coast, one of them traced his origin explicitly to Salawati forebears (Elmberg 1968:202).[11]

From the foregoing, it may be clear that these interisland and interregional contacts involved not only the export of slaves and the import of *kain timur,* but also the move—from west to east—of people, ritual practices, and ideas. Of special importance for insight into the emerging power of the immigrant big-men, however, are ideas regarding the *kain pusaka*. It was these inherited, sacred, and powerful cloths (Pouwer 1957:306; Barnett 1959:1014) that—once assimilated into the local (Ayamaru) system of ancestor worship in which a *pusaka* element already played a role (Miedema 1986)—became the new *pusaka* or, rather, the new source of mediation between the living and the dead (Elmberg 1968; Miedema 1986). Whereas the *bobot* 'big-man' could settle conflicts and arrange marriages, as banker or financier, he could either provide the *kain timur* that were needed as brideprice or be invited to settle conflicts. At the same time, as medicine man or cult leader, he could increase his control over the *kain jalan* (the wandering cloths that fly like birds) by delaying or even buying off his own obligations as a debtor through ritual services. This breakdown of reciprocity in the material sphere (the exchange of goods), even among very close relatives, could be realized by the big-men or *bobot* through the ownership of *kain pusaka*. Through their control over these cloths, the *bobot* had a monopoly in making contact with the most important ancestors. This, in turn, was a very important means of asserting power, because in Meybrat life the ancestors, and the water demon Mos, had to be continually satisfied to avoid misfortune in life (Miedema 1986:28).

In conclusion, it can be stated that, although neither the arrival and influence of coastal immigrants nor the transformation of imported cloths into *pusaka* was a necessary condition for the development of the Bird's Head *kain timur* complex as a ceremonial exchange system, these immigrants (including their ideas and practices) have played an important role in the evolution of the Ayamaru variant of the *kain timur* system as the center of the *kain timur* complex in the Bird's Head.

4. THE *KAIN TIMUR* SYSTEM AND CORRELATED PHENOMENA

In section 3, I examined the evidence that *kain timur* did not enter a static cultural setting. In this section I shall focus attention on the mutual impact of the expanding *kain timur* system and the indigenous cultural settings. Given the restricted ethnographic evidence about the Bird's Head cultures, I must confine the discussion to tribal groups and phenomena about which comparable information is available. Fortunately, the groups concerned are located in both the center and the periphery of the *kain timur* complex: the Ayamaru area and the Kebar, Ayfat, and Moi areas, respectively. Moreover, as in the case of Feil's study (1987), the subjects about which information is available are marriage systems, gender conceptions, and warfare.

Marriage Systems

In a previous study, I dealt with some general trends in the field of Bird's Head marriage systems (Miedema 1986), but I shall briefly recapitulate these trends here, as an introduction to the present subsection.

Given the Kebar data, it is now clear that before pacification (which started in the first decades of this century), in both the western and eastern parts of the Bird's Head, intratribal and intertribal marriages were often arranged through sister exchange (including classificatory sisters). Because the Bird's Head kinship groups were small localized groups, the system of obtaining a wife through sister exchange entailed severe restrictions: a man who did not have a sister could not marry.[12] Evidently pigs were not sufficiently valued to form the basis of a brideprice system, although occasionally they may have been accepted in exchange for a woman who had been married before (Kamma 1970:136). In the Kebar area, because of a shortage of free marriageable women, female slaves often became wives, but these alliances were marked by a severe restriction: through marriages, new exchange relationships are established between members of kinship groups, but slaves are not supposed to have relatives (see also Miedema 1984:99–100). As for pigs, they were not easily transportable over long distances in times of intratribal and intertribal wars. This was not the case with coastal articles of exchange like armlets, steel axes, beads, chinaware, guns, and *ikat* fabrics.

Among this coastal merchandise, *kain timur* or *ikat* fabrics must have been scarce from the start, as these trade goods were imported only by way of the south coast. Probably because of this scarcity, and because these cloths were literally equivalents for human lives (slaves), they became highly esteemed in the interior of the Bird's Head as a means of increasing social status or prestige. Through continuous importation for centuries (up to World War II), the quantities of *kain timur* increased. Although other coastal trade goods also became important as *harta maskawin* 'brideprice goods', the *kain timur* in particular caused the emergence or institutionalization of a brideprice system.These cloths became the most important brideprice goods: nowadays a brideprice without *kain timur* is unthinkable in the interior of the Bird's Head. Gradually this brideprice system became accepted all over the interior of the Bird's Head as a substitute for the rigid system of sister exchange—at least in areas where sister exchange occurred, as in the Kebar area. This can be illustrated by a remark of my Kebar informants: "formerly he who had no sister could not marry, nowadays he who has no *kain timur* cannot marry." Whereas at first *kain timur* were used to obtain a wife, subsequently women were used to acquire *kain timur,* which implies that in the peripheral eastern Bird's Head the prestige value of *kain timur* also became more important than its practical value.

Having established the background, let us now look more closely at the marriage rules in both the periphery and the center of the *kain timur* complex. In the peripheral areas, it is striking to see that, among the Kebar, exogamy is still defined consanguineously (Miedema 1984: 135), whereas among the West Ayfat, more closely connected to the center, exogamy is defined in terms of sharing brideprice: "every marriage is permitted as long as the ceremonial exchange circuits do not become too short" (Schoorl 1979:159). As J. M. Schoorl deals only with the ethnographic present of the late 1960s and the early 1970s, it cannot be determined whether preferential marriages ever occurred among the Ayfat. However, as Schoorl obtained his field data mainly in the village of Ayawasi (located directly to the north of the Ayamaru area), it is important to note what Elmberg reported about this northern area and the southern Ayfat area: "To the north of the [Ayamaru] lakes the genealogies showed a number of *sibling-exchanges*, which were said to have been *in general practice earlier*. The same was said to have been the case in the *Aifat* [Ayfat] region in the south" (Elmberg 1968:84, my italics).

The foregoing does not imply that sister exchange was the only rule for exchanging marriageable women before the *kain timur* brideprice system emerged. A Kebar informant stated that formerly a man could not marry if he did not have a sister, but I can also refer to an Akari informant from the South Kebar mountain range, who declared that "nowadays daughters of women married off to men in the plains area do not want to be married back to the mountain area." This statement refers to a marriage system in which the exchange of a woman for another woman took place over two generations.

Let us now turn our attention to the western Bird's Head. With regard to the Moi people in the northwestern periphery of the *kain timur* complex, evidence has been presented that preference is formally given to marriage between a man and his MBD, but also that the marriage relations are in fact characterized by flexibility (Haenen 1988:467–468). And although this flexibility is defined in classical structuralist terms—as being the result of combining a preferential matrilateral cross-cousin marriage with an Omaha classificatory system (ibid.:475)—Paul Haenen has elsewhere shown that among the Moi, too, *kain timur* became an exchange medium for wives and that nowadays the choice of marriage partner is also defined in terms of sharing brideprice, or rather, as an avoidance of sharing brideprice among people who are too closely related to each other. It is important here that, among the Moi, the emergence of the *kain timur* brideprice system and the accompanying elaboration of a network of exchange partners have contributed to the application of more flexible marriage rules.

Let us turn finally to the Ayamaru area. J.-E. Elmberg reported not only that sibling exchange occurred in the northern and eastern fringes of this area, but also that MBD marriages occurred among the Meysawiet in West Ayamaru, which conforms with the situation among their northern Moi neighbors. He further noted, however, that MBD marriages are *no longer* contracted in the southern Ayamaru area, as "cloths [have to] circulate in all directions, and not only within a small circle." Finally, in Central Ayamaru, the center of the Bird's Head *kain timur* system, both sibling exchange and MBD marriages were forbidden. The rule was "free choice" with a "preference for remote relatives on the maternal side" (Elmberg 1968:83, 84).

These data from both the center and the periphery of the Bird's Head exchange complex—excluding the southern part of the Bird's Head—provide strong evidence for constructing the following patterns and developments. Apparently, in the remote past, the exchange of marriageable women was realized either through symmetric exchange (directly via sister exchange or indirectly via exchange postponed to the following generation) or through asymmetric exchange (seemingly by way of an open circulating connubium, which evidently occurred only in the most western part of the Bird's Head).[13] However, because of the rise of the imported *kain timur* as articles of prestige and the emergence of the *kain timur* brideprice system, the principle of "a woman for a woman" was gradually abandoned. As free choice became the rule, people had to build an elaborate network of relationships, in order to gather a sufficient quantity of cloths to be used, when necessary, to pay brideprices or fines or as ceremonial payments on the occasion of birth, sickness, or death. The establishment of more flexible marriage rules was stimulated when, in the search for *kain timur,* women were increasingly married to nonrelatives. Since even in the peripheral Kebar area, this process has already been taking place for several generations (Miedema 1984), it can be safely described as dating from prepacification times. Only the view that at first *kain timur* were used to obtain a wife, and that women were subsequently used to acquire *kain timur,* has to be corrected. The actual sequence of events must have been as follows: initially slaves, including female slaves, were used to acquire *kain timur;* subsequently *kain timur* were used to obtain a wife; and finally free women were used to acquire surplus *kain timur.* The crucial position of women in this process will be dealt with in the following sections.

Gender Relations

In a previous study I suggested that, as far as the Bird's Head cultures are concerned, changes in gender relations in favor of women are reflected not only in the phenomenon of female cloths (that is, cloths controlled or "owned" by women, a convention reported only from the western Bird's Head; Elmberg 1968:31), but also in different myths current in the center and periphery of the *kain timur* complex. I argued that, whereas the myths current in the periphery show a struggle between characters of the opposite sex (prehuman male versus female beings), the myths most popular in the center of the *kain timur* system report a conflict between characters of the same sex (male tricksters). At the same time, however, I pointed to a striking ambiguity concerning the position of women, particularly in the center of the *kain timur* complex, expressed in the occurrence of both female cloths and accusations of witchcraft. I suggested that this had to be seen as a reflection of a basic conflict, which was postulated as a fundamental characteristic of the Bird's Head cultures: clashing interests between men as well as between men and women as a consequence of the occurrence of both warfare—inherent in the kidnapping and trading of human beings—and exchange (see Miedema 1988:505).

The crucial question is whether, in the center of the Bird's Head exchange system (as in the center of the Papua New Guinea highlands system), the emergence of the *kain timur* system has contributed to a recognition of women as pivots in intensified intratribal and intertribal marriage relations or, rather, to a change in gender relations in favor of women (Feil 1987:220). At first sight this question can be answered positively, not only because of the occurrence of female cloths in the center, but also because of the circumstance that men, including big-men, as a rule cannot exchange cloths without consulting their wives (Elmberg 1968; Schoorl 1979:170, 190, 198). At the same time, women were and are not as a rule married in directions that they themselves did or do not appreciate (Miedema 1988:500).

A difficult methodological problem, however, is that the *kain timur* system had already become an integral part of the Bird's Head cultures when these cultures were studied for the first time. Nevertheless, dealing with the Ayamaru area, two fields of study can be postulated as being representative for pre–*kain timur* gender relations: namely, the local fishing complex and the field of mythological representations.

Characteristic of the Ayamaru fishing complex is that in the present, and therefore plausibly also in the past (as we are dealing with an indigenous phenomenon), fish is only sold by women. However, like the *orang pantai* (immigrants or their offspring from the south coast) and the *orang darat* (people from the adjacent interior), women are almost completely excluded from the most important activities in fishing. Although they make the most important type of fish trap, women are not allowed to fish with this equipment. In practice, it can only be used on private, inherited fishing sites, and these sites belong to the local landowners, including the present-day big-men, who are the offspring of the first inhabitants of the area and as such the owners of the *tanah pusaka* (inherited land including fishing sites). Near these sites, special rituals are practiced to please the ancestors who are localized in the waters, to make the fish willing to be caught. Women are excluded from these rituals, as they are supposed not to know the secret words and practices, which are taught in the men's house. Women are also forbidden to eat from a first catch after a period of drought or extreme rainfall, as that would result in an "anti-effect," a disturbance of the balance between the sacred and profane spheres of life (see Miedema 1986).

So, obviously in pre–*kain timur* times, women were already active in exchange activities, but these activities were restricted to the barter of food. Nowadays, with hindsight, we can see that women also became active in the ceremonial exchange of cloths, but that this hardly resulted in an increase in their social status, or a change of gender relations in their favor. On the contrary, as far as the prepacification period is concerned, suspicions and accusations of witchcraft and trials for witchcraft are reported from areas not only on the periphery, but also and especially in the core area of the *kain timur* complex (Bergh 1964; Elmberg 1968).

We can even go a step further: until the recent past, Ayamaru social life was fiercely dominated by men, and as elsewhere in New Guinea (see Godelier 1982 [1986]), this domination was legitimated by the idea that, in the remote past, women so misused their superior power that men had to intervene.[14] This intervention went so far that witchcraft trials became the outstanding weapon for men to cope with the lethal power attributed to women. Witchcraft trials were not abandoned when women became more important as pivots in the new networks of intratribal and intertribal marriage relations. Various questions therefore present themselves about these continuous witchcraft trials. Were they—and are they still—a traditional means of coping with the lethal power of women? Or did they subsequently develop into one of the strategies, if not the strategy, of the big-men for coping with the actual power of women in the *kain timur* business?[15]

The last named possibility is suggested by Elmberg, who reported "certain tensions among the Mejprat, especially in relation to female cloth and male endeavours to possess it," and who posited a direct link between the position of women in the *kain timur* business and exchange interests of the Meybrat big-men: "The acculturated *popot* [*bobot*] form of Meyprat feasts counting out women and denouncing inconvenient females as witches who were to be killed" (Elmberg 1968:31, 26). With regard to the adjacent West Ayfat area, Schoorl also reported that "medicine-men forced women to make a confession," and a local *raja* confessed to Schoorl that he "himself often took the initiative of accusing women" (Schoorl 1979:86, 87).

The foregoing shows that in the center of the Bird's Head exchange complex, in both the long-distant and recent past, it was in particular the war leaders and the big-men who manipulated women, as female slaves and as witches and in spite of the emergence of a ceremonial exchange system and the increased intensity of intraregional and interregional marriage relations. However, as the concept of gender involves such social categories as war leaders, medicine men, big-men, followers, commoners, slaves (including female slaves), and "free" women, the position of women can be dealt with adequately only in the broader frame of intratribal and intertribal relationships in the whole interior of the Bird's Head.

These relationships were dominated by a lasting combination of warfare and exchange, and the consequences of this state of affairs will have to be elaborated. This is the object of the following subsection, where I will return, inter alia, to the problem of the ambiguous position of women in the center of the Bird's Head exchange system.

Warfare and Exchange

It makes quite a difference when an exchange system arises not through surplus production in the agricultural sphere (Feil 1987) but through "trade production," and especially when this involves the "production" of slaves. When dealing with this matter in a previous article (Miedema 1988), I referred to Barnett's article about the Meybrat and in particular to the term "warrior-capitalist" that he used to describe the Ayamaru type of leadership (Barnett 1959). This term is of interest as it combines in one notion both the idea of warfare and that of exchange, or (in the terms of Godelier) both great-men and big-men (Godelier 1986). It stresses the point that, in the Bird's Head, exchange and warfare were not mutually exclusive.

Slave trading and warfare were the very conditions that enabled the Bird's Head exchange system to emerge, and thus two questions are of interest: What were the consequences of the co-occurrence of both exchange and warfare for the development of intratribal and intertribal relationships? and How was the pre–*kain timur* war leader able to obtain and maintain a position of power?

A plausible answer to the first question is that the coexistence of warfare and ceremonial exchange would give rise to specific forms of mutual distrust between the tribes affected, and this is exactly what happened in both the periphery and the center of the *kain timur* system. This can be illustrated by the different forms of mistrust that were manifested between the Amberbaken and the Ayamaru peoples, which are of special interest for this study.[16] Whereas the Amberbaken, they said, used to mistrust both foreigners and fellow tribesmen (as reflected in their marriage rules; Miedema 1984), the Ayamaru people mistrusted especially their own people and not foreigners as such: "You had your trade friends [*tafóch*] among 'unknown' people, not among the antagonists. Antagonists were reported formerly to have practiced slave hunting in the territory of the informant or to have *cheated* in extra-regional exchange" (Elmberg 1968:19, my italics). The crucial difference, however, is that the Amberbaken people were the objects of kidnapping and slave trading (Miedema 1984), whereas the Ayamaru people were the subjects as well as the objects of these practices. Whereas the Amberbaken people did not trust each other "from mountain slope to mountain slope," because of their isolated dwelling pattern and restricted intratribal relationships, the Ayamaru people did not trust each other because their relationships were marked by an element of cheating.[17]

My point is that these cheating relationships were not restricted to the category of war leaders ("antagonists" or "rivalists"; Schoorl 1979:134) and their following, but that they affected the whole Ayamaru society. This is supported by the many examples of mutual distrust and aggression among the Ayamaru people, as reported in several studies and reports, and by the trickster stories that are most popular in the Ayamaru area. These correlations between the occurrence of kidnappings and slave trading, extreme mutual distrust, and trickster stories is remarkable, as trickster narratives are not found in the northern part of the Bird's Head. At first sight this seems to be in contradiction with the previously reported occurrence of trickster stories in the South Kebar area, but the trickster concerned, JUBEWI, is a combination of a culture hero and a trickster (Miedema 1984, 1986), and he is mentioned only in stories of the South Kebar Anari people. However, these Anari people are of Anason origin who, in turn, originate from the hinterland of Arandai, which was the easternmost center of slave trading along the south coast. This supports the idea that cheating relationships are predominantly characteristic of the southern part of the Bird's Head, or at least those regions where kidnapping and slave trading were most prevalent.[18]

Now, having provided a sketch of the intratribal and intertribal relationships in the periphery and the center of the *kain timur* complex, we can deal again with the problem of the ambiguous position of women, particularly in the center of the *kain timur* system. My starting point is the question of how the Ayamaru war leaders in the pre–*kain timur* era were able to obtain and maintain a position of power, or how they were able to create a group of loyal or, rather, dependent followers.

Focusing attention on initial conditions again, we must remember that slave trading was not restricted to male slaves, and that female slaves often became the marriage partners of free men. This matter has so far been investigated among only the Kebar plains population in the northeastern Bird's Head, a multitribal population that originates from various areas in the central and eastern Bird's Head and that is marked by frequent marriages with female slaves (including many from the western part of the Bird's Head), particularly as far as ascending generations are concerned (Miedema 1988:509). It is clear that marriage with female slaves was quite a common phenomenon in the interior of the Bird's Head.[19] This, in turn, makes it plausible that not only in the *kain timur* era but also in the pre–*kain timur* phase, war leaders had a monopoly in the distribution of a particular category of marriageable women, as only the war leaders could provide female slaves. This monopoly was clearly an important instrument of power for the war leaders: by providing female slaves and at the same time causing a shortage of marriageable free women, they were able to accommodate ordinary men and thus create groups of dependent followers.[20]

The other side of this picture is that women were already objects of exchange in the pre–*kain timur* era, and this situation hardly changed when the *kain timur* system emerged. The strategy of manipulating women (female slaves, witches, "free" women), and also their male relatives, was the crucial means by which the Bird's Head war leaders and big-men were able to obtain and maintain positions of power.

5. THE RISE AND IMPACT OF EXCHANGE SYSTEMS

In the spirit of Daryl Feil (1987), I have used the emergence, expansion, and intensity of an elaborate ceremonial exchange system as the starting point for a comparative investigation of various cultural phenomena and developments characteristic for the prepacification Bird's Head societies. By means of a description and an analysis of the beginning process of the exchange system concerned, I have tried to provide not a "simplified model of causation, but rather a constellation of elements that logically and empirically go together and exist in a complex, mutually reinforcing and continually interacting way" (Feil 1987:168). So far I am in agreement with Feil that insight into a variety of cultural phenomena and developments can only be gained by showing how the elements concerned are interrelated in a spatial and temporal perspective. However, Feil has also stated that the emergence of elaborate ceremonial exchange systems is made possible only by a specific process of production, and he suggested at least that the emergence of elaborate exchange systems goes both empirically and logically together with specific changes in the social sphere of life. I want to deal with two questions in this section: To what extent is Feil's picture of the beginning and the impact of the Papua New Guinea highlands exchange systems also valid for other New Guinea societies in which elaborate ceremonial exchange relationships are the outstanding cultural focus? And in turn, what value does this focus of research have for the comparative study of the societies concerned?

The significance of the Bird's Head data is that surplus production in the agricultural sphere, or subsistence production, is not a necessary condition for the emergence of an elaborate exchange system. Consequently, although the prepacification Bird's Head "warrior-capitalist" is evidently a combination of the great-man and the big-man (Godelier 1982 [1986]), there is no reason to agree with Feil that "Bigmen should . . . be seen as geographically specific, indeed as historically specific too, for it is *only* in those societies where intensive agriculture and linked pig production are ancient and most developed that they are most clearly in evidence" (Feil 1987:94, my italics). The Bird's Head area is marked by the lack of intensive agricultural and pig production, whereas in the prepacification era both the war leader and the big-man were clearly in evidence, which shows that these men were not necessarily mutually exclusive categories. On the contrary, warfare was the very condition that enabled the emergence of the Bird's Head exchange system and big-manship. This implies that the emergence and expansion of an elaborate ceremonial exchange system does not necessarily involve the restriction of warfare, even if this simply means a restriction of the use of visible weapons. In the Bird's Head, the restriction of warfare with military weapons was a postpacification process. Violence by other means was continued during and partly after the process of pacification, involving an excessive manipulation of people that frequently resulted in death, slavery, or lifelong dependency of these people. Violence in this broader sense was perpetuated by means such as accusations of witchcraft, beliefs in the power of sacred objects (here *kain pusaka*) or new initiation cults, imposed patronage through an unequal distribution of articles of exchange, and (last but not least) threats of sorcery.

Another point is the impact of emergent exchange systems on marriage and gender relations. Although in both the Bird's Head of Irian Jaya and the Western Highlands of Papua New Guinea the emergence of elaborate exchange systems has evidently resulted in an intensification of intratribal and intertribal marriage relations, as far as the Bird's Head area is concerned, this process has not resulted in an unambiguous or generally accepted change of gender relations in favor of women. Witchcraft accusations and trials were very common, particularly in the center of the Bird's Head exchange complex, even during the recent pacification process. Women were and have remained the object of manipulation of the Bird's Head big-men in their thought and action.

Yet, in spite of these differences, there is at least one crucial feature that the developments in the Bird's Head and in the Western Highlands of Papua New Guinea have in common, and this feature has everything to do with the emergence of an elaborate ceremonial exchange system and the linked brideprice system: in both areas prestigious exchange goods became the equivalent for human life (compare Strathern 1988:199). This raises the question, under what conditions did this equivalence occur? Confining myself to the available Bird's Head data at this point, I can only suggest that a link probably exists between surplus production or an unequal accumulation and distribution of (initially scarce) prestige goods, on the one hand, and a shortage of persons as the only means to secure the reproduction of the local group, on the other.[21] Further research will be necessary to explore whether the emergence of exchange systems is rooted in the surplus production of valuables, or in the problematic reproduction of the local group, or in a combination of these factors under specific ecological, historical, or structural conditions.

ABBREVIATIONS

AEO	Annales de l'Extrême Orient
ARA	Algemeen Rijksarchief (National Archives, The Hague)
BKI	Bijdragen van het Koninklijk Instituut voor Taal-, Land- en Volkenkunde

GKI	Gereja Kristen Injili
HKI	Hendrik Kraemer Instituut
MTZ	Mededeelingen vanwege het Nederlandsch Zendingsgenootschap (later, Tijdschrift voor Zendingswetenschappen; Rotterdam 1857–1941)
MVG	Mededeeling van de Vereeniging van Gezaghebbers bij het Binnenlandsch Bestuur in Nederlandsch-Indië
NGS	Nieuw-Guinea Studiën
NNG	Nederlands Nieuw-Guinea
NSAV	Nederlandse Sociologische en Antropologische Vereniging
TAG	Tijdschrift van het Koninklijk Nederlands Aardrijkskundig genootschap
TBG	Tijdschrift voor Indische Taal- en Volkenkunde uitgegeven door het Bataviaasch Genootschap van Kunsten en Wetenschappen
TNG	Tijdschrift Nieuw-Guinea
VKI	Verhandelingen van het Koninklijk Instituut voor Taal-, Land- en Volkenkunde

REFERENCES

Arcken, V. J. E. M.
1934 Enkele ethnografische bijzonderheden over de bevolking rond de Anggi-meren. TNG 1:370–374.

Assink, H. W.
1956 Aanvullende Memorie van Overgave van de Onderafdeling Manokwari 1953–medio 1956. (ARA).

Baal, J. van
1975 Reciprocity and the Position of Women. Assen: Van Gorcum.

Barnett, H. G.
1959 Peace and Progress in New Guinea. American Anthropologist 61:1013–1019.

Beek, A. G. van
1987 The Way of All Flesh: Hunting and Ideology of the Bedamuni of the Great Papuan Plateau. Unpublished Ph.D. dissertation. Leiden University.

Bergh, R. R.
1964 Soeangi in de Vogelkop van Nieuw-Guinea. Unpublished Masters dissertation. Oegstgeest University.

Berichten
1861–1917 Berichten Utrechtse Zendingsvereniging. Oegstgeest: HKI.

Bijkerk, J.
1931 De geheime mannenbond op Nieuw-Guinea. MTZ 75:116–140.

Boxer, C. R., and P.-Y. Manguin
1979 Miguel Roxo de Brito's Narrative of His Voyage to the Raja Empat, May 1581–November 1582. Archipel 18:175– 194.

Clerq, F. S. A. de
1893 De West- en Noordkust van Nederlandsch Nieuw-Guinea. TAG 10:151–219, 438–465, 587–649, 841–884, 981–1021.

Crockett, C.
1942 The House in the Rain-Forest. London: Hutchinson.

Dijk, H. van
1940 Algemene Memorie van Overgave van de Onderafdeling Midden-Vogelkop. Ajamaroe (ARA).

Douglas, M.
1975 Implicit Meanings: Essays in Anthropology. London and Boston: Routledge and Kegan Paul.

Dubois, J. J.
1960 De Kain Timoer revolutie in het Maibratgebied. NNG (8)1: 14–18.

Elmberg, J.-E.
1955 Field-notes on the Mejbrats (Vogelkop Western New Guinea). Ethnos 24(1):1–101.
1959 Further Notes on the Northern Mejbrats (Vogelkop Western New Guinea). Ethnos 24:70–81.
1966 The Popot Feast Cycle. Ethnos 30. Supplement.
1968 Balance and Circulation: Aspects of Tradition and Change Among the Mejprat of Irian Barat. Stockholm: Etnografiska Museet, monograph series no. 12.

Fabritius, G. J.
1854 De Papoea's van de Geelvinkbaai, J. Pijnappel, ed. BKI 2:371–3
1855 Aantekeningen omtrent Nieuw-Guinea. TBG 4:209–215.

Feil, D. K.
1987 The Evolution of Highland Papua New Guinea Societies. Cambridge: Cambridge University Press.

Forrest, T.
1780 Voyage aux Moluques et à la Nouvelle Guinée. Paris. (A Voyage to New Guinea and the Moluccas 1774–1780. Oxford: Oxford University Press.)

Fox, R.
1967 Kinship and Marriage. Harmondsworth: Penguin Books.

Galis, K. W.
1956 Nota nopens het Ajamaroe-gebied. Hollandia: Kantoor voor bevolkingszaken, no. 66 (ARA).

Geiszler, J. G.
1859 Reisbeschrijving naar Amberbaken in het jaar 1859. Licht en Schaduw in het Oosten 20:162–163.

Godelier, M.
1982 La Production des grands hommes. Paris: Librairie Arthème Fayard, Editions de la Maison des Sciences de l'Homme. (The Making of Great-Men. Male Domination and Power Among the New Guinea Baruya. Cambridge: Cambridge University Press, 1986.)

Goot, S. van der
1938–39 Enkele ethnografische bijzonderheden over de bevolking in het N.W. deel van de Vogelkop. TNG 3:414–422.
1942–43 Exploratie van de Vogelkop, voorzoover gelegen in de onderafdeling Sorong. TNG 6:26–33, 171–180.

Groenewegen, K., and D. J. van der Kaa
1964 Resultaten van het demografisch onderzoek Westelijk Nieuw-Guinea. Deel I: Nieuw-Guinea als gebied voor demografische onderzoekingen. Den Haag: Staatsuitgeverij.

Haenen, P.
1984 Eis veel en snel, maar geef weinig en traag: Ceremoniële doekenruil in de Vogelkop van Irian Jaya. *In* Antropologie en Ideologie. T. Lemaire, ed., pp. 203–222. Groningen: Konstapel.
1987a Enkele historische overwegingen met betrekking tot de Moi-samenleving: Brief aan Jan Pouwer. *In* Sporen in de antropologie. P. van der Grijp, T. Lemaire, and A. Trouwborst, eds., pp. 79–91. Nijmegen: Instituut voor Kulturele en Sociale Antropologie.
1987b Zending, "beschaving" en doekenruil bij de Moi van Irian Jaya. *In* Processen van kolonisatie en de-kolonisatie in de Pacific. A. Borsboom and J. Kommers, eds., pp. 244–264. Nijmegen: Instituut voor Kulturele en Sociale Antropologie.
1988 Marriage Alliance Among the Moi of Irian Jaya (Indonesia). BKI 144(4):464–477.
1989 Weefsels van wederkerigheid bij de Moi van Irian Jaya. *In* Liber amicorum A. A. Trouwborst: Antropologische essays. A. Borsboom and C. Remie, eds., pp. 124–138. Nijmegen: Instituut voor Kulturele en Sociale Antropologie.

Haenen, P., and J. Pouwer, eds.
1989 Peoples on the Move: Current Themes of Anthropological Research in New Guinea. Nijmegen: Center for Australian and Oceanic Studies.

Haga, A.
1884 Nederlandsch Nieuw-Guinea en de Papoesche Eilanden; Historische Bijdrage. Deel I, 1500–1817. Deel II, 1818–1883. Bataviaasch Genootschap van Kunsten en Wetenschappen. Batavia: W. Bruining en Co.; 's-Gravenhage: M. Nijhoff.

Josselin de Jong, J. P. B. de
1935 De Maleische archipel als ethnologisch studieveld. Leiden: J. Ginsberg.
1983 The Malay Archipelago as a Field of Ethnological Study. *In* Structural Anthropology in The Netherlands: A Reader. P. E. de Josselin de Jong, ed., pp. 166–182. Translations series KITLV, vol. 17. The Hague: Martinus Nijhoff.

Kalff, S.
1920 De slavernij in Oost-Indië. Onze Stemmen 3(9):1–35.

Kamma, F. C.
1939–40 Levend Heidendom. TNG.
1941 Amoelagilala: Over de oorsprong van ziekte en dood volgens de Moi Papoea's. De Opwekker 86:332–341.
1947–49 De verhouding tussen Tidore en de Papoesche eilanden in legende en historie. Indonesië 1:177–275, 360–370, 536–559.
1961 Adat bangsa Moi mengenai pernikaan. Hollandia. Report, archives Zending Nederlandse Hervormde Kerk (Missionary Society Dutch Reformed Church), Oegstgeest.
1970 A Spontaneous "Capitalistic" Revolution in the Western Vogelkop area of West Irian. *In* Anniversary Contributions to Anthropology (twelve essays published on the occasion of the 40th anniversary of the Leiden Ethnological Society WDO), pp. 132–142. Leiden: E. J. Brill.
1975–78 Religious Texts of the Oral Tradition From Western New Guinea (Irian Jaya). Vol. 3A, The Origin and Sources of Life. Vol. 8B, The Threat to Life and Its Defence Against "Natural" and "Supernatural" Phenomena. Nisaba, Religious Texts Translation series. Leiden: E. J. Brill.

Klaasen, M.
1936 Memorie van Overgave Manokwari. December 1934–March 1936. Manokwari (ARA).

Knauft, B. M.
1985 Good Company and Violence: Sorcery and Social Action in a Lowland New Guinea Society. Berkeley: University of California Press.

Kniphorst, J. H. P. E.
1875 Historische schets van den Zeeroof in den Oost-Indische Archipel. Tijdschrift voor het Zeewezen. Amsterdam, 1875–79.

Kooijman, S.
1962 Ancestor Figures From the MacCluer Gulf Area of New Guinea: A Variation of the Korwar Style. Mededelingen van het Rijksmuseum voor Volkenkunde, Leiden no. 15. Leiden: E. J. Brill.

Lamers, A.
1939 Over de pacificatie in den Vogelkop van Nieuw-Guinea. MVG 57:9–16.

Leupe, P. A.
1875 De reizen der Nederlanders naar Nieuw-Guinea en de Papoesche eilanden in de 17e en 18e eeuw. BKI:1–162, 175–311.

Leur, J. C. van
1955 [1967] Indonesian Trade and Society: Essays in Asian Social and Economic History. The Hague/Bandung: W. van Hoeve.

Lévi-Strauss, C.
1958 Antropologie structurale. Paris: Plon.

Lochem, J. T. van
1963 De Argoeniërs. Utrecht: Schotanus en Jens.

Lotgering, F. K.
1940 Memorie van Overgave van de onderafdeling Inanwatan, June 1938–July 1940. Inanwatan (ARA).

Meyners d'Estrey, C.
1878–79 Nouvelle-Guinée: Les Karons, les Kebars et les Amberbaks. AEO 1:338–343.

Miedema, J.
1979 Laporan tentang mitologi dan Kepercayaan adat di daerah budaya Kebar-Amberbaken. Manokwari: GKI. (stenciled)
1980 Injil dan Adat. Manokwari: GKI. (stenciled)
1981a Huwelijk, Verwantschap en Verwantschapsterminologie bij de Kebar in sociaal-historisch perspectief. Paper of a lecture given at the Dutch Society for Oceanic Studies, Universities of Groningen and Nijmegen. Amsterdam, May 1981.
1981b Staatsvorming en habitus in een tribale samenleving: De Kebar op 'Nieuw-Guinea. Congress NSAV Civilisatieprocessen en theorieën. Amsterdam, December 1981. (paper)
1984 De Kebar 1855–1980: Sociale structuur en religie in de Vogelkop van West-Nieuw-Guinea. VKI 105. Ph.D. dissertation. Dordrecht-Holland and Cinnaminson U.S.A.: Foris Publications.
1986 Pre-Capitalism and Cosmology: Description and Analysis of the Meybrat Fishery and Kain Timur-Complex. VKI 120. Dordrecht-Holland and Riverton-U.S.A.: Foris Publications.
1988 Anthropology, Demography and History: Shortage of Women, Intertribal Marriage Relations, and Slave Trading in the Bird's Head of New Guinea. BKI 144 (4):494–509.
1989 The West New Guinea Akari: Beyond Rule and Reality. *In* Women, Migrants and Tribals: Survival Strategies in Asia.

G. K. Lieten, O. Nieuwenhuys, and L. Schenk-Sandbergen, eds. New Delhi: Manohar Publications.

1990 Anthropologists, Missionaries and the "Ethnographic Present": The Confrontation Between Native and Christian Religious Representations in West New Guinea. *In* The Ambiguity of Rapprochement: Reflections of Anthropologists on Their Controversial Relationship with Missionaries. R. Bonsen, H. Marks, and J. Miedema, eds., pp. 45–59. Nijmegen: Focaal.

Miedema, J., and W. A. L. Stokhof, eds.

1991 Irian Jaya Source Materials. Memories van Overgave. No. 2 Series A—No. 1. Leiden and Jakarta: DSALCW/IRIS.

Miedema, J., and F. I. Welling

1985 Fieldnotes on Languages and Dialects in the Kebar District, Bird's Head, Irian Jaya. Pacific Linguistics, series A, no. 63. Papers in New Guinea Linguistics no. 22, pp. 29–52.

Müller, S.

1857 Reizen en onderzoekingen in den indischen archipel gedaan op last der Nederlandsche indische regering tussen de jaren 1828 en 1836. 2 volumes. Amsterdam: Muller.

Oosterzee, L. A. van

1904 Eene verkenning in het binnenland van Noord Nederlandsch Nieuw-Guinea. TAG (21):998–1012.

Osok, E.

n.d. Adat istiadat bangsa Moi. HKI archives.

n.d. Dalmoes Moi (1, 2; Moi myths). HKI archives.

1951 Karangan dan Pengadjaran serta Soesoenan Fasal 2 jg. Penting dalam Hal memakai Harta-Harta. Saoka. HKI archives. (report)

1953 Laporan tentang kambing [Kambik] jang terjadi pada masa ini dan bagi kaoem, serta tanda perdamaian jang dilakoekan. Saoka. HKI archives. (report)

1958 Asal usulnja bangsa Moi dan asal mulanja harta dipakai. Kelasaman. HKI archives. (report)

Pans, A. E. M. J.

1960 De Arfakkers; een volk in beweging. Maastricht (ARA). (stenciled)

Pitt, D. C.

1972 Using Historical Sources in Anthropology and Sociology. New York: Holt, Rinehart and Winston.

Ploeg, A.

1988 Legacies of an Unknown Past. BKI (4):510–522.

Pouwer, J.

1955 Enkele aspecten van de Mimika-cultuur (Nederlands zuidwest Nieuw Guinea). 's-Gravenhage: Staatsdrukkerij.

1957 Het vraagstuk van de kain timoer in het Mejbratgebied (Ajamaroemeren). NGS 1(4):295–319.

1958 Socio-politische structuur in de Oostelijke Vogelkop. Hollandia (ARA). (stenciled)

1960 Bestaansmiddelen en sociale structuur in de Oostelijke Vogelkop. NGS 4:215–234, 309–327.

1966a Toward a Configurational Approach to Society and Culture in New Guinea. Journal of the Polynesian Society 75:267–286.

1966b The Structural and Functional Approach in Cultural Anthropology: Theoretical Reflections with Reference to Research in Western New Guinea. BKI 122:129–145.

Rhijn, M. van

1956–57 Suangi en Wofle, de twee grote machten in het binnenland van Teminaboean en Berauer. HKI archives. (stenciled)

1957 Over een mogelijk verband tussen de rotstekeningen van Argoeni, enkele adat-gebruiken in Negeri Besar en het besnijdenishuis van Aitinjo. HKI archives. (stenciled)

1960 Initiatierituelen in de Vogelkop. HKI archives. (stenciled)

Roest, J. L. D. van der

1917 Van slaaf tot evangelist, de geschiedenis van Petrus Kafiar. Oegstgeest: HKI.

Rouffaer, G. P.

1902 Over ikat's, Tjinde's, Patola's en Chiné's. Het Koloniaal Weekblad. 's-Gravenhage: Gemeenschappelijk Belang.

Ruibing, A. H.

1937 Ethnografische studie betreffende de Indonesische slavernij als maatschappelijk verschijnsel. Zutphen: W. J. Thieme.

Sahlins, M. D.

1965 On the Sociology of Primitive Exchange. *In* The Relevance of Models for Social Anthropology. M. Banton, ed., pp. 139–236. London: Tavistock.

Schoorl, J. M.

1979 Mensen van de Ayfat: Ceremoniële ruil en sociale orde in Irian Jaya, Indonesia. Ph.D. dissertation. Nijmegen/Meppel: Krips Repro.

Schoorl, J. W.

1976 Shell Capitalism Among the Muyu People. Irian: Bulletin of Irian Jaya Development 5(3):3–108.

Schultz, E. L.

1956 Patrouille-verslag naar het Boven-Sibena gebied 5.12.1955–16.2.1956. Hollandia (ARA). (typed)

Strathern, A. J.

1988 Conclusions: Looking at the Edge of the New Guinea Highlands from the Center. *In* Mountain Papuans: Historical and Comparative Perspectives from New Guinea Fringe Highlands Societies. J. F. Weiner, ed., pp. 187–213. Ann Arbor: University of Michigan Press.

Tiele, P. A.

1879 De Europeëers in den Maleischen Archipel 1529–1540. BKI 27:1–69.

1887 De Europeërs in den Maleischen Archipel 1618–1623. BKI 36:199–307.

Verslag

1920 Verslag de militaire exploratie van Nederlandsch Nieuw-Guinea 1907–1915. Weltevreden: Landsdrukkerij.

Voorhoeve, C. L.

1975 Languages of Irian Jaya: Checklist Preliminary Classification, Language Maps, Word Lists. Pacific Linguistics, series B, no. 31.

1987 The Masked Bird: Linguistic Relations in the Bird's Head Area. *In* Peoples on the Move. P. Haenen and J. Pouwer, eds., pp. 78–101. Nijmegen: Center for Australian and Oceanic Studies.

Werff, H. van der

1987 Shifting Cultivation, Kain Timur and Suangi in Relation to the Position of Women. Paper given at the New Guinea Workshop, Nijmegen.

Wichmann, A.

1901–12 Entdeckungsgeschichte von Neu-Guinea: Nova Guinea. 2 volumes. Leiden: E. J. Brill.

Wolf, E. R.

1982 Europe and the People Without History. Berkeley, Los Angeles, and London: University of California Press.

NOTES

This is a revised version of a paper entitled "Warfare and Exchange. The Bird's Head of Irian Jaya in a Historical and Structural Comparative Perspective," prepared for the seminar on Research in Eastern Indonesia, Jayapura, July 1988. Participation in the ASAO seminar, Hawaii, March 1990, was made possible by the generous financial support of the Office for International Cooperation, Leiden University, and the Royal Netherlands Academy of Arts and Sciences. I am indebted to Jack Prentice for his corrections of the final text, and to the editors of this volume for their critical comments on previous versions of the paper. All translations are my own unless otherwise noted.

1. *Kain* means 'cloths'; *timur* means 'east'; the term *kain timur* refers to old *ikat*-cloths, destined for the East Indonesian archipelago, from whence they were for centuries imported into the Bird's Head in exchange for slaves and birds of paradise. These cloths became highly esteemed as brideprice goods

in the exchange of women between kinship groups, particularly in the interior of the Bird's Head area. The term *system* or *complex* refers to the very elaborate network of ceremonial exchange, dominated by surplus-manipulating big-men.

2. See Galis 1956; Pouwer 1957, 1958; Barnett 1959; Elmberg 1955, 1959, 1966, 1968; Kamma 1970; Schoorl 1979; Miedema 1980, 1981a, 1981b, 1984, 1986, 1988, 1989; Haenen 1988, 1989.

3. In Miedema 1986, it is also explained why the *kain timur* exchange complex could reach its most elaborate form in the Ayamaru culture.

4. For a detailed reference to the relevant historical sources, see Miedema 1984:254–256.

5. This practical value refers to the use of *kain timur* as money: besides being used for ceremonial exchange to consolidate social relationships on the occasion of marriage, birth, initiation, and death, these cloths are also used as money to pay for a fine, a pig, or medicines.

6. Unlike the profane cloths (the *kain jalan* or cloths for exchange, which have "to fly like birds"), the sacred cloths (the *kain pusaka*) are not exchanged. These *kain pusaka* are ancient inherited fabrics that are thought to have supernatural or protective power (Pouwer 1957:306; Barnett 1959:1014).

7. The Ogit became involved in the *kain timur* exchange relationships because of their recent marriages with the Tehit of the Teminabuan area (another example of intensified intertribal marriage relations). *Kain timur* are said to be unknown in the homeland of the Ogit, the Inanwatan area, as (according to local informants) birds of paradise did not occur in that area. Another explanation is that the people in the hinterland of Inanwatan were particularly the object of slave-trading activities.

8. The relationship between the coastal trade agents and the war leaders or big-men in the interior was characterized by the trade agents as a parent-child relationship.

9. In myths current in the western Bird's Head, Bauk is reported to be the first man who introduced new initiation cults into the interior. He is described as an "ax-man"; coming from the south coast, he married two inland women in exchange for an axe (van Rhijn 1960:24–32).

10. It is important to note that both the Uon and the Toch'mi societies are also characterized by imported elements, namely the use of a symbolic *prahu* or canoe for the Uon and the practice of circumcision for the Toch'mi. Circumcision is practiced only in the southeastern fringe of the Ayamaru area, while the use of a symbolic canoe is found in the most western part of the Bird's Head. But while circumcision is evidently a reflection of Islamic influence (see also van Rhijn 1960), the use of a symbolic canoe is no doubt an influence from the island of Salawati, where the canoe formerly played a role in the Mon cult (Kamma 1939). Both the Uon and the Toch'mi societies can thus be associated with the west.

11. The influence of Salawati, or rather of the *raja* of Salawati, was not restricted to the southwest coast: it was particularly prevalent along the

northwest coast also. This is the reason why Mon influences are also found in the Kambik or Keik Wunsemas, the secret men's societies of the northwestern Moi people (Osok 1953; van Rhijn 1960:11). It can even be expected that these Mon influences have been most manifest in the northwestern part of the Bird's Head, as this area in particular belonged to the sphere of influence of the *raja* of Salawati as the representative of the Sultan of Tidore.

12. For Ayamaru, see Galis 1956:26; Elmberg 1968:84; and Kamma 1970: 135. For Kebar, see Miedema 1984:139–140.

13. The existence of an open circulating connubium would imply another link between the western Bird's Head and the "Indonesian field of study" (de Josselin de Jong 1983:167–169).

14. I will further elaborate this topic, first mentioned by Kamma 1941 (see also Haenen 1984), in a subsequent study, after I have studied more intensively the fragmentary sources concerned.

15. Although the phenomenon of witchcraft cannot simply be reduced to a conscious intrigue on the part of the war leaders, medicine men, or bigmen, it cannot be denied that these men often played a decisive role in witchcraft accusations and witchcraft trials.

16. The Amberbaken people formerly lived in the coastal mountain range of the northeastern Bird's Head. As victims of slave-trading activities along the north coast, they themselves were hardly involved in the intertribal networks of exchange relationships. Common cotton cloths, plates, and chinaware (and not *kain timur*) became the articles of exchange and brideprice goods along the coasts of the Bird's Head. Yet, the mountain Amberbaken were partly involved in the *kain timur* complex through marriage relations with their linguistically related southern neighbors the Kebar.

17. Given the ecology of the Amberbaken mountains, marriage with the North Kebar was the Amberbaken survival strategy for coping with raids from the coast as well as from the western interior and with "coastal" diseases (Miedema 1981b).

18. Another correlation between myths and the emergence, expansion, and intensity of the *kain timur* system concerns the position of the *kain timur* in the myths. In the periphery of the *kain timur* complex among both the northeastern Kebar and the northwestern Moi, *kain timur* are only presented as a kind of civilization symbol. The culture hero orders the people to marry properly: they are told to pay *kain timur* before they marry and have children (Miedema 1984:169; Osok 1951, recapitulated in Haenen 1987b:250). By contrast, in the center of the Bird's Head exchange complex, the Ayamaru area, *kain timur* are reported to have been created by the ancestors, or the tricksters *siwa* and *mafif*.

19. These followers and their children (the *anak-anak budak* 'children of slaves', the second-lowest social class in the Bird's Head) remained dependent on the patronage of the war leaders, because of the lack of relatives on the side of the slave wife or slave mother.

20. A shortage of marriageable women is indicated by a rather large

number of marriages with female slaves in the ascending generations (see Miedema 1988:509). The interregional slave trading in the interior of the Bird's Head was dominated by war leaders acting as trade friends (Barnett 1959:1015). Examples of "trade" in female slaves are presented in Miedema 1984:107, 112, 113 (closure case 10). For an example of prepacification circumstances, see Miedema 1984:114. In the pre–*kain timur* phase, a *relative* shortage of women was caused by a combination of the limited size of the localized kinship groups and the prevailing marriage systems ("he who had no sister could not marry"). A *real* shortage of women, however, may have been caused by female suicide (Crockett 1942:106), polygyny among the war leaders, death in childbirth, witchcraft trials, and the phenomenon of *ganti manusia*: the exchange of a murdered person for human life (preferably that of a woman) when the party involved in a war wanted to make peace. In this context it is interesting to note that, with the emergence of the *kain timur* system, it became increasingly common for a death to be compensated for, not by a human being, but by a *kain pusaka* or even a large quantity of *kain jalan*. Finally, girls were formerly more appreciated than boys, when parents had a choice: when twins were born, the second child was killed, but if the second child was a girl and the first child a boy, then the boy was killed.

21. In the Bird's Head this shortage became manifest in (1) a scarcity of marriageable women, which is indicated by endogamy, marriages with female slaves, or marriage rules that became unworkable, and (2) a shortage of group members as such, indicated by the adoption of slaves. Endogamy is most clearly in evidence among the unpacified Akari people in the interior of the northeastern Bird's Head. As this group could hardly attract women from elsewhere, some of its members were forced to marry endogamously (Miedema 1984:155). But nevertheless, although the reproduction of the Akari group was in danger for years, they had given women in marriage to other groups, in spite of being aware that the daughters of these women did not want to be married back. Both the emergence of the "warrior-capitalist" type of big-manship and the co-occurrence of exogamous and endogamous marriage (as well as marriages with female slaves) seem to contradict Godelier's view that there will not emerge an exchange system, including big-manship, as long as the reproduction of the group is in danger (Godelier 1982 [1986]:xi). Further research will be necessary to find out to what extent the societies concerned can be compared.

REASSESSING COMPETITIVE LEADERSHIP AND ECONOMIC EXCHANGE IN SOUTH-COASTAL NEW GUINEA

Bruce M. Knauft

The Papuan language-culture areas of coastal south New Guinea extend along the south coast for over a thousand miles, from the Eleman language-culture area in the east to the Asmat regions in the west (see map). Except for the four small language families that comprise the Trans-Fly area, these seven culture areas correspond to the Papuan language-family boundaries compiled for New Guinea by Stephen Wurm and Shiro Hattori (1981). These regions also conform in rough measure to the existing "monographic" division of the south coastal area, that is, the ethnographic subdivision of the region into discrete populations that have been subject to separate and rigorous description in scholarly monographs.[1]

In short, these coastal culture areas have a linguistic as well as an ethnographic identity. They are well described in published accounts, for the most part in a similar "classic" ethnographic format at a roughly similar stage in the early colonial history of each area, a method that lends itself well to comparison of a number of features across the range of coastal language-culture areas.

Alternative regional configurations of south New Guinea are of course possible, and indeed if one follows Eric Wolf (1988), there are no totally "natural" boundaries between one societal group and another. In the present case, the decision to adopt an east-west axis as opposed to a more "vertical" one stretching further inland is to some extent based on a priori choice. The present configuration is also undertaken in part as an exercise to counterbalance the existing perception of south New Guinea as an area typified by ritual homosexual practices and their presumed correlates (for example, Feil 1987:ch.

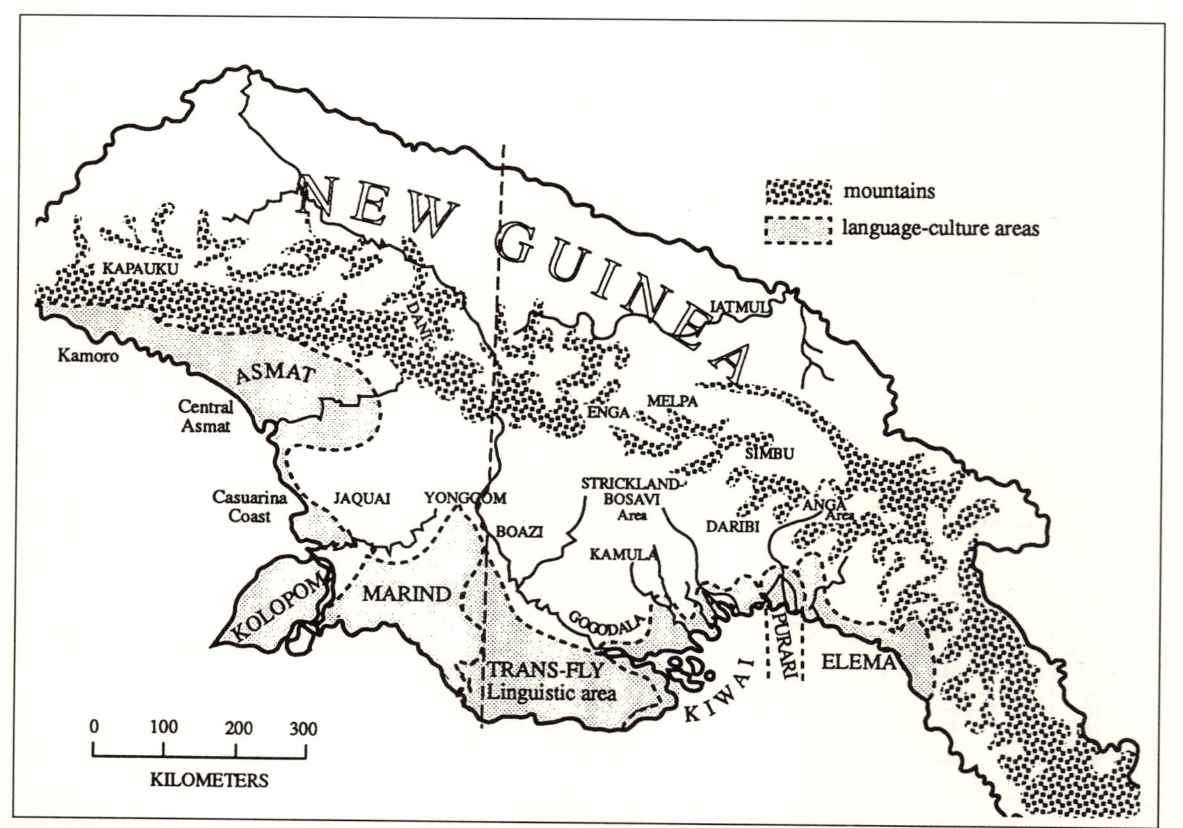

Map 1. Language-culture areas of coastal south New Guinea.

7; Lindenbaum 1984, 1987; Herdt 1984; Whitehead 1986). Ritualized homosexuality was customarily practiced along one section of south-coastal New Guinea—extending inland from the Kolopom, Marind, and Trans-Fly peoples north and northeast as far as the Strickland-Bosavi area—but was absent along the coast among the Purari, Elema, and apparently among the Kiwai and the Asmat as well (see Knauft 1990a, 1990b:appendix A).[2] Features of comparative method as well as ethnographic content are brought to light by comparing a regional configuration that emphasizes a geographically broader but shallower region along the south coast to one that emphasizes a geographically narrower but deeper region stretching further inland. The difference between these two overlapping regions is itself sometimes unclear in existing accounts, with features of one region generalized to implicitly characterize the south lowlands as a whole. It is in part for this reason that the boundaries of the present analysis are clearly delineated.

In time frame, the present work follows prominent recent analyses of south New Guinea as well as the bulk of currently available information, and it focuses on practices and beliefs that were indigenous, that is, those prevalent during the late precolonial and early colonial era. The key features chosen for analytic emphasis even at early stages of colonial history have important implications for present perceptions of the region. This is particularly true concerning the relevance of precolonial indigenous sexual customs for the present and the ethnographic artificiality of the political boundary presently separating Irian Jaya from Papua New Guinea.

A LEGACY OF HOMOSEXUAL EMPHASIS

In the past few years, in the legacy of interest in lowland Melanesian homosexuality, a chain of ethnographic assessments has been gradually reinforced in the comparative literature concerning south and southwest New Guinea.

In terms of political economy, these portrayals correspond with assessments that south New Guinea has "production systems . . . of very low intensity" (Feil 1987:177). Shirley Lindenbaum (1984:339, 343) suggests that lowland emphasis upon semen exchange and male sexuality makes male status dependent upon men's own bodily substance exchanges and labor efforts rather than on those of women. This dovetails with emphasis on marital reciprocity in sister-exchange marriage rather than payment of valuables in marital compensation (bridewealth). As a result, Daryl Feil (1987:179) suggests,

> No homosexual society has a ceremonial exchange system based on intensive, surplus production from which male prestige and renown are gained. . . . Homosexual societies are thoroughly "egalitarian" in ethos. Restricted, direct and balanced exchange predominates; asymmetrical or delayed reciprocity has no place in social arrangements. (ibid.:178)

These characterizations appear to reflect the dominant current perception of lowland south New Guinea politicoeconomic configurations as a whole as they existed in the precolonial era.

Such generalizations are analytically linked by the above authors to a selective set of sexual and marriage practices in south New Guinea, particularly the co-occurrence of ritualized male homosexuality and sister exchange in the middle part of the lowlands, including culture areas of the Kolopom Islanders, Marind, and Trans-Fly peoples. Ritualized homosexuality in the central south coast was linked to the belief that male initiate novices must be inseminated by their elders in order to receive semen as a life force crucial for their growth and adult maturation (Herdt 1984). In the existing New Guinea literature, ritualized male homosexuality is typically seen as reflecting male autonomy in both cultural reproduction and the acquisition of male status, with corresponding lack of male-status dependence on female labor and, correspondingly, low-intensity production systems. In other words, the male-status system is viewed as autonomous from, rather than dependent upon, female production. These low-intensity politicoeconomic systems, it is then reasoned, are reflected in emphasis on restricted rather than on generalized or competitive male exchange in south New Guinea, that is, sister exchange without significant wealth transaction rather than bridewealth marriage. It is in turn suggested that this produces political decentralization and fragmentation in lowlands areas (Lindenbaum 1984; Feil 1987:ch. 7).

Before I evaluate in more detail the political economic dimension of these generalizations, I would like to note, first, that they follow upon the 1960s legacy of Peter Lawrence and Mervyn Meggitt (1965) in viewing lowland New Guinea as the polar opposite of the New Guinea highlands: Feil, Lindenbaum, and Whitehead all develop their models for south New Guinea on the basis of presumed highland-lowland antinomies. Second, these generalizations tend to collapse the societies of rich coastal areas with those of much more sparsely settled lowland areas further inland. Third, like many of the Melanesian theoretical models, those of Feil and Lindenbaum are developed by ethnographers whose Melanesian fieldwork and publications focus predominantly on highland rather than lowland areas.

SUBSISTENCE INTENSITY

Concerning subsistence intensity, the reliance on sago as a starch staple among many south New Guinea groups is commonly assumed to be indicative of low-intensity food production, but this is not uniformly true (see table 1). The subsistence base of the seven south-coast language-culture areas may be briefly reviewed.

Kolopom

Kolopom subsistence entailed crop cultivation, particularly of yam and taro, in man-made garden islands reclaimed from the swamp by piling alternate layers of clay and grass on top of a floating bed constructed of cut swamp reeds (Serpenti 1977:ch. 4). The island beds were carefully and laboriously constructed to ensure the proper moisture level for various crops and different seasonal weather conditions. Vigilant attention and intensive labor were required thereafter to maintain the proper soil temperature and moisture content, the entire cropped area was regularly covered with thin layers of mud

Table 1
Basic Geographic and Subsistence Regimes of New Guinea South-Coast Language-Culture Areas

Group	*Geographic regime*	*Subsistence*	*Reference*
Asmat	Mangroves: swamp; rain forests	Sago/fish	Eyde 1967; van Arsdale 1975, 1978
Kolopom	Swamps; man-made isles; floodplain forests	Taro/yams	Serpenti 1977
Marind-anim	Grassland; savanna woodlands; swamp	Sago and yams	Baal 1966:16–21; Brookfield 1971:98f, 109; Barrau 1958:16f
Trans-Fly	Grassland; savanna woodlands	Yams/taro	Beaver 1920:88; Williams 1936:17, 218
Kiwai	Mangrove swamp; raised alluvial deposits	Sago/fish	Beaver 1920:154, 160 214f., 250; Brookfield 1971:95
Purari	Mangroves; swamp; rain forest	Sago/fish	Williams 1924:10–12; Holmes 1924:ch.20
Elema	Beach; swamp; rain forest	Sago/taro/yam	Williams 1940:12–14.

fertilizer, sifted through net strainers, and then overlaid with humus soil covered with dried grass compost. Tuber production was especially important for competitive mortuary feasts (*ndambu*).

H. C. Brookfield rates the Kolopom subsistence intensity as higher on his scale than that of others (such as the Enga and the Chimbu, for example), and he notes that the Kolopom exhibit "one of the most remarkable cultivation systems in all Melanesia" (Brookfield with Hart 1971:106, 113). The Kolopom language-culture area, like those of the Marind-anim and Trans-Fly, was one where ritualized homosexuality was practiced.

Marind-anim

A significant degree of agricultural intensity is also found among some sago-dependent peoples of the south New Guinea coast. Marind-anim made prismoid garden ridges up to 1.5 meters high surrounded by drainage ditches in which smooth-trunk sago palms were planted (Barrau 1958:16, 37; Brookfield with Hart 1971:109). Brookfield assesses Marind-anim cultivation as one of "partial intensity," that is, entailing "either the presence of intensive practices over a significant part of the total productive system, or else of a generally high level of technical competence in land management which leads to the partial creation and maintenance of a tame ecosystem." He notes that Marind subsistence "serves as a reminder that people depending on wild food [such as sago] are not necessarily at the most primitive technological level" (Brookfield with Hart 1971:109).

As Jan van Baal (1966:19–20) suggests, Marind cultivation practices beg comparison with those of the Kolopom, especially during the precolonial period when gardening and feast-giving were highly developed.

Elema

Elema subsistence combined sago utilization with intense gardening and pig husbandry. Elema had a population density of approximately 125 persons per square mile in the coastal area, making it commensurate with that of many eastern highlands areas.[3] Although it is rarely noted, the per capita pig population among Elema was equal to that of the Mae Enga of the highlands (Williams 1940:12; see Kelly 1988:150). The social significance of pigs for the Elema is poignantly captured by Williams:

> the village pig is . . . the living symbol of wealth. . . . He is the means of cementing friendship, of maintaining proper relations between kin; and at every social and ceremonial gathering of importance his dying squeals are pleasantly audible. . . . A large supply of them [pigs] all round makes for a social and ceremonial activity, and so they are highly prized. At the same time, and as a consequence, they give rise to a good many disputes and quarrels. Indeed the principal sources of joy and dissension in the life of Orokolo males are their women and their pigs. (Williams:11–12)

Such a characterization in selective ways parallels those made concerning the role of pigs in the New Guinea highlands.

Trans-Fly

In the Trans-Fly area, the subsistence base was strongly oriented around small and large yams. Among the Keraki (the Trans-Fly group studied by Williams), the collective houses built to store the yams could be over a hundred yards long, about four feet high, and three feet wide. Taking as a representative example one average man and his two wives, Williams calculated that the family amassed and put into storage about three thousand pounds of small yams for the year. Among Trans-Fly peoples as well as the Elema, Kolopom, and Kiwai, the piles of food given in feasts could be enormous. Keraki display racks presenting the food comprised up to a mile and a half of fenceline heaped with produce. One of the less extensive feasting racks was estimated to hold an exchange display at least 25–30 tons of yams (Williams 1936:233, 227, 231–35). That the seasonal Trans-Fly biotic environment could support large-scale food production is further evident in David Harris and Billai Laba's (1982) discovery of prehistoric garden mounds and large-scale drainage ditches in the southeastern Trans-Fly area.

Kiwai

Among the Kiwai, sago would appear to be the starch staple except in far-western Kiwai settlements (Beaver 1920:88, 160–162). In addition to sago, yams and taro were important for large-scale feast-giving display. Intensive cultivation practices were used for feasting gardens, including fences to protect the gardens from pigs, shading for the seedlings, and extensive drainage ditches. Sago in this area was frequently planted as a cultigen rather than harvested wild (Landtman 1927:67–68, 101). Judging from Landtman's account, crop cultivation is culturally important among the Kiwai and is linked to political achievement (to be discussed later).

It may also be noted that land reclamation for settlement sites was practiced in some eastern Kiwai areas through compost heaping and stockading (Butcher 1964:146).

Purari and Asmat

Root-crop cultivation was relatively undeveloped among the Purari and Asmat, who both relied on sago and fish. This does not appear to have compromised the intensity of their economic and political development, which among Purari included significant rank divisions and even hereditary chiefdomship (Williams 1924; Maher 1974). Purari villages could attain a size of over 2,000 persons (Maher 1961:32). (Among the Kiwai, for whom early population figures were not collected, the huge communal living houses were over 500 feet long [Landtman 1927:5].) Many Asmat villages were also fairly large: a representative village documented by Gerard Zegwaard had a population of 650 persons living in five men's houses and 59 family houses. Tobias Schneebaum (1988:168) came across one Asmat longhouse that was 90 meters in length.

Overall, subsistence intensity was relatively high in south-coast language-culture areas such as Kolopom, Marind, Elema, and possibly prehistoric Trans-Fly. In all of these areas, root crops were significant food sources, and in all, excepting Elema, ritualized homosexuality was practiced.

Of equal importance is that, where subsistence relied heavily on sago, this did not necessarily entail a correspondingly low scale and intensity of economic exchange or sociopolitical life. The ability to quickly produce a large and easily stored food source such as sago combined with water transport to allow south-coastal populations such as Purari, Kiwai, and Asmat high mobility and population aggregation in very large villages for purposes of residence, feasting, and also sometimes warfare. The Purari sustained villages of over 2,000 persons and a political system of rank differentials and hereditary chiefdomship. Asmat and Kiwai villages could support longhouses from 300 to 500 feet in length.

Among Marind, Elema, and Kiwai, the ease of sago procurement also freed labor for the cultivation of root-crop gardens that were highly important for feasting and competitive exchange. This surplus production was often critical for leadership instantiated through prestigious feast-giving. In short, the scale and organization of political life was not dependent on the extensiveness or intensity of quotidian starch staple procurement.

GIFT EXCHANGE AND LEADERSHIP

In terms of exchange and leadership, south-coast patterns diverge from the characterizations of them as economically nonintensive and politically decentralized. This view is illustrated in Daryl Feil's (1987: 179) recent comment, citing other recent works, that "No homosexual society has a ceremonial exchange system based on intensive, surplus production from which male prestige and renown are gained."

The present portrayal will hence focus on the connection in south-coast societies between male status and economic exchange, with additional attention given to the reliance of males on female labor.

Kiwai

Among the Kiwai (whom Feil considers "homosexual"), large *gaera* feasts were held on a yearly basis in preparation for heterosexual fertility rituals (*mouguru*) (Landtman 1970:ch. 26). These feasts were held by one or more leaders who had taken an oath upon challenge from a rival leader to reciprocate the gifts of a previous feast. In preparation, the leaders had special large gardens cultivated and had reserved the entire produce for distribution at the event. More generally, "an enormous quantity of food must be supplied, during which hardly any regular work can be done, except bringing home provisions from the gardens" (ibid.:383). At the feast itself, a large tree was cut down and transported to the ceremonial ground, where it was replanted in its entirety in the feasting area and festooned with huge quantities of food, shell ornaments, dog's-tooth necklaces, belts, and other valuables, both hung in the branches and piled about the base.

When all the food and valuables have been distributed, and only the empty *gaera* tree is left, the master of the feast climbs to the top, berates those who challenged him to it, and declares that the challenge has been met. If the opposing leader has not sponsored a similar feast, he challenges him:

> "I clear now; I been make *gaera* finish. Where you now? You there along water; me there along shore." No words could cut deeper than these. The man alluded to feels his honour at stake, and he and his

> people will put forth every effort to wash away the shame. They will carry on their garden work with untiring zeal during the next season. (ibid.:395)

The most successful Kiwai leaders, called "chiefs" by Landtman, were strongly polygynous and commanded the work of others to such an extent that they themselves did little labor at all (Landtman 1970:168–169). Women of successful men would indeed sometimes request co-wives to help them in their work. Thus, despite the fact that most men had only one wife, "It is by no means rare where there is only one wife for her to scold her husband for burdening her with too much work instead of procuring a second wife to share it" (ibid.: 247).

Among eastern Kiwai, Benjamin Butcher (1964:223) observed one feast at which 40 sago bundles each 10 feet in height were presented, as well as 20 pigs.

Elema

Among the Elema, very large exchanges of pork and shell ornaments were conducted in the course of numerous mortuary and costume rites. Of particular importance were the gift exchanges of the *hevehe* ceremonial cycle, during which "some forty piles [of food] were ranged in the right order, each consisting of roast sago in wrappings of palm-leaf, pots of stew, . . . piles of fresh coconuts, green and yellow bunches of areca-nut, red boiled crabs, and hunks of pork." The gift giving of food and valuables occurring at the conclusion of this event, as at other ritual feasts, was "in native eyes . . . the climax of the whole ceremony. . . . One may see the donors work themselves into what seems like a fury, while the recipients, loaded with ornaments as they are but looking very sheepish, are obliged to listen in silence" (Williams 1940:363–364, 145).

Frequent exchanges occurred between affinal or matrilateral relatives, with armshells and pearlshells given to the wife-givers, and pigs given in return (ibid.:61),

> the uncle or the brother who makes the gift likes to do so with liberality and so enhance his good name. If, on the other hand, he fails to make a creditable showing he is afflicted with *maioka,* or shame; he feels small; and he may have to endure the actual taunts of those directly or indirectly associated with the gift, for there is no convention of polite silence on such matters. (ibid.:97)

In addition to affinal gift giving were large exchanges made between Eleman nonrelatives in hereditary trading partnerships (*okeahi*). These were initiated between partners by an initial gift of "the spectacular *hoera kor*, or 'taro tree'." This consisted of a tree trunk some 60 feet long, loaded with perhaps 700 taro, "which grow to such splendid proportions at Orokolo," as well as haulms of bananas and bundles of sugarcane. The laden timber required from 70 to 80 men to carry it (ibid.:72).

Williams notes that "nothing reaches more deeply into the soul of an Elema native than does the traffic in ornaments and pigs" (ibid.: 91). Elema leadership emphasized generosity in feasting, hortatory control over female labor of the community (although polygyny was extremely rare), and incipient hereditary rank. Gerontocracy was particularly strongly developed, and "in the oldest men of the tribe we meet with something like a ruling class" (ibid.:84).

Purari

Among the Purari, just west of the Elema, a system of hereditary chieftainship existed with more general rank classification. Robert Maher (1974) found that the Purari maintained a careful chiefly genealogy of up to nine generations, tracing the origin of Purari spirit force from its origins in *imunu* 'life-force' beings to its present distribution in chiefs in the famous Purari wicker-monster Kaiemunu.

Purari politics crosscut hereditary rank with competitive leadership grounded in control of the exchange of shell ornaments and control of female labor for feast-giving. The aim of precolonial Purari exchange, according to Maher (1967:315–316) was to invest resources and establish debtor relations in order to gain wives and increase one's political power. Whereas rank was formally inherited, influence through competitive exchange was a key means of maintaining and increasing upward mobility. Maher remarks

> that a man's holdings in shell ornaments underlay much of his ability to influence his community, but if he were to have the influence appropriate to a *mari* [chief] or *amua* [man of rank], he must also maintain an extensive network of relationships to individuals through regular gifts of food. (ibid.)

At feasts, a careful investment of large-scale resources was made, creating exchange debts that were called in to underwrite major feasts by leaders at later occasions. As a result, a village of up to 2,000 persons could be galvanized into concerted action as people responded to the leader's demand that "now was the time for old obligations to be honored" (ibid.). The keen manipulation of exchange systems was particularly important.

The connection with gender in the production of food for exchange is here direct:

> for the ordinary [Purari] man, an extra wife was desirable but not usually possible. For the Purari *mari* [chief] or *amua* [man of rank], however, polygyny was essential. Although men had their significant roles in the division of labor, women were the principal providers of foodstuffs. (ibid.)

Williams records an average of 1.5 wives per married man, and chiefs could have up to eight wives. He notes "in days not long gone by certain Purari chiefs are said (possibly with some heroic exaggeration) to have had eighty wives and more apiece" (Williams 1924:55).

Asmat

Among the Asmat, polygyny was also crucial to male leadership; leaders by virtue of their many wives acquired extensive affinal land rights, controlled many sago stands, and attracted many followers (Eyde 1967:227; cf. Trenkenschuh 1982:46). These features promoted effective warfare alliances and the taking of enemy heads, which was a key dimension of male status. David Eyde states,

> It should be stressed that the equation between prowess in warfare on the one hand, and wealthy plural wives and surplus sago on the other hand, is extremely important. It is by this equation that prowess in warfare becomes transformed into the ability to make massive distributions of food, and thus into political power. . . . A successful man, thus, accumulates sago and fishing areas, and the female labor necessary to translate these areas into surplus food to be distributed, by marrying more than one wife. (Eyde 1967:228, 235)

Asmat warfare connected directly to exchange economy in that the ceremonial cycle of feasting culminated in head-hunting. Concomitantly, women disparaged and were loath to marry men who had not proven themselves by taking heads in warfare.

Kolopom

Among the Kolopom, whose sexual customs included ritualized homosexuality, success in feasts of competitive giving (*ndambu*) was the sine qua non of political status (Serpenti 1972–73; 1977:ch. 6). Factions within village wards were paired in feasting opposition and were themselves subsumed in a leveled hierarchy of feasting oppositions between whole village wards, between half-villages, and between whole villages. Competitive feasts escalated progressively to encompass larger political groups as the mortuary feast cycle progressed, and great food gifts could also be initiated ad hoc by a *warrenwundu* 'great cultivator' to challenge and defeat a rival. Many garden islands were reserved for competitive feasting exchanges, and the largely nonpolygynous men did most of the gardening work themselves.

At feasting exchanges, raw foods were heaped up in a large culinary display, including specially cultivated taro up to a meter in length and yams more than two and half meters long (Serpenti 1977: 28–38). In comparing the size and amount of food given by each side, the prestige of leaders and their competing factions were fully at stake, dependent on their ability to amass and present quantities of food equal to that of the person or faction challenging them. (Careful tallies were kept of the amounts.) Leadership depended above all else on the ability to threaten and then formally challenge and oust rivals through such competitive food exchanges. Larger competitive feasts might require a long period of time until a sufficient return feast could be mounted (Serpenti 1972–73:169). Serpenti gives a detailed case study of a feasting competition between rival leaders and their factions and notes within this process the great importance of

> the pure struggle for power and prestige. The derogatory remarks addressed to the opponent . . . arise . . . from one *warrenwundu* [great cultivator's] ambition to outdo his rivals and thus raise himself a further step on the ladder of social prestige. Not only on subjects directly or indirectly connected with agriculture, but in the most diverse matters, the opinion of the *warrenwundu* carries great weight. Less important persons will not readily contradict him or ignore his express wishes, for it is in his power at any time to "defeat" a refractory member of his *kwanda* [village ward] or *paburu* [half-village sector] at *ndambu* [competitive mortuary feast-giving], which would mean public humiliation for the man in question. (Serpenti 1977:235–236)

Keraki [Trans-Fly]

Among the Keraki, where ritualized homosexuality was also practiced, large-scale feasting was also fundamentally important to male prestige. In Keraki as well as Kolopom, huge food piles given in exchange were carefully recorded by an elaborate set of measuring devices tallying the amount of food given and the length and girth of the largest tubers.

Williams (1936:235) notes that "the headmen are expected to stand above others as food-producers and feast-makers." In elaborating this point, he remarks

> There is no doubt that the [Keraki] native is deeply impressed by the sight of a quantity of food . . . and he takes a corresponding pride in being the producer or owner of it. To cast doubt upon the food-producing capacity of an individual or group is a fertile source of quarrels; and an acknowledged type of rejoinder in any dispute is to challenge your adversaries to display as much food as you can display. (ibid.:233)

Significant here is that unlike the Kolopom, Keraki men were highly dependent upon female labor for amassing food stores. Polygyny was correspondingly highly developed: 45 percent of married men had more than one wife—an average of 1.55 wife per married man (ibid.:149). Older wives were inherited through the levirate and appear to have been more important to Keraki men as a source of labor than as sexual partners.

Marind-anim

Among the Marind-anim, by contrast, the linkage between leadership and the political economy of food and wealth exchange appears weaker than in the other south-coast culture areas. Polygyny was rare, and there appears to have been little ethic of competitive exchange in feasting.

It is true that subsistence was partially intensive, that feasts were large, and that *pakas anim* 'headmen' were leaders of the men's houses. The ideal *pakas anim* exerted decisive initiative and organization in many areas (South Pacific Commission 1952–53:56–57). His most important function, however, was as the preeminent warrior of the men's house, leading the group in organizing and carrying out head-hunting raids.

The competitive dimension of feasting and status rivalry is largely absent from Marind politics as portrayed in ethnographic accounts. This could be because of the deterioration in leadership, with the heavily armed Dutch intervention and suppression of head-hunting that began in the early 1900s, for example, which had an effect prior to Paul Wirz's observations.

As important, however, is that the above-mentioned leadership features are closely articulated with, and were in many ways subordinated to, intercommunity cooperation rather than competition in ritual, totemic, and head-hunting concerns. This reflects the overarching mythicoritual system of phratry organization that linked communities as partners in reenactment of Marind cosmology, that is, in elaborate ritual cycles enacted across Marind-anim territory. As van Baal (1966) describes, these necessarily cooperative ventures tended to cap intercommunity political rivalry through myriad crosscutting affiliations. Correspondingly, the Marind were distinctive and indeed striking among south-coast societies in that warfare was quite infrequent among Marind-anim themselves. This tendency van Baal rightly notes as being perhaps "the most remarkable of all" (1966:24). Instead, warfare was cooperatively directed against non-Marind-anim further afield in long-distance head-hunting raids (ibid.:ch. 12). Celebration feasts that concluded the head-hunt were held for allies—including distant allies—who had helped make the head-hunt possible (ibid.:720–721).

COMPARATIVE LEADERSHIP AND POLITICOECONOMIC PATTERNS

A rough composite of the relative emphases in precolonial south-coast New Guinea leadership vis-à-vis subsistence economy and control of female labor is derivable from extant ethnography as shown in table 2.

With the exception of the Marind-anim, south-coast political economies cannot be described as lacking asymmetric or delayed reciprocity, lacking major wealth transactions, lacking fervent leadership competition through exchange, or having low-intensity political economy in general. Again excepting the Marind, none of these features appear incompatible with the highly elaborate myth and ritual systems that are of such deep (and here neglected) cultural significance in all south New Guinea language-culture areas. Of the south-coast groups considered "homosexual" by Feil—including the Kolopom, Trans-Fly, Marind, Kiwai, and presumably the Asmat—all except for the Marind show major dimensions of male leadership dependent on eminence in competitive economic exchange. Among the Trans-Fly and the Kiwai, as well as the Purari, male success in exchange competition depended upon polygyny and differential access to female labor.

A cosmological system instantiated in elaborate social practice,

Table 2
Leadership and Exchange in
South-Coastal New Guinea Language-Culture Areas

Group	*Rating*	*Reference*
Asmat	++	Eyde 1967:228, 235, 349
Kolopom	+	Serpenti 1977:ch. 6, 132
Marind-anim	−	Baal 1966:65–68, 163
Trans-Fly	++	Williams 1936:149, 233, 235, 243, 99, 215
Kiwai	++	Landtman 1927:168, 247
Elema	+	Williams 1940:13, 49–51, 91, 97–98, 145
Purari	++	Maher 1967:315–16; Williams 1924:55

Notes:
++ = male leadership is highly competitive, including material-exchange competition in which male-leadership prestige is dependent upon polygyny and differential access to female labor.
+ = leaders' prestige is crucially linked (often among other things) to eminence in giving valuables or food in exchange relations, but such gifts do not depend upon polygyny or differential access to female labor.
− = leadership is not significantly dependent upon eminence in material-exchange relationships and not reliant on polygyny or female labor.

including ritual homosexuality or ritual heterosexuality, is neither indicative of nor mutually exclusive with significant dimensions of politicoeconomic intensification. In contrast to the highlands, however, in the lowlands this intensification does not depend on high population density or a high degree of subsistence localization. It is rather based on extensive subsistence exploitation and a high degree of geographical mobility both in amassing foodstuffs and aggregating population in pulsating movements. What one has, then, are contrasting configurations of politicoeconomic intensity in highlands and south-coastal New Guinea rather than polar opposition in their degree of politicoeconomic intensification.

PROBLEMS OF INTERPRETATION AND ETHNOGRAPHIC HISTORY

Given overwhelming evidence to the contrary, how has it been possible for images of low politicoeconomic intensity to become so ensconced in recent literature concerning lowland south New Guinea? Part of the issue is that such characterizations for lowland south New Guinea may be more apt in inland than in coastal areas; the difference between my characterizations and those of Lindenbaum and Feil is in part an artifact of my using a somewhat different geographical contour of the region, that is, the coast. Yet their analyses have included coastal groups such as the Kiwai, Kolopom, and Trans-Fly that appear to exemplify significant exceptions to their generalizations.

Further differences are important in the scale of analysis; Lindenbaum, Feil, and Whitehead configured lowland New Guinea by virtue of its contrast to the extremely high population densities of the core New Guinea highlands. Against this unusually elevated baseline (where else in the world does one find politically unranked horticultural societies of 200 persons or even 400 persons per square mile?), almost all prestate "tribal" political economies can be said—in relative terms—to be nonintensive. I am focusing on features of south-coast New Guinea that emerge from a perspective internal to the region rather than external to it. From this difference of perspective, south-coast political economy indeed appears more "intensive."

In addition to factors of regional-boundary configuration and comparative scale, issues of ethnographic history are also highly relevant. Notwithstanding the ethnographic evidence presented above, the very details of political economic exchange and leadership in precolonial south-coastal New Guinea were not systematically collected by ethnographers and have not been effectively analyzed. Much of the available information on south-coast New Guinea comes from classic monographs based on fieldwork between 1910 and 1940. These works—by Williams, Landtman, Wirz, and others—contain rich descriptive detail about many topics but tend to be pre–Levi Straussian and even pre-Maussian when it comes to understanding the importance of exchange politics and economy. Williams, for instance, notes that an entire monograph could have been written about the importance of production and exchange in Keraki culture, but he limits himself to the briefest of thin descriptions.[4] In his Elema monograph, Williams states that, in some respects, the enormous and elaborate exchange of gifts among men is

> the most serious and important moment in the whole [15-year ceremonial] cycle. . . . But the reader need not be wearied with a description of it. Suffice it to say that the gifts were more numerous and the throng of critical spectators far greater than at the morning presentation. (Williams 1940:330)

At an earlier period, Williams had little notion of the political significance of Purari exchange, described so vividly over two decades later by Maher. Williams laments:

> The inner meaning of this exchange of gifts must be a matter of conjecture. The only explanation ever given me by a native was that this was a suitable occasion for the husband to make a gift to his wife's relatives; he must maintain his good name in their eyes for liberality and wealth. (Williams 1924:200)

Van Baal notes for the Marind-anim that, although very large feasting exchanges were common particularly after head-hunting raids (including some at which 50 pigs were killed and sago pallets 10 meters long were cooked),

> There are only a few . . . [descriptions of Marind-anim feasts] which result from systematic observation and even these are incomplete because the marriage-relationships determining the pattern of food-exchange and the technique of the distribution of gifts remained unnoticed or were summarized in empty generalizations plainly indicating that the observer had not the slightest notion of their social relevance. (van Baal 1966:828)

Given this tendency—and that the references to political economy and its connection to leadership that are made are often buried deeply in very large descriptive monographs that focus largely on other topics—it is not surprising that these patterns have been overlooked in contemporary analyses of south New Guinea.

The larger problem is that of comparing New Guinea highlands and lowlands ethnographies collected at different times as if they were informed by similar ethnographic and theoretical agendas. An uncritical reading of the south-coast monographs based on early ethnography easily takes their dominant Frazerian emphasis on myth, ritual, and totemism to indicate a corresponding lack of highly developed competitive exchange systems. In the cases of Landtman (1917, 1927) and Wirz (1922–25, 1928), there is a general unawareness of the importance of kinship relations as well. To this, the early monographs add an emphasis on recording individual traits and customs as separable and isolated from each other, following in the strong legacy of Alfred C. Haddon and others prior to the rise of functionalism.[5] As a result, the few pieces of the politicoeconomic puzzle that are presented tend to be widely scattered and disarticulated from each other in the south-coastal ethnography.[6]

These trends contrast with the emphases that arose from the 1950s to the 1970s. By this period, the watershed of rich ethnographic fieldwork on south-coastal New Guinea had passed and was superseded among Melanesianists by intense interest in the New Guinea highlands. Theoretically, the focus shifted too, entailing waves of interest in structural functionalism, cultural materialism, and Marxism. There was correspondingly an increasing attention to politics, exchange, social structure, ecology, and processes of politicoeconomic development.

Given this, differences recently emphasized between lowland and highland New Guinea are in part a function of differing historical interests and processes in ethnographic reporting. This is in no way to deny real and significant differences that did and do exist between lowland and highland areas of New Guinea. And certainly the interest in certain features of one region and different features in another stem in significant part from the areas themselves. But the magnitude and polarity of contrast between regions is apt to become artificially magnified when perspectives for one region studied at one time become reified and then contrasted to alternative reifications from another area studied at a later time and with a different range of topical and theoretical emphases.

From this viewpoint, the contrast between conceptual labels for the New Guinea highlands ("big-man," "competitive exchange," "clan-parish," and "politicoeconomic intensification") and those of south-coastal New Guinea ("restricted exchange," "nonintensive political economy," "male-status autonomy") are in significant part due to the reification of 1970s' theoretical concerns as juxtaposed against the 1930s' ethnography of the south-coastal lowlands. The scope of regional similarities and differences is in fact much more complex and interesting than this, and I have created my regional contours in part to highlight this fact. Such a finding hopefully can sharpen further research and understanding of the differences and similarities between these cultural regions.

REFERENCES

Arsdale, Peter W. van

1975 Perspectives on Development in Asmat. *In* An Asmat Sketch Book no. 5. Frank A. Trenkenschuh, ed., parts A and B. Hastings, N.E.: Crosier Missions.

1978 Activity Patterns of Asmat Hunter-Gatherers: A Time Budget Analysis. Mankind 11:453–460.

Baal, Jan van

1966 Dema: Description and Analysis of Marind-anim Culture (South New Guinea). The Hague: Martinus Nijhoff.

1984 The Dialectics of Sex in Marind-anim Culture. *In* Ritualized Homosexuality in Melanesia. Gilbert H. Herdt, ed., pp. 128–166. Berkeley: University of California Press.

Barrau, Jacques
1958 Subsistence Agriculture in Melanesia. Bernice P. Bishop Museum, bulletin no. 219. Honolulu: Bishop Museum.

Beaver, Wilfred N.
1920 Unexplored New Guinea. London: Seeley Service.

Brookfield, H. C., with Doreen Hart
1971 Melanesia: A Geographical Interpretation of an Island World. London: Methuen.

Butcher, Benjamin T.
1964 My Friends, the New Guinea Headhunters. Garden City, N.Y.: Doubleday.

Eyde, David B.
1967 Cultural Correlates of Warfare Among the Asmat of South-West New Guinea. Ph.D. dissertation. Anthropology, Yale University.

Feil, Daryl K.
1987 The Evolution of Highland Papua New Guinea Societies. Cambridge: Cambridge University Press.

Feld, Steven
1982 Sound and Sentiment: Birds, Weeping, Poetics, and Song in Kaluli Expression. Philadelphia: University of Pennsylvania Press.

Haddon, Alfred C.
1911 The Wanderings of Peoples. Cambridge: Cambridge University Press.
1920 The Migrations of Cultures in British New Guinea. Journal of the Royal Anthropological Institute of Great Britain and Ireland 50:234–280.
1927 Introduction. *In* The Kiwai Papuans of British New Guinea. Gunnar Landtman, ed., pp. ix–xx. London: Macmillan. Reprinted by Johnson Reprint Co., New York, 1970.
1936 Introduction. *In* Papuans of the Trans-Fly. F. E. Williams, ed., pp. xxiii–xxxiv. Oxford: Clarendon Press.

Harris, David R., and Billai Laba
1982 The Mystery of the Papuan Mound-Builders. Geographical Magazine 54:386–391.

Herdt, Gilbert H.
1984 Ritualized Homosexual Behavior in the Male Cults of Melanesia, 1862–1983: An Introduction. *In* Ritualized Homosexuality in Melanesia. Gilbert H. Herdt, ed., pp. 1–81. Berkeley: University of California Press.

Holmes, J. H.
1924 In Primitive New Guinea. London: Seeley Service.

Kelly, Raymond C.
1977 Etoro Social Structure: A Study in Structural Contradiction. Ann Arbor: University of Michigan Press.
1988 Etoro Suidology: A Reassessment of the Pig's Role in the Prehistory and Comparative Ethnology of New Guinea. *In* Mountain Papuans: Historical and Comparative Perspectives from New Guinea Fringe Highlands Societies. James F. Weiner, ed., pp. 111–186. Ann Arbor: University of Michigan Press.

Knauft, Bruce M.
1985a Good Company and Violence: Sorcery and Social Action in a Lowland New Guinea Society. Berkeley: University of California Press.
1985b Ritual Form and Permutation in New Guinea: Implications of Symbolic Process for Sociopolitical Evolution. American Ethnologist 12:321–340.
1990a The Question of Homosexuality Among the Kiwai of South New Guinea. Journal of Pacific History 25:188–210.
1990b Reassessing South New Guinea. Paper presented at the Annual Meetings of the Association for Social Anthropology in Oceania. Hawaii.

Landtman, Gunnar
1917 The Folk-Tales of the Kiwai Papuans. Vol. 47, Acta Societatis Scientiarum Fennicae. Helsinki: Finnish Society of Literature.
1927 The Kiwai Papuans of British New Guinea: A Nature-Born Instance of Rousseau's Ideal Community. London: Macmillan. Reprinted by Johnson Reprint Co., New York, 1970.

Lawrence, Peter, and Mervyn J. Meggitt
1965 Introduction. *In* Gods, Ghosts and Men in Melanesia. Peter Lawrence and Mervyn J. Meggitt, eds., pp. 1–26. Melbourne: Oxford University Press.

Lindenbaum, Shirley
1984 Variations on a Sociosexual Theme in Melanesia. *In* Ritualized Homosexuality in Melanesia. Gilbert H. Herdt, ed., pp. 337–361. Berkeley: University of California Press.
1987 The Mystification of Female Labors. *In* Gender and Kinship: Essays Toward a Unified Analysis. Jane F. Collier and Sylvia J. Yanagisako, eds., pp. 221–243. Stanford: Stanford University Press.

Maher, Robert F.
1961 New Men of Papua: A Study in Culture Change. Madison: University of Wisconsin Press.

1967 From Cannibal Raid to Copra Kompani: Changing Patterns of Koriki Politics. Ethnology 6:309–331.

1974 Koriki Chieftainship: Hereditary Status and Mana in Papua. Ethnology 13:239–246.

Schieffelin, Edward L.

1976 The Sorrow of the Lonely and the Burning of the Dancers. New York: St. Martin's Press.

Schneebaum, Tobias

1988 Where the Spirits Dwell: An Odyssey in the New Guinea Jungle. New York: Grove Press.

Serpenti, Laurent M.

1966 Headhunting and Magic on Kolepom. Tropical Man 1:116–139.

1972–73 Ndambu, the Feast of Competitive Giving. Tropical Man 5:162–187.

1977 Cultivators in the Swamps. 2d ed. Assen, The Netherlands: Van Gorcum. (Original edition, 1965.)

1984 The Ritual Meaning of Homosexuality and Pediphilia Among the Kimam-Papuans of South Irian Jaya. *In* Ritualized Homosexuality in Melanesia. Gilbert H. Herdt, ed., pp. 292–336. Berkeley: University of California Press.

South Pacific Commission

1952–53 Marind-anim Report: An Investigation into the Medical and Social Causes of the Depopulation Amongst the Marind-anim. Microfilm no. WP14, Western Pacific Archives, Government House Grounds, Suva, Fiji. (This manuscript is a partial translation and partial emendation of South Pacific Commission 1955, below, but is dated 1952–53.)

1955 Rapport van het Bevolkingsonderzoek onder de Marind-anim van Nederlands Zuid Nieuw Guinea. Population Study S-18 Project. Unpublished manuscript.

Trenkenschuh, Frank A. (Fr.)

1982 Asmat Sago Gathering Practices. *In* An Asmat Sketch Book no. 1. Frank Trenkenschuh, ed., pp. 45–54. Hastings, N.E.: Crosier Missions.

Weiner, J., ed.

1988 Mountain Papuans: Historical and Comparative Perspectives from New Guinea Fringe Highlands Societies. Ann Arbor: University of Michigan Press.

Whitehead, Harriet

1986 The Varieties of Fertility Cultism in New Guinea. Parts 1 and 2. American Ethnologist 13:80–99, 271–289.

Williams, Francis E.

1923 The Pairama Ceremony in the Purari Delta, Papua. Journal of the Royal Anthropological Institute of Great Britain and Ireland 59:379–397.

1924 The Natives of the Purari Delta. Territory of Papua, Anthropology Report no. 5. Port Moresby: Government Printer.

1936 Papuans of the Trans-Fly. Oxford: Clarendon Press.

1939 Seclusion and Age Grouping in the Gulf of Papua. Oceania 9:359–381.

1940 Drama of Orokolo: The Social and Ceremonial Life of the Elema. Oxford: Clarendon Press.

Wirz, Paul

1922–25 Die Marind-anim von Hollandisch-Sud-Neu-Guinea, 1–4. 2 volumes. Hamburg: Friederichsen. (Hamburgische Universität, Abhandlungen aus dem Gebiet der Auslandskunde, Band 10 und 16 [Reihe B, Band 6 und 9].)

1928 Dämonen und Wilde in Neuguinea. Stuttgart: Strecker und Schorder.

Wolf, Eric R.

1988 Inventing Society. American Ethnologist 15:752–761.

Wurm, Stephen A., and Shiro Hattori, eds.

1981 Language Atlas of the Pacific Area. Pacific Linguistics, series C, no. 66. Canberra: Australian Academy of Humanities/Japanese Academy.

Zegwaard, Gerard A.

1959 Headhunting Practices of the Asmat of West New Guinea. American Anthropologist 61:1020–1041.

1982 An Asmat Mission History. Transl. Joseph de Louw of "De Missie Geschiedenis Asmat Missie." *In* An Asmat Sketch Book no. 2. Frank A. Trenkenschuh, ed., pp. 5–15. Hastings, N.E.: Crosier Missions.

Zegwaard, Gerard A., and J. H. M. C. Boelaars

1982 Social Structure of the Asmat People. Annotated translation by Frank A. Trenkenschuh and J. Hoggebrugge of "De Sociale Structuur van de Asmatbevolking." *In* An Asmat Sketch Book no. 1, Frank A. Trenkenschuh, ed., pp. 13–29. Hastings, N.E.: Crosier Missions/Asmat Museum of Culture and Progress.

NOTES

Financial support for the research upon which the present work is based is acknowledged with gratitude from the Harry Frank Guggenheim Foundation and the Emory University Research Committee. I thank several persons who read and commented thoughtfully on a previous version of the present manuscript, particularly Terence Hays, Raymond Kelly, Stuart Kirsch, Andrew Strathern, James Weiner, and the members of the 1990 ASAO symposium on Migration and Transformations.

1. For example, by Francis Williams for the Elema (1940, cf. 1939), the Purari (1924, cf. 1923), and the Trans-Fly area (1936); by Gunnar Landtman (1927, cf. 1917) for the Kiwai; by Jan van Baal (1966, cf. 1984) following Paul Wirz (1922–1925, 1928), Verscheuren and others for the Marind-anim; by Laurent Serpenti (1977 [1965], cf. 1966, 1972–73, 1984) for the Kolopom; and by Gerard Zegwaard (1959; Zegwaard and Boelaars 1982 [1954]) and David Eyde (1967) for the Asmat.

2. The name Purari is geographically associated with the people of the like-named river and has been adopted both by Francis Williams (1924) in the title of his monograph and by Stephen Wurm and Shiro Hattori (1981) in their designation of the Purari Language Family. Although the name Namau is in some ways a more accurate ethnic designator of these people (Weiner 1988), I have retained the older term because of its familiarity and its precedence in the ethnographic literature. The Strickland-Bosavi area has been subject to intense ethnographic research from the late 1960s to the early 1980s. See monographs published by Raymond Kelly (1977), Edward Schieffelin (1976), Steven Feld (1982), and myself (1985a, cf. 1985b).

3. Williams (1940:2, 27) tabulated 4,465 western Elema in 1937, and his maps and text suggest that this population inhabits approximately eighteen miles of beachfront up to two miles inland.

4. This brief description is capped by "the sound if somewhat platitudinous conclusion that food is sociologically as well as biologically an important thing in Keraki life" (Williams 1936:235).

5. Haddon's influence on the development of south-coast New Guinea ethnography was particularly strong (see Haddon 1911, 1920, 1927, 1936).

6. This neglect and disarticulation of the south-coast political economy is most striking in the primary ethnography for the Elema, Purari, Kiwai, and Marind-anim. Robert Maher's later work (particularly his 1967 and 1974 articles) mark important advancements concerning Purari political economy during the early colonial and precolonial period. Concerning Asmat, the relative recentness of study is crosscut by the relative dearth of ethnographic publications generally and the rather topically bounded interests that various researchers have had in art and ecology. Eyde's (1967) thesis forms a partial exception, however. The Kolopom are perhaps the south-coastal group that have been the best researched from the vantage point of gift exchange and political economy; Serpenti's (1977 [1965]) monograph presents important information on many points, if in topically discrete segments.

ETHNOHISTORICAL AND MYTHOLOGICAL TRADITIONS OF PLACES OF ORIGIN, PATHS OF MIGRATION, AND FORMATIONS OF COMMUNITIES AMONG THE BIMIN-KUSKUSMIN, WEST SEPIK SANDAUN PROVINCE, PAPUA NEW GUINEA

Fitz John Porter Poole

INTRODUCTION

This essay focuses upon certain ethnohistorical and mythological portraits of historical permanence and transience within that complex, multi-ethnic mosaic of the Mountain-Ok region of the western and eastern "fringe" highland areas of Papua New Guinea and Irian Jaya. The cultural map of migration, settlement, expansion, contraction, intrusion, dispersal, reconsolidation, and other processes affecting the movement of sociocultural groups into, within, and beyond this region is portrayed from a particular sociocentric perspective—that of the Bimin-Kuskusmin near the upper Strickland Gorge on the middle eastern flank of the Mountain-Ok, roughly south of the Oksapmin, east of Feramin, and north of Kwermin and Faiwolmin (Poole 1976, 1983, n.d.a, n.d.b, n.d.c, n.d.d).[1] This territory, *abiip mutuuk* 'center place', constitutes the focus of the mythicohistorical narratives of the social making of the Bimin-Kuskusmin as a culturally distinct people.

This chapter is primarily concerned with tracing the cultural contours of the sociocultural and "natural" ecology of place and of passage, the social pressures toward movement and settlement, and the sociocultural forms and forces variously constituting and reconfiguring ethnic identities in local understandings of the history of human emergence and migration, within a region that transcends the boundaries of the central highland border of Papua New Guinea and Irian Jaya at the very hub of the island of New Guinea.[2] The analysis attends to several more or less distinctive ethnohistorical and mythological traditions that create vital linkages among ecological milieu, material culture, subsistence pattern, sociomoral order, and the process and structure of migration, settlement, cultural transformation, and social reconfiguration and consolidation. Such mosaics of linkages are variously configured in constructing a map of ethnic identity, similarity, and differences vis-à-vis stability and change among human groups of the Mountain-Ok over space and time.

This culturally constituted map, however, is drawn from the contemporary perspective of a particular Mountain-Ok community, located on the eastern fringe of the region, and no doubt reflects in important ways the Bismin-Kuskusmin's own ideological sense of regional identity, uniqueness, hegemony, and privilege. The contours of this complex map, nonetheless, may yield some tentative clues to more general patterns of areal movement and settlement when seen in the context of other and quite limited information on archaeological, ecological, and linguistic variation within and beyond the Mountain-Ok (including selected images drawn from the hypothesized prehistory of the New Guinea highlands and the Sepik-Ramu basin). Although these more general speculations about prehistoric migration and settlement have a vastly greater time depth (from millennia to centuries) than the more proximal images depicted in Bimin-Kuskusmin ethnohistory and mythology (perhaps a few centuries at most), there are some intriguing similarities in the contours of the maps of movement that each portrays.

This local map may also reveal something of the particular historical formation of the Bimin-Kuskusmin—an ethnic group both integrated and distinctive in the mosaic of Mountain-Ok communities. The somewhat peculiar sociocultural characteristics represented by the Bimin-Kuskusmin community within the Mountain-Ok may be the consequence of a confluence of contacts, migrations, and influences from both east and west, the western pathway perhaps also encompassing southward migrations from the Sepik north. Indeed, although most of their social contacts in the present face westward, southward, and northward into the Mountain-Ok, the Bimin-Kuskusmin have maintained important, if infrequent and limited, relationships of trade, marriage, alliance, and warfare with a variety of small groups on the eastern flank of the Strickland. They have also maintained relations with some groups of Hewa to the northeast and of Duna to the southeast (see also Poole 1976 and Stürzenhofecker this volume). In mythicohistorical accounts, these contemporary relationships are seen as vestiges of once more frequent, extensive, and formative contact with *khyrkhymin* 'primordial ancestors' and their descendants, marking ancient paths of migration out of the highlands of Papua New Guinea. Indeed, certain important rituals are oriented to the east to draw upon the power of these ancestors, and *sacrae* from trade with the east are given special markings and places of ritual significance in cult houses. Beyond ritual, continued trade with the east produces key resources—most notably shells, skins, feathers, bones, drums, rare hardwoods, stone, and materia medica—that Bimin-Kuskusmin then deploy in intraregional trade within the Mountain-Ok.

THE ARCHAEOLOGICAL CONTEXT

The archaeological exploration of the Mountain-Ok is from scant to nonexistent, and much evidence of earlier patterns of material culture consists of attention to cave paintings along the Strickland, patterns of trade in various genres of stone implements from distant quarries, and surface finds (sometimes collected traditionally by local peoples and enshrined in cult houses).[3] These surface finds include curious and limited assemblages of mortars and pestles, stones inscribed with abstract designs, stones carved into animal and human heads or bodies, artifactually transformed fossils, diverse kinds of club heads, axes, adzes, stone amulets, nose-plugs, pendants, and the like. It should be noted, however, that evidence of mortars, pestles, and carved stones—not often present, much less of recent manufacture, in the material culture of contemporary Mountain-Ok peoples and distributed far to the west into the highlands of Irian Jaya—bear marked affinity with similar finds to the east in the highlands of Papua New Guinea (Bulmer 1964, 1975; Bulmer and Bulmer 1964).

Beyond such naturally decontextualized or deliberately translocated surface finds, there remains remarkably little firm archaeological evidence of past human habitation in the Mountain-Ok, although B. Craig's (1984) distributional studies of Mountain-Ok material culture and Pamela Swadling's (1983, 1984, 1986, 1988) attention to artifacts in reconstructing the prehistory of both the Mountain-Ok and the Sepik-Ramu basin offer some preliminary clues to the sociocultural past and passage of Mountain-Ok peoples (see especially Swadling 1983). Nonetheless, the likelihood of discovering early sites on the Fly platform is potentially perhaps greater than in the Sepik-Ramu basin. Indeed, most of the latter area was extensively flooded some 5,000 or 6,000 years ago (Swadling 1983), although this dramatic change of landscape in the Sepik-Ramu basin may have created conditions for contact, migration, and influence between the Austronesian-speaking lowlands (in the Sepik-Ramu basin) and the Papuan-speaking highlands (including the Mountain-Ok) within recent millennia (see Swadling 1988). By way of the Sepik and its southern tributaries and the Sepik Hills, it has long been and remains possible to ascend into the eastern highlands of Irian Jaya, the western highlands of Papua New Guinea, and the Mountain-Ok and to move east or west along either the northern or southern flanks of the central range. Small migrations from the Sepik Hills into the vicinity of the Bimin-Kuskusmin continue into the present, and important trade with peoples of the Sepik Hills and beyond seems long to have been marked as a significant source of scarce resources of several kinds—especially quarried stone or stone implements.

E. Löffler (1977) suggests that the Fly platform is covered by a sequence of terrestrial Pliocene and early to middle Pleistocene sediments, with underlying Miocene limestone, and that the Fly and Strickland rivers have cut into and deposited upon these sediments. Yet, as Swadling (1983) notes, this promising archaeological opportunity has never been exploited. In contrast, the probability of finding early sites in the vicinity of the Hindenburg Wall is slight, for this formation appears to be and to have been steadily retreating at a rate of some two or three meters a century, affected by the combined effects of high rainfall and frequent earthquakes or massive landslides, leaving aprons of colluvial debris in its wake (see Gillieson 1983). Other areas of potential archaeological importance within and immediately encompassing the Mountain-Ok, with some exceptions around the Telefomin valley and plateau (see Swadling, Mawe, and Tomo 1990), have rarely been identified or surveyed, much less systematically explored.

Yet, much of this scant and heterogeneous evidence suggests that a major influence upon and perhaps migratory source of many Mountain-Ok peoples may have been the Sepik north (either directly, or indirectly by way of the Irian Jaya and Papua New Guinea highlands to the west and east), an influence perhaps also affected by social migrations and cultural transmissions from the Sepik through the tributaries and foothills along the northern flank of the central range. The archaeological evidence for contact, migration, or cultural influence across the Strickland from the highlands of Papua New Guinea, however, rests on only some very tentative inferences from quite limited and heterogeneous fragments of complexes of material culture.

THE ECOLOGICAL CONTEXT

The recent appearance of a growing corpus of information on the early ecological character of the Mountain-Ok region may be more promising in depicting the potential of the landscape and its shifting resources and constraints for accommodating human habitation and exploitation. The key subarea of Telefomin is often imagined to be a hub from which, under pressures of demographic expansion within severe ecological constraints, populations radiated throughout the Mountain-Ok. Until some twelve thousand years ago, this subarea bordered on a more or less unbroken expanse of subalpine grasslands extending as far west as Paniai Lake and exhibiting an eastward rift in the vicinity of the Sepik-Strickland headwaters before again resuming its profile in the area of the Central Range and the Müller Mountains (Hope 1977). This gap in the central mountain expanse of the grasslands may indicate why the Strickland is considered to be a major fault line within contemporary highland societies and cultures, for the requisites of ecological adaptation within the gap are dramatically different from those on either side of it.

Indeed, gradients of historical population density inferred from various indices of human habitation suggest a long-term east-west distribution: from high-density population in the highlands of Papua New Guinea to low-density population in the Strickland, low density in the Mountain-Ok and eastern highlands of Irian Jaya, and a gradual increase far westward toward the Grand Baliem valley, with marked declines in population farther west. There are some rough correlations between this pattern of population density and both the profile of deforestation and the evidence of intensive cultivation (Larson 1987).

Another correlated factor in this apparent pattern of highland habitation may be the somewhat uneven distribution of intermontane valleys along the mountainous spine of New Guinea. Such valleys are generally concentrated east and west of the central montane hub of the island, perhaps encouraging the more or less distinctive development of the eastern Tari-Lai-Wahgi-Asaro sphere of "classical" Papua New Guinea highland societies, the central realm of the Mek-Ok groups encompassing the Mountain-Ok, and the western domain of the Baliem-Paniai. Although these relatively distinctive spheres of sociocultural efflorescence are generally recognized, both in the archaeological and in the ethnographic record, little account is generally taken of the Mountain-Ok (or, indeed, of the eastern highlands of Irian Jaya) in most profiles of the prehistoric or recent pattern of sociocultural similarity and variation among societies and cultures of the New Guinea highlands (see Brown 1978; Feil 1987).

Within the Mountain-Ok, clearance fires around Telefomin (perhaps produced anthropogenically by gardening or hunting practices or by accident) seem evident over the last 20,000 years and particularly from between 15,000 and 17,000 years ago (Hope 1983; Swadling 1983; Swadling, Mawe, and Tomo 1990).[4] These occurred at about the same historical time that populations seem to have been expanding and migrating within the Asaro, Wahgi, and Lai intermontane valleys (Swadling 1983; Golson 1977, 1982). About 12,000 years ago, forest began to replace the subalpine grasslands, and the modern grasslands of various parts of the Mountain-Ok—especially on the Telefomin alluvial fan complex and along and in the Strickland Gorge—appear also to be anthropogenic, the result of burning centered on gardening and hunting activities, and accidents.[5] A decline in soil fertility in such areas may have discouraged cultivation in the grasslands and also hindered the reinvasion of the grasslands by new forest growth (Hope 1983; Landsberg and Gillieson 1980). Indeed, there seems to be archaeological evidence that soil fertility has been poor in the grasslands for some four thousand years (Swadling 1983), and there are widespread ethnohistorical accounts of the infertility of the grasslands extending back more than a century (Poole 1976, 1986).[6] These local traditions, however, suggest that such poor soils can variously be improved over short spans of time by planting casuarinas, by techniques of ash or leaf-mulch fertilization, and by more or less elaborate ritual means focused on soil or plant fertility, although such traditions tend also to recognize that gardening in the grasslands holds little promise for long.[7] Contemporary traditions in Telefomin and its environs note an ever-increasing infertility of the soil in the Telefomin valley, an early and fragmented and then intensifying and consolidating pattern of grassy intrusions appearing in stands of forest growth, and a gradual tendency of the widening grasslands to expand into ever-higher reaches of the valley slopes and ridges as cultivation ascended beyond the infertile perimeter of prior invasions of grasses and toward its altitudinal limits.[8] In response, and as cultivation in and around the alluvial fan complex extending southward from the Mittag Mountains into the Telefomin valley had become—by virtue of heavy erosion, invasive grasslands, and declining soil fertility—less and less viable, Telefolmin gardening activities had slowly begun to shift toward the west into the Urapmin area, toward the east approaching Feramin, toward the south in the vicinity of the Nong River valley, and toward the northeast of the upper Om River valley. Accordingly, settlement patterns began to exhibit an outward radiation to accommodate pragmatic needs of proximity to gardens.

The local but expanding ecological constraints in and near the Telefomin valley seem to have substantially diminished the potential for intensifying cultivation and, thus, for elaborating pig husbandry and increasing pig herds, as well as for more or less expanding and concentrating settlements. Without an apparent Ipomoean revolution and its hypothesized entailments and consequences for pig husbandry, settlement structure, political organization, pig feasts, ceremonial exchanges, and related sociocultural phenomena, social relationships among ethnic groups were largely constituted through the ritual integration of cult elaborations, trade, marriage, and war—creating intragroup boundaries of differing form, force, and permeability and intergroup alliances and networks of varying focus, extent, solidarity, and duration.[9]

Within perhaps the last three hundred years, however, an outward expansion from the center of Telefomin may also have been related to the incipient impact of the sweet potato.[10] Such population expansion radiating outward from Telefomin seems to have led to increasingly endemic warfare, resulting in smaller peripheral groups being either destroyed or forced to move to higher altitudes or southward toward the lower areas of the middle Fly River.[11] These fringe groups, nonetheless, often continued to expand (albeit at a slower rate and under different demographic and ecological circumstances) under the constraints of less than favorable environmental conditions and may variously either have developed their own spheres of outward expansion or else have declined for reasons beyond their control or adopted practices to limit the growth of population or both.[12]

Thus, the expansion in the area of Telefomin—both demographically at the center and then through warfare, colonization of new lands, and forced dispersal and migration at the periphery, under certain changing ecological conditions at different periods in the process—may have developed in such a manner that this more or less dramatically expanding population center increasingly displaced groups at its periphery. Either these displaced groups were then immediately destroyed through warfare or experienced a new set of ecological conditions and consequent demographic collapse resulting in some form of "population sink" at certain points on the periphery; or else they themselves migrated, colonized, and expanded, to a lesser extent and at a slower rate, forcing further displacements.[13] Local conditions of increasing taro-leaf blight and parasites, drought, and episodic famine, in turn, may have periodically affected the character of this centripetal expansion, and the search for new taro lands seems primarily to have resulted in a complex pattern of migrations and displacements toward the east and south of Telefomin, which perhaps reached its greatest elaboration and force some three hundred years ago.[14]

THE LINGUISTIC CONTEXT

Linguistic evidence, based largely on lexicostatistical or glottochronological appraisals of degrees of cognate sharing and inferred historical language divergence, also roughly indicates a local south-southeastern pattern of migratory radiation from the Telefomin area. According to A. Healey (1964), a reconstructed Proto-Ok language may have differentiated into its Mountain-Ok and Lowland-Ok forms some 5,000 years ago, with the latter being subsequently represented primarily from the upper to middle Fly. In turn, Telefol and Faiwol (spoken to the southeast of the Telefol speakers) may have become significantly distinctive some 2,000 years ago, with the Bimin-Kuskusmin language, in turn, becoming differentiated from Faiwol some 1,500 years ago. Further evidence (Bromley 1967; Wurm 1982) suggests that the earlier history of Ok languages—given their present distribution and diversity—may have involved myriad paths of migration from the linguistically complex Sepik north. The contours of these possible patterns of linguistic diversification not only exhibit some affinity with certain suspected patterns of migratory movement—into the Mountain-Ok and beyond, from the Sepik hinterland, the eastern highlands of Irian Jaya, and toward the large population center at Telefomin—but also are traced, mutatis mutandis, in the ethnohistorical and mythological traditions of a number of Mountain-Ok groups, traditions that also richly portray a vast array of other sociocultural similarities and differences constituting approximate (albeit shifting) ethnic boundaries that are more or less aligned with the linguistic correlates of ethnicity.[15]

MORE GLOBAL SPECULATIONS ON PREHISTORIC MOVEMENT INTO THE MOUNTAIN-OK

Enfolding these regional patterns of migratory movement, however, is an image—both in the archaeological, ecological, and linguistic evidence and in the mythicohistorical traditions of local people—of a more encompassing migration of peoples in New Guinea.[16] With respect to this image, the general assumption about the primary path of migration and settlement has been a movement along the north coast of the island from west to east, with subsequent southern migrations into the central mountain chain and then beyond toward the south coast. Many Mountain-Ok ethnohistorical and mythological traditions trace paths of migration implicated in the early settlement of the region from the north and west primarily, but such traditions also commonly depict their versions of the great ancestor Afek coming from at least the proximate east (see Bercovitch 1982). From the west, a portrait emerges of a general eastward flow of successive and expanding migrations that radiate in a north-south fan somewhere to the immediate west of the present Irian Jaya border and then begin to converge on the Mountain-Ok within and along the flanking foothills of the central mountains. From the north, both distinctive and interlocking paths of migration follow the Sepik, August, Idam, Green, May, Frieda, Wario, Wogamush, and April rivers, with secondary paths of eastward and westward migration along the Om and westward migration along the Lagaip from the northern Sepik Hills hinterland. In general, the migrations eastward out of the west depict a continuous flow of peoples similar in sociocultural character to ancestral portraits of more or less contemporary Mountain-Ok ethnic mosaics and also a continuity of trade, ritual, and sociocultural influence along these paths of migration into the present era.

These migrations seem to have been the movements of primary significance in the settlement of the Mountain-Ok and to have been mostly restricted to the ecological conditions of the high mountain corridor, constrained both on the north flank and on the south by unfamiliar and inhospitable environments, the higher prevalence of malaria at the lower altitudes, and the pressures of warfare directed upslope by groups of marked ethnic difference. The marked migrations southward out of the north—also associated with continuing trade in the most proximate regions, but with ritual and other cultural influence only in the distant past—are generally represented as secondary intrusions of more recent historical circumstances into the west-east stream of primary waves of successive migrations, which in turn may have a heritage of yet earlier migrations from the Sepik north. Occasional reckonings of migrations from the south seem often to be deflections of the general sweep of migrations from the west or of northeastward migrations of peoples displaced to the south from the western Mountain-Ok; and migrations from the east are usually cast as deflections in an east-south-west arc of the most easterly of southern migrations from the north. Indeed, the general migratory pattern seems to conform to the apparent Mek-Ok sociocultural orientation to the west and, perhaps earlier, to the north, with only occasional (and always ambiguous) eastern forms of influence noted. The Bimin-Kuskusmin portrait of their historical position in the Mountain-Ok is unusual, however, in emphasizing a significant path of migration westward from the east out of the Southern and Western highlands. Indeed, the special local significance of migrations from the east is marked both in narrative performance and in ritual action and is held to represent a particular distinctiveness of the Bimin-Kuskusmin among Mountain-Ok cultures and societies. In fact, this eastern path of migrations may illuminate some otherwise curious sociocultural forms characteristic of this ethnic group at the eastern edge of the Mountain-Ok and on the western flank of the Strickland.

THE CYCLE OF AFEK MYTHS

In shifting toward the temporal range of ethnohistorical and mythological images, it should be noted that the Bimin-Kuskusmin narrate several more or less distinctive genres of apparently long traditional accounts, which portray their sense of their historical origins and migrations within the Mountain-Ok and beyond. The most elaborate, ritually marked, and mythically enshrined set of these narratives depicts the primordial origin of the Bimin-Kuskusmin—as a single community directly ancestral to the present community—as occurring within their present territory of the *abiip mutuuk* 'center place' or *afek yemen am* 'Afek's taro home', and their recognition of the ritual sanctity and boundedness of this *aiyem* 'sacred' sense of a traditional, contiguous, territorial domain.[17] Indeed, this sense of continuity of place and people is intricately articulated with a reckoning of the enduring stability of its key ecological features throughout remembered, ethnohistorically marked, and mythologically apprehended time, and Bimin-Kuskusmin have come to associate certain recent ecological changes—especially the advent of new kinds of grasses and a particular species of bee—with an apparent erosion of the *alyem'khaan buurugaamak* 'sacred integrity' of their landscape, an erosion foreshadowed in mythic portrayals of a gradual decline in the efficacy of ritual and in the performative powers of its mortal practitioners.[18]

The recent intrusions of grasslands and bees, appearing first in a narrow strip along the Strickland and gradually encroaching westward, are believed to emanate from the highlands to the east of the Strickland and are mythically represented as a magical attempt of the descendants of early ancestors to reestablish a once complex set of enduring social relationships and political-economic transactions, facing eastward, that have diminished over time to a limited trade network of little eastern depth and some relations of intermarriage extending across the Strickland.[19] These early ancestors are depicted as adorned with netted aprons and rear grass coverings, complex feather headdresses or wigs, and large shell pendants; as once living in large and sometimes multinucleated settlements along the slopes and ridges of vast grassland valleys; as subsisting primarily both on taro and on sweet potatoes; as rearing and feasting upon large numbers of domesticated pigs; and as entering into complex exchange transactions involving great displays of shells and pigs. Indeed, the ordeals of their westward migratory passage out of the eastern highlands are seen in these accounts to have fragmented their once large groups, disabled the reestablishment of their complex settlements, disrupted their political-economic elaboration, and impoverished their material culture. Bimin-Kuskusmin cult house displays of fragments of large *Pinctada* shells are associated with these eastern migrations.

This ritually embedded mythological tradition is centered on the complex cycle of *afek sang* 'Afek myths' focused on the primordial androgynous ancestor Afek and her male consorts (but not her sisters, as among some other Mountain-Ok groups). Afek came from the east before her androgynous "father," the great monitor lizard Daarkru, cut the great gorge of the Strickland to bound her domain and to impede her return to the east. Portrayed as a giant cassowary, and being more female than male in appearance but endowed with more masculine than feminine powers of agency, she gave birth to the founders—both human and totemic—of all of the original sixteen patriclans of the Bimin and the Kuskusmin ritual moieties. Once these great immortal ancestors were assembled, she laid down the foundations of an important set of traditions that she had brought from the east and that mark certain more or less unusual and distinctive sociocultural attributes of the Bimin-Kuskusmin within the pattern of Mountain-Ok societies and cultures. She introduced the cultivation secrets of the sweet potato, including certain ditching, mounding, and terracing techniques, but relegated the primordial sweet potato to the realm of *oor fuutan'ok* 'famine foods' (or literally 'watery shoot feces' or 'sprout diarrhea'), possessing neither *kitiirnam ben'kha* 'ritual strength' nor *kitiirnam fom'sokeirey* 'bodily strength'.[20] She also brought taro and designated it as the center of valued subsistence and of a ritual complex, but she withheld the esoteric secrets of its cultivation and its ritual significance.[21] She instituted certain modes of pig husbandry not dependent upon sweet potato cultivation.[22] She then illuminated the character of pig feasts and exchanges, bound to ceremonialized exchanges of *Pinctada* pearl shells and to certain aspects of bridewealth transactions (see Poole 1981), and she anchored such matters to the role of the *kamok* 'political-economic transactors' in interpersonal networks, intergroup relations, and the enhancement of male prestige.[23]

She articulated an ideology of gender that emphasized and elaborated male-female difference in terms of notions of female pollution and the entailed grounds for more or less rigid rules and understandings of male-female segregation in residential, ritual, garden, and other social spaces. She delineated a dominant and pervasive ideology of patrilineality bound to matters of procreation, bodily substance, social identity, the boundedness of more or less corporate categories that were constituted in part as localized exogamous groups, and related aspects of inheritance, succession, political leadership, warfare, marriage, exchange, and other social activities shaped by the patrilineal contours of institutional forms (Poole 1984b). Virtually all of these sociocultural characteristics are relatively distinctive of the Bimin-Kuskusmin, comparatively within the Mountain-Ok, and exhibit a certain marked affinity with sociocultural patterns more typical of the east and the so-called classic highlands of Papua New Guinea (Brown 1978; Feil 1987). Even with respect to material culture, she introduced a complex of mortars and pestles, grass loin-wrappings, minuscule wigs, and chest decorations, more characteristic of possible eastern influences, and she enshrined assemblages of mortars and pestles among the *sacrae* of cult houses as relics of that eastern passage.

After having founded the original clans of the Bimin-Kuskusmin, Afek journeyed to the west to found other groups of the Mountain-Ok, to Telefomin, and beyond. Upon her subsequent return to the east and to the 'center place', however, she brought a new set of traditions, which were now marked mythically and embedded ritually so as to dominate the traditions introduced earlier. She told of the cultivation secrets of taro and of cults focused on taro, establishing a taro hearth at the center of cult houses and now relegating the once central sweet potato hearth to the periphery and the cultivation of sweet potato to the realm of women.[24] In contrast, taro became associated with the domain of men and with preeminent cultural elaboration as the most valued nutrient and ritual cultigen.

Pig husbandry was entirely separated from the sweet potato complex, and techniques of encouraging pig foraging in the forest and in taro gardens turned to fallow were introduced. As ritual rules concerning the castration of domestic boars were articulated, the pig became secondary in feasts and exchanges except for its central role as a sacrificial creature in ritual and the importance of its relics—notably mandibles and skulls—in cult houses. The emphasis on pig domestication gave way to a highly ritualized focus on pig hunting. In important ways, however, the symbolic emphasis on the pig in the context of political-economic transactions was transformed into a focus on marsupials in ritual transactions, under which less elaborate political-economic transactions were largely subsumed.

The role of the male *kunum aiyem* 'ritual elder' and of the *kunum kusem* 'male diviner' became paramount in an elaboration of ritual commissions that fused political, economic, and ritual authority and power in a gerontocracy associated with an elaborate, hierarchical sociology of knowledge supported by extensive rules of secrecy and entitlement to disclosure (Poole 1982b, 1987b). The *kamok* became more a pathway to becoming a *kunum aiyem* 'ritual elder' than a status or office of high male prestige in its own right. Ritual, and especially rites of male initiation, became the focus of the central institutions of social life. Ceremonial exchanges became more simplified and a mechanism of intragroup redistribution in the service of intergroup ritualized trade. Conceptions of gender were encompassed by myths of primordial matriarchy, notions of androgyny, and statuses of powerful female ritual elders and diviners, all of which transformed key aspects of pollution beliefs, sexual segregation, and the possibilities of female power and authority (Poole 1981, 1984a).

A ritual moiety organization was much elaborated in ordering interclan transactions, reciprocities reflected in initiation rites, territorial configurations and the bundles of rights in and over them, and certain aspects of marriage exchanges among the paramount ranking clans of each moiety. The once strict and highly elaborated patrilineal ideology became significantly transformed by certain cognatic emphases, with implications for a variety of category, group, and network transactive arrangements. Even in regard to material culture, the phallocrypt and other ritually ordained emblems of personhood came to modify or obliterate eastern influences.

In summary, the cycle of Afek myths provided representations of and charters for a complex of sociocultural forms and forces more characteristic of western influences on more pan-Mountain-Ok patterns of Bimin-Kuskusmin culture and society, all of which, nonetheless, were transformed distinctively among Bimin-Kuskusmin by traditions mythically relegated to an earlier stratum of eastern influences emanating from the Papua New Guinea highlands. Indeed, a western emphasis on highly localized endogamous patterns of marriage—although sometimes focused preferentially on congeries or more or less contiguous hamlets of different clan-associated parishes—found its greatest elaboration in beliefs concerning the distinctiveness and boundedness of Bimin-Kuskusmin as an ethnic category and community beyond which intermarriage was deemed culturally anathema and socially disintegrative and the sociomoral order encompassing proper personhood was extended rather thinly and weakly (in Read's [1955] sense of a distributive morality).[25]

Before her final departure to the ancestral underworld, Afek celebrated an elaborate rite of mourning oriented toward the east and focused on her eastern passage. She ritually marked the Strickland Gorge as a boundary of Bimin-Kuskusmin ethnic identity and instituted a set of taboos on the kind and extent of interaction with peoples on the eastern flank of the Strickland. Yet, she also transmitted to the primordial ancestors a wealth of lore about their eastern origins, a set of myths concerning the essential orientation of the sun and its powers toward the east, and a complex of rites that focused on harnessing ancestral power from the east. Then, by creating the mists commonly overhanging the Strickland and marking the Strickland as the source of rain, she enfolded the eastern heritage of the Bimin-Kuskusmin in a cloak of almost impenetrable secrecy. She then adorned herself with a large decorated phallocrypt, cut the septum of her nose, sprinkled the flow of blood into the Strickland, placed a live centipede in her pierced septum, and journeyed to the ancestral underworld—having marked her orientation to the west and vowing never to return to her origins in the east.

ETHNOHISTORICAL NARRATIVES OF MIGRATION

Changes in the sociocentric map of the ethnic landscape of the Mountain-Ok region, however, are foreshadowed and reflected in interesting ways in other sets of narratives, which illuminate a migratory history of once differing social groups that ultimately became politically and ritually consolidated as the Bimin-Kuskusmin, gradually converging on the 'center place' from diverse origins beyond the pale of this traditional territory. These narratives of migratory *khaa'tebemaam* 'historical events' are sharply distinguished from the *aiyem sang* 'sacred myths' (most notably the cycle of Afek myths) that are ritually embedded and that portray the Bimin-Kuskusmin as a single, culturally homogeneous, sociopolitically integrated people originating and forever dwelling in the 'center place'. Indeed, these ethnohistorical tales are never told in the central contexts of ritual, and they are marked by an open-ended, speculative character.

Passage from the East and the Papua New Guinea Highlands

One ethnohistorical account traces a migration from the Papua New Guinea highlands to the east along two paths: one from south of Lake Kopiago across the Strickland Gorge into the southern Oksapmin and then deflected further southward into the 'center place' by warfare pressing from the north, and another from far down the eastern flank of the Strickland, crossing the river westward, and moving north through uninhabited territory toward the 'center place'. These narratives essentially portray the same sociocultural complex from the east as is depicted in the Afek myths, but the descriptions of terrain and peoples are much more detailed and vivid. Vast grassland valleys and large settlements are associated with extensive sweet potato gardens and some taro gardens, large domestic pig herds and much feasting and exchange focused on pigs, and distinctive concentrations of flora and fauna gathered and hunted. As the passage progresses and is marked by settlement, ecological maladaptation or ritual failure or war, and renewed movement, the passing panorama slowly shifts to smaller riverine valleys, diminished grasslands in the midst of heavy stands of forest, lower concentrations of population, smaller and more scattered and impermanent settlements, different gardens emphasizing taro, increased dependence on hunting and foraging, and varying styles of dwellings—including longhouses. Much descriptive attention is directed toward headdresses (from great lattice constructions of feathers and furs to decorated wigs of human hair) and toward fighting styles and implements, often in the context of a difficult passage marked by incessant warfare. These descriptions are reminiscent of the ecological contours of a possible east-west migration somewhat northward and southward through the Papua New Guinea highlands. Recognition is given to trade and intermarriage with certain Hewa and Duna groups as consequences of this passage.

The convergence of these two migratory paths in the 'center place', after an initial period of confrontation, peace, and exchange of women and wealth, eventually yields an ethnic group—the Bimin—with a variety of eastern characteristics, in relative isolation, except to the north from which successive waves of small groups flowing out of the Sepik Hills exerted more or less constant pressure through raiding. Thus, the Bimin are recognized in these accounts as having a primacy of settlement, although not of ritual, in the creation of the territory of the 'center place'. In turn, it is the Bimin who hold primary rights over the control of trade with the east, although they are dependent on rites associated with the later Kuskusmin migrants from the west to launch and to sustain such trade. Intermarriages with groups from the eastern flank of the Strickland are also understood to be restricted to the Bimin.

MIGRATIONS FROM THE SEPIK HINTERLAND

Another ethnohistorical tradition illuminates a set of migratory paths constituting a prolonged, gradual movement from the north, southward from the upper Sepik River in the west to the April River in the east, then moving through the higher foothills and following the Lagaip-Om rivers and northern flank of the ranges from east to west, converging on the Telefomin valley and its western environs, and moving south-east-northeast toward the 'center place' to constitute the Kuskusmin ethnic group. The Kuskusmin are portrayed as first fighting, then intermarrying, exchanging with, and finally forging an alliance with the Bimin, in form of a ritual moiety system seemingly bearing some affinity with middle to upper Sepik patterns.

These new immigrants brought important and distinctive ritual secrets and stocks of sago and yam, but in their negotiation of alliance with the Bimin, both sago and yam were consigned to the category of famine foods and deleted from the category of ritual foods. It was their introduction of taro and aspects of the taro cult that became central to newly forming ritual institutions. These complex and sometimes intertwined stories of migrations depict ancestors who first came by river and then by land through dense malarial swamps and other lowland forests, fighting their way into the high mountain corridor toward Telefomin and further west and then being displaced southward to move eventually through sparsely populated or uninhabited terrain toward the 'center place'.

Descriptions abound of riverine expanses giving way to dangerous swamps and dense lowland forests, although there are relatively few portrayals of people or settlements. Depictions of flora and fauna give special prominence to mosquitoes and other noxious insects, fish, crocodiles, venomous snakes, and to yams, sago, breadfruit, and bananas. Crop stocks of these foods, ideas about ritual organization, and crocodile bones as cult *sacrae* accompanied these migrations and became assimilated in some respects among the Bimin-Kuskusmin, who essentially were formed as a politically and ritually consolidated, yet still multi-ethnic group in the wake of these migrations.

Movements from the West and the Irian Jaya Highlands

A different ethnohistorical portrait marks successive waves of a massive migration out of the west toward the east, with paths moving through the Red Digul and Sibil river areas, winding through narrow river valleys toward the Telefomin valley and beyond, eastward, toward the southeast through the Fly headwaters south of the Hindenburg Wall and ascending toward the northeast. An offshoot reached the western flank of the middle Strickland, and then moved north, and east. The northeast migrations from the Digul-Sibil area ultimately followed the northern flank of the Om River and turned south through the Oksapmin area. Both the terrain and the peoples encountered by these numerous migrations of large and small populations are distinctively Mountain-Ok and subsequently slightly Mek in an intricate complex of sociocultural characteristics centered on and coordinated through an efflorescence of ritual forms involving marsupial and cassowary and pig and human relics; complexes of permanent and temporary cult houses; elaborate male initiation rites; lesser rituals focused on hunting, foraging, taro gardening, human fertility, and war; and the prominence of "great- men" (in Godelier's [1986] sense). This complex was transformed into various configurations throughout the Mountain-Ok, and several migratory versions of this complex became variously incorporated and integrated, over perhaps the course of several centuries, into the Sepik-Highlands pattern of the early Bimin-Kuskusmin, through the gradual but more or less continuous incorporation of small groups of emigrants from the west.

In time, as Bimin-Kuskusmin began to constitute a variety of social relations with other Mountain-Ok groups to their south, west, and north, and to form the rudiments of an increasingly elaborate ritual integration of the region, the western influences began to dominate myriad cultural models and social forms and forces, nonetheless affected and given distinctive shape by earlier historical migrations. As the ritual coordination and integration of the Mountain-Ok progressed and became encompassing of other relations of trade and exchange, war and peace, and intermarriage, two key ritual centers began to form, each with its own more or less distinctive orbit of ethnic groups ritually focused and dependent on it. The major center among the Telefolmin was acknowledged by all groups throughout the Mountain-Ok, mutatis mutandis, as being paramount in ritual importance, but this western pole of the region had its lesser but eastern counterpart in the ritual center elaborated among the Bimin-Kuskusmin. Perhaps only in the 1940s and 1950s, as the Telefolmin ritual center was seen to be eroded—by disasters and desecrations resulting from the early accidental destruction of a cohort of initiates by fire and the later intrusion into cult houses by colonial officers and police—was the Bimin-Kuskusmin ritual center elaborated. This center was claimed to ascend in ritual importance as the rites among Telefolmin declined in efficacy—at least in Bimin-Kuskusmin perceptions of the matter.

THE PATTERN OF PATHS OF MIGRATION

Each of these ethnohistorical traditions of migration is narratively focused on a more or less detailed panorama of the passing ecological and sociocultural scene as various ethnically diverse ancestors are seen to migrate, to settle, and to move again: either because their ecological milieus are judged inappropriate for defense, health, hunting, trapping, gathering, gardening, constituting sociopolitical relations, constructing ritual forms, and so on, or because they are forced along a migratory path by other, larger, expanding, warring groups. In time, these ethnically diverse immigrants, arriving in successive waves to the 'center place', were transformed: through sociopolitical necessities, aspirations, and negotiations, or through initial settlement and subsequent attachment to, alliance with, or incorporation into a distinct Mountain-Ok group, prominent in the ritual organization and structure of the region yet clearly distinguishable as a complex synthesis of its variegated sociocultural past. Since this gradual set of alignments and consolidations probably occurred over the last many centuries, it seems that the community—its expansive and centripetal demographic tendencies more or less held in check to some extent by war, drought, famine, disease, and culturally constituted means of limiting population growth—has developed a kind and a degree of cultural cohesiveness, social solidarity, ritual prominence in the region, and ecological adaptation so that immigrants are more or less systematically integrated into the community through recognized processes of affiliation, assimilation, and incorporation; internal forces generating fission and segmentation do not often result in the dispersal of emigrants beyond the pale of the 'center place' to be forever lost to the community; long-term emigrants tend to remain domiciled in the 'center place', however long they may be resident elsewhere; and territorial expansion has been slight, infrequent, and into contiguous terrain that is ritually incorporated into the 'center place'.

CONCLUSION

On the basis of my brief representation and analysis of these local ethnohistorical and mythological traditions and, as their more distal context, of other archaeological, ecological, and linguistic understandings of the inhabitants and historical habitation of the Mountain-Ok (and both sets of materials markedly converge on certain roughly similar patterns of migration and settlement despite their considerable differences in time depth), it may be suggested that the Bimin-Kuskusmin narratives yield significant and defensible clues to some possible migratory and settlement patterns in the Mountain-Ok region. In particular, it is the cycle of Afek myths and ethnohistorical narratives depicting eastern origins and their accounts of migrations and influences from the highlands to the east that give the corpus its most distinctive character.

Through both narratives of migration and the cycle of 'Afek myths', Bimin-Kuskusmin represent a complex sense of their past founded on their cultural imagination of historicity and historiography (Poole 1992). One vision depicts a confluence of peoples converging over a long span of historical time and constituting a community from what once was marked sociocultural diversity. On occasion, this corpus is known as *daib ok'ban sang* 'tales of many river paths'. Another vision, cast in the form of 'Afek myths', portrays a single people forever within the 'center place'. On the one hand, these narratives are sharply distinguished as genres, are performed in mutually exclusive contexts, and serve quite different functions in the marking of Bimin-Kuskusmin identity. On the other hand, these narratives exhibit a similarity of pattern in encasing the formative travels and exploits of significant culture heroes in the contours of a rich geographical map extending throughout the Mountain-Ok and beyond and being marked by the sociocultural characteristics of numerous groups. For Bimin-Kuskusmin, images of space and place enfold and punctuate imaginations of historical time, and at times, these images—and the mosaic of sociocultural anchorages that are bound up with their narrative portrayals—often converge in tantalizing ways with patterns now being recognized in the archaeological, ecological, and linguistic understandings of their region and of the relationship of that region to broader patterns of a wider historical portrait of peoples and places in New Guinea.

The Bimin-Kuskusmin now dwell in a cultural region that, although still affected on occasion by some migratory exodus and invasion, not only exhibits considerable and complex ritually focused sociopolitical and economic integration but also reveals a historical legacy of diverse ethnic groups who migrated into the Mountain-Ok under differing circumstances and from different regions beyond its pale, entering into relations of peace and war with one another and circulating through vast stretches of the region before establishing relatively stable settlements under intertwined demographic, ecological, and sociocultural conditions.

In turn, certain cultural and social characteristics of the variability yet similarity among contemporary Mountain-Ok groups may be rendered more comprehensible, in part, by attending to how the region has been constituted and reconstituted historically through patterns of successive waves of migration from beyond its periphery. The sociocentric narrative perspective of the Bimin-Kuskusmin, therefore, facilitates some understanding of their sociocultural distinctiveness as a nonetheless recognizably Mountain-Ok group and also of the cultural region of which they are both an integral and a distinctive ethnic part. These local narratives also reveal more generally that the Strickland may not have formed the impenetrable barrier in the development of highland societies and cultures so long suspected, and that migrations and cultural influences from the east—only tantalizingly and fragmentarily suggested in the archaeological, ecological, and linguistic record of the prehistory of the New Guinea highlands—may have contributed to the shaping of at least some subregions within the Mountain-Ok.

REFERENCES

Barth, F.
1971 Tribes and Intertribal Relations in the Fly Headwaters. Oceania 41:171–191.
1987 Cosmologies in the Making: A Generative Approach to Cultural Variation in Inner New Guinea. Cambridge: Cambridge University Press.

Bayliss-Smith, T.
1985 Subsistence Agriculture and Nutrition in the Bimin Valley, Oksapmin Sub-District, Papua New Guinea. Singapore Journal of Tropical Geography 6:101–115.

Bercovitch, E.
1982 A Regional Perspective on the Narrative Traditions of the Min Peoples of Papua New Guinea. Unpublished manuscript. Institute of Papua New Guinea Studies.

Bromley, H. M.
1967 The Linguistic Relationships of Grand Valley Dani: A Lexico-Statistical Classification. Oceania 27:296–308.

Brookfield, H. C.
1972 Intensification and Disintensification in Pacific Agriculture: A Theoretical Approach. Pacific Viewpoint 13:30–48.

Brookfield, H. C., and J. P. White
1968 Revolution or Evolution in the Prehistory of the New Guinea Highlands? Ethnology 7:43–52.

Brown, P.
1978 Highland Peoples of New Guinea. Cambridge: Cambridge University Press.

Bulmer, S.
1964 Prehistoric Stone Implements from the New Guinea Highlands. Oceania 34:246–268.
1975 Settlement and Economy in Prehistoric Papua New Guinea: A Review of the Archaeologlcal Evidence. Journal de la Société des Océanistes 31:7–75.

Bulmer, S., and R. Bulmer
1964 The Prehistory of the New Guinea Highlands. American Anthropologist 66(4), part 2, pp. 39–76.

Cape, N.
1981 Agriculture. *In* Oksapmin. S. Weeks, ed., pp. 149–190. Port Moresby: Educational Research Unit, University of Papua New Guinea.

Clarke, W. C.
1966 From Extensive to Intensive Shifting Cultivation: A Succession from New Guinea. Ethnology 5:347–359.

Craig, B.
1981 Report of Mountain-Ok Field Survey. Unpublished manuscript. Department of Anthropology, Papua New Guinea National Museum.
1984 Is the Mountain-Ok Culture a Sepik Culture? Paper presented at the Sepik Symposium, Basel.

Feil, D. K.
1987 The Evolution of Highland Papua New Guinea Societies. Cambridge: Cambridge University Press.

Gillieson, D. S.
1983 Geomorphology of Limestone Caves of the Highlands of Papua New Guinea. Unpublished Ph.D. dissertation. University of Queensland.

Godelier, M.
1986 The Making of Great Men. Cambridge: Cambridge University Press.

Golson, J.
1977 The Making of the New Guinea Highlands. *In* The Melanesian Environment. J. Winslow, ed., pp. 45–56. Canberra: Australian National University Press.
1982 The Ipomoean Revolution Revisited: Society and the Sweet Potato in the Upper Wahgi Valley. *In* Inequality in New Guinea Highlands Societies. A. J. Strathern, ed., pp. 109–136. Cambridge: Cambridge University Press.

Healey, A.
1964 The Ok Language Family of New Guinea. Ph.D. dissertation. Australian National University.

Hope, G. S.
1977 Observations on the History of Human Usage of Subalpine Areas near Mt. Jaya. Irian 6:41–72.
1983 New Guinea Mountain Vegetation Communities and Historical Influences. *In* Alpine Flora of New Guinea. P. Van Royen, ed., pp. 111–248. Munich: Kramer Verlag.

Landsberg, J. J., and D. S. Gillieson
1980 Toksave bilong Graun: Common Sense or Empiricism in a Folk Soil Knowledge from Papua New Guinea. Capricornia 5(8):13–23.

Larson, G. F.
1987 The Structure and Demography of the Cycle of Warfare Among the Ilaga Dani of Irian Jaya. Unpublished Ph.D. dissertation. University of Michigan.

Löffler, E.
1977 Geomorphology of Papua New Guinea. Canberra: Commonwealth Scientific and Industrial Research Organisation and Australian National University Press.

Pearson, M., and B. M. Thistleton
1981 Taro Diseases in the Hotmin Area, East Sepik Province, and the Telefomin Area, West Sepik Province, Papua New Guinea. Unpublished manuscript. Report on a field visit. Library of the University of Papua New Guinea.

Poole, F. J. P.
1976 The Ais Am. 5 volumes. Unpublished Ph.D. dissertation. Cornell University.
1981 Transforming "Natural" Woman: Female Ritual Leaders and Gender Ideology Among Bimin-Kuskusmin. *In* Sexual Meanings. S. B. Ortner and H. Whitehead, eds., pp. 116–165. Cambridge: Cambridge University Press.
1982a Couvade and Clinic in a New Guinea Society: Birth Among the Bimin-Kuskusmin. *In* The Use and Abuse of Medicine. M. W. deVries, R. L. Berg, and M. Lipkln, Jr., eds., pp. 54–95. New York: Praeger Scientific.
1982b The Ritual Forging of Identity: Aspects of Person and Self in Bimin-Kuskusmin Male Initiation. *In* Rituals of Manhood. G. H. Herdt, ed., pp. 99–154. Berkeley: University of California Press.
1983 Cannibals, Tricksters, and Witches: Anthropophagic Images Among Bimin-Kuskusmin. *In* The Ethnography of Cannibalism. P. Brown and D. Tuzin, eds., pp. 6–32. Washington, D.C.: Society for Psychological Anthropology. (Special publication of the Society for Psychological Anthropology)
1984a Cultural Images of Women as Mothers: Motherhood Among the Bimin-Kuskusmin of Papua New Guinea. Social Analysis 15:73–93. (Special issue on Gender and Social Life)
1984b Symbols of Substance: Bimin-Kuskusmin Models of Procreation, Death, and Personhood. Mankind 14(3):191–216.
1985 Among the Boughs of the Hanging Tree: Male Suicide Among the Bimin-Kuskusmin of Papua New Guinea. *In* Culture, Youth and Suicide in the Pacific. F. X. Hezel, D. H. Rubinstein, and G. M. White, eds., pp. 152–181.
Honolulu: Working Paper Series of the Pacific Island StudiesProgram of the Center for Asian and Pacific Studies of the University of Hawaii at Manoa and the Institute of Culture and Communication of the East-West Center.
1986 The Erosion of a Sacred Landscape: European Exploration and Cultural Ecology Among the Bimin-Kuskusmin of Papua New Guinea. *In* Mountain People. M. Tobias, ed., pp. 169–182, 208–210. Norman: University of Oklahoma Press.
1987a Morality, Personhood, Tricksters, and Youths: Some Narrative Images of Ethics Among Bimin-Kuskusmin. *In* An-

thropology in the High Valleys. L. L. Langness and T. E. Hays, eds., pp. 283–366. Novato: Chandler and Sharp Publishers Inc.

1987b Ritual Rank, the Self, and Ancestral Power: Liturgy and Substance in a Papua New Guinea Society. *In* Drugs in Western Pacific Societies. L. Lindstrom, ed., pp. 149–196. Association for Social Anthropology in Oceania Monograph Series, no. 11. Lanham: University Press of America.

1992 Wisdom and Practice: The Mythic Making of Sacred History Among the Bimin-Kuskusmin of Papua New Guinea. *In* Discourse and Practice. F. Reynolds and D. Tracy, eds., pp. 13–50. Albany: State University of New York Press.

n.d.a Ethnohistory and Myths of Migration, Settlement, and Origin. Unpublished manuscript.

n.d.b The Mythological Character of Bimin-Kuskusmin Ethnohistory. Unpublished manuscript.

n.d.c Places of Origin and Paths of Migration in Bimin-Kuskusmin Myth. Unpublished manuscript.

n.d.d Ethnohistorical Accounts of the Bimin-Kuskusmin Ritual Center. Unpublished manuscript.

Read, K. E.

1955 Morality and the Concept of the Person Among the Gahuku-Gama. Oceania 25:233–282.

Swadling, Pamela

1983 How Long Have People Been in the Ok Tedi Impact Region? Papua New Guinea National Museum Record no. 8.

1984 Sepik Prehistory. Paper presented at the Wenner-Gren Symposium, Sepik Research Today. Basel, Switzerland.

1986 Glimpses of Pre-Historic Contacts Within and Beyond the Sepik-Ramu. Paper presented at the Sepik Symposium, Mijas.

1988 The Sepik-Ramu. Boroko: Papua New Guinea National Museum.

Swadling, Pamela, T. Mawe, and W. Tomo

1990 Archaeology of Telefolip. *In* Children of Afek. B. Craig and D. Hyndman, eds., pp. 109–114. Sydney: Oceania Monographs.

Watson, J.

1965 From Hunting to Horticulture in the New Guinea Highlands. Ethnology 4:295–309.

1977 Pigs, Fodder and the Jones Effect in Post-Ipomoean New Guinea. Ethnology 16:57–70.

Wurm, S. A.

1982 Papuan Languages of Oceania. Tübingen: Gunter Narr Verlag.

NOTES

1. The field research among the Bimin-Kuskusmin (from 1971 to 1973, in 1979, and in 1982) from which the data for this chapter were drawn was generously supported by the National Institutes of Health, the Cornell University–Ford Foundation Humanities and Social Sciences Program, the Center for South Pacific Studies of the University of California at Santa Cruz, and the University of Rochester. The New Guinea Research Unit of the Research School of Pacific Studies of the Australian National University, the Department of Anthropology and Sociology of the University of Papua New Guinea, and later the Papua New Guinea Institute of Applied Social and Economic Research provided much valuable assistance. Above all, however, an immeasurable debt of gratitude is owed to those senior ritual elders, renowned repositories of the knowledge of past and place, who shared such vivid and intricate mythicohistorical portraits of patterns of origin, migration, and settlement, and who wondered why my questions seemed to imply that ethnohistorical accounts and mythic narratives revealed different images of the past or that there was only one single past. For insightful and useful remarks on and criticisms of an early version of this paper, I am especially grateful to Tim Bayliss-Smith, Murray Chapman, Andrew J. Strathern, and Gabriele Stürzenhofecker.

2. In contemporary ethnographic and linguistic studies, the coherence and integrity of the Mountain-Ok as a cultural region has variously been cast in terms of a marked similarity in sociocultural forms (Poole 1976), ritual institutions, particularly cult organizations and rites of male initiation (Barth 1971, 1987), and language structures (Healey 1964). Despite a striking isomorphism in the maps drawn of this region from these different perspectives, however, there are notable intraregional differences, which may suggest significant sociocultural affinities of various Mountain-Ok groups with different aspects of the periphery of the region and beyond. Indeed, it has been argued that the northern, western, and southern boundaries of the Mountain-Ok often seem to be blurred and to be more or less constituted as ethnic continua or gradients, with only the eastern boundary of the Strickland Gorge having formed an effective barrier to migration, interaction, and influence (see Bulmer and Bulmer 1964). The Bimin-Kuskusmin ethnohistorical and mythological evidence, as well as contemporary practices of bridge-building, trade, and intermarriage, however, suggest that the Strickland did not represent a barrier to contact, migration, and sociocultural influence.

3. For example, Bimin-Kuskusmin engage in a form of "ethnoarchaeology." Having identified signs of early sites of human habitation within the 'center place', ritual elders organize or commission deliberate excavations of such sites in order to increase stocks of *sacrae* associated with early ancestors, when it is deemed necessary to enhance the efficacy of the rituals of particular cult houses. The local interpretation of the ancestral identity and significance of particular artifacts that are unearthed is based upon a rather crude

notion of stratigraphic context, and careful attention is focused on the character of the soil, the mountain elevation of the site, the evidence of identifiable flora and fauna, the coexistence of different artifacts, and other characteristics that lend meaning to a stratum and locate it in a series of strata associated with ancestral eras. Such artifacts typically include axes, adzes, clubheads, mortars, pestles, iron pyrite fire-making stones, carved or inscribed stones, flint or chert chisels or pounders, and bone or stone nasal ornaments, and each is given an ancestral identity and thus a place among the *sacrae* of a clan cult house.

4. Among contemporary peoples of the Mountain-Ok, loss of control over fires set to clear gardens, to drive game, or to provide for cooking or comfort in garden or forest is common and often has devastating ecological effects in small areas over at least limited periods of time. Uncontrolled fires set by lightning are also locally recognized to have similar effects.

5. Bimin-Kuskusmin tend to view the relatively recent appearance of areas of grassland within the sphere of their gardening and residential areas as a slow encroachment from the older and more extensive grasslands along the western flank of the Strickland at the eastern periphery of their territorial domain. In turn, these Strickland grasslands are seen as historical intrusions emanating from the highlands to the east, accompanied by the appearance of a new, honeyless kind of bee, bound up with the advent of colonial exploration, and affecting the ritual integrity and soil fertility of their domain (see Poole 1986). Indeed, they recognize a decline in soil fertility following the appearance of the grasses and have taken extensive ritual measures to halt or slow the invasion of such grasslands. They do not recognize as causal in the matter, however, the fact that they have long used fire as a technique to drive game along the Strickland and to clear patches of forest in the vicinity for stands of semicultivated fruit trees.

6. Bimin-Kuskusmin ethnohistorical and mythological narratives describe the successive spread of barren grasslands around Telefomin before the appearance of bird-of-paradise hunters late in the last century. They attribute the expansion and barrenness of these grasslands to the ritual "attacks" of intruders from the south, bringing destructive powers up the Fly.

7. Many local traditions in the Mountain-Ok, especially in the western areas of the region, seem to recognize, mutatis mutandis, that the advent of the grasslands and consequent evidence of soil infertility are a result of human clearing and gardening activity—perhaps exacerbated by a decline in the efficacy of local ritual performances and a rise in strange alien influences from the periphery.

8. It should be noted that the expansion of grasslands in the area of the Bimin-Kuskusmin is far less extensive and more recent than in the vicinity of Telefomin—perhaps a combined result of later human habitation and cultivation, different ecological conditions, somewhat different and less disruptive practices of swidden cultivation, a smaller and more dispersed population, and a gardening cycle that exhibits shorter active and

longer fallow cycles. Long aware of the more extensive and expanding grasslands to the west and of historical circumstances seen to accompany this ecological change, Bimin-Kuskusmin attribute this progressive transformation to a steady erosion of the efficacy of ritual among the Telefolmin and, thus, among groups within the immediate orbit of the Telefolmin ritual system.

9. See Watson 1965, 1977; Brookfield 1972; Brookfield and White 1968; Clarke 1966; Golson 1977, 1982. For a local mapping of categories of ethnic groups, their sociocultural characteristics, their concentric arrangements, and their interactions with Bimin-Kuskusmin, see Poole 1983. One mode of marking ethnic difference among these ritually identified and aligned groups is, from the Bimin-Kuskusmin perspective, the character of their secret knowledge concerning the esoterica of taro and marsupials—not sweet potatoes and pigs.

10. Although, with the notable exception of certain communities among the southern Oksapmin, most of the Mountain-Ok groups appear to emphasize the paramount nutritional and ritual significance of taro (*Colocasia esculenta*) as the primary subsistence crop of importance and although taro is given the greatest cultural elaboration and social anchorage (both symbolically and transactively), the amount of sweet potatoes grown and consumed is considerable and increasing (see Bayliss-Smith 1985). There is some evidence for suggesting, however, that the western Mountain-Ok, particularly in the vicinity of Telefomin, may have experienced an invasion of certain taro diseases and parasites emanating from farther to the west, which, when coupled with other ecological constraints emerging on the terrain most suitable for the cultivation of taro, may have led to further reliance on sweet potato. The matter of the relationship between sweet potatoes and domestic pig herds, nonetheless, is more complex, although most groups in the region associated with sweet potato cultivation do appear to feed pigs the tubers at least to some extent. With an expanding population, a proportionally greater emphasis on the exploitation of game through hunting, a diminishing forest habitat of game with the advent of expanding grasslands, and a consequent decline in protein harvested by hunting, in the western Mountain-Ok around Telefomin, both ethnohistorical and archaeological evidence suggest that increases in sweet potato cultivation were accompanied by expansions of domestic pig herds. In the eastern Mountain-Ok as represented here by the Bimin-Kuskusmin, both sweet potatoes and domestic pigs were less prevalent, and more extensive tracts of forest—less eroded by expanding areas of grassland—were richer in game. Nonetheless, among Bimin-Kuskusmin the feeding of pigs is substantially focused on encouraging them to forage in areas of grassland, forest, and gardens long turned to fallow. Furthermore, Bimin-Kuskusmin and their domestic pigs tend to reside at or beyond the upper limit of the altitudinal range of feral boars, and ritual prescriptions enforce a castration of all domestic boars when they are probably still reproductively immature. Thus, small domestic pig herds must be replenished primarily through the arduous cap-

ture of feral piglets—a comparatively inefficient strategy for building sizable pig herds however they may subsequently be fed.

11. Such altitudinally variable enforced migrations may confront pronounced kinds of variation in the malarial character of the environment. Groups moving from high areas where malaria is essentially nonexistent or quite low in prevalence to lower altitudes where malaria is endemic may suffer population declines both in the short term (from dramatic increases in malaria-induced mortality) and in the long term (when survival to reproductive age, fecundity, and infant and child mortality are all implicated in the epidemiological pattern).

12. Such practices seem to include infanticide, postpartum conception taboos, prolonged breastfeeding, food taboos denying certain protein to women, and various techniques of contraception or abortion or patterns of sexual abstinence to ensure widely spaced birth intervals (see Poole 1982a). Bimin-Kuskusmin birth intervals in the early 1970s were consistently between three and five years, and one of twins—divined to be not human—was killed at birth.

13. Bimin-Kuskusmin traditions represent all of these processes at different mythicohistorical moments in their local portrait of expansion from the Telefomin center.

14. Bimin-Kuskusmin narratives represent various disasters befalling taro since the end of the primordial era when the advent of mortality brought a progressive erosion of the efficacy of rituals focused on taro. The periodic misfortune of longest duration appears to be drought, necessitating the complete harvesting of taro from all gardens and the embedding of stalks in the mud of riverbeds to preserve these stocks for further planting. Over a time period probably covering the better part of the last century, however, there are detailed mythicohistorical accounts of the ravages of feral pigs in the lower-altitude taro gardens, the periodic appearance of taro-leaf blight (*Phytophthora colocasiae*) and possibly the Dasheen mosaic virus with the last seventy years, and invasions of the taro beetle (*Papuana* spp.) in gardens cultivated in the expanding grasslands shortly thereafter. Dispersed outbreaks of taro-leaf blight inhibiting corm growth continue to appear (Cape 1981; Pearson and Thistleton 1981).

15. Ethnohistorical tracings of paths of migration among Bimin-Kuskusmin often include not only detailed descriptions of named rivers, waterfalls, mountains, and other geographic features of passage, and attention to diverse sociocultural features of populations on these paths, but also the serial transformations of the cognates of selected lexical items that figure prominently in the narratives. Indeed, the initial narrative marking of a centripetal path of historical migration toward the 'center place', many of which are also seen to trace centrifugal paths of trade from the 'center place', is often noted as a *takhaak weeng* 'line of speech', connoting an ancestral connection.

16. This more general image is drawn from aspects of more synthetic portraits of New Guinea prehistory that appear possibly linked to the pre-

history of the Mountain-Ok (see Brown 1978; Bulmer 1964, 1975; Bulmer and Bulmer 1964; Craig 1981, 1984; Feil 1987; Swadling 1983, 1988).

17. The 'center place' is invariably portrayed mythologically as a stable, contiguous territory constituted by an underground system of capillaries through which course oil (the 'semen' of Afek), integrated by rites to ensure the flow of oil and the fertility of land, and founded and bounded by Afek in the primordial era (Poole 1986). However, ethnohistorical accounts reveal a constant reconfiguration of the 'center place' as territories are gained and lost through various forms of conflict and subsequent movement. Most notably, Bimin-Kuskusmin note previous occupations of territories now under the dominion of other ethnic groups to their north (in what is the present Oksapmin area), toward the west (in the present Feramin domain), and a gradual encroachment toward the south in their own expansion (see Poole 1976).

18. The notion of a gradual, implacable decline in the efficacy of ritual is common throughout much of the Mountain-Ok (Barth 1987). Among Bimin-Kuskusmin, such decline is marked both in a moral and cognitive impoverishment of human capacity and agency since the primordial era of immortality (Poole 1984b, 1985, 1987a) and in a consequent decline in the powers of ritual knowledge and performance (Poole 1982b, 1987b).

19. It should be noted that Bimin-Kuskusmin build and maintain both permanent and semipermanent bridges across the Strickland for purposes of trade with several small groups on the eastern flank of the river gorge and believe that these shallow direct trade relations ultimately connect them to more extensive trade networks extending eastward, both north and south across the Lagaip, beyond Kopiago, and down the Strickland, more deeply into the highlands. These trade networks yield distinctive sets of drums, shells, plumes, skins, quarried stones, pendants, pig relics, and sweet potato stocks, some of which represent Bimin-Kuskusmin trade monopolies as they enter into local regional transactions extending westward into the Mountain-Ok and perhaps beyond. A shallow network of intermarriage across the Strickland is commonly said to be *taak'kuun*, the 'spine' of such trade.

20. In this primordial era, the sweet potato did not yet appear in its subsequent forms but was disguised as forms of *Pueraria* and *Dioscorea* and other no longer extant tubers. It was an important ritual secret of women, who then controlled the major cults and rites. It is claimed that women continue to hold these undisclosed secrets. Thus, for women, the sweet potato, *Pueraria*, and certain yams form a powerful ritual complex, and this complex possesses both 'ritual strength' and 'bodily strength' when brought into the arenas of secret female rites.

21. Afek did not disclose the secrets of taro until she had developed the secrets of the sweet potato-*Pueraria*-yam complex and revealed them to women, journeyed to the west to create the myriad kinds of taro in secret gardens in deep caverns, and returned to the east to present the taro and its secrets to men—who had by then gained control of the cults and rites in her absence.

22. Such modes of pig husbandry included the enticement of pigs to forage in forest and fallowed garden, the deliberate cultivation of stocks of earthworms and grubs as pig fodder in rotting stumps of felled trees, and secret preparations of sago, bananas, yams, and *Pueraria*.

23. The term *kamok* is cognate to Enga terms for big-man status far to the east (A. J. Strathern pers. comm.). Indeed, there are aspects of the Bimin-Kuskusmin status of *kamok*, especially as the status is portrayed in mythico-historical terms of earlier eras, that are reminiscent of some features of the so-called big-man complex in the Western Highlands, although never as elaborated as among the Enga-speaking groups. The contemporary sense of *kamok*, however, stands in marked contrast to the more ritually embedded statuses of *kunum aiyem* and *kunum kusem*, which exhibit more the qualities of the "great-man complex."

24. Once the primordial matriarchy had been overturned and men controlled the primary cults and rites, the sweet potato became *yemen yangus* 'female food', and sweet potato gardens the exclusive domain of women. Yet, because of the secret power of the sweet potato-*Pueraria*-yam complex in women's rites, the sweet potato hearth was retained in male cult houses as a necessarily complementary hearth to the hearth associated with taro. Men, nonetheless, acknowledge that the ritual significance of these sweet potato hearths is ambiguous and is bound up with women's ritual secrets to which they are not privy. In some women's secret rites, however, temporary hearths are constructed with sweet potato at the center and taro at the periphery.

25. See Poole 1983, 1987a.

DUNA IN BETWEEN

Scales of Variation in Montane New Guinea

Gabriele Stürzenhofecker

Comparative surveys of societies and cultures in the highlands region of New Guinea have tended to focus on hypotheses linking material factors to aspects of social structure. A recent summation of this approach has been provided by Daryl Feil (Feil 1987), building on earlier work by James Watson (see Watson 1977), H. C. Brookfield (Brookfield with Hart 1971), and Paula Brown (Brown 1978). These authors have provided sophisticated analyses of variables (for example, M. Meggitt's hypothesis linking population density, agrarian pressure, and effective patrilineality [Meggitt 1965]) as a means to refine earlier impressions and arguments concerning the determinants of variation. Brown, drawing on her collaborative work with Aaron Podolefsky, has shown an association between individual rules of land tenure and population density or agricultural intensification; while Feil has sought to demonstrate a systematic east-west continuum in the Papua New Guinea highlands that corresponds to different trajectories of social evolution. Feil has also built his work explicitly around an attempt to match prehistorical data with the analysis of contemporary patterns of social structure and has drawn a series of pictures of a gestalt kind, which suggest that the greatest evolution of societal forms has occurred in the Melpa and Enga areas at the western end of his continuum.

Classificatory exercises of this kind have great virtue, in that they enable us to obtain a synoptic view of intersocietal variation and to make a coherent interpretation of it. However, the enterprise inevitably raises other problems, which center on cases and areas that remain anomalous and refractory to Feil's classificatory methods. J. Weiner's edited volume on Mountain Papuans pointed to some of these problems, as seen from the southern fringes of the highlands—

where distinct forms of sociality have emerged (centered on longhouse residence and exchange relations between small lineal units), coupled with cultural features (ritual homosexuality, for example) that are absent throughout most of the highlands (Weiner 1988). Maurice Godelier has recently attempted to integrate all comparative discussions under two categories of "big-man" and "great-man" societies, an approach that follows his earlier ethnographic placement of the Baruya (Godelier 1982; Godelier and Strathern 1991). These approaches all involve an intuitive choice of core variables for discussion, and an attempt to build around the core a number of further variables in such a way as to present "structural complexes" of features that can then be imaginatively linked to ideas of evolution or prehistory, in a two-way movement between past and present.

The present paper seeks to add to this existing literature in two ways: first, to employ a number of statistical methods through which a more graphic and detailed mode of depicting structural complexes can be achieved; and second, to use these methods to illuminate the anomalous categorization of the Duna people, who belong to the far western end of the highlands region in Papua New Guinea (see maps 1 and 2). Further, these methods—multidimensional scaling and cluster analysis—can be used to tackle a problem of considerable difficulty and interest, that of the relationship between linguistic and cultural differentiation in the highlands (for discussion on data from the Northern New Guinea coast, see R. L. Welsch, J. Terrell, and J. A. Nadolski 1992). To date, little has been established on this topic, beyond I. Dyen's (Dyen 1965) original proposition of a correlation between language size and origin points, by which the eastern highlands become the original source and the western highlands the areas of most recent diffusion. In these terms, as in others, the Duna are anomalous, however, and I will look for explanations as to why this should be so.

I will first give some ethnographic background on the Duna. Then I will look at linguistic and ethnohistorical information that poses the problem of the Duna's classificatory status in regional terms. I will then show how statistical methods can be used to situate the Duna more accurately in relation to their neighbors and thus to cluster them with some of these neighbors in ways that are comparable to what is suggested from the linguistic and ethnohistorical spheres.

THE DUNA

Some 15,000 speakers of the Duna language live in three main river valleys in the region immediately east of the Strickland River, stretch-

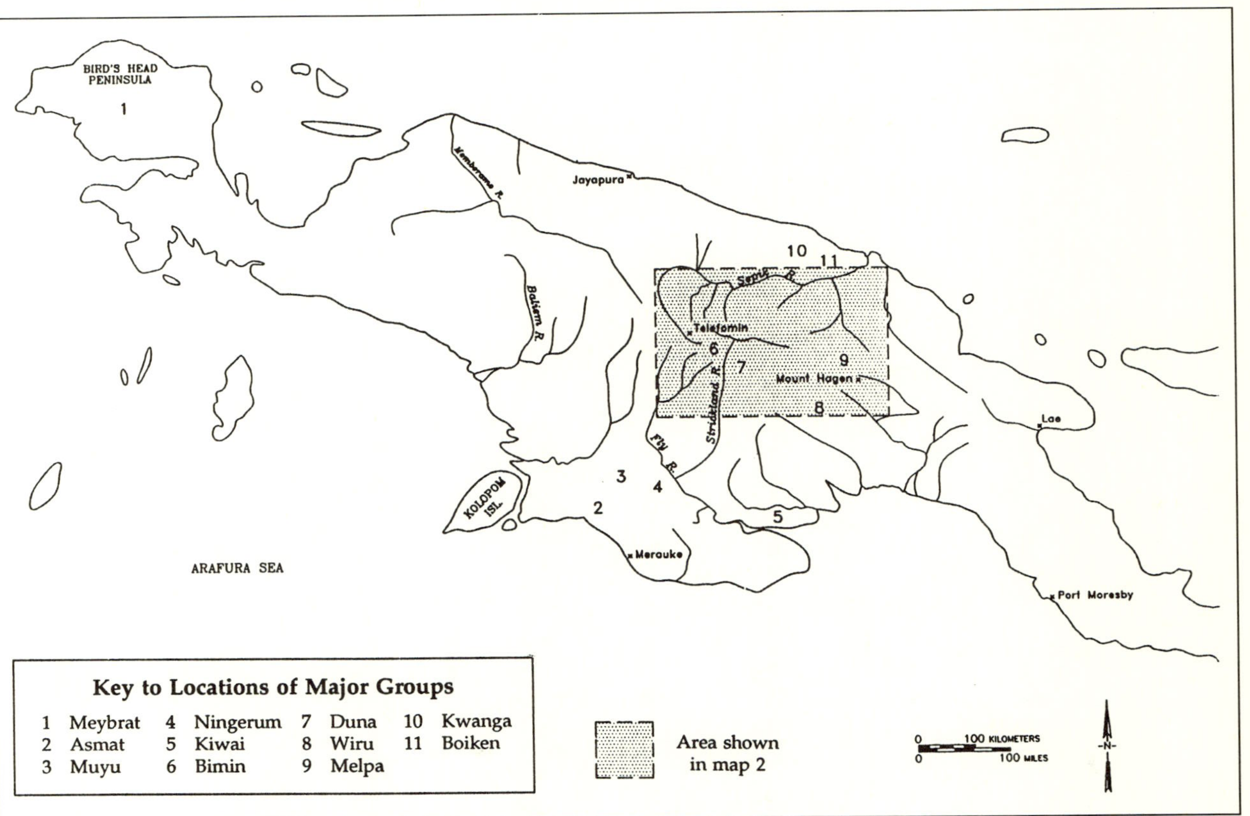

Map 1. Adapted from Swadling, 1983.

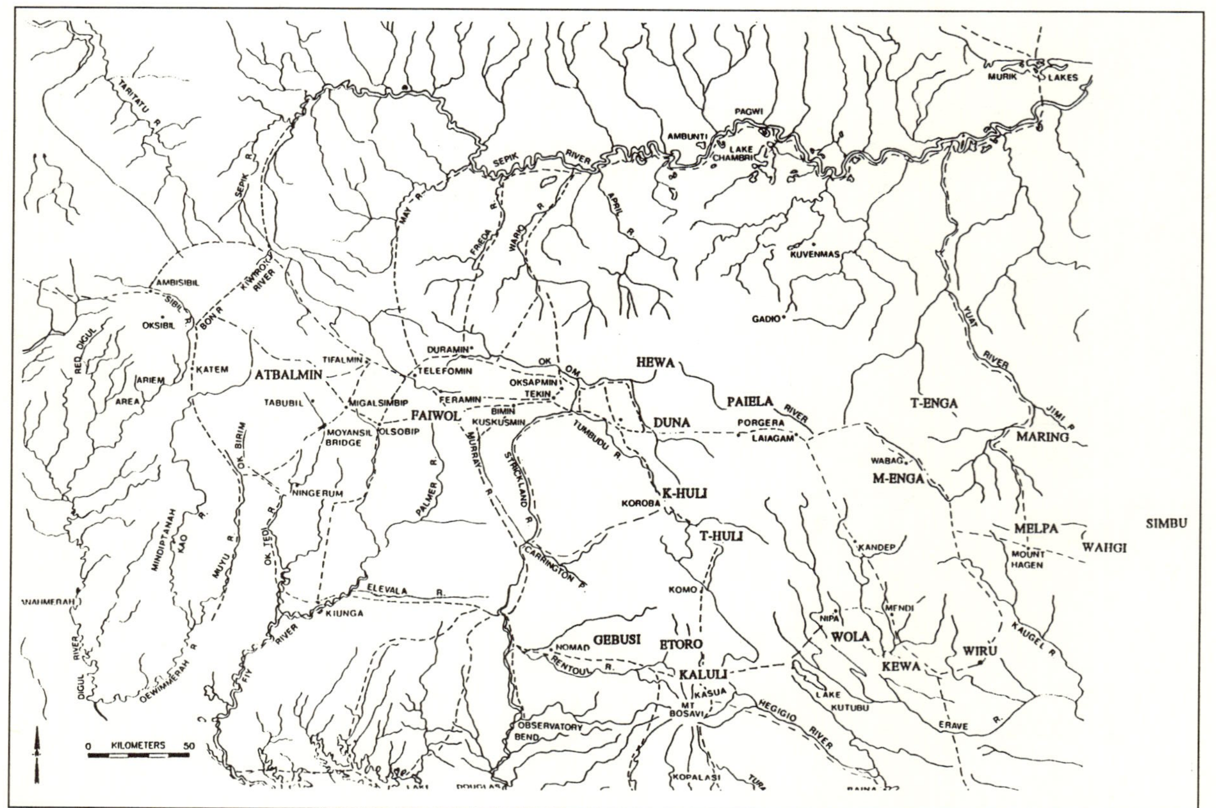

Map 2. Adapted from Swadling, 1983.

ing from the crest of the Müller Range to the low divide between Lake Kopiago and the Lagaip River and extending from the Strickland River to the headwaters of the Tumbudu and Logoiya (Modjeska 1977:1–15). The immediate neighbors of the Duna are the Huli to the south, the Hewa in the north, and the Paiela to the east. Across the Strickland their closest neighbors are the Oksapmin and the Bimin-Kuskusmin. Their residential mobility extends beyond the limits of Duna country and into the territories of neighboring ethnic and linguistic groups, with whom the Duna intermarry. According to C. N. Modjeska (1977: 11), descent affiliations are traced to Bogaia and Oksapmin ancestors, as well as to Hewa, Huli, and Paiela groups. Traditionally, Duna were intermediary in the trade networks linking the Hewa and Paiela to groups across the Strickland—to the Oksapmin and the Bimin, for example (Swadling 1983:90–111; Poole this volume). Considerable interchange of cultural and linguistic elements is reported along the transitional boundary with Huli country (Modjeska 1977:12).

The Duna are an intriguing case to be considered in classificatory exercises on highland societies because of their structural ambiguity in the linguistic picture as well as with respect to sociocultural traits. The linguistic picture appears equivocal if we look at the percentages of cognates the Duna share with their neighbors: Huli 31 percent, Bogaia 28 percent, Paiela 27 percent, Hewa 2 percent, Bimin 1 percent, Oksapmin 1 percent (Modjeska 1977:12). With respect to structural features, however, the Duna language is more closely related to the Ok and Bosavi languages than to either Huli or Paiela. Accordingly two different linguistic classifications have been presented. Stephen Wurm (1964) initially classified the Duna language as the sole member of the aberrant western family of the East New Guinea Highlands (ENGH) Stock, and it was later designated by him as a family-level isolate within this stock (Wurm 1964; Wurm and Laycock 1970). C. L. Voorhoeve, on the other hand, includes Duna in the Central and South New Guinea (CSNG) Stock on grounds of structural similarity with Ok and Bosavi languages (Voorhoeve 1975). More recently, Wurm (1982) has agreed to this classification of the Duna language and argues that the apparent inconsistency in the classification of Duna appears justifiable because the lexical relationship between Duna and languages of the West-Central Family of the ENGH Stock is overall fairly low. However, this fact seems to have been obscured by heavy borrowing by Duna from Huli of the West-Central Family. At the same time, Duna differs structurally and typologically from the ENGH Stock languages and is more similar to some languages of the CSNG Stock (Wurm 1982:117).

Thus the linguistic picture is anything but straightforward; it may, however, be indicative of a history of intermeshing of cultural and linguistic forms originating from the Western Highlands and the Fly and Strickland rivers area. Modjeska (1977:12) suggests that the Duna represent an ethnological amalgam of ancestral forms originating from their eastern and western neighboring regions, resulting in a dual influence that contributed to the societal and linguistic formation of the Duna people and their culture. Ethnohistorically, the idea can be supported by the Duna origin myths of local parishes, suggesting a mixing of both western and eastern-southeastern populations in the settlement of Duna country:

> Some founders are said to have originated from the regions west of the Strickland or south of the Müllers, while others originated from Huli country or Ipili-Paiela to the east. The former are portrayed in the origin stories as magical, capable of travelling underground, changing form and influencing the fertility of the soil. The latter are mundane immigrants without magical powers. (Modjeska 1977:7)

According to Modjeska's interpretation of the Duna narratives, the Strickland was seen as the primal origin place of all humanity, and from there people scattered and dispersed. Earliest parish histories in the Tumbudu Valley, where Modjeska worked, date from between nine and fifteen generations back, and Modjeska suggests that the Duna language and culture may have developed under the influence of a Huli spillover dating from the adoption of the sweet potato cultivation in the Tari basin and acting upon an already present population substratum of western and eastern populations (Swadling 1983:32; Modjeska 1977:12, 13, 30).

In this context it is interesting to note some aspects of the archaeological situation outlined briefly by Pamela Swadling (1983). She suggests that within the Duna area only the Lake Kopiago basin may have had a taro-time.[1] (The lake, according to mythology, was created by a boy pulling out a huge taro, leaving a big hole that filled up with water.) The remains of a 38-square-kilometer ditch complex found at the Lake Kopiago seem to support this idea. Swadling further notes that Kopiago may have a considerable antiquity of human settlement (Swadling 1983:33). One of the intriguing aspects emerging out of the Ok Tedi impact study is the likelihood that many members of the CSNG Stock may have a common ancestry (ibid.:29).

REGIONAL ANALYSIS

In order to situate the Duna more clearly within their overall region, I constructed a matrix consisting of 16 attributes distributed among 21 groups. (For further discussion on attribute selection and coding see the appendix at the end of this chapter.)[2] The groups chosen came from the two language categories the Duna have variously been classified with, that is, the CSNG Stock and the ENGH Stock. Although language data for these areas are incomplete in terms of percentages of shared cognates, it is nevertheless possible to produce a dendrogram based on available taxonomies that will show farthest-neighbor relationships. In this representation, the Duna language has been assigned membership of the CSNG Stock, as agreed by both Wurm and Voorhoeve (see figure 1).

The problem, therefore, is to determine the extent of overall agreement or correspondence between this taxonomy and the

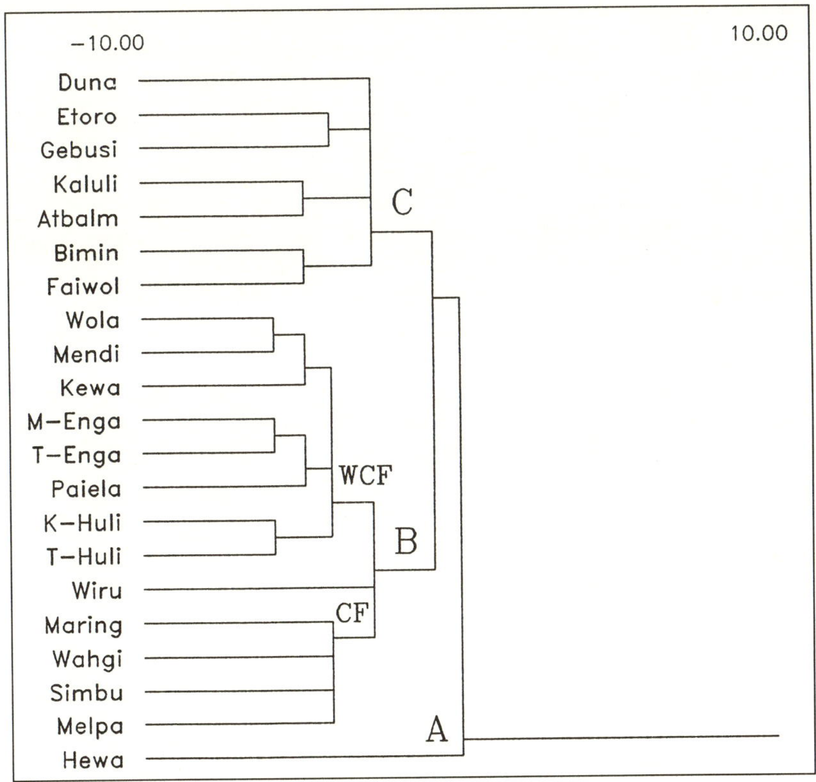

Fig. 1. Linguistic affiliation dendrogram (complete linkage method): A = Sepik-Ramu phylum; B = East New Guinea Highlands stock; C = Central and South New Guinea stock; WCF = west-central family; CF = central family.

groups that emerge from the scaling analysis of sociocultural attributes.

MULTIDIMENSIONAL SCALING

Figure 2 shows the patterns of association when using Multi-Dimensional Scaling (MDS), a multi-variate data-reduction technique used to tease out underlying relationships among a set of observations. Its particular advantage is that it produces a graphic display of the relationships among a set of variables.

By superimposing the patterns of association in the cluster-analysis on MDS, we see that two major clusters appear, each containing a number of subclusters. Cluster 1 contains two smaller subclusters: one (1a) is formed by the Wahgi and Maring groups (L and N), and the other (1b) consists of the Melpa, Mendi, Wiru, Kewa, and Wola groups. The association of the Melpa with the Mendi, Wiru, Kewa, and Wola is not predictable from the linguistic picture. Linguistically, the Melpa are more closely related to the Wahgi, Simbu, and Maring (see figure 1), but here they are differentiated from their own language family and are associated in sociocultural terms southward with the Mendi, Wiru, Kewa, and Wola. The reason for this may be found in three structural variables, whose presence or absence the Melpa share with the Mendi, Kewa, Wiru, and Wola, but which set them apart from their own language group: circulating cults, bachelor cults, and women's participation in exchange.[3] The linkage of Melpa with the four southern groups, however, cuts across two language families within the ENGH Stock, that is, the Central Family and the West-Central Family (CF and WCF in figure 1). The Wiru are an aberrant member of the West-Central Family, showing linguistically and here also culturally almost as much linkage with the Melpa (20 percent shared cognates) as with any of the groups within the West-Central Family. Historically the Wiru maintained many ties with the Ialibu area, the southernmost part of the Hagen language area (Clark 1985; Strathern, this volume).

The Maring and Wahgi subcluster (1a) in cluster 1 does not require any special explanation since it does not show surprising features but is in accordance with linguistic affiliations and geographic proximity. The Maring, for example, are linguistically more closely related to the Wahgi (and Simbu) than to the Melpa. We know separately from the patterns represented in figure 3 that the Maring have greater similarities with their Wahgi neighbors than with the Melpa. The large Enga and Simbu populations (B, C, and M in figure 2) do

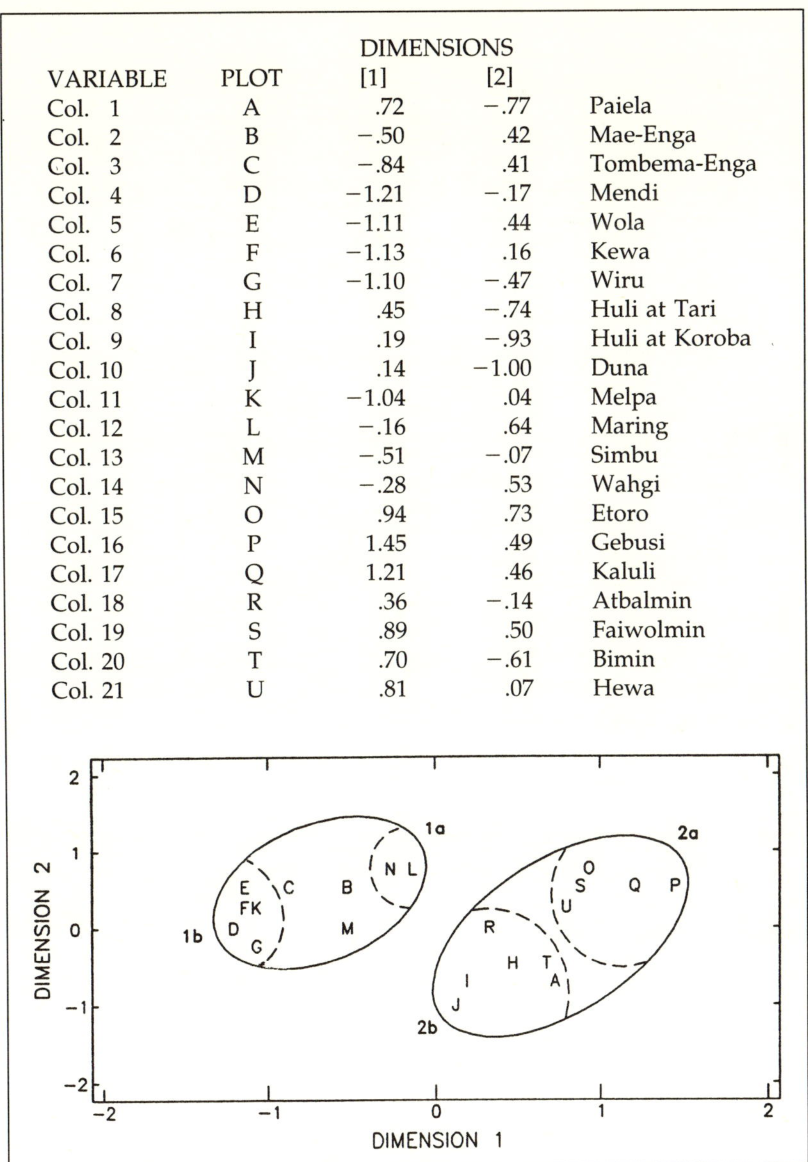

VARIABLE	PLOT	DIMENSIONS [1]	[2]	
Col. 1	A	.72	−.77	Paiela
Col. 2	B	−.50	.42	Mae-Enga
Col. 3	C	−.84	.41	Tombema-Enga
Col. 4	D	−1.21	−.17	Mendi
Col. 5	E	−1.11	.44	Wola
Col. 6	F	−1.13	.16	Kewa
Col. 7	G	−1.10	−.47	Wiru
Col. 8	H	.45	−.74	Huli at Tari
Col. 9	I	.19	−.93	Huli at Koroba
Col. 10	J	.14	−1.00	Duna
Col. 11	K	−1.04	.04	Melpa
Col. 12	L	−.16	.64	Maring
Col. 13	M	−.51	−.07	Simbu
Col. 14	N	−.28	.53	Wahgi
Col. 15	O	.94	.73	Etoro
Col. 16	P	1.45	.49	Gebusi
Col. 17	Q	1.21	.46	Kaluli
Col. 18	R	.36	−.14	Atbalmin
Col. 19	S	.89	.50	Faiwolmin
Col. 20	T	.70	−.61	Bimin
Col. 21	U	.81	.07	Hewa

Fig. 2. Multi-dimensional scaling of all groups according to sociocultural attributes.

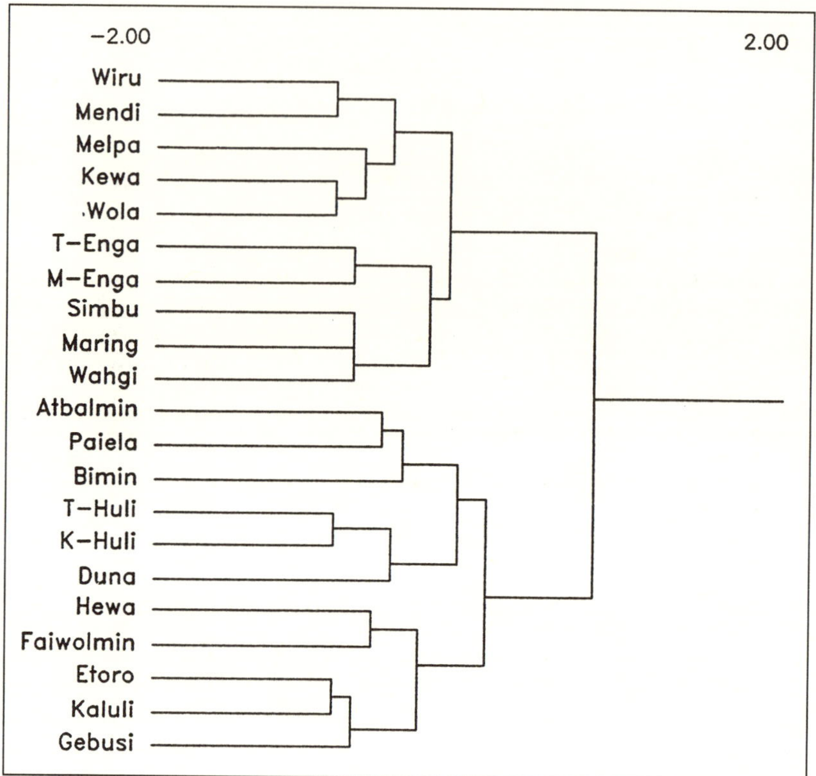

Fig. 3. Dendrogram of all groups according to sociocultural attributes (complete linkage method; farthest neighbor).

Note: The computer facilities available to me offered only nearest- or farthest-neighbor relationships for cluster analysis. Both algorithms generate the same major clustering patterns while differing in minor details that are not relevant for the discussion of this paper.

not exhibit any particular clustering with the other groups; however, they still belong clearly to the major cluster 1.

In cluster 2, three of the groups (O, Q, and P) in one subcluster (2a in figure 2) belong geographically to the Strickland/Bosavi area, stretching from Nomad Patrol Post in the northwest to Mount Bosavi in the southeast. The Etoro and Kaluli (O and Q) live close together along the northern slopes and immediately to the north of Mount Bosavi, the Gebusi farther away and close to Nomad (see map 2). All of them are closely related linguistically and culturally, however, and one of the sociocultural attributes they share is absent in all the other groups on the matrix, that is, ritualized homosexuality (see appendix). The Faiwolmin (S) and Hewa (U) clearly belong to this subcluster. The two groups are neither geographically nor linguistically related. Geographically the Hewa are closer to the Duna, and the Faiwolmin are linguistically and culturally related to the Bimin and Atbalmin and live in geographic proximity to those peoples (see map 2). Their presence in this subcluster may be a result of shared conditions of low population density and demographic fragility.

The two Huli groups (I and H) are to be expected to co-associate. They speak dialects of the same language, share the same wider territory, and are strongly akin culturally. For the Huli, as for the Paiela, their cultural affiliations link them with societies that belong to the CSNG Stock, and thus also across the barrier of the Strickland River.

The second subcluster (2b in figure 2) shows overall some intriguing patterns of configuration and is most relevant for the purpose of this paper. The link between the Duna and the Paiela is surprising on the basis of linguistic relationships. Overall it is very clear that, in terms of the attributes chosen, the Duna do indeed cluster with CSNG Stock categories, rather than with the bulk of the ENGH Stock cases. However, interesting aspects also appear: for example, the Paiela belong linguistically to the ENGH Stock category, but in terms of sociocultural attributes, they cluster with the Duna and within the overall CSNG Stock set. This type of association is paralleled by other parts of the matrix: for example, the Mendi and the Wiru cluster much more closely in sociocultural attributes than in terms of language. A similar pattern holds for the Atbalmin (R) in cluster 2.

These correlates are not immediately predictable or evident from a cursory scan of either linguistic or cultural data. Overall the data set shows a clear bifurcation, placing together on one hand most of the ENGH Stock cases minus the Paiela and the Huli, and on the other hand the CSNG Stock cases plus the Duna, the Paiela, and the Huli (see figure 2).

Looking at the MDS representation, we can see clearly that the data set divides along two major axes, creating distinct units. The most distinct overall division is made by a vertical axis that decisively demarcates societies with the "big-man" form of leadership from societies without it. In cluster 2, the subcluster to which the Duna belong (2b) is also clearly characterized by the strong presence of cognatic features in the system of descent and kinship.[4]

This representation therefore gives us the main outline of divisions within the overall set, while cluster analysis further pinpoints the more detailed linkages. Thus from cluster analysis we can see that the linkage of Duna, Paiela, and Atbalmin is unequivocally a unique point of articulation between the two stocks. Furthermore, there are clear cultural associations that in general link Ok populations west of the Strickland with highlands populations to its east. This finding clearly strengthens the supposition of an ancient connection between Duna and Ok, since the Duna are immediate neighbors of the Ok peoples. The dendrograms of linguistic affiliations and the multidimensional scaling of sociocultural traits show that cultural and linguistic classifications are not necessarily isomorphic.

DISCUSSION: THE DUNA AS AN INTERMEDIATE CATEGORY

The impetus for this paper came from the discovery of a change in classification of the Duna language by linguists over time. The change not only involved the switching of Duna from one family or subfamily to another, but rather to a completely different stock. This shift was made on the grounds of structural (grammatical) elements as opposed to shared cognation percentages. Given all this, it therefore became intriguing to know which stock the Duna were more closely associated with in terms of cultural attributes.

The statistical methods I used indicated the points at which there is or is not a concordance between language and culture. The points where there is not a concordance are the interesting ones because they suggest research problems. The investigation using MDS and cluster analysis clearly shows the Duna's association with the cultures of the CSNG Stock, and that there are cultural affinities that tie them in the CSNG direction rather than in any other. Whether this sharing of cultural features reflects a shared ancestry is another matter. Archaeological data from the Duna drainage system could provide further background to this problem. For the meantime, the ethnohistorical association with Ok cultures is also confirmed, on one hand, while there is also, on the other hand, a clear association with Paiela and Huli, who do belong to the ENGH Stock.[5] It is apparent, therefore, that the Duna are truly very much in between these two large categories, both linguistically and culturally.

Finally, looking at the more detailed picture and patterns of association overall we have discerned a subcluster (2b in figure 2) consisting of the Huli, Duna, Atbalmin, Bimin, and Paiela. One significant feature of this assemblage is that they all share the attributes of cognatic ideology and/or cognatic land inheritance (plus witchcraft).

One might be tempted to suggest that we can set up a geographical category here, previously unrecognized, that we might call the western cognatic belt, placing together societies east and west of the Strickland that have hitherto been considered quite separately.

This last point calls for a more detailed discussion of the cultural affinity and elements shared by groups on both sides of the Strickland. This can most convincingly be illustrated in the case of the Duna and their Ok neighbors. I have already noted that some parish groups among the Duna claim that their founder originated from the regions west of the Strickland and are portrayed in the original stories as magical beings capable of traveling underground and influencing the fertility of the soil (Modjeska 1977:7). Furthermore, in these groups west and east of the Strickland we find a strong cognatic element in relational reckoning.

Further traces of the Duna's culturally in-between status can be found at the level of specific ritual elements. Bachelor cults among Huli and Paiela trace their power to a female spirit or culture heroine, and this element is shared by the Duna in the form of the Palena cult (Stürzenhofecker 1993). Across the Strickland to the west, the same element of a female spirit appears, greatly enhanced, in the powerful figure of Afek whose cult predominates among all the Ok societies. One of the routes Afek is supposed to have taken in entering Ok is from the east, which means the Duna area itself. Further research would enable us to trace this ritual track in more detail. The same motif with a reversed geographical marker is said to be found in the traditions of the Duna Kiria Pulu cult, a cult performed only rarely and not by all the Duna groups. This cult "was linked with the myth of an early ancestress who traversed the world from Ok-country to Tari in pursuit of her pig. At each place where she slept, an *auwi* 'sacred stone' appeared and these places became the sites for Kiria houses" (Modjeska 1991:8). Here then is another "mythically encoded track" (ibid.) showing historic connections between Duna and Ok. Although these facts are fragmentary, they indicate clearly that the Strickland was by no means an impermeable barrier and that there were vigorous social relations conducted to and fro across it.

POSTSCRIPT 1992

The above paper was written prior to fieldwork among the Duna, which I carried out during 1991. A field site, Aluni, was selected within the wider Duna-language area, precisely because it was geographically contiguous with the Strickland River and was also linked—via the small Bogaia-language area—with Strickland/Bosavi peoples. During the course of the fieldwork, it became abundantly evident that at least for Aluni the suggestion that emerged from the earlier statistical analysis—of an in-between status for the Duna—had been essentially correct. Connections through trade, rituals, marriage, and ceremonies with both Oksapmin and Bogaia brought many elements of these cultures into Aluni, and what one uncovers is a mosaic of motifs of various linkages with areas both to the west and southeast. In one respect only does the account have to be modified. According to my Aluni informants, the narrative of the ancestress who traversed Duna-land from the Strickland eastward is not in fact the charter for the Kiria cult but belongs rather to the origin story of a particular clan, the Songwa. The ancestress was linked in a general way to the founding of sacred sites, however, and she is definitely said to have come from Ok, in fact from a place known as Sipuyambo not far from the territory of the Bimin people (Strathern 1993; Strathern in press; Stürzenhofecker 1993; Stürzenhofecker in press).

In general we may observe that this study shows an interesting instance of how quantitative library-based studies may point to and dovetail with intensive ethnographic investigation in the field.

APPENDIX

Brief Notes on the Data Base

1. The matrix for the linguistic affiliations, on page 223, is a similarity matrix, with degrees of closeness of association ranging from 0 to 6. Thus:

Same language but different dialect	6
Same subfamily but different language	5
Same family but different language	4
Same family but different subfamily	4
Same stock but different family	3
Same subphylum but different stock	2
Same phylum but different stock	1
Different phyla	0

2. The matrix for the cultural associations is a present-absent matrix featuring 21 groups and 16 sociocultural traits. The traits are here listed in alphabetical order. Numbers in parentheses indicate the order of appearance of traits in the data matrix.

Bachelor Cults: Boys' temporary seclusion, followed by a public ceremonial parade indicating their manhood. The Huli have a particular version of this, where boys enter the cult and emerge, but some continue as senior bachelors (1).

Bridewealth: Definite payments made by husband's side to wife's side in

DATA MATRIX

GROUPS	1	2	3	4	5	6	7	8	9	10	11	12	13	14	15	16
Paiela	1	0	1	0	0	0	0	0	1	1	1	1	0	1	1	0
M-Enga	1	1	1	0	0	0	1	0	0	0	1	0	0	0	1	1
T-Enga	1	1	0	1	0	0	1	0	0	0	1	0	0	0	1	1
Mendi	0	1	0	1	0	0	1	0	0	0	1	1	1	1	1	1
Wola	0	1	0	0	0	0	1	0	0	0	1	0	1	0	1	1
Kewa	0	1	0	0	0	0	1	0	0	0	1	0	1	1	1	1
Wiru	0	1	0	1	0	0	1	0	0	0	1	1	1	1	1	0
Huli-Tari	1	0	1	0	1	1	0	0	0	0	1	1	0	1	1	0
Huli-Krb	1	1	1	0	1	1	0	0	0	0	1	1	0	1	1	0
Duna	1	1	1	1	0	1	0	0	1	0	1	1	0	1	1	0
Melpa	0	1	0	1	0	1	1	0	0	0	1	0	1	1	1	1
Maring	1	0	0	0	0	1	1	0	0	1	1	1	1	0	1	1
Simbu	1	0	0	0	0	1	1	0	0	0	1	1	1	1	1	1
Wahgi	1	0	0	0	0	1	1	0	0	1	1	0	1	1	1	1
Etoro	1	0	1	0	0	1	1	1	0	1	1	0	0	0	0	0
Gebusi	1	0	1	0	0	1	0	1	0	1	0	0	0	0	0	0
Kaluli	1	0	1	0	0	1	0	1	0	1	1	0	0	0	0	0
Atbalmin	1	0	1	1	0	1	1	0	1	1	1	1	0	1	1	1
Faiwol	0	0	1	0	0	1	1	0	1	1	1	0	0	0	0	0
Bimin	1	0	1	1	1	1	1	0	1	1	1	1	1	1	1	0
Hewa	0	0	1	0	0	1	0	0	0	0	1	0	0	0	0	0
	1	**2**	**3**	**4**	**5**	**6**	**7**	**8**	**9**	**10**	**11**	**12**	**13**	**14**	**15**	**16**

ATTRIBUTES
(1 = present, 0 = absent)

a marriage as a means of effecting the marriage itself whether or not reciprocated with return gifts (11).

Circulating Cults: Cults moving through a region, traded from group to group (see Strathern this volume) (2).

Cognatic Land Inheritance: A formal recognition as well as practice of bilateral principles of land inheritance (12).

Graded Initiation: Gradual transmission of ritual knowledge, encompassing the complete life cycle in stages (9).

High Sexual Segregation: Strict spatial segregation as well as menstrual taboos (3).

Long Genealogies: Ten generations or more. This applies also if long genealogies only appear in a ritual context, as among the Bimin, for example (5).

Matrilateral Payments: Definite payments made by husband's side to wife's side on the birth of children to secure either the child's affiliation or its health (generalized affinal exchanges do not qualify here) (7).

Payments to Allies: Reparation payments made to allies for losses in warfare (15).

Pig Festivals: Climactic occasions where people kill a considerable number of pigs and distribute them. These occasions have to be distinct from compensation payments. The Etoro pig killing for affinal exchanges does not qualify here, because of its very small scale (Kelly 1977:223–224). The Bimin-Kuskusmin pig killing with a maximum of 57 pigs killed—of which most were hunted and not domesticated—does, however, qualify (Poole pers. comm.) (13).

Ritualized Homosexuality: Homosexuality occurring in the context of initiation rituals (8).

Segmentary Territoriality: Territories arranged in accordance with an oppositional hierarchy of groups defined in terms of descent or kinship (16).

Spouse Exchange: The type case of this is known in the literature as sister exchange, but delayed forms of patrilateral cousin marriage are also included as well as the Wahgi rule that in some way a woman must be returned for a woman (10).

Witchcraft: This is a complex variable coded for whenever the source ethnography mentions it with this term, and also in a few cases (Gebusi, for example) where the author uses the term *sorcery,* but the phenomenon is closely akin to what other authors call witchcraft. In general a notion of unconscious, usually cannibalistic malevolence is involved (6).

Women as Healers: Women holding positions as mediums or curers (14).

Women in Exchange: A situation in which women can act as givers and receivers of wealth items in their own right as well as along with men (4).

General Note on Attributes

All these attributes are chosen as formal structural categories that have cultural underpinnings, and not just as statistical tendencies. The attributes have been chosen to delineate enduring cultural features that are linked to significant social practices. It is not implied that they represent all the significant features of the societies chosen; but they do enable us to make viable comparisons between these groups. The exercise could be improved by adding further attributes; but it is difficult to find attributes for which the data can be coded in all the cases chosen. I scanned data in available sources (as listed in the bibliography) and decided upon a coding in terms of the presence or absence of the attributes. In most instances this could be done unambiguously, in line with the definitions of attributes given above. In some cases, I had to exercise my judgment (in relation to witchcraft among the Gebusi, for example).

REFERENCES

Barth, F.
1975 Ritual and Knowledge Among the Baktaman of New Guinea. New Haven: Yale University Press.

Bercovitch, E.
1989 Disclosure and Concealment: A Study of Secrecy Among the Nalumin People of Papua New Guinea. Ph.D. dissertation, Stanford University.

Bernard, R.
1988 Research Methods in Cultural Anthropology. Newbury Park, London, and New Delhi: Sage Publications.

Biersack, A.
1980 The Hidden God: Communication, Cosmology, and Cybernetics Among a Melanesian people. Ph.D. dissertation. University of Michigan.

Brookfield, H. C., with D. Hart
1971 Melanesia. London: Methuen.

Brown, P.
1978 Highland Peoples of New Guinea. New York: Cambridge University Press.

Brown, P., and A. Podolefsky
1976 Population Density, Agricultural Intensity, Land Tenure and Group Size in the New Guinea Highlands. Ethnology 15:211–238.

Clark, J.
1985 From Cults to Christianity. Ph.D. dissertation. University of Adelaide.

Dyen, I.
1965 A Lexicostatistical Classification of the Austronesian Languages. Indiana University Publication in Anthropology and Linguistics 19. IJAL Memoir 19.

Feil, D. K.
1978 Holders of the Way: Exchange and Partnership in an Enga Tee Community. Ph.D. dissertation. Australian National University.
1980 When a Group of Women Takes a Wife: Generalized Exchange and Restricted Marriage in the New Guinea Highlands. Mankind 12:286–299.
1987 The Evolution of Highland Papua New Guinea Societies. Cambridge: Cambridge University Press.

Foley, W. A.
1986 The Papuan Languages of New Guinea. Cambridge Language Surveys. Cambridge: Cambridge University Press.

Frankel, S.
1986 The Huli Response to Illness. Cambridge: Cambridge University Press.

Glasse, R. M.
1965 The Huli of the Southern Highlands. *In* Gods, Ghosts and Men in Melanesia. P. Lawrence and M. Meggitt, eds., pp. 27–49. London, New York, and Melbourne: Oxford University Press.
1968 Huli of Papua. A Cognatic Descent System. Paris: Mouton.

Godelier, Maurice
1982 Social Hierarchies Among the Baruya of New Guinea. *In* Inequality in New Guinea Highlands Societies. A. J. Strathern, ed., pp. 3–34. Cambridge: Cambridge University Press.

Godelier, Maurice, and M. Strathern, eds.
1991 Big Men and Great Men. Personifications of Power in Melanesia. Cambridge: Cambridge University Press.

Jones, B. A.
1980 Consuming Society. Ph.D. dissertation. University of Virginia.

Kelly, R.
1977 Etoro Social Structure: A Study in Structural Contradiction. Ann Arbor: University of Michigan Press.

Knauft, B.
1985 Good Company and Violence. Berkeley: University of California Press.

Meggitt, M.
1965 The Lineage System of the Mae-Enga of New Guinea. New York: Barnes and Noble.

Modjeska, C. N.
1977 Production Among the Duna. Aspects of Horticultural Intensification in Central New Guinea. Ph.D. dissertation. Australian National University.

1991 Post-Ipomean Modernism: The Duna Example. *In* Big Men and Great Men: Personifications of Power in Melanesia. M. Godelier and M. Strathern, eds., pp. 234–255. Cambridge: Cambridge University Press.

Poole, F.J.P.
1981 TAMAM: Ideological and Sociological Configurations of "Witchcraft" Among Bimin-Kuskusmin. Social Analysis 8:58–76.
1982 The Ritual Forging of Identity: Aspects of Person and Self in Bimin-Kuskusmin Male Initiation. *In* Rituals of Manhood. G. Herdt, ed. pp. 99–154. Berkeley: University of California Press.

Rappaport, R. A.
1968 Pigs for the Ancestors. New Haven: Yale University Press.

Schieffelin, E. L.
1976 The Sorrow of the Lonely and the Burning of the Dancers. New York: St. Martin's Press.

Steadman, L.
1971 Neighbors and Killers: Residence and Dominance Among the Hewa of New Guinea. Ph.D. dissertation. Australian National University.

Strathern, A. J.
1971 Wiru and Daribi Matrilateral Payments. Journal of the Polynesian Society 80:449–462.
1972 One Father, One Blood. London: Tavistock.
1993 Great Man, Big Man, Leader: The Link of Ritual Power. Journal de la Société des Océanistes 145–158.
in press Ritual Movements Reconsidered: Ethnohistory of Aluni. *In* Papuan Borderlands: Huli, Duna, and Ipili Perspectives on the New Guinea Highlands. A. Biersack, ed. University of Michigan Press.

Stürzenhofecker, Gabriele
1993 Times Enmeshed: Gender, Space, and History Among the Duna. Ph.D. dissertation. University of Pittsburgh.
in press Sacrificial Bodies and the Cyclicity of Substance. Journal of the Polynesian Society.

Swadling, Pamela
1983 How Long Have People Been in the Ok Tedi Impact Region? Port Moresby: Papua New Guinea National Museum Record no. 8.

Voorhoeve, C.
1975 Central and Western Trans-New Guinea Phylum Languages. Pacific Linguistics, series C, no. 38, pp. 354–459.

Watson, J.
1977 Pigs, Fodder and the Jones Effect in Post-Ipomoean New Guinea. Ethnology 16:57–70.

Weiner, J., ed.
1988 Mountain Papuans. Ann Arbor: University of Michigan Press.

Welsch, R. L., J. Terrell, J. A. Nadolski
1992 Language and Culture on the North Coast of New Guinea. American Anthropologist 94(3):568–600.

Wurm, Stephen
1964 Australian New Guinea Highlands Languages and the Distribution of Their Typological Features. American Anthropologist no. 66 4(2):79–97.
1982 The Papuan Languages of Oceania. Acta Linguistica 7. Tübingen: Gunter Narr.

Wurm, Stephen, ed.
1975 New Guinea Area Languages and Language Study. Vol 1, Papuan Languages and the New Guinea Linguistic Scene. Pacific Linguistics, series C, no. 38.

Wurm, Stephen, and D. Laycock, eds.
1970 Papuan Linguistic Studies in Honor of Arthur Capell. Pacific Linguistics, series C, no. 13.

NOTES

Andrew Strathern has provided great assistance in designing the matrix and gathering coding information for this chapter. Fitz John Porter Poole provided valuable coding information for the Bimin-Kuskusmin. Paul Roscoe's critical reading of an earlier version of this chapter provided the stimulus for further refinement of the matrix. I am grateful to all of them for their input; all errors, however, remain my own.

1. The term *taro-time* is generally used in the literature to refer to the prehistoric period in New Guinea when taro was the staple crop in several parts of the highlands. The sweet potato, which perhaps arrived about three hundred years ago, replaced taro in most regions as a staple crop (but see also Soto and Scaglion this volume).

2. Establishing the variables involved a subjective appraisal of available ethnographic data and required me to code these data in a binary manner, as attributes present or absent. Obviously this reduces the rich complexities of social facts and processes to a simple form. However, this is inevitable if we are to apply this version of cross-cultural analysis to the ethnographic record, while doing our best to present clear definitions and honest assessments of the information presently to hand.

3. Circulating cults are reported in all of the five societies, while bachelor

cults are absent in all of them. Women's participation in exchange is seemingly absent among the Wola and Kewa but is present among the Mendi, Wiru, and Melpa.

4. This finding is a robust one, since neither big-manship nor cognatic ideology appear themselves as attributes in the matrix. We are not therefore dealing simply with a tautologous result.

5. Poole (this volume) provides evidence of one permanent and several temporary bridges across the Strickland, which are maintained by Bimin-Kuskusmin and which enable trade networks between Duna and Bimin to continue over time. My own research in 1991 showed that connections of this kind are very much a part of contemporary life also.

LINES OF POWER

Andrew J. Strathern

INTRODUCTION

In Melanesian societies the drive for self-differentiation has led local populations endlessly to define emic categories in terms of which to contrast themselves with others around them. The dialectical opposite of this process has been their equally strong tendency to communicate with their neighbors by means of ritual cooperation and gift exchanges, which bring them into a commonality of culture. The result of this dialectic at any given time is the ethnographic present. In analysis, also, we can follow this dialectic, alternately attempting to see what makes one set of people different from others and, per contra, in what ways they can be seen as the same. One way of tracking one's way through this problem is to look specifically at those cultural practices and ideas that can be shown to have moved between local populations over time and space. We can ask what has been the dynamic of their movement and how it has modified the relative isolation of these populations from one another. A conclusion that emerges from this perspective is that the boundaries (however they are perceived) between linguistic and cultural units were much more permeable than might be imagined. It follows that the case for a regional time- and space-oriented viewpoint is strengthened by contrast with the ethnographic localism that was our earlier focus. This does not mean, of course, that small-scale studies are invalidated. It merely indicates a better way to contextualize these investigations.

The chief example I will use to illustrate this theme is the geographical dispersion of a particular cult known as the Female Spirit cult, which I first observed during 1964 in the Mount Hagen area of the Western Highlands Province in Papua New Guinea. The example will be set into a wider viewpoint on the spatial tracks of ritual power in areas surrounding the Western Highlands; hence my title, "Lines of Power" (see map on p. 233).

THE FEMALE SPIRIT CULT

This has been described in two previous publications of mine (A. J. Strathern 1970, 1979), as well as in the earlier German ethnographies on Hagen (Vicedom and Tischner 1943–48; Strauss and Tischner 1962). Here I give a schematic account. The cult centers on sacred stones, which are discovered in the environment by cult participants, under the guidance both of local leaders, who are supposedly visited by the Spirit (or Goddess) in dreams, and of ritual experts from outside the local group, who are paid to establish these stones in a secret cult site and perform rituals over them to ensure the fertility of women, crops, and pig herds.

The cult has a male agnatic bias in Hagen, since it is supposed to help men obtain sons by their wives, and it is performed by men alone, women being forbidden to enter the cult site. There is a supposed antipathy between the Goddess and human women that is based on the model of jealousy between *wölik*, 'co-wives'. This is explained by the fact that the Goddess appears in dreams and offers to come to a local group of men as their bride. In Hagen she is said to appear in the costume of a woman from the Tambul area south of Hagen, which is the supposed origin point for the cult. The Goddess has the power to protect men from the dangerous force of women's menstruation. In logical keeping with this idea, she herself is held to be a perpetual virgin. She comes as a bride, but this marriage is not, like a human marriage, consummated by sexual intercourse. Instead, she brings the power of granting fertility to others, acting like a third operator on the human female-male pair. She also gives protection to men against the possibly harmful effects of contact with the menstrual fluids of human females. This notion of the virgin goddess also works in another way, to facilitate the movement of the cult from place to place. As she remains intact, so she can be passed on again to another group of men and continue circulating indefinitely. As an expression of the general passage of female fertility from one area to another, she remains the logical opposite of each individual human female who after marriage stays in the place of her husband and there bears children for him.

Despite the exclusion of women from the cult, the male cultists clearly recognize the female principle in their society by dividing themselves sharply into two moieties, the "men's house" and "women's house" sides, paralleling the conventional residential division of men and women in secular life. Each side is headed by a leader, and each individual has a partner on the other side with whom he

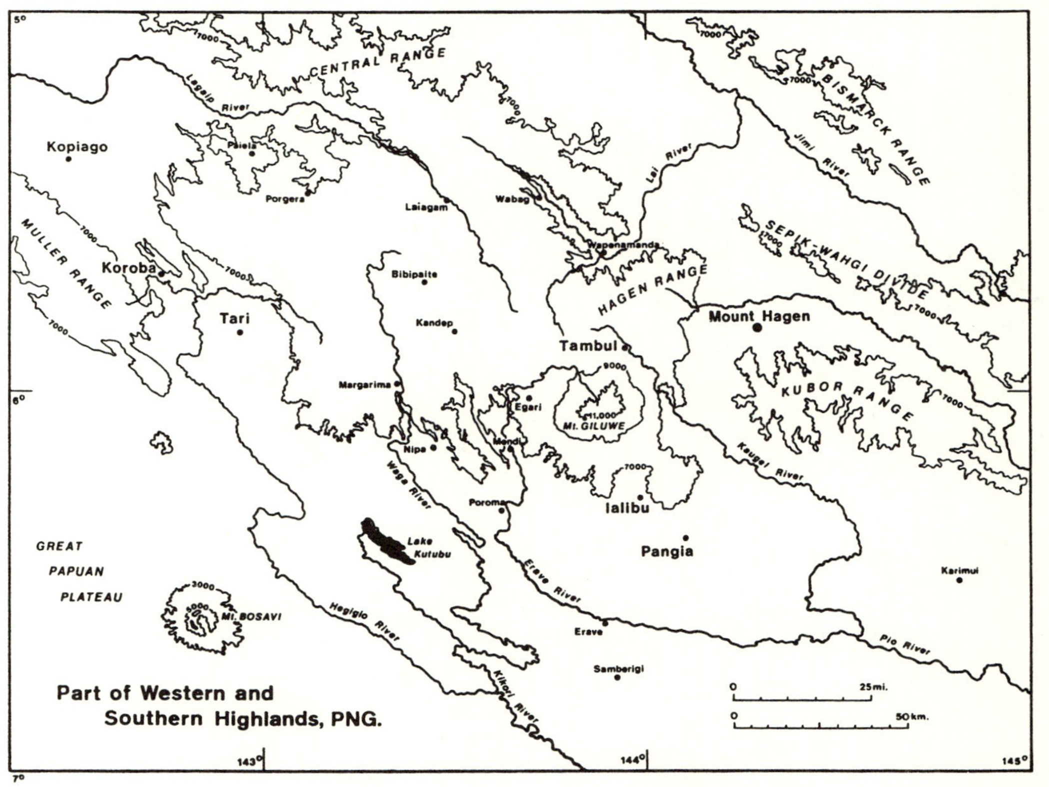

Part of Western and Southern Highlands, PNG.

must enter and exit from the cult site. No one can enter by himself. The two sides sit separately, facing each other in the main cult house where the cooking of sacrificial pork takes place. In the innermost sanctum a small house is built, which is known as "the men's and women's house," and in this are piled separately the stones belonging to individuals of the two moieties. These cult acts and structures present a picture of both separation and cooperation between the two sides, which is in some way both a "model of" and a "model for" social life. The power of the cult seems to come simultaneously from the absolute separation of the moieties and from their meticulous bonding into one unity, marked by the "men's and women's house" structure.

Ritual experts who serve the local cultists fall into two categories. There is a set of local friends of the performers, who have carried out the cult earlier and now come as confidants, advisers, and sponsors, sometimes supplying stones and ritual paraphernalia needed for the cult. There is also, however, a chief ritual expert who has superior knowledge of the sacred invocations to the Goddess and detailed ways of handling the stones that are identified with her power. This chief expert is usually recruited specially from one of the groups near to the putative origin point of the cult in Tambul. Both categories of expert have to be paid handsomely for their services, with pork and other forms of wealth, and these payments are described as analogous to brideprice, paid for the Goddess as the bride to all the local male participants.

The performance is completed by a spectacular dance in which the moieties emerge from the cult site in two parallel lines, stamping the ground with their feet, with whitened head nets and plumes of both the lesser bird of paradise (white and yellow in color) marking the Goddess and the Raggiana bird of paradise (red) marking themselves. This is then followed by a general distribution of meat from high platforms around the dancing ground. The performers offer their lesser-bird-of-paradise plumes to any group who might wish to enter the cult cycle next. The stones themselves are buried carefully in the cult site. Only a few men know the location where they are kept; and these men, after an interval of some twenty years, are expected to disinter them and renew the cult's power with a repeat performance. The cult has thus an intentional extension both in space and in time, within and between local groups.

The chief ritual experts come from an area where a different dialect is spoken from that used in the Central and Northern Melpa–speaking areas where I have worked; and in the 1950s, as reported by

Hermann Strauss, the cult had not yet reached the Northern, or Kopon, part of Hagen at all (Strauss and Tischner 1962:62–63), although the myth of the "young virgin" was known in folktales there, as in all parts of the wider language area that encompasses the Hagen and Tambul peoples. I witnessed a first performance of the cult in 1964 in the far western part of Kopon among the Ukini people, and from there it spread in a chain fashion eastward to the Kawelka people, and successive clans among the Kawelka performed it from 1973 through to 1984. Its microdiffusion is thus clear and is documented within the span of my own field experience. Questions remain, however, regarding its wider regional diffusion, which I now consider.

THE GODDESS AND THE SWEET POTATO

Richard Werbner earlier established the category of "regional cults," which serve a region, crossing over local boundaries of ethnicity, community, and language, but which possess a single main ritual center (Werbner 1977). Such regional cults have often emerged as a means of controlling economic resources in times of social change. They may be elitist and hierarchical, as in the case of the Gaan Tata cult, which arose in the 1880s among the Bush Negroes of Surinam (Van Velzen 1977:98); or they may be egalitarian, giving more significance to secondary ritual centers.

Melanesian circulating cults of the kind I am describing here, with the Female Spirit cult as my type-case, extend the egalitarian principles of some regional cults by having no true ritual center. However, they preserve the idea of priority or source of power in the person of the hired ritual expert, and the tracks the cult makes across the landscape are lines of power, leading back through a chain of experts to an imputed source or ideological center.

As we have established, a cult of this kind moves on a geographical track. It migrates, and in doing so leaves behind it a wake of innovative practices that amount to a form of cultural diffusion. If the cult succeeds in one area but not in another, reasons have to be suggested for this pattern, and these should give us insight into general questions of cultural change. It is necessary, therefore, first to establish the geographical distribution of these cults. I chose the Female Spirit or Goddess Cult for particular discussion because it appears to have been the most widespread of a set of cults found radiating out from Tambul in the Western and Southern Highlands. As it spread, this cult seems to have articulated certain historically emergent values in its region. It was practiced in Mount Hagen, in Tambul, further south in Pangia, and westward in some parts of the Enga area, notably among the Kyaka of the Baiyer Valley, to whom it had diffused in the 1950s (Bulmer 1965:148–151). In all cases its transmission followed the lines of already established networks of trade, alliance, and ceremonial exchange. What circumstances could have stimulated its successful diffusion?

Irrespective of circumstances, one thing is clear. All the references to the cult suggest that its origins lay not in a dim and distant past but within the horizon of generational memories. In this respect the cult can be compared to stories of volcanic ash falls throughout the Highlands; the most recent of these has been dated archaeologically to about 250 years BP, from evidence found at Kuk in the Western Highlands (Blong 1982:47–56; Golson 1982:130). This ash fall, known as Tibito Tephra from the Tibi Creek at Kuk where it was first found, also correlates, according to Golson, with prehistoric evidence of environmental changes that fit with the possible spread of sweet potato cultivation in the Highlands of Papua New Guinea. Memories of this precipitation were preserved orally in a story that the Hagen people themselves distinguished from the category *ka:ng*, 'folktale', calling it an *ik teman*, 'oral account'. G. F. Vicedom also bills the story as a *Geschichte* and adds a note that it relates to actual historical events, known because the early explorer and goldminer Michael Leahy "often had to work through as many as ten feet of ash layers before he came to the layers bearing gold" (A. J. Strathern 1977:67). The story notes that the ash fall was harmful: people and crops died, and after the disaster, the survivors had to begin again, so that the crops of today were derived from the new crops planted at that time. It has been suggested that this last part of the story may reflect the actual spread of the sweet potato at the time of the fall. Versions of the story are widespread in the Highlands.

Sweet potato cultivation, it is agreed, must have transformed Highlands agricultural systems in a number of ways: by making cultivation possible in drier land and at higher altitudes than before, by enabling continuous harvesting, by encouraging the domestication of pigs, and by stabilizing a division of labor between the sexes such that women became increasingly responsible for the reproduction of tilled garden areas reworked over time. There was certainly a lengthy evolution of gardening in the Highlands; and the sweet potato alone did not produce the "revolution" originally suggested by James Watson (1965). However, the pattern of work and social relations that emerged in complex, step-by-step fashion from the introduction of this crop probably had, at least, a marked effect on the division of labor and hence on gender relations as a whole. If that effect meant an objective increase in male dependence on female labor coupled with an attempt by men to define for themselves especially a sphere of political activity based not just on internally ordered and inward-looking descent principles but on externally enchained and outward-looking exchange ties, then a new ideological gap could have arisen (or an existing one widened) that was eventually to be filled by the invention of the Female Spirit cult. By its very logic, this cult seems designed both to recognize and give high value to female fertility and creativity, as an essential part of the dichotomous order of social life, and at the same time to "keep women in their place," out of immediate participation in the cult and observant of menstrual taboos that remind the women to be circumspect in their dealings with men.

The sweet potato itself was one of the items subject to taboo during the cult, both in Hagen and in Pangia. Sweet potatoes were not permitted inside the cult enclosure, and after a major performance of the cult, the participants were not allowed to eat sweet potatoes baked in the ashes of a fire but could consume them only if they were steamed in an earth oven. In Pangia, one informant explained this as *Aroa Ipono-ne kirau* 'a taboo thing of the Goddess', carrying with it the danger of death. He went on to say that the Goddess herself is female and so the human females and the crop closely associated with them were forbidden to enter her enclosure. This ritual separation between the sacred female and her profane counterparts highlights their underlying identity as well as their opposition. The Female Spirit cult is the only one among a set of otherwise similar cults in the region in which there is a special focus on the sweet potato as a food laden with taboo significance.

In making such a historical and functional argument, I recognize that other cults could and did perform similar functions to those I impute here to the Female Spirit cult. We cannot date any of these cults with any precision; we do not know if they are all to be regarded as post-Ipomoean. What we do know is that the Female Spirit cult tends to be represented as the most recent in a given area, and it therefore becomes plausible to regard this cult as especially associated with other recent historical changes that can be identified in oral history or from the prehistoric record. We have to note also, however, that other cults also spread historically throughout the region. The major track for these other cults appears to have been from south to north, where valuable pearl shells also made their way through trade routes into the central Highlands.

UNCOVERING THE TRACKS OF CULTS: TIMP AND TIMBU

Rena Lederman refers to a complex of cult practices in Mendi similar to those found in Hagen and Pangia:

> A number of fertility cults are followed in the Mendi Valley. Two, called Pim and Kupia, have their sacred places in the Upper Mendi, on Yansup and on Surup territories. . . . According to older informants, Kupia was performed four times since just before the Australians came to Mendi in 1950 until the mid-1960s and about four times during the period from the 1940s back to the 1920s. These cults are associated with mythic origin stories, and may well predate the *mok ink* [major pig-killing festival]. (Lederman 1986:182).

Pim and Kupia cults may perhaps be related to the cults known in Hagen as Palyim and Kopiak, practiced in the lower Nebilyer Valley among a roster of other cults. Lederman continued, "During the 1950s and 1960s, a new cult called Timp swept through the valley, proceeding from south to north" (ibid.). In an earlier reference in the same book she wrote:

> Social alignments dramatically at odds with the segmentary hierarchy model were produced by a number of "fertility" cults, performed by Upper Mendi men from at least the turn of the century until the late 1960s. Occurring every eight years or so, these cults operated in structural counterpoint to *sem* [clan] alignments. . . . During performances, the participants were divided into moieties without regard to their clan or tribal affiliations. (ibid.:46)

It is unclear from this reference whether the Timp cult is included or excluded. If it were especially referred to, we might link it both to pacification and the crosscutting ties exemplified in cult affiliations, but Lederman here refers to the whole period from the turn of the 19th century onward through the 1960s, so presumably the other cults are included as well. At any rate, the Timp cult was recent in Mendi, and as with the Amb Kor or Female Spirit cult in Hagen, we have to ask why it spread so rapidly in the 1950s.

For the Timp cult, it seems inevitable that one should link it to colonial change, if only because this facilitated the spread of the cult. If one asks why cults of this kind should emerge and spread at all, one can give an answer similar to answers given for cargo cults: in situations of change and uncertainty, when there are perturbations in the conditions of social life, new cults may be adopted as solutions to perceived problems. This is certainly true of cults described for the Enga by M. J. Meggitt (Meggitt 1973) and P. Gibbs (Gibbs 1977).

What is clear is that these cults all tend to have an element built into them that guarantees the possibility, even likelihood, that they will be exported. Once a group has performed a cult, its men become the new owners of the cult's secret procedures. As they were required to pay ritual experts from elsewhere for its acquisition, so they now can pass it on to others and command similar payment. In the case of the Female Spirit cult in Hagen, two levels of expert are usually involved: the first, a master expert from some area considered close to the origin point of the cult (in this case always places close to Tambul in the southwest part of the overall Hagen region); and the second, a neighboring group of men who have acquired some degree of expert knowledge in the way I have described. Both categories of specialists receive pay for their services. If this mechanism by which the Female Spirit cult moves from group to group holds also for other cults, we can classify them all as intrinsically circulating. The direction, speed, timing, and total track of their circulation still remains to be examined.

As it happens, the Timp cult, so recent in Mendi, has certainly a longer history in Pangia; that is, if we can make a rough equation between the Wiru Timbu cult and the Timp. In Pangia, both Tapa and Timbu cults are usually presented by informants as the two main religious cults, and the Female Spirit cult—there known as *Laiaroa* 'Woman from the Lai or Ialibu area'—is presented as definitely more recent, introduced precisely from the direction of Ialibu and Kagua by men described as *Kewa* (a term applied both to speakers of the Kagua language and to bilingual speakers of Kewa and Wiru north of Pangia government station).

The Tapa cult (reminiscent of the Melpa term *rapa*, 'men's house') was a cult of community ghosts and was closely associated with the enduring internal political structure of groups. The ghosts were thought to impinge on the living largely by making them sick, thus requiring sacrifices of pigs in the classic manner of materialist-minded Highlands ancestors elsewhere. Bones of individual dead were kept in a single *tapa* house and were sacrificed to as appropriate. In addition to these bone relics, cult practices also centered on the *tapa mu*, 'testicles of the *tapa*', smooth, hard, round stones usually dark in color. *Tapa* stones were accorded the ability to move through the ground and appear to a specific person, who would then take them and use them in the cult. I know of no stories suggesting that *tapa* practices were in any way extraneous to, or introduced into, the Wiru area. They correspond to what we may recognize as the basic local forms of ghost cults found throughout the Highlands. If we could assign temporal priority to any part of the religious complex (which we cannot do, other than speculatively), cults like the Tapa cult would be the obvious candidates. Their political significance lies within the sphere of control of social relations within units.

The Timbu cult, on the other hand, was more outward looking and involved what Thorsten Veblen would have called "conspicuous consumption," or at least a conspicuous record of consumption. Over a considerable period of time, pigs were sacrificed at the cult house and their bones were hung on its walls, until the whole cult building was covered with them. Only then could the final rituals (including dancing) take place, as a form of display and hospitality to surrounding groups. There were visiting cult experts who officiated at these rituals, and the cult moved from place to place. At its conclusion, people made wickerwork figures representing the Timbu spirit, painted them with ocher colors, and wore them as a part of their dance decorations. After this performance the figures, known as *timbu wara* 'spears of the *timbu*' were generally destroyed, though some might be kept. The cult had a number of general aims, which do roughly correspond to "fertility," but its emphasis was partly apotropaic, to the effect that "if we don't do this, then sickness will result." Sickness as the inverse of health is the underpinning factor in many of the Highlands cults of a circulating kind. The cult objects in the Timbu cult were also stones. One of my informants told me:

> The Timbu cult and the Laiyeroa [Laiaroa] cult are recent. Timbu was brought from Koinda [an outlying Wiru place, toward Erave] when I and my brother were about the size of Ewa, Longai's son [about ten years old]. We made the Timbu at Makuliyondo [an earlier settlement place of the Peri people of Tunda]. The Pakiri [who also form a small immigrant group in Tunda] brought it from Koinda. Previously it was made at Iaro, Kapele, Koyapu, Weriko, Takuru, . . . Marapini, Laiapu, Noiya, Timbari, Pupi, and Wiliame. In the Tunda area it was performed first here at Kerepali settlement, this was a 'little' or 'short' Timbu. The first time the bananas were cooked dry and they didn't like it, so they removed this *timbu*. They paid for it with pearl shells and pigs. Pakiri Oe [a cult leader] said that their *timbu* was too dry [that is, it would not make fertility, which depends on 'grease'], and they should remove their old *timbu*, and he gave more stones, new stones, from his place. [As a trial] we made a little house, *ware yapu*, and killed a few pigs. They could not finish all of the meat, there was plenty of pork, and they said therefore that the *timbu* was a good one. They gave plenty of pearl shells, pigs, salt packs, bailer shells, bush

> knives, and axes, and the Pakiri took off everything to Koinda. The father of Longai [an old man of the Windiperi subgroup] was in charge of this *timbu,* he was the *timbu karukango* [leader of the *timbu*]. . . . The Timbu spirit also sent dreams to Wipai [another old ritual expert] and he learned from these the incantations that are for the cult.

The informant here knows the places where the Timbu cult was performed prior to its arrival in his own place or village, Tunda. He lists places where it was performed, although we cannot be sure that these constitute a single track leading to Tunda itself. His group obtained it directly from one of the source points to the southwest, in the Erave area. This same area might have served as a source toward Poroma and upward into Mendi, where Lederman recorded the arrival of the Timp cult in the 1950s. The text also allows us to glimpse the pragmatic, almost entrepreneurial context in which new cults like Timbu were imported: if it works, buy it and keep it; if it doesn't work, buy it (for less) but throw it out and replace it. In such a volatile context we can understand why it was worthwhile for experts to maintain their trade and seek continually to expand its range. This gives us another dynamic for the spread of cults, an experts' "push factor."

The Kewa had a number of ancestral cults, the most pervasive being the Ribu cult. According to Lisette Josephides, "*Ribu* stands for a collectivity of male ancestors not individually honored, or a collection of ancestor-chiefs whose memory of heroic achievements in tribal war and leadership should be remembered by future generations." There were several Ribu cults in the Sugu area: *Adalu* 'long' Ribu; *Salu* or *Mae* 'short' Ribu; *Koi* 'bad' Ribu:

> The ritual practice in all cases was similar and followed a cycle lasting five to seven years. In the beginning, after some major disaster, a clan might feel that its established Ribu cult was not a powerful one and decide to purchase another from a neighboring clan. The cult house would be built in two to three days, and the cult owners would hand over power in the form of painted sacred stones which with due ceremony and sacrifice were buried in the house. During the following years small numbers of pigs would be killed from time to time while large numbers were bred for the final celebrations, at which time as many as a hundred might be killed. All but three were killed outside the spirit house and eaten by everyone. Three were sacrificed inside and eaten only by cult participants. The cult would then be phased out, to be revised, or perhaps replaced, when another disaster occurred. (Josephides 1985:76–77)

Josephides' account depicts a cult essentially like that described by my Wiru informants in 1967. In particular, the designations 'long' and 'short' Timbu were found also in Pangia, referring to the length of a central house pole to which pig bones from sacrifices were tied until it was covered. She does not mention the *timbu wara,* although figures like them were made in both the Kagua and Enga areas (Dosedla 1984). Finally, the notion that Ribu stands for a collectivity of ancestors may be questioned, by analogy with Pangia, where the Tapa and Timbu cults were clearly differentiated and nonoverlapping in reference.

In the case of Timbu, it is at least possible to regard its invention and diffusion into the Highlands as a result of two factors: one, an increase in introduced forms of sickness to which people had low immunity. Sacrifices to established cults would then fail, in their eyes, to restore patients to health and would lead to a faster turnover of new versions of cults. The other factor may have been a desire on the part of cult inventors in the south to claim back some of the wealth of their northern neighbors, as these came more into contact with European sources of wealth based in the Western Highlands.

The same explanations might also hold, indeed, for the Female Spirit cult, but I differentiate between the Timbu and the Female Spirit cults in two ways: first, the Female Spirit cult spread more widely than the Timbu; second, it may be rather more ancient, although it was diffused into Pangia within living memory of older men alive in the 1960s. I attach some significance, also, to the special character of taboos associated with the Female Spirit, specifying the necessity of separating women from men at the times of menstruation and childbirth, prohibiting them from cooking or having intercourse at menstruation, and forbidding them to pass over the round log (in Pangia *pokou kango*) at the entrance to the veranda of men's houses. Kapu, my Tunda informant, put it like this: all these taboos were introduced by the experts from the Ialibu area who first brought the Female Spirit cult southward down to the Wiru. They also introduced the classic division of the cult membership into two sides, the *ali yapu* 'men's house' and *aroa yapu* 'women's house', each with its *kalueli* 'ceremonial leader' who stood at the head of their line of celebrants. The *kalueli* also functioned in cases where the Female Spirit was approached individually, at times in between cult performances because of sickness in the family of a cult member. All of these structural features, as we have seen, are clearly found also in the Hagen versions of this cult. Parallel evidence of this kind suggests indeed that we are dealing with the same cult, spreading north and south from the Tambul area in historical times.

The question of why the Wiru, as a Highlands people speaking a language belonging to the Enga family, should have lacked those menstrual taboos that appear so characteristic of Hagen and Enga (and have dropped them again since they turned to Christianity), can be approached from another starting point, with the aid of speculations made by Jeffrey Clark (1985). Clark suggests that ancestors of the present-day Wiru, while having originally migrated in from some proto-Engan homeland, earlier lived to the south and east of their present location, closer to the then territory of the ancestors of the Daribi (now living at Karimui). At that time, they could have been influenced by patterns of custom more reminiscent of the Erave and Samberigi areas, which stretch toward Lake Kutubu (which could be called "Papuan" features, in this sense). But, as the sweet potato cultivation spread from about 250 or 300 years BP, the ancestors of the present-day Wiru were drawn more into the nexus of the Highlands societies to their north. Their intermediate status between "Papua" and "the Highlands" might explain the absence, as well as the presence, among them of characteristic Highlands practices. The intrusion of the Female Spirit cult into Pangia could then be seen as a late phase of an ongoing process of "Highlandization," which began earlier, was strengthened either by the actual inmigration of large numbers of people from Ialibu (a motif that often appears in origin stories) or at least by a post-hoc representation of history in these terms, and was stimulated by the desire to be associated northward rather than southward (a point that Clark suggests).

In this version of the argument, the Female Spirit cult is a later arrival than sweet potato cultivation but is still a part of one overall process of cultural diffusion and migration of populations, in this instance north to south, running in the opposite direction to the Timbu in the Southern Highlands, which traveled south to north. In the Western Highlands, however, the movement of the Female Spirit cult is definitively south to north also—and to an ingenious indigenous explanation of this pattern I now finally turn.

RELIGIOUS PRACTICES AS EXPORTS

Boyope Kangie Didi published two accounts of cults in his home place Tambul in the journal *Oral History* (Didi 1982a, 1982b). The first account deals with the Kuru Kopiaka cult (the same as the Melpa cult Kor Kopiak). Didi's informants, mostly men over sixty years old, traced this cult back to the Upper Kaugel Valley, associating it with "two women from the Wagoma tribe and an unknown man from the Yano tribe in the Upper Kaugel." The original experience of these cult founders was to find a lake with red cordylines growing in it at the edge of a new garden, and in the lake a double-headed snake. It was thought this lake contained the spirit of Ye Waigono, a supernatural dwarf who had been killed and buried earlier; and sacrifices were made in order to appease this spirit and avert disasters such as epidemics, which he might choose to inflict on the community. The name Kopiaka appears to have been derived from the fact that certain kinds of rats, including those known as *kopiaka,* might appear in the cult place of this spirit. The chief stone used in the cult came—according to one informant, Peaa Yapu, who was about sixty-six years old—from the Lake Ekari area (in the Upper Mendi Valley to the south of Tambul) and was obtained from there by trading in the time of his grandfather. Other stones were added continuously, some being of the classic 'mortar' type associated with various spirit cults in the overall Hagen area. Some also appeared first in the guise of rats or bandicoots but then turned into stones when people approached them. Cult members refrained from eating dog meat or red pandanus fruit and acquired dog's ears and dry pandanus leaves for use in the cult all the way from the lower Nebilyer Valley to their northwest.

One of Didi's informants actually came from Upper Mendi. This man told him that the Kopiaka cult was known there as Kumbe Reke, and he also "claimed that the cult flowed into the upper Mendi area and to Komea from their trading partners from Kandep in the Enga provinces" (Didi 1982a:29).

Many of the features of the Kopiaka cult are shared with the Female Spirit cult (and other congeners). For instance, the cult stones are decorated and painted; the house in which they are displayed is decorated with fern leaves; and special items, known as *kuru opipi* (in Melpa *kor uipip*) had to be collected in distant bush areas—from as far away as Mendi and the hillsides of Mount Giluwe. Other features were peculiar to Kopiaka, such as the practice of placing the cult stones and ancestral skulls and bones at the bottom of an earth oven and then cooking pork and fine greens on top of these. Sacrifices to Kopiaka were also made before going out to war. If sacrifices were not made, Kopiaka might emit a long warning noise to the people and follow this with frost or epidemics of pneumonia. The Tambul area lies at an altitude of over 7,000 feet above sea level and is subject to such disasters. To avert these, "when planting a new garden, after clearing virgin forest, rats, opossums and piglets were taken to the cult site, cooked, and offered to the spirits to ensure a good harvest" (Didi 1982a:36).

Didi notes that Kopiaka was similar to the Wapu (the Melpa Wöp) cult, but that *wapu* stones were acquired through a well-developed trading system while those for the Kopiaka were found mostly on the spot (1982a:40). He thinks that Kopiaka could have emerged as a variant on Wapu. Wapu was established earlier and spread further north into the Hagen area proper, whereas Kopiaka was confined to Tambul and a few parts of the lower Nebilyer Valley.

In his second article, an overview of spirit cults in Tambul, Didi refers to the story of Anda Kopa, a tribal founder:

> Long, long ago there lived a man named Anda Kopa. He lived and mastered all the lands and bushes and cultivated all sorts of food crops. His hide-out was somewhere in the midst of Mount Giluwe. . . . Once upon a time his crops were ready to be harvested, so he sent word around inviting the people to a big feast where he was going to cook all his food crops and some of his pigs. He cooked each variety of crop and animal at the top of Mt. Giluwe, and his cooking area stretched right along the mountain summit. Thousands of people came, and some had to leave before he had distributed to them, because they had nowhere to stay. In the event, he distributed the best food crops to the people from far distances, such as Ialibu in the Southern Highlands, Melpa in the Western Highlands, and others from further away. And Anda Kopa himself got other poor yielding crops. . . . Those crops shared to the people of far distant areas are the crops and other foodstuffs which nowadays are not found in the lower Kaugel Valley. . . . Anda Kopa's own surrounding areas were given poor yielding crops, so to secure the good harvest and high productivity religious cults were necessary, and so these were developed or obtained from their trading partners. It was thought that technology alone could not give high production. (Didi 1982b:51–52, adapted)

Anda Kopa and his descendants are thus proved to be good Malinowskians, requiring ritual to meet uncertain circumstances beyond their control. (This, however, may be Didi's own interpretation of the story, based on anthropology classes he had taken with me at the University of Papua New Guinea.)

In the same article, Didi notes that both Wapu and Kopiaka cults preceded the Amb Kuru or Female Spirit cult. Another cult, Kuru Paleme, had reached the Upper (but not the Lower) Kaugel Valley by the time the Christian missions banned all cults and halted their development in the area after 1945. The first major *wapu* stone was obtained from Ekari also, supposedly in the time of Nabile-Eru, the son of Anda Kopa. Kuru Paleme also came across from Ekari, and before that from Kandep, another high-altitude area in Enga Province.

Didi's view of the Female Spirit cult, gleaned from his informants, was that this cult was put together with stones and practices similar to those used in Wapu and Kopiaka. The practices he reported for this cult differed in some respects, however, from those for the older cults. He wrote:

> In other religious institutions women were not allowed to participate to eat the pig that was slaughtered and cooked inside the enclosure. But in the *Amb Kuru* this was allowed. Furthermore children before their teenage were not allowed to enter the sacred place but in the *Amb Kuru* it was allowed conditionally here to abide by the rules and regulations of the cult. (Didi 1982b:62)

So the Female Spirit cult, according to Didi, was a home-made job, first put together in the Tambul area itself. If so, it was nevertheless the most successful version, if one can judge by the extent of its spread to other areas. It may be that the feature he incidentally mentions—that of allowing women to eat at least a part of the meat that had been steamed inside the cult enclosure— was instrumental in giving a greater popularity to this cult than others.

From Didi's account, and from my own field investigations in the lower Nebilyer, it is clear that Tambul was indeed a ritual switch point, through which practices from the Southern Highlands and Enga flowed into the Hagen area. The myth of Anda Kopa is intended as an ecological and economic fable. Anda Kopa gave away the best crops to other areas, so in his own area rituals were needed to boost production; but also, we may add, since these cults were imported into Tambul and exported out again, they became a part of the total traffic of exchange, running on the tracks of the interchange between the Enga *tee* and the Hagen *moka* exchange systems. By this means, also, wealth would flow back into Tambul, an otherwise poor area. The 'lines of power' of the cults were also vectors for other exchanges of wealth.

Of all the cults, the Female Spirit cult appears from the available evidence to deal most explicitly with the question of relations between the sexes and to give a recognition to the contribution of females to the social structure, by dividing the cult place into the 'men's house' and 'women's house' sides. The men's side is given preeminence, but integration between the two is greatly stressed. It is in this sense, rather than in terms of any strict correspondence in time, that we can suggest that this cult was well suited to the epoch of the sweet potato, which increased men's dependence on female labor and on female links for multiplying alliance. The Female Spirit cult both recognizes the importance of females and yet still excludes them from the line of power that comes from sacrifice to the Goddess herself.

We do not know for sure that any of these cults predated the sweet potato. All of them might, in one way or another, be inventions in response to perturbations experienced since the crop switch occurred. Truly high-altitude areas such as Tambul could hardly have been occupied at all by horticultural populations prior to the sweet potato. For the same reason, it is unlikely that the *tee* and *moka* systems could have been interlinked through Tambul before that time. (Even in recent historical times, these links have scarcely approached a systemic character but rather consist of the networks made by individual men of enterprise.) Both these ceremonial linkages and the passage of cults from Enga to Mendi to Tambul to Hagen should then be relatively recent, post–Tibito Tephra phenomena.

LINES OF POWER

The two main examples of circulating cults here adduced have been the Female Spirit cult and the Timp. The Female Spirit cult appears to have been literally invented in Tambul by bricolage from elements found in other cults such as Kopiaka, Paleme, and Wapu, all of which diffused from Tambul into the Nebilyer Valley but did not proceed further north and south into the Hagen and Pangia areas, as the Female Spirit cult did. The Timp cult seems to have expanded northward from somewhere in the Erave area, though this cannot be established, into the Kewa, Wiru, and Mendi areas but not to have moved further north into Tambul itself or into Hagen. Of the two cults, it is possible that the Female Spirit cult is older and associated with the aftermath of the spread of sweet potato cultivation in this part of the highlands, while Timp is more recent and linked with changes in sickness patterns since European contact.

Aside from other considerations, a major factor in ensuring the export of cults has been the entrepreneurship of ritual experts. One can only speculate that over a longer time period, for example, the Female Spirit cult might have reached the Maring or Wahgi areas. If it had done so, it might have blended in with existing religious conceptions such as the Maring *kun kaze ambra* 'smoke woman' (Rappaport 1968; C. Healey pers. comm.) or the Wahgi *golyomba* spirit girl, as pointed out by Michael O'Hanlon (O'Hanlon 1989:91). If so, however, as O'Hanlon also suggests (ibid.), it is likely that its elements and their relative prominence might have been altered in line with local ethos and values. Such transformations of meaning in the elements of migrating cults have been little studied so far. On the other hand, the existence of regional traditions and themes in both myth and cult is well established, and more detailed fieldwork could be carried out on any one of these themes in order to pinpoint answers to the more detailed questions my discussion has been able to raise but not solve. Some examples of these regional traditions are now given.

Souw

Roy Wagner links the Souw theme, which he found at Karimui among the Daribi, with Papuan hero tales of Sido (Hido, Iko, Saur, Sosom) originating far south on the Papuan coast and found also in the Torres Straits (Wagner 1972:17–37). The name Tiro was known also in Pangia among Wiru speakers where it was applied to the Uelali, a spirit of water courses and pools, who could shoot people with his arrows and make them sick. Related notions appear further north among the Koroba Huli, whose ideas of Iba Tiri "show homologous relations with the mythic complex detailed by Wagner" (Goldman 1983:222). Iba Tiri is a spirit linked to water (as L. R. Goldman points out), and his name is found among the Duna as well as the Wiru and Huli. As Goldman argues, the "water" association may be peculiar to the Wiru-Huli-Duna part of the tradition. In Huli also, Iba Tiri is linked to disorder, sickness, and irresponsibility. Here we find traces of at least minor transformations in a theme across geographic space. Among the Duna in Lake Kopiago in 1989 we found the name Tsiri or Siri applied to a friendly spirit who had benefited a Duna man by revealing to him a powerful stone carved in the shape of a human head, which is now in the Papua New Guinea National Museum (Stürzenhofecker and A. J. Strathern, field notes, 1989). Subsequent fieldwork in 1991 has confirmed the salience of Ipa Tsiri as a powerful spirit category among the Duna, associated with low-lying watercourses.

Dindi Gamu

Stephen Frankel has reported that the Huli people at Tari recognized an exceptionally long line of power stretching from the Papuan plateau to the central highlands. He wrote:

> Key sacred sites are said to be joined by the 'root of the earth', which has the physical form of a thick liane entwined by a python, and pro-

> vides a channel through which flow water and, during performances of *dindi gamu,* smoke [*dindi gamu* was a major ritual sequence that ideally linked all these sites together]. . . . The source of ritual power is said to lie in the lowlands of the Papuan Plateau. The major *dindi gamu* cycle capable of summoning *mbingi* [a new volcanic ash fall] is said to be initiated by ritual activity on the Plateau. (Frankel 1986:19)

The ritual sites start in the territory of the Onabasulu people, continue in the Tari Basin, into Mount Ambua, and thence to Bibipaite where Enga speakers live.

The Huli have their particular theory of entropy, that they have reached the thirteenth generation from the founders and the world is worn out and its fertility could be renewed only by revivifying *dindi gamu* and bringing back *mbingi.* We might interpret this as a memory of social and cultural renewal brought about initially by the sweet potato. If this plant did indeed arrive into the Southern Highlands by some route from the south rather than the north, we would finally gain some understanding also of why the lines of ritual power run often in that direction, a direction taken also, by and large, by the valued pearl shells in their track from the Papuan coast up into the interior of the highlands. In that case we could reaffirm the likelihood that all the spirit cults we have discussed for Tambul may also derive from this same historical moment, amplified by the exigencies of high altitude and the opportunities of the *moka.* We have certainly seen, at any rate, that these lines of power are historical and parts of their history can even be recovered, giving us again a picture of a volatile, changing world rather than one of static adaptations, of boundaries crossed as well as maintained, and of the dynamics of entrepreneurial activity in the transmission of ideas as much as in the migrations of persons and the exchange of gifts.

Afek and Congeners

Mythical female figures who travel over a landscape, modifying it and leaving behind descendants, appear in a number of parts of the Southern Highlands Province and in the Ok region. The best known is Afek, whose story is known throughout the Mountain Ok area and is most clearly tied to Telefomin where the *telefolip* cult house, center of a regional cult, became established (Swadling 1983:14). Afek is reputed to have come from the east, and thereby possibly hangs a tale, or another line of power, since Pamela Swadling notes that,

> The people in the Mendi and Nipa areas also have a story about a woman who left behind an altered landscape, descendants and cultural

> precedents. . . . It is curious that she was also travelling westwards. Whether there is any linkage with the culture heroine of the Mountain Ok and Sepik Hill speakers is not known. (ibid.:32)

Such a connection may be less implausible than one might think. T. Mawe's longer discussion of the Mendi story (1985), on which Swadling draws, makes it reasonable to suggest possible connections between the Mendi "heroine" and both the Female Spirit and a similar heroine who appears in a Huli story (Frankel 1986; see also Sillitoe 1993:175). (A male character in this set of stories from Mendi is called Sunda Owil or Sunda Kowil, where *Kowil* seems to refer to the Köwul or Tambul area, from which the Female Spirit cult came.) In the Huli story, the heroine is actually a Duna woman. She bore a perfect son, Bayebaye, who was killed in error during a *dindi gamu* performance. His mother was upset, and as she left to return to her Duna home, she cursed the Huli with incest, famine, and disease. Frankel noted, "*Bayebaye* means 'perfect', here referring to great fertility of crops, people and pigs, but also to social harmony" (Frankel 1986:23). The Huli believe that as a result of the Duna woman's curse, their world is on the decline and can only be renewed through a correct revival of the *dindi gamu* line of power, preceded by a payment of compensation to the Europeans for Bayebaye's death. In this part of the complex Bayebaye is nowadays equated with Jesus.

Here, one of the most interesting features is simply that the woman was a Duna woman. The Duna in fact have a comparable story, but it indicates the departure of a heroine eastward across the Strickland into the Duna area from Ok, and the story is tied to the origin myth of a particular group, the Songwa. The Duna story thus reverses the direction of lines of power. Regardless of the particular form of directionality involved, the story breaches the usually conceptualized divide between the Highlands and the Ok cultures; and this idea fits with suggestions emerging from Gabriele Stürzenhofecker's typological examination of languages and cultural attributes in this part of New Guinea (Stürzenhofecker this volume, and in press). We can also see, again, how mythical and ritual themes can be subject to metamorphosis.

In Tambul and Hagen a myth of sacred sisters becomes attached to a ritual complex that we know as the Female Spirit cult. While the elder sisters become wives of human men, the youngest sister retains her virginity and becomes the Spirit or Goddess. A similar set of motifs appears in the Mendi story of Sunda Owil as recounted by Mawe, with a further interesting twist. Sunda Owil is a traveling culture hero, who introduces a set of women to the practice of cooking and eating pigs instead of regarding these as their husbands. He then marries all the "black" (dark-skinned) women, but one woman who is "white" (light-skinned) escapes from him and travels westward, and her resting places later become sacred cult sites. She strikes a range with her walking stick to form a passage in it and finally disappears into a cave in the Nipa area west of Mendi. In the Nipa people's version, the elements of the story are rather different, but the character of the "white woman" is preserved, as Mawe notes. He also remarks that folktales of light-skinned women are found also in Hagen and in Enga, sometimes associated with the sky, sometimes appearing as dangerous creatures. These features are abundantly documented by G. F. Vicedom and H. Strauss, in fact (Vicedom and Tischner 1943–48:vol. 3; Strauss and Tischner 1962). Mawe concludes his review of the story as follows: "Perhaps the white woman reemerged from the cave . . . because there are stories of a similar light-skinned woman further west in the Huli district" (Mawe 1985: 67). It is possible that he is here referring to the story of the mother of Bayebaye, the "perfect boy," whose Duna mother left the Huli and returned to Kopiago. Modjeska (1977:295) also refers to a tradition—regarding the Kiria cult in the Koroba area south of the Duna—that the sites of its cult houses "are said to have been the sleeping-places of an ancestral woman who traversed the country following a striped pig." (This is in fact the ancestress of the Songwa.) In the Ok region itself, the ancestress Afek becomes associated with a regional cult center connected with the control of taro production. We have no comparative time scales here, but perhaps, since taro preceded the sweet potato, we can see the figure of Afek as the patron goddess of this more ancient crop and the Female Spirit as the patroness of the sweet potato. Ok remained the stronghold of taro long after the sweet potato presumably reached the Highlands, and Afek correspondingly remained its Goddess (but see Poole this volume, where it is pointed out that in one tradition Afek is associated with the sweet potato). Perhaps challenges to the supremacy of Telefolip as a regional cult center (rather an unusual arrangement, converting lines of power into a concentric set of spokes of power) coincided with the spread of the sweet potato. Sweet potato might then be seen as having favored big-manship on the one hand and the decline of ritually established hierarchy with graded initiations on the other (see Modjeska 1987).

One final suggestion, from more recent times, can be made. Possibly, circulating cults have a better chance of survival against the inroads of world religion than do cults of the regional type as discussed by R. P. Werbner. Regional cults usually have a single major sacred center to which, for example, pilgrimages are made. The center may also depend on tribute from its branches or from visitors. A priestly hierarchy tends to emerge, at risk from changes of fortune. In the Telefomin case the Telefolip house was regarded by some of the surrounding groups as a ritual center from which the power for taro magic flowed out to outlying parts. Hence, when this cult house was put out of action by mission-inspired Christians, the regional cult based on it was also threatened with collapse. With circulating cults, this is not so. Although the lines of power are indeed traced back to certain major sites, the replication and the transmission of the cults do not depend directly on continuing contact with these points of origin. New experts are created with each transmission, and if the cult is dormant in one place, like a snake it can raise its head elsewhere. Cult stones can be "found" as well as brought to a group. Many are prehistoric "mortars," whose distribution in the Highlands has probably been profoundly affected by their use in rituals for an unknown period of time. The Female Spirit cult is performed in any case by a group only once every twenty years or so. It remains potential and latent as long as the cult stones lie buried in a clan's territory and are not stolen or lost. Although the whole area appears currently to be turning more and more to the new, highly emotional, and "salvationist" Christian sects, one should not lightly presume that the indigenous lines of power have died out rather than simply remaining dormant for the time being (A. J. Strathern 1991); although it has to be admitted that by the end of 1991 the cult enclosure of the Goddess had been breached by men in search of scarce gardening land, and the site of the cult stones was not overtly preserved at all (the site location was deliberately kept secret). At the same time, the influence of the charismatic sects continued to grow rapidly, and they themselves spread in a chainlike fashion from group to group, which inscribed a transformed version of the older lines of power.

REFERENCES

Blong, R.
1982 The Time of Darkness: Local Legends and Volcanic Reality in Papua New Guinea. Seattle: University of Washington Press.

Bulmer, R. N. H.
1965 The Kyaka of the Western Highlands. *In* Gods, Ghosts and Men in Melanesia. P. Lawrence and M. J. Meggitt, eds., pp. 132–161. Melbourne: Oxford University Press.

Clark, Jeffrey
1985 From Cults to Christianity. Ph.D. dissertation. University of Adelaide.

Didi, B. K.
1982a Kuru Kopiaka, Goddess Cult in the Lower Kaugel Valley of the Tambul Sub-District, Western Highlands Province. Oral History 10(1):5–43.
1982b An Overview of the Traditional Cults in the Lower Kaugel Valley of the Tambul Sub-District, Western Highlands Province. Oral History 10(1):44–87.

Dosedla, H. C.
1984 Kultfiguren aus Flechtwerk im zentralen Hochland von PNG (Papua-Neuguinea). Abhandlungen und Berichte des Staatlichen Museums für Völkerkunde Dresden 41:86–98.

Frankel, Stephen
1986 The Huli Response to Illness. Cambridge: Cambridge University Press.

Gibbs, P.
1977 The Cult from Lyeimi and the Ipili. Oceania 48(1):1–26.

Goldman, L. R.
1983 Talk Never Dies. London: Tavistock.

Golson, J.
1982 The Ipomoean Revolution Revisited: Society and the Sweet Potato in the Upper Wahgi Valley. *In* Inequality in New Guinea Highlands Societies. A. Strathern, ed., pp. 109–136. Cambridge: Cambridge University Press.

Josephides, L.
1985 The Production of Inequality, Gender and Exchange Among the Kewa. London: Tavistock.

Lederman, Rena
1986 What Gifts Engender: Social Relations and Politics in Mendi, Highland Papua New Guinea. Cambridge: Cambridge University Press.

Mawe, T.
1985 Mendi Culture and Tradition: A Recent Survey. Port Moresby: Papua New Guinea National Museum.

Meggitt, M. J.
1973 The Sun and the Shakers. Oceania 44:1–37, 109–126.

Modjeska, C. N.
1977 Production Among the Duna. Ph.D. dissertation. Australian National University.
1991 Post-Ipomoean Modernism: The Duna Example. *In* Big Men and Great Men: Personifications of Power in Melanesia. M. Godelier and M. Strathern, eds., pp. 234–255. Cambridge: Cambridge University Press.

O'Hanlon, M.
1989 Reading the Skin. London: British Museum Publications.

Rappaport, R. A.
1968 Pigs for the Ancestors. New Haven: Yale University Press.

Sillitoe, P.
1993 A Ritual Response to Climatic Perturbations in the Highlands of Papua New Guinea. Ethnology 32(2):169–185.

Strathern, A. J.
1970 The Female and Male Spirit Cults in Mount Hagen. Man n.s. 5:571–585.
1977 Myths and Legends from Mount Hagen (transl. of G. Vicedom, Die Mbowamb, vol. 3). Port Moresby: Institute of PNG Studies.
1979 Men's House, Women's House: The Efficacy of Opposition, Reversal and Pairing in the Melpa Amb Kor Cult. Journal of the Polynesian Society 88:37–54.
1991 Fertility and Salvation. Journal of Ritual Studies 5(1):51–64.

Strauss, H., and H. Tischner
1962 Die Mi-Kultur der Hagenberg-Stämme. Hamburg: Cram de Gruyter and Co.

Stürzenhofecker, Gabriele
in press Dialectics of History: Female Witchcraft and Male Dominance in Aluni. *In* Papuan Borderlands: Huli, Duna, and Ipili Perspectives on the New Guinea Highlands. A. Biersack, ed. (Submitted to University of Michigan Press.)

Swadling, Pamela
1983 How Long Have People Been in the Ok Tedi Impact Region? Port Moresby: Papua New Guinea National Museum Record no. 8.

Van Velzen, B. T.
1977 Bush Negro Regional Cults: A Materialist Explanation. *In* Regional Cults. R. P. Werbner, ed., pp. 93–118. ASA Monograph 16. London: Academic Press.

Vicedom, G. F., and H. Tischner 1943–48
Die Mbowamb. 3 vols. Hamburg: Friederichsen, de Gruyter and Co.

Wagner, R.
1972 Habu: The Innovation of Meaning in Daribi Religion. Chicago: University of Chicago Press.

Watson, James
1965 From Hunting to Horticulture in the New Guinea Highlands. Ethnology 4:295–309.

Werbner, R. P., ed.
1977 Regional Cults. ASA Monograph 16. London: Academic Press.

NOTE

I am grateful to Gabriele Stürzenhofecker for incisive discussion of the ideas in this paper and for drawing my attention to Ok and to Afek. I am also grateful to Terry Hays for comments and bibliographic references, especially to the work of H. C. Dosedla on cult figures.

A PREHISTORIC INTRODUCTION OF THE SWEET POTATO IN NEW GUINEA?

Richard Scaglion and Kimberly A. Soto

> In general the introduction of the sweet potato into New Guinea is something of an enigma.

INTRODUCTION

At least since the 1920s (see Safford 1925; Dixon 1932) the question of where sweet potatoes (*Ipomoea batatas*) originated and how and when they spread to other parts of the world has been of concern to both physical and social scientists.[1] In 1974, Douglas E. Yen, a botanist, published *The Sweet Potato and Oceania: An Essay in Ethnobotany*. This classic work—based on extensive historical, genetic, linguistic, and botanical data—focused on the problem of the origin and subsequent diffusion of the sweet potato in the Pacific Islands. Yen's conclusion that the sweet potato was domesticated in South or Central America and then diffused prehistorically to the eastern Pacific is well supported and widely accepted. However, his hypothesis for the 16th-century diffusion of the plant into New Guinea from Europeans via Indonesian traders remains rather speculative.

Although the evidence examined by Yen was inconclusive, many Melanesian scholars favor this hypothesis of an Indonesian (western) route of introduction.[2] In this chapter, we examine new linguistic data that bear on this problem. We argue that an alternative hypothesis—positing that the sweet potato was traded or otherwise diffused from the Pacific Islands to eastern New Guinea before the arrival of Europeans—is equally plausible and certainly cannot be precluded by currently existing historical, archaeological, ethnographic, and linguistic evidence. The possibility of a prehistoric introduction could have major implications for the interpretation and reconsideration of agricultural intensification and social evolution, particularly in the New Guinea Highlands. Considerably more time depth might be possible than a purely European-Indonesian hypothesis would suggest.

PLAUSIBILITY OF A PREHISTORIC ROUTE OF INTRODUCTION

The evidence for the pre-Colombian presence of sweet potatoes in Polynesia is fairly compelling.[3]

The earliest reports from Hawaii, Easter Island, and New Zealand, at the apexes of the Polynesian triangle, describe plants that were well-established staple crops at or soon after European discovery. Dixon (1932:44–45) reports that Jacob Roggeveen observed large sweet potato plantations on Easter Island in 1722 and indicates that the sweet potato was a mainstay of the diet. Captain James Cook, upon his discovery of Hawaii in 1778, reported elaborate methods of cultivation of sweet potatoes. The plant featured prominently in origin myths and was mentioned in several rituals that used an archaic form of speech. While Abel Tasman's 1642 contact in New Zealand was very brief, Cook, Banks, and Parkinson report the importance of sweet potatoes in Maori horticulture in 1769.

In addition to these historical accounts, there is also good archaeological evidence suggestive of considerable antiquity for sweet potato cultivation in these three locations. Rosendahl and Yen (1971: 381–383) report on a carbonized sweet potato from the island of Hawaii assayed at 295± 90 BP Skjolsvold (1961:297, 303, cited in O'Brien 1972) reports on charred sweet potato remains from a fireplace on Easter Island dating to the sixteenth century. Jack Golson (1959:45) believes that, in New Zealand, pits dated to the 14th century may have been sweet potato storage pits, and Law (1969:245) reports evidence that suggests intensive sweet potato cultivation by AD 1300 (see also Law 1970).

Perhaps the strongest archaeological evidence for the early existence of sweet potatoes anywhere in Polynesia derives from the recent work of P. V. Kirch, J. R. Flenley, D. W. Steadman, and others on a site in the Cook Islands. Excavations at Tangatatau, a large, well-stratified rock-shelter site, produced several specimens of carbonized sweet potato tubers in unquestionably prehistoric contexts.

> In short, sweet potato remains are represented throughout the deposits, in securely dated contexts that leave no doubt as to the presence of

> this cultigen during the last millennium of Mangaian prehistory. As the MAN-44 site does not extend back to the initial colonization of Mangaia (believed to be at least 1600 BP, based on pollen profiles indicative of major forest clearance; Lamont 1990), the date of first introduction of *Ipomoea batatas* to the island remains unknown. (Hather and Kirch 1991:889)

The above-cited ethnohistorical and archaeological evidence suggests a pre-European sweet potato culture firmly established at the far limits of Polynesian settlement well before European contact. Linguistic evidence also supports this view. Since the term for sweet potato is similar in different Polynesian languages (*kumar[a], umara, uma's, kumala, umala,* and *uwala* [Conklin 1963:130]), it can be argued that the term was present in Proto-Polynesian (O'Brien 1972:353). Still further evidence is given by Yen (1961:339–342), who argues that considerable time would be necessary for sweet potato cultivation and storage techniques to develop so that the tubers could be grown in the temperate climate found in present-day New Zealand.

While estimates of sweet potato antiquity in Polynesia vary, even before the recent findings of Hather and Kirch cited above, most researchers have suggested at least a millennium. Peter Bellwood (1978:185), for example, estimated a date of introduction before AD 1000. In summarizing most of the evidence presented above, O'Brien (1972:353) concluded that the sweet potato was most likely introduced into Polynesia, possibly to Samoa, by AD 1. Yen (1974:259) suggested a date of introduction between AD 400 and 700. Citing the work of Davidson (1979:230), Kirch (1979:289; 1982), McCoy (1979: 144), and Yen (1974), White with O'Connell (1982:183) found "good evidence of the presence of sweet potato in Polynesia 600–1000 years ago." A current consensus view might place sweet potatoes in eastern Polynesia as long ago as 1500 BP (see also Ayres 1975; Bellwood 1987:6).

Demonstrating plausible links through which sweet potatoes may have passed between Polynesia and eastern Melanesia is much more problematic, however. It is unfortunate that the early European explorers of islands in Outlier Polynesia and the eastern Melanesian islands rarely left records of their visits that could establish the precontact existence of sweet potatoes. However, the archaeologically known Lapita Cultural Complex, dating from ca. 1600 to 500 BC, was characterized by extensive long-distance trading networks during its early west-to-east expansion phase, as Lapita peoples strove to maintain ties with parent populations in the west:

> Elsewhere I have argued that the long-distance exchange networks that linked Lapita sites in the Bismarcks with settlements farther to the east were an integral part of the colonization strategy of this rapidly expanding population. "The importance of exchange for Lapita communities did not lie in assuring access to certain material resources such as obsidian or temper, but as a formal mechanism assuring a 'lifeline' back to larger and more securely established homeland communities" (Kirch 1988:113). (Kirch 1991:159, quoting his own work)

Later, these networks began to erode:

> Throughout the last 2000 years of Melanesian prehistory, there is evidence of gradual or episodic retraction or reduction in the geographic scale of exchange networks, accompanied by subsequent increases in the magnitude or intensity of exchange within these progressively smaller systems. (Kirch 1991:155–156)

While any possible sweet potato transfer between Polynesia and eastern Melanesia would have been a late (if not post-) Lapita phenomenon, it is at least possible that the reduced Lapita long-distance exchange networks in place at the time might have been sufficiently overlapping as to allow for such transfer.

Thomas Michel (1987:231) believes that sweet potatoes were present in the Solomon Islands by AD 1200–1300 and may have reached New Guinea via the Bismarck Archipelago. However, most other researchers (Ross 1977, for example) reject this view. The Polynesian Outliers are perhaps more fertile ground to search for nodes of diffusion. For example, obsidian from New Britain, metavolcanic adzes and chert from the Solomon Islands, volcanic glass and pottery from the northern New Hebrides, impressed sherds probably from Fiji, and basalt adzes probably originating in Samoa have all been found on Tikopia (Kirch and Yen 1982:339), albeit in different time frames. It is certain that archaeological sequences in this area are quite complex and involve considerable external contacts:

> The prehistoric sequences of Tikopia and Anuta, combined with the results of archaeological study of Bellona, Rennell, Taumako, Kapingamarangi, and Nukuoro, leave no room for doubt as to the complexities of culture change on the Polynesian Outliers. The time-depth for settlement is as long as three millennia, and cultural replacements, immigration from multiple sources, and a general diversity of external contacts are all likely possibilities for any Outlier sequence. . . .
>
> The significance of such complex sequences must not be underestimated. Anthropologists have been accustomed to thinking of the Outliers as peripheral to the mainstream of Polynesian, and even Oceanic,

> culture history. The term "outlier" connotes something apart, removed from the center of culture change and innovation. Yet it is clear that what transpired on an Outlier such as Tikopia was a reflection of several major eras of southwest Pacific prehistory. Although the term is too thoroughly ingrained in the Oceanic literature to seriously suggest a change, we would nevertheless like to offer the viewpoint that the true "outliers" of Polynesia are not Tikopia, Anuta, and the other Polynesian-speaking communities on the Melanesian fringe, but rather the marginal outposts of triangle Polynesia itself: Hawai'i, Easter Island, and New Zealand. (Kirch and Yen 1982:345)

Thus, while no evidence of actual sweet potato transfer exists at this time, complex pre-Magellanic trade networks linked Polynesian Outliers and the eastern Melanesian islands, which in turn were linked to the New Guinea mainland. Facilitated by efficient sailing vessels, trade networks along the eastern New Guinea coast and adjacent islands were well established by the first millennium AD. For example, obsidian from Fergusson Island has been found near Port Moresby, at sites dating to over 1000 years BP (Allen 1977:389, 411). Other evidence suggests that trade networks in the interior of New Guinea are even more ancient. Coastal shell had reached the New Guinea Highlands as early as 9000 BP (ibid.:389). Obsidian flakes from Fergusson Island and New Britain have been found in sites in the Papua New Guinea Highlands in levels dated to the last 5,000 years. In fact, obsidian from New Britain has been widely traded for the last 11,000 years (White with O'Connell 1982:189–190). Thus we argue that, based on circumstantial evidence, a prehistoric introduction of sweet potatoes into New Guinea from the east cannot be summarily discounted. We proceed to review the New Guinea literature bearing on this problem.

SWEET POTATOES IN NEW GUINEA

The relative antiquity of the sweet potato in the Highlands of New Guinea and the impact that its adoption may have had on the ecology, economics, and social organization of the region have been the subject of considerable discussion and debate. James B. Watson (1965a, 1965b, 1967, 1977) was one of the first to argue for a relatively recent introduction and significant impact. Basing his initial (1965a) argument primarily on ethnographic and ethnohistoric data, Watson reasoned that pre-Ipomoean horticulture in the Highlands was probably a seasonal, intermittent, or supplementary practice of foraging people until sweet potato gardening brought about revolutionary changes. In at least one group, the Huli, sweet potatoes are expressly recognized as an "introduced" crop recently found growing in a wild state.

In examining the possible significance of the introduction of sweet potato cultivation in Highlands populations, other researchers (summarized in Golson 1982) stressed the properties of the cultivar itself: it is quicker to mature and more productive at higher altitudes than the older crops, its rooting system allows for partial harvesting with subsequent development of additional tubers, and it is more tolerant of agriculturally degraded soils (Golson 1982:131). Thus W. C. Clarke (1977:161) argued for both extensive and intensive changes in the Highlands horticultural base. Cultivation could not only move into higher altitudes and on to poorer soils, but sweet potatoes could also be used as a follow-up crop in a rotational system. Additionally, they provide excellent fodder for pigs, adding to the impetus for intensification (Watson 1977).

The possibility of revolutionary changes in the Highlands horticultural base might suggest that the social organization of the Highlands at contact, if indeed linked with an "Ipomoean revolution," could have been merely a transitional phase. If so, the "big-man"–type society, comprised of densely populated cultivators but lacking complex social hierarchies or social stratification, may not really be a stable type of social organization. Of course, other researchers (for example, Clarke 1966, 1971; and especially Brookfield and White 1968) take a less revolutionary view of the changes precipitated by sweet potato cultivation, preferring to interpret these changes as the result of more long-term processes. Nevertheless, the prevailing view is that the sweet potato has probably been in Highland New Guinea for only a few hundred years (Barrau 1957; Conklin 1963; Yen 1974) and that it did precipitate widespread changes in the horticultural base.

A distinctly minority view holds that the presence of the sweet potato in New Guinea may be considerably older than three hundred years. Golson initially (Powell et al. 1975:46; Golson 1977a:52) proposed an introduction of the sweet potato by about 1200 BP. However, he later revised this view (1977b:626–628; Golson and Gardner 1990:407). Golson (1982:131–132) interprets certain changes apparent in phase 6 of the Kuk drainage sequence as marking the incorporation of sweet potatoes into the swamp gardens. Charred fragments of tubers are first found in this level. Golson places phase 6 shortly after the fall of "Tibito ash" from the volcanic eruption on Long Island, which Blong (1982:193–194) and Polach (1982) estimate at about 300 years BP. In contrast to Golson, however, Paul Gorecki chooses to interpret the Kuk and related evidence as suggesting a much earlier introduction. He states (1986:164):

> The end of Phase C is notable for two events. One is a marked increase in forest clearance in many parts of the Highlands, and particularly at altitudes higher than Kuk; the second is the possible introduction of a tree-fallowing system on drylands (Powell 1982[a]:29–30). Both events occurred at around 1,200–1,000 BP. For reasons detailed below, these two events can be correlated with the possible introduction of the sweet potato into the Highlands.

Perhaps because of the lack of hard evidence for sweet potato antiquity in the New Guinea Highlands, prevailing opinion seems to favor a historical route of introduction from Southeast Asia via Indonesia. L. J. Brass (cited in Watson 1965a:299) "believes there is little doubt that the sweet potato reached New Guinea from the west, through bird-of-paradise hunters, traders, and other Malays. He estimates its arrival on the coast of West New Guinea (Irian Barat) about 350 years ago." Similarly, Pamela Swadling (1986:45) states,

> The sweet potato, now the staple food in the densely populated Highlands, was introduced here about 300 to 400 years ago from eastern Indonesia. . . . The Spaniards took the sweet potato to Europe and Africa. From there the Portuguese and Spaniards took it to Ambon, Timor and the Moluccas in the 15th and 16th centuries. . . . Papuan pirates, other people from the coast of the Cendrawasih Peninsula paying tribute to Tidore, or Malay traders, may have introduced the sweet potato to coastal areas of Irian Jaya, and from there it was traded to the Highlands.

This interpretation also seems to be favored by Yen (1974:259), who proposes a tripartite hypothesis accounting for the observed Pacific distribution. The Indonesian or Western route of introduction described above Yen calls the "Batata Line," from a Caribbean lexical item for sweet potato. It is this route of introduction that he believes accounts for the presence of the sweet potato in New Guinea.

Despite the persistence of this viewpoint, however, there is evidence suggestive of other possible routes of introduction of the sweet potato into New Guinea. Drawing upon palynological evidence, J. M. Powell made the following observation:

> Flenley's (1967) evidence for forest reduction probably due to human activities at Lake Inim at 2530m altitude at an inferred date of 1600 years ago may be associated with the cultivation of sweet potato there,

> and the Hopes' (1974) record of *Casuarina* being grown in Chimbu from circa 1200 years ago may be interpreted in similar terms. Such a sequence requires the sweet potato to arrive in New Guinea from the direction of Oceania rather than South-east Asia. While this is not generally accepted, there is no real evidence against it and such an entry is quite feasible if the early dates for its presence in Polynesia are correct. (1976:179–180)

Naturally, high-altitude forest clearing does not necessarily establish the existence of sweet potatoes, but it can be interpreted in this way. Powell does not repeat her original interpretation in a later (1982) publication, but Gorecki (pers. comm.) continues to maintain this view.

Other indirect evidence for an early introduction of sweet potatoes derives from oral histories relating to the eruption of Long Island, dated to approximately 300 years BP (Blong 1982:191). Ten of the legends collected by Blong from areas throughout the Highlands relate the effects of the Tibito ash fall on sweet potato gardens. The fact that so many groups accurately reported the serious impacts of ash fall on sweet potato cultivation and considered it a catastrophic event at the time suggest that sweet potatoes may well have been an important staple crop in the New Guinea Highlands by some three hundred years ago.

While there are numerous reports by patrol officers of extensive sweet potato cultivation present at contact in many areas of New Guinea, such reports do not provide evidence for pre-Magellanic cultivation since the cultivar may have spread throughout the island before extensive European contact. Nevertheless, it is interesting to note that there are some quite early accounts, such as the published reports on the Cambridge Expedition to the Torres Straits (1888–89). This expedition took place only fourteen years after the first South Sea Islands missionaries arrived in the area. A. C. Haddon (1929) reports several specific legends (17:28–30, 18:31–35), related by elderly informants, describing how a particular culture hero, Sida, brought sweet potatoes and other vegetable crops to the Murray Islands from the New Guinea mainland.

A related and interesting argument is made by Dan Jorgensen (1990:4) in examining why the Ipomoean revolution failed to take place among the Telefolmin and many of their Mountain Ok neighbors. Jorgensen points out that other New World crops such as maize, *Xanthosoma* taro, and cassava would have made their appearance at roughly the same time as a post-Magellanic sweet potato. Yet they are recognized as having exogenous origins by people in widely scattered parts of New Guinea, whereas sweet potatoes are "regarded by a good many peoples—including Telefolmin—as an ancient and thoroughly indigenous crop." There do not appear to be as many oral histories of the arrival of sweet potatoes as there are for these other crops.

We now turn our attention to the linguistic evidence for possible routes of introduction of the sweet potato into New Guinea. We believe that sufficient linguistic diversity exists in the terms used for the sweet potato in New Guinea to cast doubt on a purely Indonesian route of introduction in only the past three hundred years. Furthermore, the terms do not resemble Indonesian terms as closely as such a hypothesis might predict. Rather, many terms are more suggestive of a possible route of introduction through Polynesia.

LINGUISTIC EVIDENCE FOR THE PACIFIC HYPOTHESIS

Considering the substantial amount of ethnographic, ethnohistoric, botanical, and archaeological data employed in the investigation of the introduction and distribution of sweet potato cultivation in the Highlands, it is surprising that relatively little linguistic evidence on this problem has been collected or examined. This section represents the results of our most recent work in compiling, organizing, and analyzing such linguistic data.

We began by compiling about 1700 generic terms for "sweet potato" from about 450 languages in New Guinea and adjacent areas, from many different sources. Many of these terms were elicited by persons who were not trained linguists; hence these data must be interpreted with considerable caution. Nevertheless, by using these data, we identified roughly sixty phonetically similar sets, mapped the present locations of the languages in the largest sets, and inspected them for patterns in distribution. The sets most important for our arguments are presented in the tables and maps accompanying the text.

As can be seen from table 5, there seems to be relatively little similarity between the terms found in Western Indonesia and Malaysia and those found in western New Guinea. We found relatively little similarity between either of these areas and Papua New Guinea. If sweet potatoes were first introduced to western New Guinea via Indonesia or Malaysia in the seventeenth century, one might expect noticeable traces of the introduction to be preserved in the words indigenous peoples of the area use or used for sweet potatoes. Although our data from Irian Jaya are far from complete, we do not find any clear evidence for such patterns. Contrary to what might be predicted from a west-to-east historical-diffusion hypothesis, we find terms suggestive of an early historical introduction, such as *ubi kastela* and *katela,* to be relatively common in the west, but not found at all in Irian Jaya.

On the other hand, there are some plausible (but as yet unsubstantiated) connections between southeastern New Guinea and the New Guinea Highlands. These patterns, although open to other interpretations, are consistent with the Pacific hypothesis.

1. The Kumara Set

We have found that the Polynesian word for sweet potato, *kumara,* and related terms are used in many of the Austronesian and Non-Austronesian (NAN) languages of southeastern Papua. Table 1 and map 1 provide a list of the *kumara* linguistic terms and their present geographical locations. Naturally, the set of *kumara* terms could have

Table 1
The *Kumara* Set

Language	*Term*	*Source*
DOBU	komwara	Dutton 1973
ENATAULU	kumwala	Dutton 1973
GALEYA	komuara	SIL
	kumuara	Dutton 1973
GUMASI	koumwala	SIL
KEHELALA	kumara	Armstrong 1923
	kumala	SIL
Kiwai	kamara	Dutton 1973
	gamara	Murray 1919
Koiari	kumara	Dutton 1973
MUYUW	komalo	Murray 1919
SEWA BAY	kumuara	Dutton 1973
	kumuala	SIL
TABARA	kumala	Dutton 1973
TAWALA	kumala	Dutton 1973
TUBETUBE	tumwala	SIL
	kumwala	Dutton 1973
WEDAU	kumara	King 1894
	kumara	MacGregor 1892

Note: In the tables and text, SIL is an acronym for Summer Institute of Linguistics. All SIL data were provided by Terry Hays. Austronesian (AN) languages are in upper case, non-Austronesian (NAN) languages are in lower case.

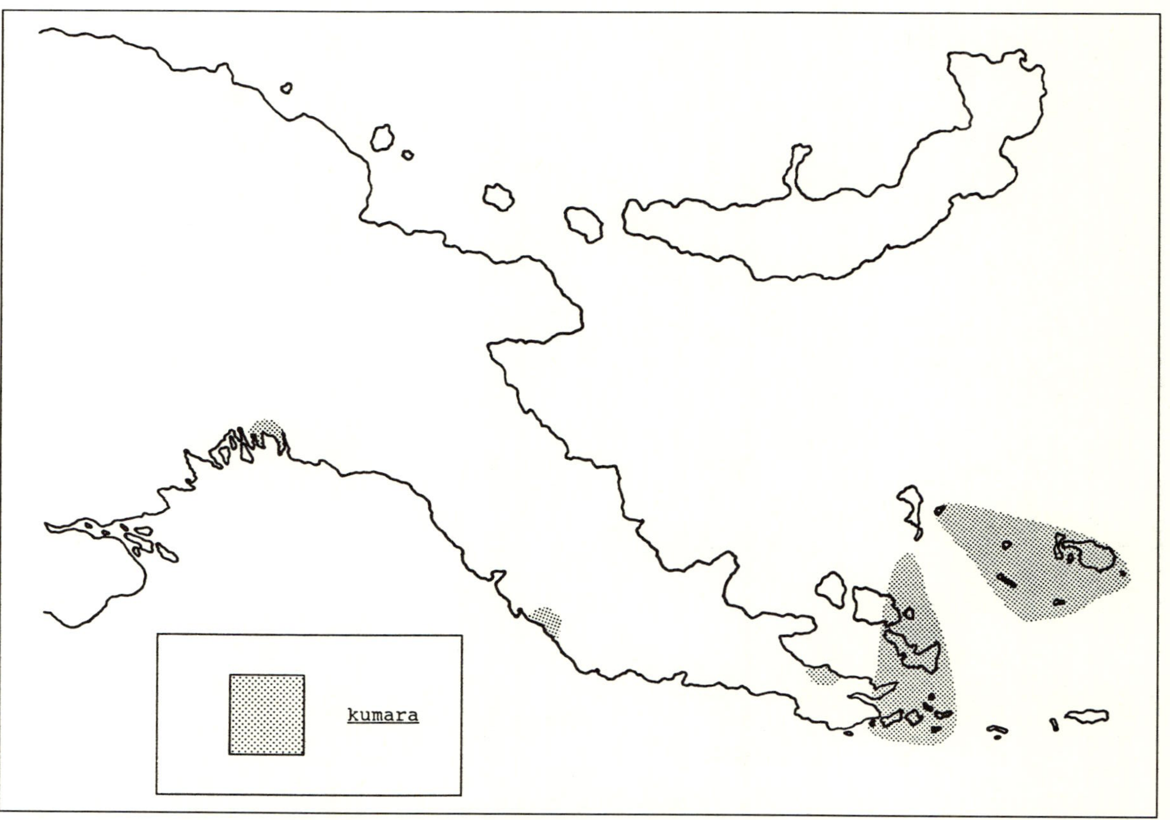

Map 1. Geographical distribution of the *kumara* set.

resulted from an early historical introduction of sweet potatoes. This view may also be supported by the fact that terms other than *kumara* have also been recorded for a number of the languages found in table 1. Variants of the term *kanukanua* are particularly common, for example. Nevertheless, we maintain that the observed linguistic pattern can also be explained as a result of a possible prehistoric introduction from Polynesia.

Some of the words in this set may have been borrowed from Polynesian languages spoken by South Sea Island missionaries in the late 19th and early 20th centuries who may have introduced the crop (see Latukefu 1978 for a discussion of SSI missionaries in Melanesia). However, the term from Wedau (MacGregor 1890; King 1894) was recorded very shortly after the first missions were established in the area. According to Latukefu (1978:91–93) and Rowley (1966:134–135), the earliest missions in New Guinea with Polynesian workers were (1) in 1872, in Manu village on the Papuan coast east of Saibai Island, with mission workers from Rarotonga and Niue; (2) in 1875, a Wesleyan Methodist mission in the Duke of York Islands, with nine Fijians and two Samoans, some with their wives; (3) in 1882, thirteen Rarotongans, Port Moresby; and (4) in 1891, a Methodist mission on Dobu Island. The last-established Dobu Island mission was geographically closest to the mainland Wedau speakers contacted by MacGregor and King. MacGregor actually recorded the Wedau term *kumara* before the establishment of this mission.

Certainly Polynesian missionaries as well as early whalers and traders, who knew the word from their Polynesian travels, could have had some influence in spreading the term and the crop. However, as we have argued earlier, the geographical area represented by the *kumara* set would have been a likely point of introduction from Polynesia in prehistoric times. An east-to-west prehistoric diffusion hypothesis would predict some trace of a *kumara* term to be present in this area, just as we have observed.

2. The Kaima Set

Table 2 and map 2 present the *kaima* set of terms. This set includes *kaima* (2a), *kama* (2b), and *kampek* (2c). The relatedness of these three subsets has not yet been confirmed through historical-linguistic investigation, but the two most geographically distant sets, *kaima* and *kama,* seem, on surface inspection, to be the most similar, while the geographically intermediate and most limited subset, *kampek,* is less like the others. The *kaima* set may be historically related to the *kumara*

Table 2
The *Kaima* Set

Language	*Term*	*Source*
A. *kaima*		
Ambasi	kaema	SIL
Bariji	kaima	Dutton 1973
Baruya	kaɛma	Dutton 1973
Binandere	kaéma	SIL
Boazi	kaieb	SIL
Domu	kaeyomo	SIL
Gahuki	kemba	SIL
Gogodala	kaema	SIL
Koita	kaema	SIL
Komba	kemba	SIL
Kuini	kaimba	Dutton 1973
Minanibai	kaima	Dutton 1973
MOTU	kaema	Dutton 1973
	kaemadahu	Lawes 1890
NARA	kaema	Dutton 1973
Notu	kaema	SIL
RORO	kaema	Dutton 1973
	ta:kaema	Lawes 1890
Siane	komba	SIL
SINAGORO	kaima	SIL
Sirio	kaɛma	SIL
Suki	kaima	SIL
Waia	kaima	Dutton 1973
Yareba	kaema	SIL
Yega	kaika	SIL
Zimakani	kaima	SIL
B. *kama*		
Binumarien	kama	Cappell 1949
	kama:	SIL
Gadsup	kama	SIL
	kamai	Capell 1949
	kamami	SIL
Tairora	ka:ma	Hays (p.c.)
	ama	Cappell 1949
Usarufa	kama:ma	Bee 1965
C. *kampek*		
Biangai	kampek	SIL
Tauade	kampek	Dutton 1973

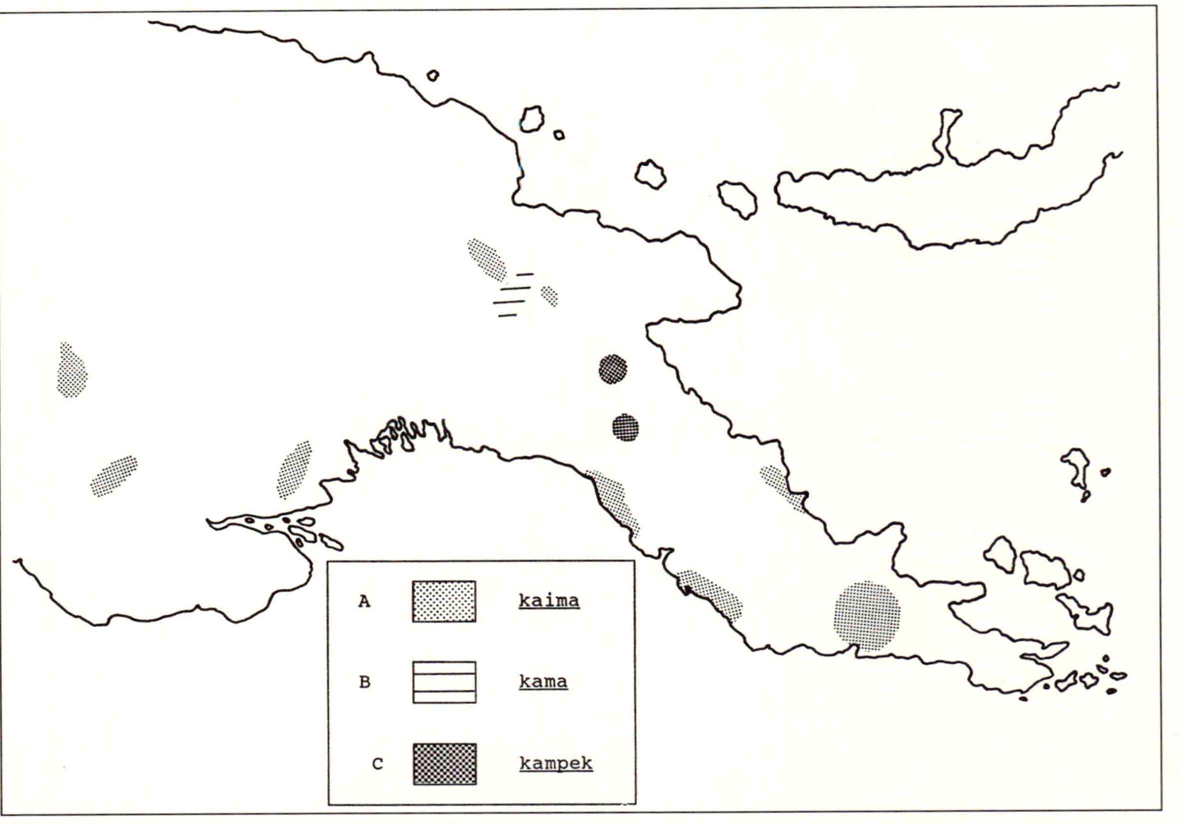

Map 2. Geographical distribution of the *kaima* set.

set. If so, one could easily posit a prehistoric diffusion from Polynesia through the Massim and Papuan Coast areas and into the Highlands (based on the trade routes pictured in map 4). Of course, historical diffusion cannot be precluded either, especially since the Hiri Motu term for sweet potato, *kaema,* was widely used by government officers and police after contact.

The *kaima* and *kama* subsets, if related, suggest a diffusion of the term between southeastern Papua and the Eastern Highlands. While the actual direction of the linguistic transfer cannot be ascertained without further research, a prehistoric transfer from lowland coastal Papua into the Highlands is plausible, especially given the fact that the Motu (whose generic term for sweet potato is *kaema*) were extremely active traders in prehistoric times. The NAN-speaking Koiari (the Koita term is also *kaema*) were participants in the Western Motu trade network. If the *kampek* subset is historically related to the other two, we could posit the Koiari, Tauade, and Biangai (among others) as mediators in the transfer to the Eastern Highlands.

3. The Siabulu Set

Table 3 and map 3 provide the terms and geographical distribution of the *siabulu* set. This set is concentrated in the Southern Highlands and Western Provinces of Papua New Guinea, with representatives in the Irian Jaya Highlands, and far-flung members in Gulf, Central, Milne Bay, West and East Sepik, and Madang Provinces. T. E. Dutton (1973:491) reports that reflexes of "**(t)isiaburu*" occur in NAN languages of the Bird's Head area of Irian Jaya but does not provide examples. The geographical distribution of the *siabulu* set strongly suggests a north-south or south-north transfer across the Western Highlands in Papua New Guinea.

Map 4 (from Brookfield with Hart 1971) illustrates early 20th-century trade routes in eastern New Guinea. Trade from the Fly River Delta to the central *siabulu* region pictured in map 3 was well established prehistorically. On this basis, we posit that the linguistic transfer probably occurred in a south-to-north direction, and west to Irian Jaya, rather than through the Sepik, where linguistic evidence suggests a relatively recent introduction.

4. The ToToTe Set

The *ToToTe* set, presented in table 4 and map 5, is subdivided into *tokote* (4a), *bokoko* (4b), and *bako* (4c). The *bako* subset, found in

Table 3
The *Siabulu* Set

Language	*Term*	*Source*
Agala	sibalu	SIL
	si'bii	SIL
Bainapi	siapuri	Dutton 1973
	siapri	SIL
Beami	siabulu	Dutton 1973
	siapuru	Dutton 1973
	sabulu	SIL
Biaka	sußulu'	SIL
	siΦεro'	SIL
Fasu	siabulu	Dutton 1973
	supuru	SIL
G. V. Dani	sepoeroe	Stokhof 1983
Hattam	sieba	Loukotka 1966
Honibo	siyabul	Dutton 1973
Kaluli	siabulu	Dutton 1973
	siapuru	Dutton 1973
Kamula	se'yabεlu	SIL
	saipru	SIL
Kasua	siabulu	Dutton 1973
	siapulu	Dutton 1973
Konai	sa'buyu	SIL
	sibu'yu	SIL
	siyi'bulu	SIL
Kubo	siyafu:	Dutton 1973
Lower GV Dani	supuku	Bromley 1972
Mianmin	siripuεte[a]	SIL
Nomad	siyabul	SIL
	siyofulu	SIL
Onabasulu	isabulu	SIL
Pesechem	soemberoe	Snell 1913
Rocky Peak	siblu	SIL
	sibalo'	SIL
Samo	siyafulu	Dutton 1973
Soba	suburu	Godschalk p.c.
Sonia	sibeii	SIL
Telefol	saburup	Champion 1932
Tomu	siyobulu	Dutton 1973
Yali	suburu	Zollner 1977

Note: [a]Morren (pers. comm.) sees this as merely the English sweet potato, and notes that the actual term is wan + variety.

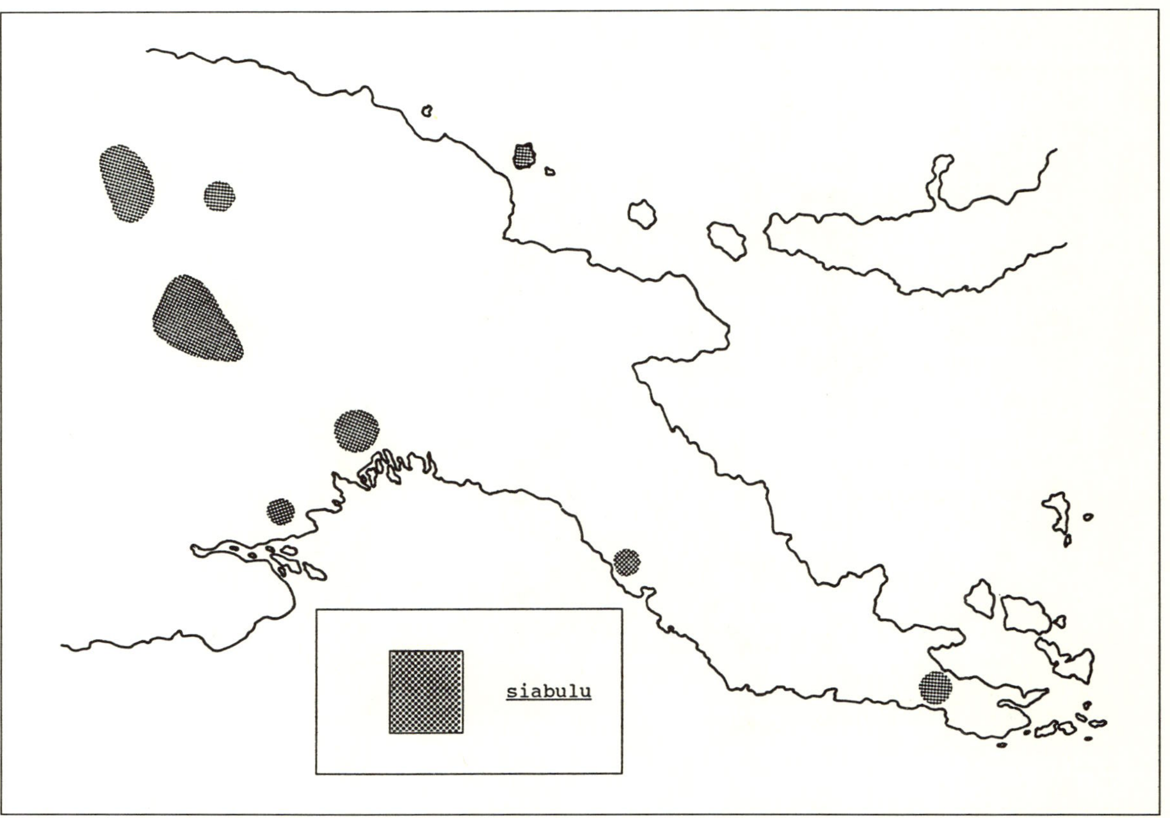

Map 3. Geographical distribution of the *siabulu* set.

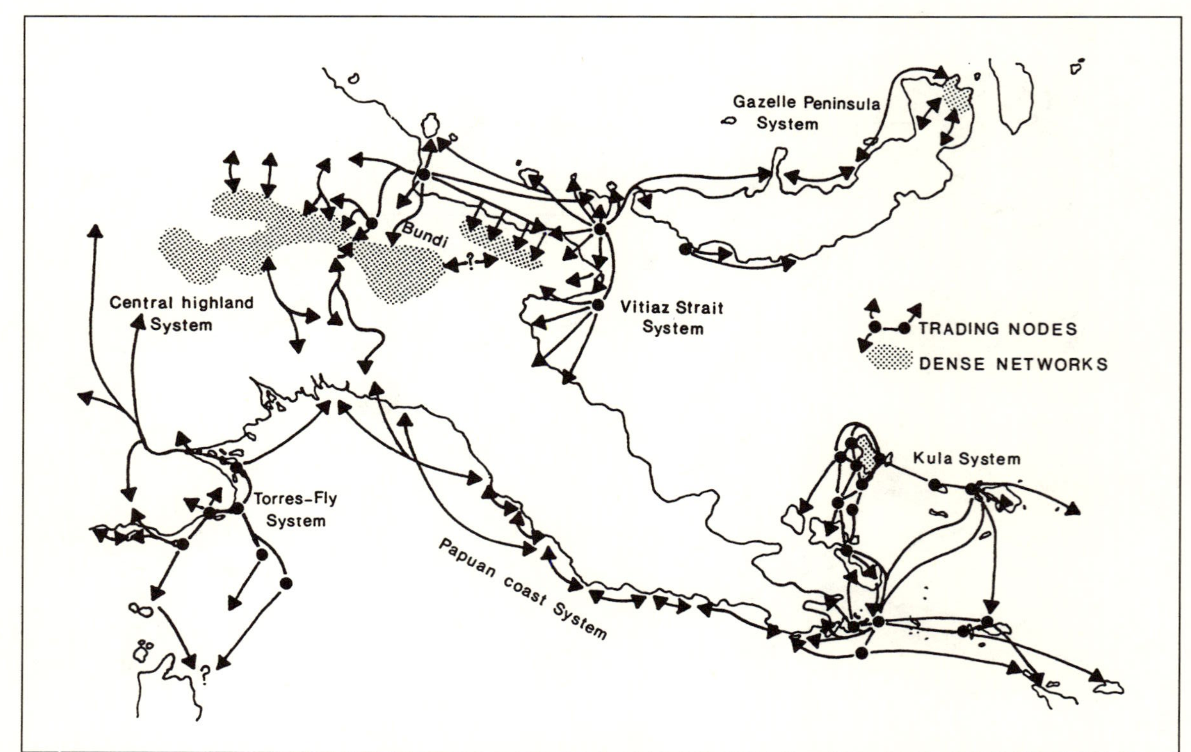

Map 4. Early twentieth-century trade routes in Papua New Guinea. *Source:* Brookfield & Hart (1971).

Table 4
The *ToToTe* Set

Language	*Term*	*Source*
A. *Tokote*		
Ari-Wauna	totobe	SIL
Dugeme	tokose	Dutton 1973
Gira	tokote	SIL
Gogodala	tokobi	Ray 1913
	tokobe	SIL
Karima	kokose	Dutton 1973
Mena	kokore	Murray 1920
	tokose	Murray 1925
Nahu	tokote	SIL
Omati	sokose	Dutton 1973
Tirio	tokobe	Ray 1913
Ufim	togodɛ	SIL
B. *bokoko*		
Kâte	bokoko	SIL
Koiari	takoko	Dutton 1973
	takokwa	Dutton 1973
Managalasi	ßakok^{w}a	SIL
Mape	bokokoc	SIL
C. *bako*		
Morafa	bako:	SIL
Nahu	mbako	SIL
Rawa	bak	SIL
	mbako	SIL
	mbak^{h}o	SIL

Madang Province, is the most linguistically divergent but is geographically circumscribed by the *tokote* set. *Tokote* is found in two clusters, in the western Gulf and Fly River Delta regions, and in the border area between Madang and Morobe provinces. The *bokoko* set is found primarily on the tip of the Huon Peninsula and in the interior of Central Province. While we could plausibly imagine links between the Koiari and the western Gulf via Austronesian-speaking traders, links between these two areas and the Morobe-Madang clusters are less clear. One possible explanation is that the distribution of the

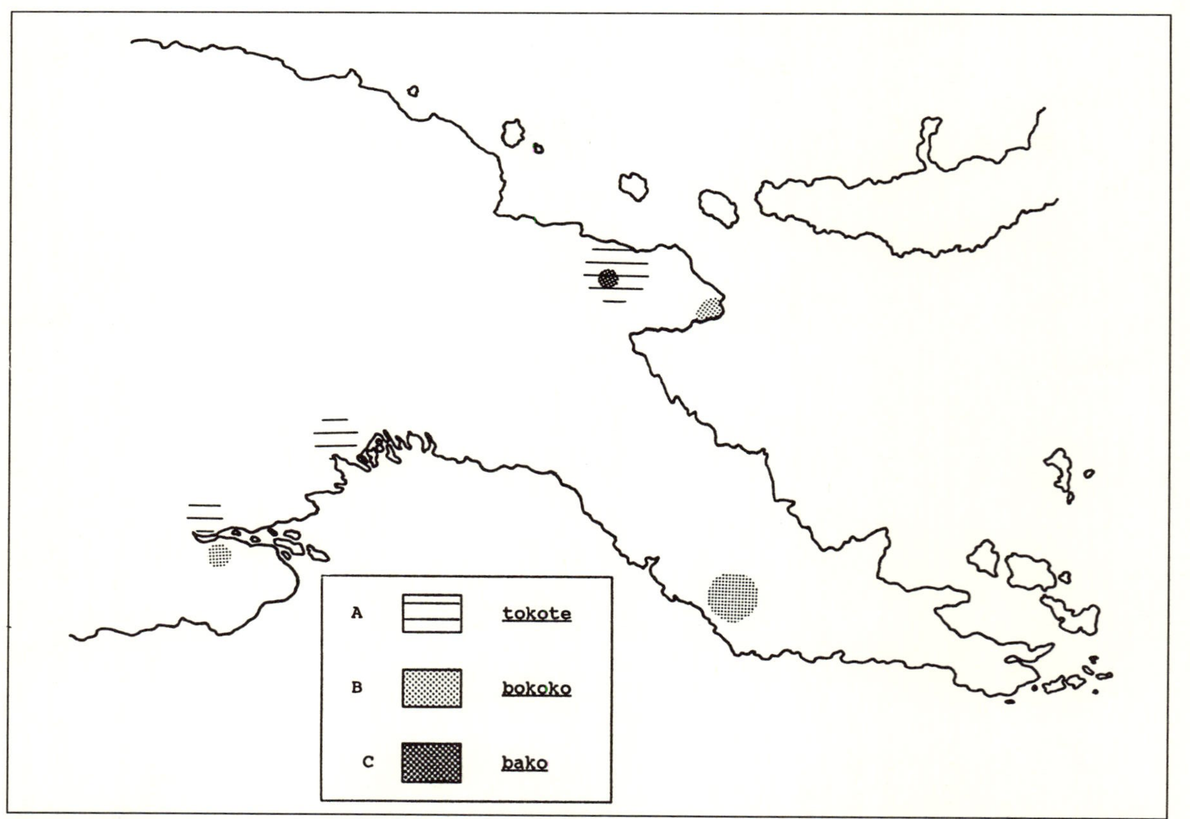

Map 5. Geographical distribution of the *ToToTe* set.

terms in these sets was once more widespread but that subsequent events in the Highlands and elsewhere have obscured this pattern.

WESTERN NEW GUINEA

Since our data for Irian Jaya and adjacent areas to the west were much less complete than for Papua New Guinea, we tended to be more inclusive in constructing our sets. The resultant sets are smaller and somewhat less homogeneous than those constructed for Papua New Guinea, with a greater probability of including erroneous members and of suggesting spurious patterns. The patterns we did identify were somewhat less clear than those previously described for Papua New Guinea. Because the data are somewhat more manageable, however, we have decided to present them in some detail in table 5 and in maps 6 and 7, in order to facilitate further research.

There are some clear clusters in the Irian Jaya Highlands, some of which have outlying members. These outliers are few in number, however, and by no means positively related. For example, the apparent connection between terms from Irian Jaya and island Indonesia suggested by set B may well be spurious. The Irian Jaya language terms found in set F are probably related to the *siabulu* set previously described. Given the strong affinity of these set F words with nearby linguistic terms to the east, we cannot confidently credit the inclusion of outliers to the west.

There are clusters such as H, I, and J, centered in Western Indonesia and Malaysia, that suggest very recent introduction. Interestingly, set H (a *batata/patata* cluster) is common in the Moluccas, a likely site for sweet potato transfer into New Guinea from the west. Yet we found no trace of this term in Irian Jaya. We likewise found a *patete* cluster in northwestern coastal Papua New Guinea (not otherwise reported here), which we also took to be a recent introduction, and which did not seem to have broader affinities in PNG. Set G, indicating a possible connection between Java and Irian Jaya, we found interesting but much too small to credit without many more intervening terms. From our point of view, the set most suggestive of sweet potato transfer from west to east into New Guinea is set L, which links Tidore with several groups in northwestern Irian Jaya. This set seems very localized, however, without evidence of broader links. In short, we found no strong linguistic support for an early western route of diffusion of the sweet potato into New Guinea.

Table 5
Terms and Term Sets for the Sweet Potato

Term	*Language*	*Source*
A.		
bei	W. Dani	Wirz 1924, Stokhoff 1983, le Roux 1950
bieh	W. Dani	Wirz 1924
bijem	Dem	le Roux 1950
bijem	Dem	Damm 1961
boei	Grand Valley Dani	Stokhof 1983
mbi	Baliem Valley	Temple 1962
mboi	Grand Valley Dani	le Roux 1950
bieh	Pesechem	Stokhof 1983
biejen	Dem	Stokhof 1983
boei	Ndani	Stokhof 1983
pei	W. Dani	le Roux 1950
peya	W. Dani	le Roux 1950
mbi	W. Dani	Larson 1987
B.		
bonden	Yonggom	Austen 1923
poteng	Yonggom	SIL
boreng	Ninggirum	Austen 1926
pondeng	N. Kati	Drabbe 1954
bondeng	S. Kati	Austen 1921–22
omborop	S. Kati	Drabbe 1954
boneng	Ngalum	SIL, Hylkema 1974
bondol	Eipomek	Heeschen et al. 1983
bodin	Java	Dwyer 1957
boled	Sunda	Dwyer 1957
hoewi boled	Sunda	Oostroom & Hoogland 1954, Dwyer 1957
C.		
hiperi	Grand Valley Dani	Matthiesen 1963
balerei	Moni	Damm 1961
balerai	Moni	le Roux 1948–51
D.		
farenggend	Waropen	Held 1957
farengend	Waropen	Anceaux 1961
farekio	Waropen	Anceaux 1961
farkiam	Wandamen	Anceaux 1961
farkia	Biak	Anceaux 1961

Table 5
Terms and Term Sets for the Sweet Potato (continued)

Term	*Language*	*Source*
paringgeni	Ambai	Anceaux 1961
parinnge	Serui-Laut	Anceaux 1961
paringke	Ansus	Anceaux 1961
E.		
elom	Uhunduni	le Roux 1948–51
errom	W. Dani	le Roux 1948–51
erom	W. Dani	Larson 1987
eroem	Grand Valley Dani	Stokhof 1983
F.		
suburu	Yali	Zollner 1988
supuku	Lower G. V. Dani	Bromley 1972
sepoeroe	Grand Valley Dani	Stokhof 1983
soemberoe	Nduga (Pesechem)	Snell 1913
suburu	Soba	Godschalk p.c.
sieba	Hattam	Loukoutka 1966
sabrang	Java	Steiner 1961
sabbheang	Sunda	Dwyer 1957
G.		
toendoe	Nduga	Stokhof 1983
toendoe	Dauwa/Nduga	Stokhof 1983
toenda-woelong	Java	Dwyer 1957
H.		
batata	Celebes	Oostroom & Hoogland 1954, Steiner 1961
watata	Celebes	Oostroom & Hoogland 1954, Steiner 1961
batate	Moluccas	Conklin 1963
batata	Ambon	Conklin 1963
patatas	Ambon	Oostroom & Hoogland 1954, Steiner 1961
watata	Ambon	Conklin 1963
ihim basala	Seram	Oostroom & Hoogland 1954, Steiner 1961
patatas	Timor, Alfur	Salaman 1949
batata	Timor	Salaman 1949, Conklin 1963
watala	Timor	Salaman 1949
watata	Timor	Salaman 1949, Conklin 1963

(*continued*)

Table 5
Terms and Term Sets for the Sweet Potato (continued)

Term	*Language*	*Source*
I.		
ubi	Malayan Peninsula	Dwyer 1957
ubi keladi	Malayan Peninsula	Oostroom & Hoogland 1954, Steiner 1961
ubi djawa	Minangkabau	Oostroom & Hoogland 1954
ubi ketelo	Minangkabau	Oostroom & Hoogland 1954
ubi pelo	Minangkabau	Oostroom & Hoogland 1954
ubi djawa	N. Sumatra	Oostroom & Hoogland 1954, Steiner 1961
ubi pelo	N. Sumatra	Oostroom & Hoogland 1954, Steiner 1961
ubi tjina	E. Sumatra	Oostroom & Hoogland 1954, Steiner 1961
ubi kastela	Seram	Oostroom & Hoogland 1954, Steiner 1961
ubi	Bauri (Bauzi)	Briley 1976
J.		
'achila	Malaysia	Conklin 1963
kastila	Malaysia	Conklin 1963
katela	Malaysia	Conklin 1963
katela rambat	Malayan Peninsula	Dwyer 1957
katelo	Minangkabau	Oostroom & Hoogland 1954
ubi ketelo	Minangkabau	Oostroom & Hoogland 1954
katelo	N. Sumatra	Oostroom & Hoogland 1954, Steiner 1961
katela	Java	Dwyer 1957
ketela	Java	Oostroom & Hoogland 1954, Dwyer 1957, Steiner 1961
ketela pendem	Java	Oostroom & Hoogland 1954, Dwyer 1957
ketela rambat	Java	Oostroom & Hoogland 1954, Dwyer 1957, Steiner 1961
tela	Java	Dwyer 1957
tela loeng	Java	Dwyer 1957
keledek	Java	Oostroom & Hoogland 1954, Dwyer 1957, Steiner 1961
setilo	Lampong	Oostroom & Hoogland 1954
longga tela	Sunda	Dwyer 1957
katela	Sunda	Dwyer 1957
kasela	Bali	Oostroom & Hoogland 1954

Table 5
Terms and Term Sets for the Sweet Potato (continued)

Term	*Language*	*Source*
asitela	Seram	Oostroom & Hoogland 1954, Steiner 1961
kaitela	Seram	Oostroom & Hoogland 1954, Steiner 1961
kastera	Seram	Oostroom & Hoogland 1954, Steiner 1961
uwi kastela	Seram	Oostroom & Hoogland 1954, Steiner 1961
kesera	Busami (< Malay)	Anceaux 1961
K.		
keladek	Malayan Peninsula	Oostroom & Hoogland 1954, Steiner 1961
keladi	Malayan Peninsula	Oostroom & Hoogland 1954, Steiner 1961
Keledek	Malayan Peninsula	Dwyer 1957
ubi keladi	Malayan Peninsula	Oostroom & Hoogland 1954, Steiner 1961
L.		
daso	Tidore	Oostroom & Hoogland 1954
daso	Halmahera	Oostroom & Hoogland 1954
sasu	Brat (Ayfat)	Schoorl 1979
sasu	Brat (Mejprat)	SIL
ranso	Biak (Noef)	Oostroom & Hoogland 1954
(r)ansio	Biak	Anceaux 1961
M. Isolated terms		
aga	Riantana	Drabbe 1949
avi	Serui-Laut	Anceaux 1961
badagaj	Moni	Drabbe 1949
bage	Celebes	Oostroom & Hoogland 1954, Steiner 1961
bwisbwis	Berik (Berrik)	Westrum 1975
demabde	Awembiak (?)	Stokhof 1983
dien	Dem	Stokhof 1983
doeri	Wodani (Wolani)	le Roux 1948–51
esa	Uria (Sawi)	Stokhof 1983
en mav	Kei	Oostrom & Hoogland 1954
gadong	N. Sumatra	Oostroom & Hoogland 1954, Steiner 1961

(*continued*)

Table 5
Terms and Term Sets for the Sweet Potato (continued)

Term	*Language*	*Source*
gumbili	Moluccas	Conklin 1963
heis-kaf	Marind	Drabbe 1954
hoewi mandang	Sunda	Oostroom & Hoogland 1954, Dwyer 1957
ima	Ternate	Oostroom & Hoogland 1954
ingge	Sentani	Stokhof 1983
joknim	Ndom	Drabbe 1949
kamma	Moi	Stokhof 1983
karipiani	Wandamen	Anceaux 1961
kasfin	Berik (Berrik)	Stokhof 1983
katabang	Sumbawa	Salaman 1949
katabang	Sunda	Steiner 1961
kepileu	N. Sumatra	Oostroom & Hoogland 1945, Steiner 1961
kibdek	Moi	Stokhof 1983
lame djawa	Celebes	Oostrom & Hoogland 1954, Steiner 1961
lame kamumu	Celebes	Oostroom & Hoogland 1954, Steiner 1961
lame kandora	Celebes	Oostroom & Hoogland 1954, Steiner 1961
loli	Timor, Alfur	Oostroom & Hoogland 1954, Steiner 1961
lolir	Timor, Alfur	Oostroom & Hoogland 1954, Steiner 1961
makupa	Yaqay	Drabbe 1954
mamber	Mor	Anceaux 1961
mangat	Tamagario (Buru)	Oostroom & Hoogland 1954, Steiner 1961
mekuk	Matbrat (Mejprat)	Elmberg 1968
momai	Ekagi (Kapauku)	le Roux 1948–51
mou	Meax	Wirz 1923
n'gane	Yaqay	Nevermaun 1940
ndu-kaf	Marind	Drabbe 1954
ningkoy	Kemtuik (Kemtuk)	van der Wilden 1976
nota	Ekago (Kapauku)	Drabbe 1949, le Roux 1948–51, Damm 1961, Pospisil 1963, Stokhof 1983
olananin	Nimboran	Anceaux 1965
ornaning	Nimboran	Anceaux 1965

Table 5
Terms and Term Sets for the Sweet Potato (continued)

Term	*Language*	*Source*
paara tukale	Ambon	Oostrom & Hoogland 1954, Steiner 61
pamea	Kamoro (Mimika)	Pouwer 1955
piek	N. Sumatra	Oostroom & Hoogland 1954, Steiner 1961
sampoessah	Sobei (Sarmi)	Stokhof 1983
sane	Wetar	Oostroom & Hoogland 1954, Steiner 1961
siane fatabre	Irahutu (Irarutu)	Anceaux 1961
takao	Tumawo (Sko)	SIL
tales-kenari	Java	Dwyer 1957
tambawa	Awembiak (?)	Stokhof 1983
tebiki	Moi	Stokhof 1983
tingalan	Java	Dwyer 1957
urlau	Aru	Oostroom & Hoogland 1954, Steiner 1961
usu	Aru	Oostroom & Hoogland 1954, Steiner 1961
vee kuni	Kimaghama	Drabbe 1949
wamberi	Wandamen	Anceaux 1961
waning	Mekwei (Mek)	Bromley 1972
watibor	Amberbaken (Kebar)	Miedema & Welling 1985
wob	Arsotami (?)	Stokhof 1983

Note: These terms and term sets are from Irian Jaya and adjacent areas in Indonesia and Malaysia (pictured in figures 6 and 7).

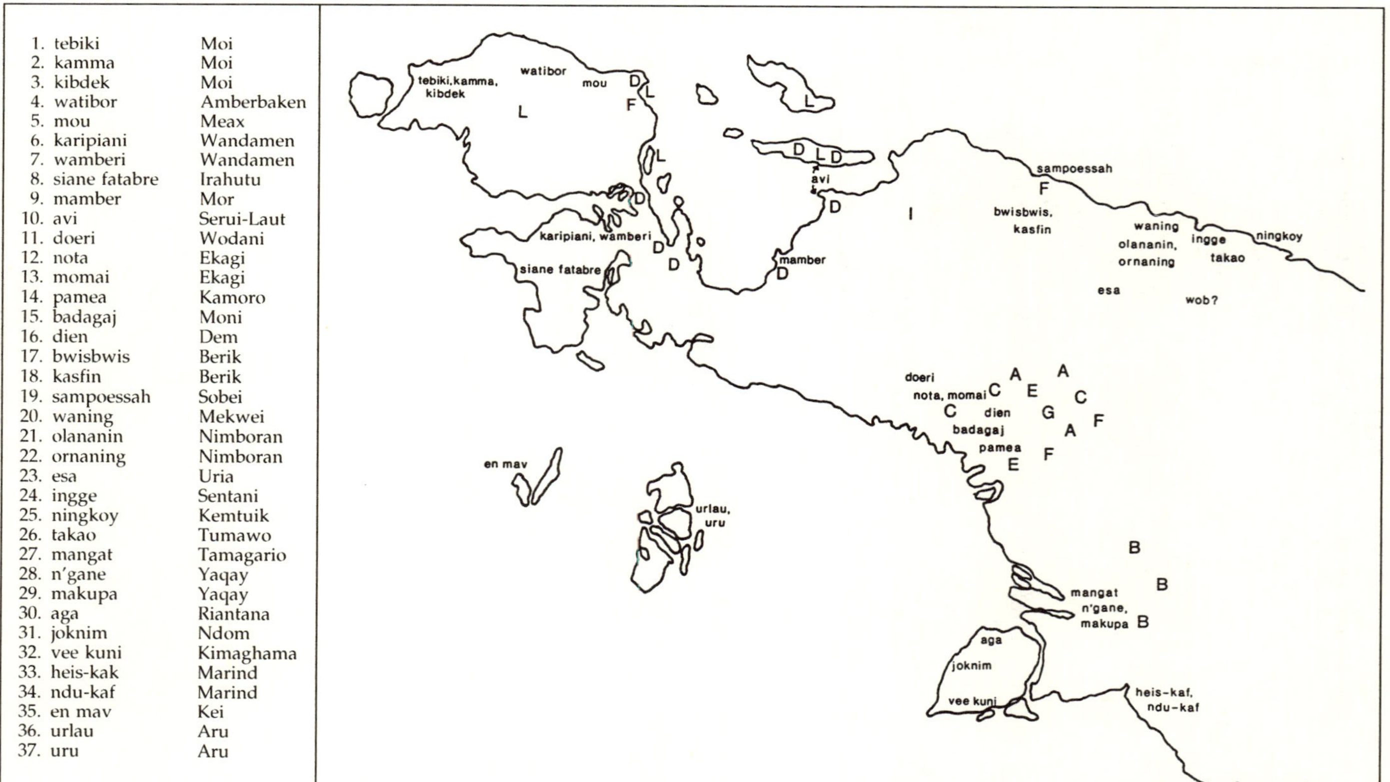

Map 6. Geographical distribution of terms for sweet potato in Irian Jaya.

1. gedong	N. Sumatra	8. lolir	Timor, Alfur	15. gumbili	Moluccas
2. kepileu	N. Sumatra	9. loli	Timor, Alfur	16. mekuk	Matbrat
3. piek	N. Sumatra	10. lame djawa	Celebes	17. paara tukale	Amborn
4. howei mandang	Sunda	11. lame kamumu	Celebes	18. en mav	Kei
5. katabang	Sunda, Sumbawa	12. lame kandora	Celebes	19. sane	Wetar
6. tales-kenari	Java	13.bage	Celebes	20. urlau	Aru
7. tingalan	Java	14. ima	Ternate	21. uru	Aru

Map 7. Geographical distribution of terms for sweet potato in Malaysia and Insular Indonesia, including terms in common with Irian Jaya.

CONCLUSIONS

As previously stated, the prevailing opinion of most researchers seems to favor an introduction of the sweet potato into New Guinea from the west, through Irian Jaya. Assuming a historical introduction, this would allow a time depth of no more than four hundred years for sweet potato cultivation in the Highlands. In this scenario, the development of intensive agricultural systems based on sweet potatoes and pig husbandry and the concomitant growth of large, stable populations and complex ceremonial systems might have proceeded very rapidly. By considering other possible routes of introduction, however, other scenarios can be entertained, allowing for alternative interpretations of the archaeological and ethnohistoric data.

We have attempted to demonstrate that other routes of introduction are equally plausible and at least as consistent with our linguistic data. It is quite likely that there were multiple introductions of the sweet potato into New Guinea, in different places at different times. Indeed, we think it likely that there were in fact historical introductions from the west. Yet we find it hard to explain the complex linguistic patterns present in eastern New Guinea as the result of only a few hundred years' time depth.

We believe that the widespread and early reports of the term *kumara* provide evidence for a possible introduction from Polynesia, perhaps via the Outliers into Milne Bay, with a possible route of diffusion into the Highlands of the *kaima* form. The *siabulu* term may represent a transfer of sweet potatoes from the south coast of Papua New Guinea into the Southern Highlands area, and possibly into the Highlands of Irian Jaya. The *ToToTe* set, while difficult to interpret, may provide evidence for the existence of widespread relationships of considerable time depth involving sweet potatoes in eastern New Guinea.

Little more can be said about the precise time of introduction of sweet potatoes into New Guinea without the benefit of further archaeological and linguistic research. Historical-linguistic investigations hold promise for unraveling the details of the time of introduction and direction of diffusion through relative chronologies for sound changes, and conservative glottochronological dates for the divergence of languages. In addition, much better macro- and microfloral recovery techniques now in use in archaeological field research may facilitate the identification of early traces of sweet potatoes in the prehistoric record. In the meantime, we maintain that the possibility of a prehistoric introduction of sweet potatoes in New Guinea merits serious consideration.

REFERENCES

Allen, J.
1977 Sea Traffic, Trade and Expanding Horizons. *In* Sunda and Sahul: Prehistoric Studies in Southeast Asia, Melanesia and Australia. J. Allen, F. Golson, and R. Jones, eds., pp. 387–417. London: Academic Press.

Anceaux, J. C.
1961 The Linguistic Situation in the Islands of Yapen, Kurudu, Nau and Miosnum, New Guinea. s'Gravenhage: Nijhoff.
1965 The Nimboran Language: Phonology and Morphology. The Hague: Nijhoff, 16, Verhandelingen Koninklijk Instituut voor Taal-, Land- en Volkenkunde 44, Diss. Leiden. (Cited in Yen 1974.)

Armstrong, W. E.
1923 Report on Anthropology of the South-Eastern Division (excluding Woodlark 1), Engineer Group, Bosilai, East Cape, Normanby Island (south coast), Fergusson Island (Morima). Papua, annual report for 1921–22, pp. 26–39; also Territory of Papua, anthropology report no. 2 (pt. 1), pp. 1–31.

Austen, L.
1923 Vocabularies. Papua, annual report for 1921–22, App. 9, pp. 159–163.
1926 Comparative Vocabularies of the N. W. District of Papua. *In* Territory of Papua, annual report for 1924–25, App. D, p. 75.

Ayres, W. S.
1975 Comments on Bellwood's "The Prehistory of Oceania." Current Anthropology 16:17–18.

Barrau, J.
1957 L'Enigme de la patate douce. Etudes d'Outre-Mer 40:83–87.

Bee, D.
1965 Comparative and Historical Problems in East New Guinea Highlands Languages. *In* Papers in New Guinea Linguistics, pp. 1–37. Pacific Linguistics, series A, no. 6. Canberra: Australian National University.

Bellwood, P.
1978 Man's Conquest of the Pacific. Auckland: Collins.
1987 The Polynesians: Prehistory of an Island People. London: Thames and Hudson.

Blong, R. J.
1982 The Time of Darkness: Local Legends and Volcanic Reality in Papua New Guinea. Seattle: University of Washington Press.

Briley, J.
1976 An Overview of the Bauzi Verb Phrase. Irian 5:3–17.

Bromley, H. M.
1972 The Grammar of Lower Grand Valley Dani in Discourse Perspective. Ph.D. dissertation. Yale University.

Brookfield, H. C., with D. Hart
1971 Melanesia: A Geographical Interpretation of an Island World. London: Methuen.

Brookfield, H. C., and J. P. White
1968 Revolution or Evolution in the Prehistory of the New Guinea Highlands: A Seminar Report. Ethnology 7:43–52.

Capell, A.
1948–49 Distribution of Languages in the Central Highlands, New Guinea. Oceania 19:104–129, 234–253, 349–377.

Champion, I. F.
1932 Across New Guinea from the Fly to the Sepik. London: Constable.

Clarke, W. C.
1966 From Extensive to Intensive Shifting Cultivation: A Succession from New Guinea. Ethnology 5:347–359.
1971 Place and People: An Ecology of a New Guinea Community. Berkeley: University of California Press.
1977 A Change of Subsistence Staple in Prehistoric New Guinea. *In* Proceedings of the Third Symposium of the International Society for Tropical Root Crops. C. L. A. Leaky, ed., pp. 159–163. Ibadan.

Conklin, H. C.
1963 The Oceanian-African Hypothesis and the Sweet Potato. *In* Plants and the Migrations of Pacific Peoples. J. Barrau, ed., pp. 129–136. Honolulu: Bishop Museum Press.

Davidson, J. M.
1979 New Zealand. *In* The Prehistory of Polynesia. J. D. Jennings, ed., pp. 222–248. Cambridge: Harvard University Press.

Dixon, R. B.
1932 The Problem of the Sweet Potato in Polynesia. American Anthropologist 34(1):40–66.

Drabbe, P.
1949 Bijzonderheden uit de talen van Frederik-Hendrik-eiland: Kimaghama, Ndom en Riantana. Bijdragen tot de Taal-, Land- en Volkenkunde 105:1–24.
1954 Talen en dialecten van Zuid-West Nieuw-Guinea. Micro-Bibliotheca Anthropos 11. Freiburg: Anthropos Institut.

Dutton, T. E.
1973 "Cultural" Items of Basic Vocabulary in the Gulf and Other Districts of Papua. Part 1, Foodstuffs and Associated Agricultural Terms. *In* The Linguistic Situation in the Gulf District and Adjacent Areas, Papua New Guinea. K. Franklin ed., pp. 411–538. Pacific Linguistics, series C, no. 26. Canberra: Australian National University.

Dwyer, R. E. P.
1957 Vernacular and Common Names of Plants. Paper presented to the Ninth Pacific Science Congress (Bangkok). (Cited in Yen 1974.)

Elmberg, J. E.
1968 Balance and Circulation: Aspects of Tradition and Change Among the Mejprat of Irian Barat. Stockholm: Etnografiska Museet Monograph series no. 12.

Flenley, J. R.
1967 The Present and Former Vegetation of the Wabag Region of New Guinea. Ph.D. dissertation. Australian National University.

Golson, J.
1959 Culture Change in Prehistoric New Zealand. *In* Anthropology in the South Seas: Essays Presented to H. D. Skinner. J. D. Freeman and W. R. Geddes, eds., pp. 29–74. New Plymouth, N.Z.: Thomas Avery and Sons.
1977a The Making of the New Guinea Highlands. *In* The Melanesian Environment. J. H. Winslow, ed., pp. 45–56. Canberra: Australian National University Press.
1977b No Room at the Top: Agricultural Intensification in the New Guinea Highlands. *In* Sunda and Sahul: Prehistoric Studies in Southeast Asia, Melanesia and Australia. J. Allen, J. Golson, and R. Jones, eds., pp. 601–638. London: Academic Press.
1982 The Ipomoean Revolution Revisited: Society and the Sweet Potato in the Upper Wahgi Valley. *In* Inequality in New Guinea Highlands Societies. A. Strathern ed., pp. 109–136. Cambridge: Cambridge University Press.

Golson, J., and D. S. Gardner
1990 Agriculture and Sociopolitical Organization in New Guinea Highlands Prehistory. Annual Review of Anthropology 19:395–417.

Gorecki, Pawel P.
1986 Human Occupation and Agricultural Development in the Papua New Guinea Highlands. Mountain Research and Development 6(2):159–166.

Haddon, A. C.
1929 Reports of the Cambridge Anthropological Expedition to the Torres Straits. Volume 5. Cambridge: Cambridge University Press.

Hather, J., and P. V. Kirch
1991 Prehistoric Sweet Potato (*Ipomoea batatas*) from Mangaia Island, Central Polynesia. Antiquity 65:887–893.

Heeschen, V., and W. Schiefenhövel
1983 Wörterbuch der Eipo-sprache: Eipo-Deutsch-Englisch. Berlin: Deitrich Reimer.

Held, G. J.
1957 Papuas of Waropen. s'Gravenhage: Nijhoff.

Hylkema, S.
1974 Mannen in het draagnet: Mens-en wereldbeeld von de Nalum (Sterrengebergte). 's-Gravenhage: Martinus Nijhoff.

Jorgensen, Dan
1990 Production and the Aims of Exchange: Telefol Crop Regimes in Historical Perspective. Paper presented at "The Mek and Their Neighbours" Conference in Seewiesen, Germany, in October 1990. Revised version.

King, C.
1894 Vocabulary of Words Spoken by Tribes of Wedau, Wamira, and Jiwari, Bartle Bay, on the Northeast Coast of British New Guinea. British New Guinea annual report for 1892–93, pp. 92–100.

Kirch, P. V.
1979 Subsistence and Ecology. *In* The Prehistory of Polynesia. J. D. Jennings, ed., pp. 286–307. Cambridge: Harvard University Press.
1982 Ecology and the Adaption of Polynesian Agricultural Systems. Archaeology in Oceania 17:1–6.
1988 Long-Distance Exchange and Island Colonialization: The Lapita Case. Norwegian Archaeological Review 21:103–117.
1991 Prehistoric Exchange in Western Melanesia. Annual Review of Anthropology 20:141–165.

Kirch, P. V., and D. E. Yen
1982 Tikopia: The Prehistory and Ecology of a Polynesian Outlier. Bishop Museum Bulletin no. 238. Honolulu: Bishop Museum Press.

Lamont, F.
1990 A 6000 Year Pollen Record from Mangaia, Cook Islands, South Pacific: Evidence for Early Human Impact. Unpublished B.Sc. dissertation. School of Geography and Earth Resources, University of Hull.

Larson, G. F.
1987 The Structure and Demography of the Cycle of Warfare Among the Ilaga Dani of Irian Jaya. Ph.D. dissertation. University of Michigan.

Latukefu, S.
1978 The Impact of South Sea Islands Missionaries on Melanesia. *In* Mission, Church, and Sect in Oceania. J. A. Boutilier, D. T. Hughes, and S. W. Tiffany, eds., pp. 91–108. ASAO Monograph no. 6. Boston: University Press of America.

Law, R. G.
1969 Pits and Kumara Agriculture in the South Island. Journal of the Polynesian Society 78(2):223–251.
1970 The Introduction of Kumara to New Zealand. Archaeology and Physical Anthropology in Oceania 5:114–127.

Lawes, W. G.
1890 Comparative View of New Guinea Dialects. British New Guinea annual report for 1888–89, pp. 158–167 (App. 12).

Loukotka, C.
1966 Renseignements inconnus sur le Hatam. Journal of Austronesian Studies 2:49–51.

McCoy, P. C.
1979 Easter Island. *In* The Prehistory of Polynesia. J. D. Jennings, ed., pp. 135–166. Cambridge: Harvard University Press.

MacGregor, W.
1890 Native Dialects. British New Guinea annual report for 1888–89, App. 10, pp. 117–157.

Matthiesen, P.
1963 Under the Mountain Wall. London: Heinemann.

Michel, T.
1987 Taro und Süsskartoffel auf Neuguinea. *In* Neuguinea: Nützung und Deutung der Umwelt. M. Münzel, ed., pp. 227–237. Frankfurt: Museum für Völkerkunde.

Miedema, J., and F. I. Welling
1985 Fieldnotes on Languages and Dialects in the Kebar District, Bird's Head, Irian Jaya. Pacific Linguistics, series A, no. 63. Canberra: Australian National University.

Murray, J. H. P.
1917–19 Vocabularies. Papua, annual report for 1917–18, Appendix E, pp. 85–99.
1920 Vocabularies. Papua, annual report for 1918–19, Appendix D, pp. 106–117.
1923 Vocabularies. Papua, annual report for 1921–22, Appendix 9, pp 159–166.
1925 Patrol to the Palmer River Natives of the Upper Fly at Daru. Papua, annual report for the year 1923–24, p. 8.

Nevermann, H.
1940 Die Sohur. Zeitschrift für Ethnologie 72:169–196.

O'Brien, P. J.
1972 The Sweet Potato: Its Origin and Dispersal. American Anthropologist 74(3): 342–365.

Oostroom, S. J. van, and R. D. Hoogland
1954 Convolvulaceae. *In* Flora Malesiana 6(4). C. G. G. J. van Steenis, ed. Djakarta: Noordoff-Kolff. (Cited in Yen 1974.)

Polach, H. A.
1982 Radiocarbon Dating of Long Island and Tibito Tephras. *In* Cooke-Ravian Volume of Vulcanological Papers. R. W. Johnson, ed., pp. 108–113. Port Moresby: Geological Survey of Papua New Guinea, Memoir 10.

Pospisil, L.
1963 Kapauka Papuan Economy. Yale University Publications in Anthropology no. 67. New Haven: Yale University, Department of Anthropology.

Pouwer, J.
1955 Enkele aspecten van de Mimika-cultuur (Nederlands zuidwest Nieuw Guinea). 's-Gravenhage: Staatsdrukkerij.

Powell, J. M.
1976 Ethnobotany. *In* New Guinea Vegetation. K. Paijmans, ed., pp. 106–183. Canberra: Australian National University Press.

1982a Plant Resources and Palaeobotanical Evidence for Plant Use in the Papua New Guinea Highlands. Archaeology in Oceania 17(1):28–37.

1982b History of Plant Use and Man's Impact on the Vegetation. *In* Biogeography and Ecology of New Guinea, part 1. J. L. Gressitt, ed., 207–227. The Hague: Junk.

Powell, J. M., A. Kulunga, R. Moge, C. Pono, F. Zimike, and J. Golson
1975 Agricultural Traditions of the Mount Hagen Area. Occasional Paper no. 12. Department of Geography, University of Papua New Guinea.

Ray, S. H.
1913–14 The Languages of the Papuan Gulf District, Papua. Zeitschrift für Kolonialsprachen 4:20–26.

Rosendahl, P., and D. E. Yen
1971 Fossil Sweet Potato Remains From Hawaii. Journal of the Polynesian Society 80(3):379–385.

Ross, H. M.
1977 The Sweet Potato in the South-Eastern Solomons. Journal of the Polynesian Society 86(4):521–530.

Roux, C. C. F. M. le
1948–51 De Bergpapoea's van Nieuw Guinea en hun Woongebied. Leiden: Brill. (Cited in Yen 1974.)

Rowley, C. D.
1966 The New Guinea Villager: Impact of Colonial Rule on Primitive Society and Economy. New York: Praeger.

Safford, W. E.
1925 The Potato of Romance and of Reality. Parts 2 and 3. Journal of Heredity 16(5):175–183, 16(6):217–229.

Salaman, R. N.
1949 The History and Social Influence of the Potato. Cambridge: Cambridge University Press. (Cited in Yen 1974.)

Schoorl, J. M.
1979 Mensen van de Ayfat: Ceremoniële ruil en sociale orde in Irian Jaya, Indonesia. Meppel: Krips.

Skjolsvold, A.
1961 Site E-2, a Circular Dwelling, Anakena. *In* Archaeology of Easter Island, vol. 1. T. Heyerdahl and E. N. Ferdon, Jr., eds, pp. 181–219. Santa Fe: Monographs of the School of American Research and the Museum of New Mexico, no. 4, part 1.

Snell, L. A.
1913 Eenige gegevens betreffende de kennis der zeden enz. der Pesechem van Centraal Nieuw Guinee. Bulletin Treub Maatschappij 68.

Steiner, M. L.
1961 A Dictionary of Vernacular Plant Names of Pacific Food-Plants. Philippines: Pacific Science Association and UNESCO. (Cited in Yen 1974.)

Stokhof, W. A. L., ed.
1983 Holle Lists, Vocabularies in Languages of Indonesia. Pacific Linguistics, series D, no. 53. Canberra: Australian National University.

Swadling, Pamela
1986 Papua New Guinea's Prehistory: An Introduction (revised version). Port Moresby: National Museum and Art Gallery, and Gordon and Gotch.

Temple, P.
1962 Nawok. London: Dent.

Watson, James B.
1965a From Hunting to Horticulture in the New Guinea Highlands. Ethnology 4:295–309.
1965b The Significance of a Recent Ecological Change in the Central Highlands of New Guinea. Journal of the Polynesian Society 74:438–450.
1967 Horticultural Traditions in the Eastern New Guinea Highlands. Oceania 38:81–98.
1977 Pigs, Fodder, and the Jones Effect on Post-Ipomoean New Guinea. Ethnology 16:57–70.

Westrum, P., and S. Westrum
1975 A Preliminary Berik Phonology. Irian 4:1–37.
White, J. P., and J. F. O'Connell
1982 A Prehistory of Australia, New Guinea and Sahul. Sydney: Academic Press.
Wilden, J. van der
1976 Some Inter-clausal Relations in Kemtuik. Irian 5:39–58.
Wirz, P.
1924 Anthropologische und ethnologische Ergebnisse der Zentral-New-Guinea Expedition 1921–22. Nova Guinea 16:1–148.
Wurm, S. A., and S. Hattori, eds.
1981 Language Atlas of the Pacific Area. Part 1, New Guinea Area, Oceania, Australia. Pacific Linguistics, series C, no. 66. Canberra: Australian National University.
Yen, D. E.
1961 The Adaptation of Kumara by the New Zealand Maori. Journal of the Polynesian Society 70(3):338–348.
1974 The Sweet Potato and Oceania: An Essay in Ethnobotany. Bishop Museum Bulletin no. 236. Honolulu.
Zollner, S.
1988 (1977) The Religion of the Yali in the Highlands of Irian Jaya. Jan A. Godschalk, transl. Goroka: Melanesian Institute.

NOTES

First and foremost, we would like to gratefully acknowledge the special contribution of Terry Hays, who provided us with his own lists of sweet potato terms in literally hundreds of New Guinea languages. He also provided detailed suggestions throughout our research. Jan Godschalk was invaluable in checking our linguistic data on Irian Jaya, and for providing data suggesting that the *siabulu* set may extend into the Irian Highlands. Andrew Strathern and Gabriele Stürzenhofecker helped us refine our ideas during the early stages of this project. Rob Welsch, James B. Watson, Dan Jorgensen, Bill Thurston, Jim Roscoe, and Tim Bayliss-Smith provided helpful suggestions along the way. We are most grateful to Jack Golson, and to Tim Bayliss-Smith, Paul Gorecki, Pat Kirch, George Morren, and Chris Ballard for particularly helpful comments on previous drafts of the manuscript. Since most of these reviewers overtly disagree with some of our interpretations, none should be held responsible for the opinions expressed herein. We would also like to thank the many ASAO members who provided us with unpublished linguistic data on various groups.

1. The epigraph is from Patricia J. O'Brien 1972:356.

2. See, for example, Watson 1977; Ross 1977; Golson 1982; Swadling 1986; but for exceptions, see also White and O'Connell 1982:183 and Gorecki 1986.

3. The literature review in this section is based largely on O'Brien (1972).

MELANESIAN INTERACTION AT THE REGIONAL SCALE

Spatial Relationships in a Fluid Landscape

Tim Bayliss-Smith

This book is a pioneer attempt by New Guinea ethnographers to examine patterns and processes of social interaction at a regional scale. It is an exploration of precolonial interactions, and the resulting diffusion of goods, people, ideas, and cultural practices. My object is to review this project from a geographical and ecological perspective, and to make some suggestions about where it might lead in the future.

For a geographer, the first obvious question to ask is whether, in traveling along this pioneer trail, we have gone beyond the point reached by Harold Brookfield in his innovative synthesis of more than twenty years ago (Brookfield with Hart 1971). In *Melanesia: A Geographical Interpretation of an Island World,* Brookfield's major focus was on the use of the natural environment as a resource, and on the organization of production and distribution at various scales. His book was therefore primarily about economic rather than social interactions, with a heavy emphasis on agriculture and trade. From a starting point in the precolonial world, which he termed "Old Melanesia," Brookfield traced the transformations in indigenous agriculture and trade that followed from Melanesia's gradual and incomplete integration into the world economy during the colonial era. His principal interest in Melanesian prehistory was to use it to establish the extent of historical continuity in economic processes. As he later described it, "my long-promised book on Melanesia [was] the product both of a decade of empirical research and of a set of ideas about long-term and short-term change" (Brookfield 1984a:30). The long-term change he measured in terms of agricultural intensity, and he later went on to theorize about intensification in ways that explored much more explicitly the linkages between economic intensity and social hierarchy (Brookfield 1972, 1984b, 1986; Blaikie and Brookfield 1987).

However, as in the present volume, much of the discussion in Brookfield's *Melanesia* refers to indigenous processes of spatial diffusion, an emphasis on space that is absent in the more recent intensification debates. So it is worthwhile to see how far the ten authors of this present book are still operating within Brookfield's conceptual framework. His focus was on the production and movement within Melanesia of 'goods', for example the indigenous trade in foodstuffs, stone tools, salt, and items of decoration. As well as 'goods' he discusses 'services', but he felt that in the precolonial period there was actually little scope for services to be transferred beyond local areas:

> Goods may readily be passed on from hand to hand, in 'trade'. Services, on the other hand, are limited in the main to a single 'transfer' from one person to another, within a single contact field. Within a contact field, services may be reciprocated for goods, and vice versa, but there is little scope for 'trade' in such services, through introduction from one contact field to another. Such might occur in a wider society, under centralized authority, but in a society such as that of 'old Melanesia', little but goods could travel through a chain of contact fields. (Brookfield with Hart 1971:315)

Some of the examples discussed in this present book show that Brookfield was wrong to exclude as difficult or impossible the movement of anything other than goods. Such movements do happen in Melanesia, even in areas of low population density and low production intensity. From this we can infer that these processes of cultural diffusion probably happened throughout the Holocene period with various other kinds of change. We now have available a range of evidence about paleoenvironments and the prehistory of the Melanesian people that could scarcely have been imagined in the 1960s, covering landforms, sea level, climate, vegetation, fauna, diseases, human populations, genes, and languages and other cultural artifacts. While Brookfield could merely point to some unsolved problems in cultural distribution patterns and confess that "we can say nothing about these question" (1971:80), today a more ambitious project is unfolding: the study of long-term regional transformation. An outline of this project emerges strongly from the chapters of this present volume.

We can now see that Brookfield's focus on the movement of goods as the main symptom of regional interaction reflects a certain materialist ideology as well as data constraints. Nevertheless there is much to be learned from the conceptual framework that he established in order to analyze communication and movement in Melanesia. His chapter on this subject is entitled "Location, Transfer and Trade in Old Melanesia" (Brookfield with Hart 1971:314–334). "Location" refers to the various characteristics of a place, including its location relative to other places, the nature of production to be gained from its immediate hinterland, and the possibilities for surplus production.

Brookfield went on to explore the relevance to Melanesia of theories of agriculture intensification, seeing this process as the key to explaining the existence of larger populations at certain locations, populations that themselves could generate a greater surplus and more exchange activity (Brookfield 1972, 1984b, 1986). We see from Paul Roscoe's and Robert Welsch's chapters in this present book that regional integration via intense networks of exchange can emerge in ways other than through the generation of "social" production surpluses from intensive agriculture (see chapters 3 and 4). Nevertheless the ecology of particular places and their relative location is often significant, as clearly demonstrated by Fitz John Porter Poole, Gabriele Stürzenhofecker, and Andrew Strathern for the highlands (chapters 7, 8, and 9), and by Paul Roscoe and Bruce Knauft for the lowlands (chapters 3 and 6).

How can we conceptualize the various processes of interaction between individuals and groups, interactions that may or may not be stimulated by the special character of some locations? Brookfield distinguishes between two types of interaction. One is "transfer," by which he means a type of transaction between someone who is the originator and someone who is the receiver. They are both known to each other, and therefore this transfer will normally occur within the same community or group. In Melanesia the vast bulk of interactions are of this kind (or were, before more impersonal market exchanges began to intrude). They involve a redistribution or an exchange usually of food or of labor, and they occur almost entirely within local areas. These local areas provided for most Melanesians the entirety of their action space.

There is a second form of interaction, termed by Brookfield "trade." For present purposes, in this volume, we can expand the concept of trade from the movements of goods to include people (chapters 1, 4, and 6), their languages (chapters 2 and 7), their beliefs and ritual practices (chapters 3, 5, and 8), and their plants and plant names (chapters 7 and 9). Trade in this sense involves more than a single local transfer between two people. It involves a series of transfers involving multiple interpersonal links. These chains of interaction can extend over long distances, between ecological zones, or even in a circular "ring" such as the Kula of southeast Papua. No one person involved in such trade links fully perceives how the series of linkages are articulated. Moreover, the potential is obviously considerable for a shift to take place in whatever meaning is attached to the thing that is being traded, the more distant the trade links become from their origin in time and in space.

Rather than reiterate points about "location," "transfer," and "trade" that are already well made in the particular case studies in this book, I will now turn to some more general issues about transformation in Melanesian prehistory. Each "location" has a geomorphic, an ecological, and a demographic dimension as well as its purely spatial relationships to other places, and rather than assume that these are static variables, we need to explore their potentially fluid nature. Recent work in environmental science, archaeology, and human biology provides important clues to the transformations that different Melanesian locations have undergone in recent prehistory. Under the headings of evolving landscape, expanding grasslands, and the ebb and flow of malaria, I will consider the general implications of these transformations for regional interaction via "transfer" and "trade."

TRANSFORMATION: AN EVOLVING LANDSCAPE

In Melanesia all patterns of human interaction are based on shifting sands: the landscape itself is changing, in slow, insidious, but irrevocable ways. We cannot begin to understand without some appreciation of geomorphology, particularly in coastal areas, as is elegantly demonstrated by Pamela Swadling, J. Chappell, G. Francis, N. Araho, and B. Ivuyo (1989), and by Roscoe (this volume) in relation to the Sepik basin.

Atolls are perhaps an extreme case. As recently as twenty years ago, the biological anthropologist William Howells could plausibly hypothesize a prehistoric settlement of high-island Polynesia by migration through the chain of atolls that runs from Micronesia through Kiribati and Tuvalu (Howells 1973:254). Today the very existence of land on atolls at this period in the past seems doubtful: atoll islands are regarded as a very recent phenomenon, deriving almost entirely from storm deposition during the period of falling sea level that has characterized the last 2,000 years (Bayliss-Smith 1988; Nunn 1988;

Pirazzoli and Montaggioni 1988; Woodroffe et al. 1990). The map of the Pacific looked very different at the time that Lapita culture began to expand, a process of "migration" that, contrary to Howells's assertion, we now believe took place from a Melanesian heartland starting some 3,500 years ago.

The coasts of high islands have also been transformed over this period by changes in sea level and by storm deposition. The best researched examples come from Island Melanesia. Tikopia in the eastern Solomons has been studied by P. V. Kirch and D. E. Yen (1982). They showed that the island increased its land area by 40 percent over a period of 2,000 years, through the formation of coastal dunes and storm deposits, augmented by colluvial spreads of soil derived from slope wash following deforestation inland. These new coastal flats provided the land on Tikopia that was being cultivated intensively in the most recent period. As the island grew, there was a corresponding reduction in the area of reef flats. An entire bay of the sea was cut off and transformed into a freshwater lake, Te Roto, between A.D. 1600 and 1800: "The creation of Te Roto precipitated major shifts in human settlement patterns and, indeed, enters into the great Tikopia epic tales of the ascendancy of Nga Ariki over their rivals" (Kirch and Yen 1982:332). Since intensive agriculture on such islands would be impossible without this history of geomorphic change, M. J. T. Spriggs (1985) describes it as "landscape enhancement" rather than "land degradation." On Tikopia the archaeologists conclude that "man's prehistory . . . is as much a sequence of landscape transformation as of culture change in the usual sense" (Kirch and Yen 1982:349).

Aneityum in southern Vanuatu is another spectacular example of the same process (Spriggs 1986). Following initial settlement at 2900 BP, forest clearance for shifting cultivation and the use of fire on inland slopes led to accelerated soil erosion. The products of erosion accumulated in valleys, which were originally swampy but by about 2,000 years ago had become suitable for new settlements based on dry-land agriculture. By 500 or 600 BP, massive alluviation had formed the extensive Aname floodplain on top of what had previously been reef flat. This area became the focus for a new and more intensive technology of cultivation. Spriggs considers that the growth of chiefly power and the expansion of irrigation on the island went hand in hand:

> As a chief's prestige grew he would become more able to command labor to expand the conditions of agricultural production by the build-

> ing of new canals and the extension of irrigation systems. . . . It is hard to imagine that the social system at European contact . . . could have existed on anything like the same scale even five hundred years previously. Human interference with natural environmental processes had led, not to ecological disaster, but to a greatly expanded potential for agricultural intensification and social stratification. (Spriggs 1986:16)

Fiji provides several further examples of recent geomorphological change (Nunn 1988). On Lakeba, for example, the degradation of interior forests and consequent slope wash resulted in catastrophic erosion and the rapid infilling of valleys and coastal reefs, to form the land later used for intensive taro production (Latham and Bayliss-Smith 1988). We can infer a growth in population and the emergence of more centralized chiefdoms, culminating about a thousand years ago in the construction of massive hill forts such as Ulunikoro (Best 1988). Inevitably the archaeological evidence for population movement and trade is more ambiguous, but oral histories suggest that the Lau polity centered on Lakeba established links with communities as far away as Viti Levu to the west and Tonga to the east (Reid 1983).

Thus it seems that in eastern Fiji sea-level change, soil erosion, and the emergence of new landforms is very much part of the "migration and transformation" story in recent prehistory. When information becomes available for coastal New Guinea through multidisciplinary studies comparable in scope to those carried out in Tikopia, Aneityum, and Lakeba, we shall no doubt have similar cause to revise our notions about the shifting sands upon which recent prehistories have been based.

TRANSFORMATION: THE EXPANDING GRASSLANDS

In many parts of New Guinea, it is likely that there have been equally dramatic geomorphic and cultural changes, as demonstrated by the example of the Sepik basin (Swadling et al. 1989; Roscoe, chapter 3). In the highlands, extensive clearance of forests in the zone around sixteen-hundred-meter altitude had already occurred by 5500 BP. Even earlier impacts have been proposed for the Baliem valley (Haberle, Hope, and DeFretes 1991).

In the pre–sweet potato economy of the highlands, replacement of forest by grassland implies a severe reduction in opportunities for hunting, gathering, and the production of taro (*Colocasia esculenta*) from swiddens (see figure 1). This transformation in the vegetation cover therefore created an ecological crisis for highlands populations.

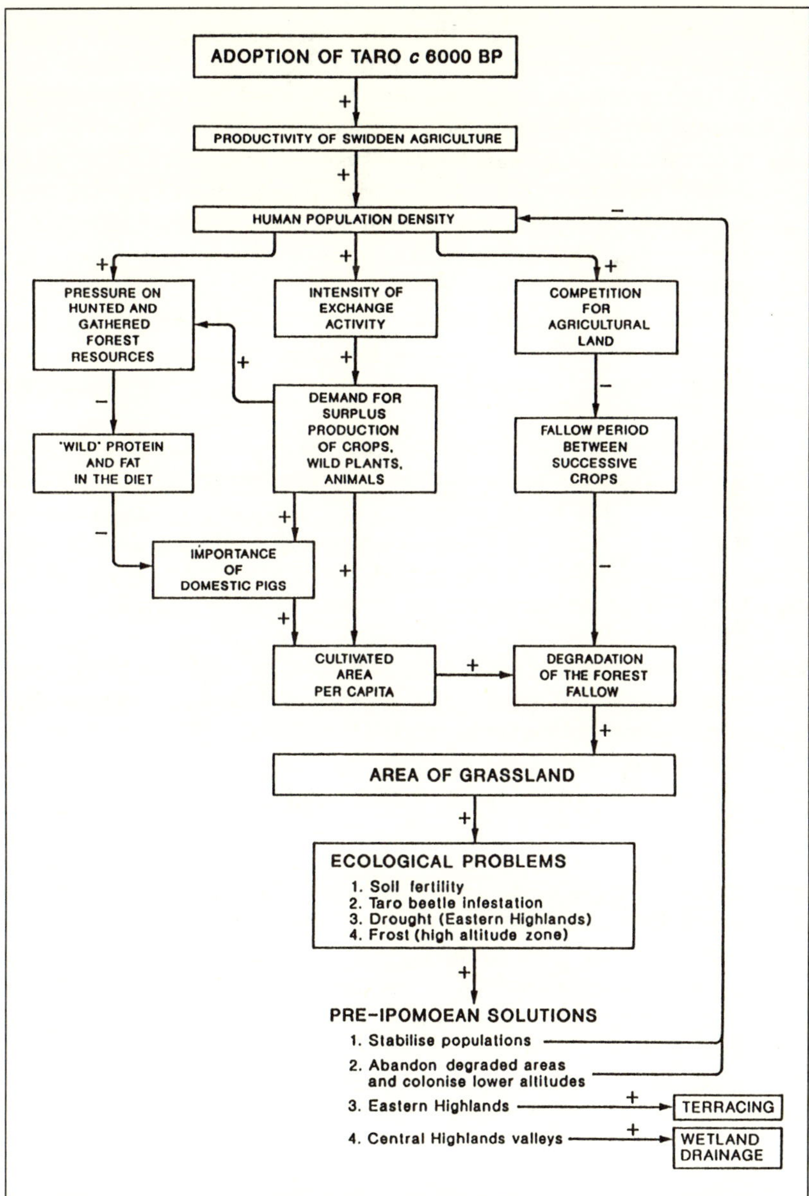

Fig. 1. The Colocasian Revolution in the New Guinea Highlands, Interaction Between Social Processes, Ecological Problems, and Technical Solution at Regional Scale.

By two thousand years ago, an open landscape of degraded grasslands had become established in all the major highlands valleys, and this transformation in the productive base must have represented a severe crisis for those highlands populations unable to maintain access to forest swiddens. Agroforestry systems, some of them based on *Casuarina,* were one response to this crisis. The groves of planted trees helped replenish the soils, probably for taro or yam cultivation, and provided timber and fuelwood supplies. In the Wahgi valley, the archaeological evidence from Kuk indicates that cultivation of wetlands there offered a secure substitute for taro swiddens, and one that was capable of intensification. In the Eastern Highlands, terrace cultivation may have fulfilled the same role (Golson and Gardner 1990).

We can reconstruct the technology used at this time by highlanders for taro production in wetlands by using the evidence from Kuk in the upper Wahgi valley (Bayliss-Smith and Golson 1992a, 1992b). The period known as Kuk Phase 4 began some time after 2000 BP and ended at 1200 BP. During this period, the wetland component of the agricultural system centered on intensive taro cultivation with swamp fallow. Land was reclaimed through swamp drainage by means of networks of small ditches articulating with larger disposal channels, the whole forming a grid pattern of drained gardens within which the water table was lowered. This made available fertile soils free from weeds and pests, notably the taro beetles (*Papuana* spp.) that find a habitat in the roots of tussock grasses in deforested dryland areas. The Phase 4 technology of wetland reclamation established a new geography of relative location in the highlands, with a new contrast between the wetlands, which became islands of high taro productivity, and the surrounding oceans of infested, drought-prone, and infertile grasslands.

The archaeological evidence does not allow us to trace the origins let alone the migration of this new technology, but it is interpreted as constituting a revolutionary change for those communities having secure access to wetland sites. As such, there are possible implications for a whole range of demographic and social variables:

> Phase 4 . . . did have the potential to be a catalyst for social change. Its agricultural base had the capacity to sustain a high density of pigs and people in stable, sedentary settlements and to permit regular exchange, in what was otherwise a quite empty landscape of degraded grasslands with shifting cultivation in scattered swiddens. (Bayliss-Smith and Golson 1992a:18)

This transformation in technology could therefore have been a veritable "Colocasian Revolution," foreshadowing the later and more widespread effects of the Ipomoean revolution (see figure 1). We must envisage highlands prehistory as involving successive revolutions in technology, such as wetland cultivation, dryland soil tillage, and agroforestry (Golson 1977). New crops with revolutionary potential include the introduction of southeast Asian yams (Yen 1990), perhaps at the start of Phase 2; wetland taro cultivation in Phase 4, as discussed above; and the more recent sweet potato (Oldfield, Appleby, and Thompson 1980; Golson 1982; Bayliss-Smith 1985; Feil 1987).

At present the whole chronology of these successive transformations in highlands cultures remains uncertain (see chapter 10), but preliminary work on the trade in stone axes indicates that Phase 4 may have been implicated in the beginnings of regional integration in the Central Highlands zone. John Burton (1984) has suggested that the opening up of specialized stone axe quarries was a reflection of demand for bridewealth generated from the dynamic economy centered on the upper Wahgi valley wetlands. This trade in stone therefore represents archaeologically visible exchange. It is the 'goods' component within regional systems of social and ideological integration that Burton's evidence shows developed some time between 2500 and 1500 BP, in other words well before the sweet potato transformation. This evidence needs to be extended, just as the Kuk site reconstruction needs to be replicated in other wetlands. However, as J. Golson and D. S. Gardner (1990:404) note, the evidence for specialized stone-axe production seems to begin "within the period that has been identified as decisive for interconnected developments in the spheres of environment, agriculture and pig husbandry." There is the beginning here of a history of regional culture that feeds off ethnoarchaeology for insights, but that relates to a period in the past too remote to be directly related to modern ethnography.

TRANSFORMATION: THE EBB AND FLOW OF MALARIA

Alongside the changing landforms and spreading grasslands are some more hidden ecological factors that influence the quality of a location: factors of epidemiology. From the 19th century until thirty years ago, malaria was the most important cause of illness and death in Melanesia, but was this always the case? Authoritative and recent reviews of the evidence from human biology, epidemiology, and archaeology by Leslie Groube (1993a, 1993b) come to the important conclusion that malaria's importance has been far from unchanging in the recent past. It is a disease that has the power to influence not only demography but also settlement dispersal, mobility, marriage patterns, and exchange networks. If its influence has ebbed and flowed in Melanesian prehistory, then its changing impact is something that we need to consider most carefully.

The following outline is based on Groube's work (1993a, 1993b) and the sources that he cites, including S. W. Serjeantson, R. L. Kirk, and P. B. Booth (1983) and F. B. Livingstone (1985). Four separate types of malaria are present in Melanesia, all of which coexist on mainland New Guinea. Infection by the commonest, the benign malaria *Plasmodium vivax,* produces spontaneous immunity that is strain specific. The same feature occurs with *P. falciparum,* which is the most malignant and fatal of the malarial parasites. Groube (1993a:4) argues that the development of local immunities to both malignant and benign malarial parasites is of great importance in Melanesian prehistory, affecting among other things the degree of mobility and the nature of intermarriage between groups. The disease must therefore be seen as a potentially major constraint on the movement of people and consequently a brake on the spread of cultural artifacts.

Nor can we assume a uniform effect. The impact of the four parasites upon human morbidity and mortality probably fluctuated in time and space. The dependence of the most serious form of the disease, *falciparum* malaria, upon large nucleated settlements—for its effective transmission via mosquito vectors—means it is very likely to be a relative newcomer to the Pacific (Livingstone 1985). Following its spread out of Africa since the Neolithic, *falciparum* malaria reached Melanesia via Southeast Asia perhaps as recently as two thousand years ago, according to Groube's (1993b) estimate. This proposal finds support in the very weak development in Melanesian populations of any effective inherited response such as hemoglobin S or sickle-cell hemoglobin. It is argued that despite *falciparum*'s powerful selection effect today through high infant-mortality rates, this intense natural selection pressure has only operated during a comparatively brief period of prehistory.

In contrast to *falciparum* malaria, the more benign forms are probably more ancient, and Melanesians have learnt to live with them quite effectively via a set of biological and cultural adaptations. These are likely to include, first, aspects of settlement and housing such as raised house construction, villages situated on ridge tops, on small islands, or over saltwater; a dispersed settlement pattern; and the keeping of domestic animals, which act as alternative sources of blood for mosquitoes. All these cultural features have been shown to reduce the malaria-transmission rate to a level that is more tolerable.

Second, there is the avoidance of overnight residence in hazardous places, and restrictions on the extent of mobility for the most vulnerable group, the young children. Third, there are practices that enable a community to withstand high infant-mortality levels. Exogamous marriage is seen as a particularly risky practice in malarial areas. Women (or men) moving from one area to another upon their marriage would be the likely victims of renewed infection by strains to which they had little or no immunity. Without resorting to determinism, one could argue that other things being equal, those Melanesian communities that incorporated these cultural adaptations would have thrived if they were in competition with others that did not. The early German, British, and Australian colonists in Melanesia were subject to similar cultural selection pressures.

Population movements from nonmalarial to malarial areas are particularly dangerous. We know from Europe that Italian migrant labor moving into the malarial wetlands of the Po valley, or wives moving into the Essex marshes and the English Fenland, were extremely vulnerable to even the so-called benign forms of malaria. In Melanesia, with the spread of people and parasites in the colonial period, very severe mortality was recorded. Examples include the spread of malaria to offshore islands like Ontong Java, where it became endemic, and to highlands valleys like the Wahgi during short-lived epidemics (Bayliss-Smith 1975; Gorecki 1979). Throughout prehistory highlander-lowlander interactions in New Guinea must have taken place against the same background of sickness, fear of sorcery (that is, infection), and the consequent avoidance by travelers of overnight stays in malarial areas.

These examples show that *vivax* and *malariae,* the benign and probably ancient malarias of Melanesia, are nonetheless serious diseases if a population is not immune. In the endemic phase, high population densities sustain frequent malaria transmission (assuming *Anopheles* mosquitoes are present); infant-mortality levels are high and must be balanced by high fertility; and everyone develops a degree of acquired immunity, at least to local strains. Long-distance mobility remains hazardous, but with these other adaptations populations can thrive and even expand.

Unless and until this endemic stage is reached, avoidance of malarial localities is the best response to the lack of immunity. This may account for some "black holes" in the map of prehistoric settlement. For example, Groube (1993a:42) points out that there is an extraordinary lack of occupation evidence from the Papuan south coast until the last two thousand years, despite rich reef and lagoonal resources, and the floodplains and deltas seem to have been even more empty of people. Geomorphic change may have obscured some of the archaeological evidence. On the other hand the communities may still have been in the "pre-endemic" stage:

> It is possible that only the fringes of the large alluvial flood plain systems (the Fly/Purari and the Sepik/Ramu) would have been exploited, as penetration beyond this would have involved many days of high risk activity. Trackways and trade routes through such areas would also have been in jeopardy. . . . The Kikori area subject to annual flooding and high mosquito concentrations, would have been formidable in the "pre-endemic" stage; the rich resources would become accessible only when endemic malaria became firmly established and human populations could tolerate the conditions. (Groube 1993a:42–43)

According to Groube, the distribution and age of sites in the Sepik-Ramu basin suggests it was in north New Guinea that a transition first took place toward endemic malaria. The genetic evidence also provides support for this model, as it is in the Madang region that we find some of the highest frequencies of most of the inherited immunities found in Melanesia (Hill et al. 1989; Serjeantson et al. 1983; Livingstone 1985). Groube proposes that the Lapita culture itself was made possible by cultural strategies that enabled people to live with malaria and so permitted the rich resource base of coastal areas to be utilized.

It is against this background that we must assess the "migrations" across lowland New Guinea space that are discussed in this volume. People achieved some degree of regional integration even in highly malarial areas of low resource availability such as the Upper Fly-Digul plain (chapter 4), and they did so despite the hazards of mobility and interaction at the pre-endemic stage. In contrast, it is the opposite situation that Groube predicts as the norm:

> One can hypothesize that one of the effects of endemic malaria, depending on how exclusive the strain boundaries are, is a reduction in mobility, increased sedentarism, and cultural isolation, resulting in less contact between various communities. This could well be one of the most important factors promoting language isolation and particularly the small size (and therefore multiplication) of languages in Melanesia. . . . With endemic malaria the distance a man may travel to seek a wife before getting too sick to enjoy the nuptials is limited. (Groube 1993a:52–53)

As well as this pressure toward endogamy, the lack of incentive for highlanders to interact with malarial lowland communities is obvious. A consequence is that one might expect some effective gene flow and language movement from the coast into the interior but little of the reverse. Above all, the ebb and flow of malaria must now be recognized as a factor of prime importance in assessing the quality of a location, and hence its capacity to sustain the migrations of cultural phenomena discussed in this volume.

CONCLUSION

These examples of long-term transformation indicate that Brookfield's conceptual framework of "location/transfer/trade" needs to incorporate the changing character of Melanesian locations. Swept along by the enthusiasm of geographers in the 1960s for locational analysis, Brookfield was drawn in his book *Melanesia* toward an emphasis on modeling spatial relationships as if they occurred between locations (not people) and within static ecological space.

If, however, we revise this rigid assumption, then, as Brookfield (1984a) himself recognized, we are left with a rather different task. We are forced to reconstruct in a more holistic way the emic view of location within a Melanesian space economy in which social distance is often more important than spatial distance. We have to do this in the context of a reconstructed landscape of shifting landforms and retreating forests and a fluctuating boundary of disease prevalence. In these ways we can appreciate better the meaning of the historical drama, by studying the interactions between actors in terms of the actors' own worldview, and by considering the continual changes of scenery that are taking place within the ecological theater. Both actors and scenery influence the drama that is unfolding of local versus regional integration. By following this road, we can better meet the challenge of reconstructing for whole regions the migrations and transformations of Melanesian prehistory.

REFERENCES

Bayliss-Smith, T. P.

1975 Ontong Java: Depopulation and Repopulation. *In* Pacific Atoll Populations. V. Carroll, ed., pp. 417–484. Honolulu: University of Hawaii Press.

1985 Pre-Ipomoean Agriculture in the New Guinea Highlands Above 2000 Metres: Some Experimental Data on Taro Cultivation. *In* Prehistoric Intensive Agriculture in the Tropics. I. S. Farrington, ed., pp. 285–321. British Archaeological Reports International Series no. 232, Oxford.

1988 The Role of Hurricanes in the Development of Reef Islands, Ontong Java, Solomon Islands. Geographical Journal 54, 377–391.

Bayliss-Smith, T. P., and J. Golson

1992a A Colocasian Revolution in the New Guinea Highlands? Insights from Phase 4 at Kuk. Archaeology in Oceania 17: 1–21.

1992b Wetland Agriculture in New Guinea Highlands Prehistory. *In* The Wetland Revolution in Prehistory. B. Coles, ed., pp. 15–27. The Prehistoric Society and WARP, University of Exeter.

Best, S. B.

1988 Lakeba: The Prehistory of a Pacific Island. Ph.D. dissertation. University of Auckland.

Blaikie, P., and H. Brookfield

1987 Land Degradation and Society. London: Methuen.

Brookfield, H. C.

1972 Intensification and Disintensification in Pacific Agriculture: A Theoretical Approach. Pacific Viewpoint 13:30–48.

1984a Experiences of an Outside Man. *In* Recollections of a Revolution: Geography as Spatial Science. M. Billinge, D. Gregory, and R. Martin, eds., pp. 27–38. London: Macmillan.

1984b Intensification Revisited. Pacific Viewpoint 25:15–44.

1986 Intensification Intensified. Archaeology in Oceania 21:177–180.

Brookfield, H. C., and D. Hart

1971 Melanesia: A Geographical Interpretation of an Island World. London: Methuen.

Burton, John

1984 Axe Makers of the Wahgi: Pre-Colonial Industrialists of the Papua New Guinea Highlands. Ph.D. dissertation. Australian National University.

Feil, D. K.

1987 The Evolution of Highland Papua New Guinea Societies. Cambridge: Cambridge University Press.

Golson, J.

1977 No Room at the Top: Agricultural Intensification in the New Guinea Highlands. *In* Sunda and Sahul: Prehistoric Studies in South-East Asia, Melanesia, and Australia. J. Allen, J. Golson, and R. Jones, eds., pp. 601–638. London, New York, and San Francisco: Academic Press.

1982 The Ipomoean Revolution Revisited: Society and the Sweet Potato in the Upper Wahgi Valley. *In* Inequality in New Guinea Highlands Societies. A. Strathern, ed., pp. 109–136. Cambridge: Cambridge University Press.

Golson, J., and D. S. Gardner
1990 Agriculture and Sociopolitical Organization in New Guinea Highlands Prehistory. Annual Review of Anthropology 19:395–417.

Gorecki, P. P.
1979 Population Growth and Abandonment of Swamplands: A New Guinea Highlands Example. Journal de la Société des Océanistes 35:97–107.

Groube, L.
1993a The Role of Malaria in Melanesian Prehistory. Antiquity (forthcoming).
1993b Contradictions and Malaria in Melanesian and Australian Prehistory. *In* A Community of Culture: The People and Prehistory of the Pacific. M. Spriggs et al., eds. Occasional paper no. 21, Department of Prehistory, Research School of Pacific Studies, Australian National University, Canberra.

Haberle, S. G., G. S. Hope, and Y. DeFretes
1991 Environmental Change in the Baliem Valley, Montane Irian Jaya, Republic of Indonesia. Journal of Biogeography 18:5–40.

Hill, A. V. S., D. F. O'Shaughnessy, and J. B. Clegg
1989 Haemoglobin and Globin Gene Variants in the Pacific. *In* The Colonization of the Pacific: A Genetic Approach. A. V. S. Hill and S. W. Serjeantson, eds., pp. 246–288. Oxford: Clarendon Press.

Howells, W.
1973 The Pacific Islanders. London: Weidenfeld and Nicolson.

Kirch, P. V., and D. E. Yen
1982 Tikopia: The Prehistory and Ecology of a Polynesian Outlier. Bernard P. Bishop Museum Bulletin no. 238, Bishop Museum Press, Honolulu.

Latham, M., and T. P. Bayliss-Smith
1988 The Island Landscape. *In* Islands, Islanders and the World: The Colonial and Post-Colonial Experience of Eastern Fiji. T. P. Bayliss-Smith, R. D. Bedford, H. Brookfield, and M. Latham, eds., pp. 12–43. Cambridge: Cambridge University Press.

Livingstone, F. B.
1985 Frequencies of Haemoglobin Variants. New York: Oxford University Press.

Nunn, P. D.
1988 Recent Environmental Changes Along Southwest Pacific Coasts and the Prehistory of Oceania: Developments of the Work of the Late John Gibbons. The Journal of Pacific Studies 14:42–58.

Oldfield, F., P. G. Appleby, and R. Thompson
1980 Palaeoecological Studies of Lakes in the Highlands of Papua New Guinea. Vol. 1, The Chronology of Sedimentation. Journal of Ecology 68:457–477.

Pirazzoli, P. A., and L. F. Montaggioni
1988 Holocene Sea Level Changes in French Polynesia. Palaeogeography, Palaeoclimatology, Palaeoecology 68:153–175.

Reid, A. C.
1983 The Chiefdom of Lau: A New Fijian State Built on Lakeba Foundations. Journal of Pacific History 18:183–197.

Serjeantson, S. W., R. L. Kirk, and P. B. Booth
1983 Linguistic and Genetic Differentiation in New Guinea. Journal of Human Evolution 12:77–92.

Spriggs, M. J. T.
1985 Prehistoric Man-Induced Landscape Enhancement in the Pacific: Examples and Implications. *In* Prehistoric Intensive Agriculture in the Tropics. I. T. Farrington, ed., pp. 409–434. British Archaeological Reports, International Series no. 232.
1986 Landscape, Land Use and Political Transformation in Southern Melanesia. *In* Island Societies: Archaeological Approaches to Evolution and Transformation. P. V. Kirch, ed., pp. 6–19. Cambridge: Cambridge University Press.

Swadling, Pamela, J. Chappell, G. Francis, N. Araho, and B. Ivuyo
1989 A Late Quaternary Inland Sea and Early Pottery in Papua New Guinea. Archaeology in Oceania 24:106–109.

Woodroffe, C. D., D. R. Stoddart, T. Spencer, T. P. Scoffin, and A. W. Tudhope
1990 Holocene Emergence in the Cook Islands, South Pacific. Coral Reefs 9:31–39.

Yen, D. E.
1990 Environment, Agriculture and the Colonization of the Pacific. *In* Pacific Production Systems: Approaches to Economic Prehistory. D. E. Yen and J. M. J. Mummery, eds., pp. 258–277. Occasional Papers in Prehistory 18, Department of Prehistory, Research School of Pacific Studies.

NOTE

I am most grateful to Les Groube for permission to draw upon his arguments so extensively in the final section of this chapter. Discussions with him, and also with Jack Golson and John Muke in particular, have greatly influenced my recent thinking and have kept me in touch with archaeological reality. I regret not having had any recent opportunity for discussion with Harold Brookfield, whose influence on my understanding of Melanesia is not fully acknowledged by the references to his work in this paper.

Notes on Contributors

Index

Notes on Contributors

TIM BAYLISS-SMITH is a lecturer in the Geography Department, University of Cambridge, England. His research has focused on indigenous strategies, past and present, for the management of tropical rain forests (in Melanesia and Costa Rica), coastal environments (in eastern England, Ontong Java atoll, and the western Solomons), tropical mountains (especially the New Guinea Highlands), and the boreal forest zone of northern Sweden. He has done collaborative work with archaeologists on the prehistory of agriculture in New Guinea, and on reindeer herding in Lapland. His books include *The Ecology of Agricultural Systems* and *Islands, Islanders and the World.*

KAREN BRISON is an assistant professor in the Department of Sociology and Anthropology at Union College, Schenectady, New York. She received her Ph.D. in anthropology at the University of California, San Diego, in 1988 after completing a dissertation based on two years of field research (from 1984 to 1986) among the Kwanga of the East Sepik Province, Papua New Guinea. She has written on village politics, meetings, gossip, bereavement, and sorcery. She is currently studying ethnic and national identity in Papua New Guinea and in other Pacific Island nations, interests that she developed as a postdoctoral fellow at the East-West Center and as a Rockefeller Humanities fellow at the University of Hawai'i.

BRUCE KNAUFT is associate professor of anthropology at Emory University. He received his B.A. from Yale University in 1976, conducted fieldwork among the Gebusi of Papua New Guinea from 1980 to 1982, and received his doctorate from the University of Michigan in 1983. Author of two books, Dr. Knauft's interests include cultural theory, practice, and power; Melanesian ethnography; the comparative study of sexuality, gender, and political economy; the evolution of human violence; and the history of anthropological theory.

JELLE MEDIEMA studied anthropology at Groningen University and received his Ph.D. from Nijmegen University in 1984. He is coordinator of an Irian Jaya Studies Project in the Projects Division of the Department of Languages and Cultures of South-East Asia and Oceania, Leiden University. He is also the co-editor of a series, Irian Jaya Source Materials. He did extensive fieldwork in the Bird's Head peninsula of Irian Jaya from 1975 through 1980 and is the author of *The Kebar 1855–1980* and *Pre-Capitalism and Cosmology.*

FITZ JOHN PORTER POOLE is an associate professor of anthropology at the University of California, San Diego. He studied in the United States and Europe, and finished his Ph.D. in anthropology and social psychology at Cornell University. His research focuses on issues of cultural representation and understanding, especially matters of personhood, selfhood, individuality, gender, and ritual structure and experience. His primary field research has been conducted among the Bimin-Kuskusmin of Papua New Guinea. He is currently completing a study of rites of passage and the ritual dimensions of identity among Bimin-Kuskusmin children.

PAUL B. ROSCOE is associate professor of anthropology at the University of Maine and research associate in the Department of Anthropology, American Museum of Natural History. He was educated at Manchester University and the University of Rochester. He has taught at Hobart and William Smith colleges, and the University of Maine, and he held the Richard Lounsbery Fellowship in the Department of Anthropology, American Museum of Natural History. He has done two years of ethnographic fieldwork among the Yangoru Boiken of Papua New Guinea.

RICHARD SCAGLION is associate professor of anthropology at the University of Pittsburgh. His major field research has been with the Abelam people of the East Sepik Province of Papua New Guinea, whom he has revisited frequently for some twenty years. He was the director of the Customary Law Project of the Law Reform Commission of Papua New Guinea from 1979 to 1981. Although his primary expertise is in tribal systems of law, he has very broad interests within both anthropology and Pacific studies.

KIMBERLY SOTO received a B.A. in Anthropology from Humboldt State University in 1988, and is studying anthropology and linguistics at the University of Pittsburgh. She has conducted field research with the Pame, a conquered hunting and gathering people of north-central Mexico. She is currently writing her Ph.D. dissertation, a formal description of the Pame language. Her other interests include the social and linguistic histories of native peoples, Pacific and Native American Indian ethnology, and the study of cultural contact.

ANDREW STRATHERN obtained his Ph.D. at Cambridge University in 1966, and has subsequently held posts at the Australian National University, the University of Papua New Guinea, University College London, the Institute of Papua New Guinea Studies, and the University of Pittsburgh where, since 1987, he has held the post of Andrew W. Mellon Professor of Anthropology. He is editor for the ASAO Monograph Series and also co-editor of the Journal of Ritual Studies. He has done long-term fieldwork in three language areas of Papua New Guinea, and his interests include politics, religion, kinship, social change, medical anthropology, the anthropology of the body, and most recently the anthropology of Europe. His latest books are *Landmarks* and *Voices of Conflict,* and he is currently working on a book entitled "Body Thoughts."

GABRIELE STÜRZENHOFECKER was educated at the universities of Munich and Hamburg, F.R.G., and the University of California at San Diego before receiving her Ph.D. from the University of Pittsburgh in 1993. She has conducted fieldwork during 1991 among the Duna-speaking people of Papua New Guinea and is completing a monograph based on her fieldwork on history and gender among the Duna. She was co-editor of the translation of Hermann Strauss, *The Mi-Culture of the Mount Hagen People.* Her interests encompass gender studies, historical anthropology, symbolism, kinship studies, and medical anthropology. She is currently expanding her interests for work on national identity and gender in Western Europe, and is teaching in the Anthropology Department at the University of Pittsburgh.

ROBERT L. WELSCH received his Ph.D. in anthropology from the University of Washington (Seattle) after completing nearly three years of research in Papua New Guinea among the Ningerum people of the Western Province (1977–79) followed by research on the impact of the Ok Tedi mine (1980). He has also conducted research among the

Mandar people of South Sulawesi, Indonesia (1985–87). Subsequently, he had been studying regional networks along the North Coast of Papua New Guinea as part of the A. B. Lewis Project at Field Museum of Natural History, where he is currently a Visiting Associate Curator of Anthropology. In 1993–94 he conducted collaborative field research on the Aitape coast with John Terrell (Field Museum) and Wilfred Oltomo (PNG National Museum and Art Gallery).

Index

Association of Social Anthropology in Oceania Monograph Series

Andrew J. Strathern, General Editor

Aging and Its Transformations: Moving Toward Death in Pacific Societies
Dorothy Ayers Counts and David R. Counts, Editors

The Business of Marriage: Transformations in Oceanic Matrimony
Richard A. Marksbury, Editor

Clowning as Critical Practice: Performance Humor in the South Pacific
William E. Mitchell, Editor

Migration and Transformations: Regional Perspectives on New Guinea
Andrew J. Strathern and Gabriele Stürzenhofecker, Editors